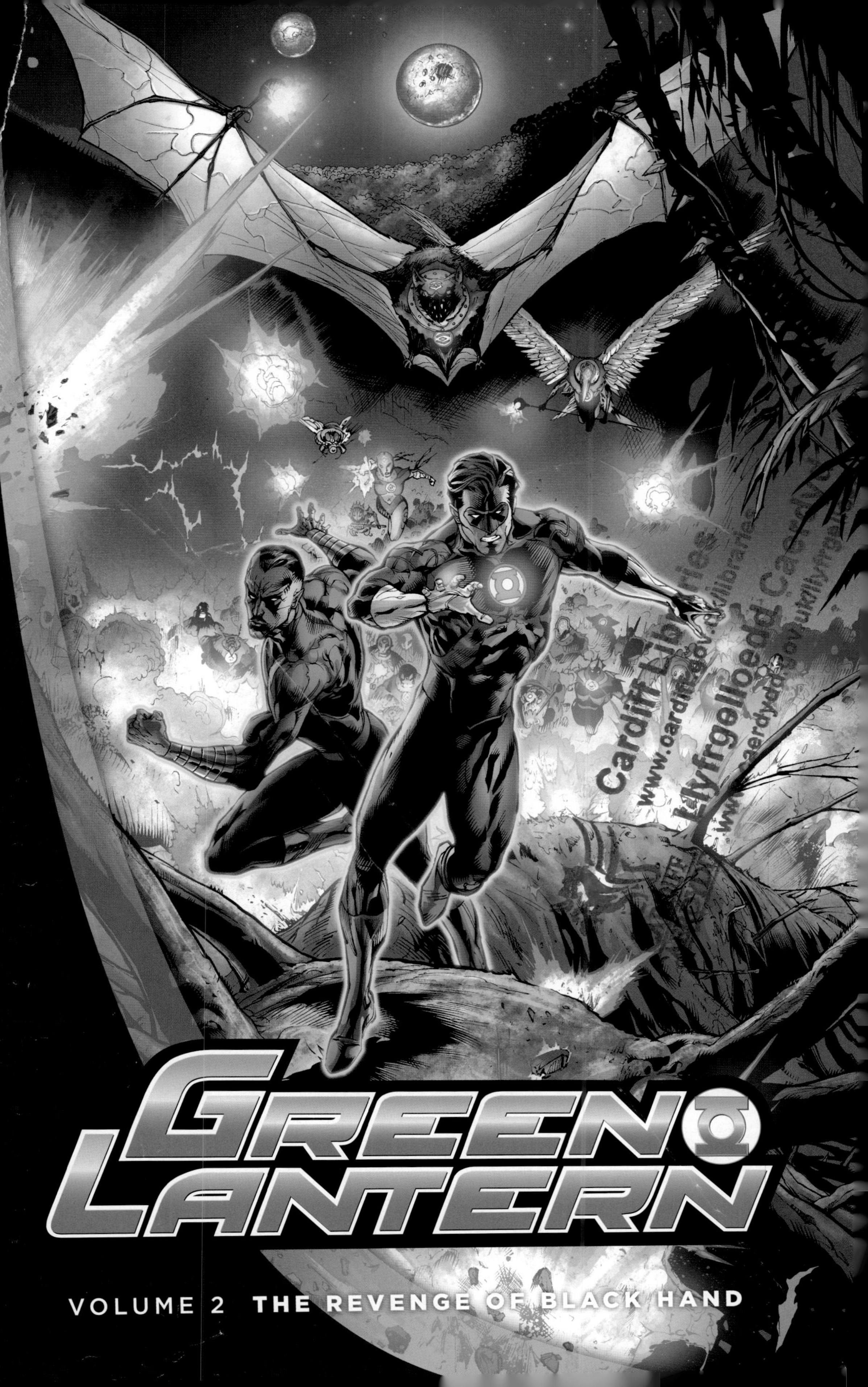

GREEN LANTERN

VOLUME 2 **THE REVENGE OF BLACK HAND**

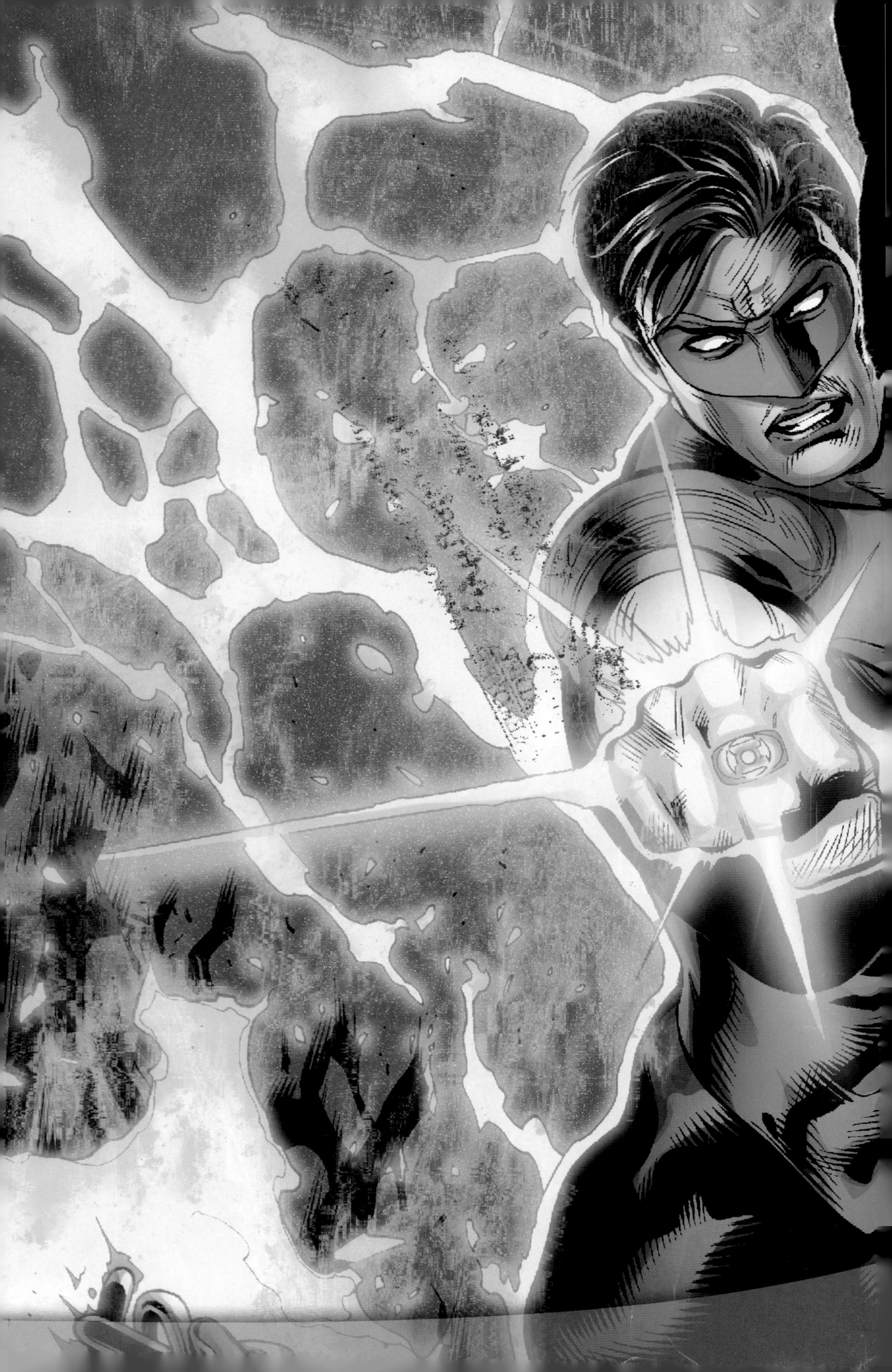

GREEN LANTERN

VOLUME 2
THE REVENGE OF BLACK HAND

GEOFF **JOHNS** writer

DOUG **MAHNKE** ETHAN **VAN SCIVER**
PETE **WOODS** RENATO **GUEDES**
JIM **CALAFIORE** pencillers

KEITH **CHAMPAGNE** CHRISTIAN **ALAMY** MARK **IRWIN**
DOUG **MAHNKE** TOM **NGUYEN** ETHAN **VAN SCIVER**
RENATO **GUEDES** JIM **CALAFIORE** CAM **SMITH** inkers

ALEX **SINCLAIR** HI-FI TONY **AVINA** colorists

SAL **CIPRIANO** letterer

DOUG **MAHNKE**, MARK **IRWIN** & ALEX **SINCLAIR**
collection cover artists

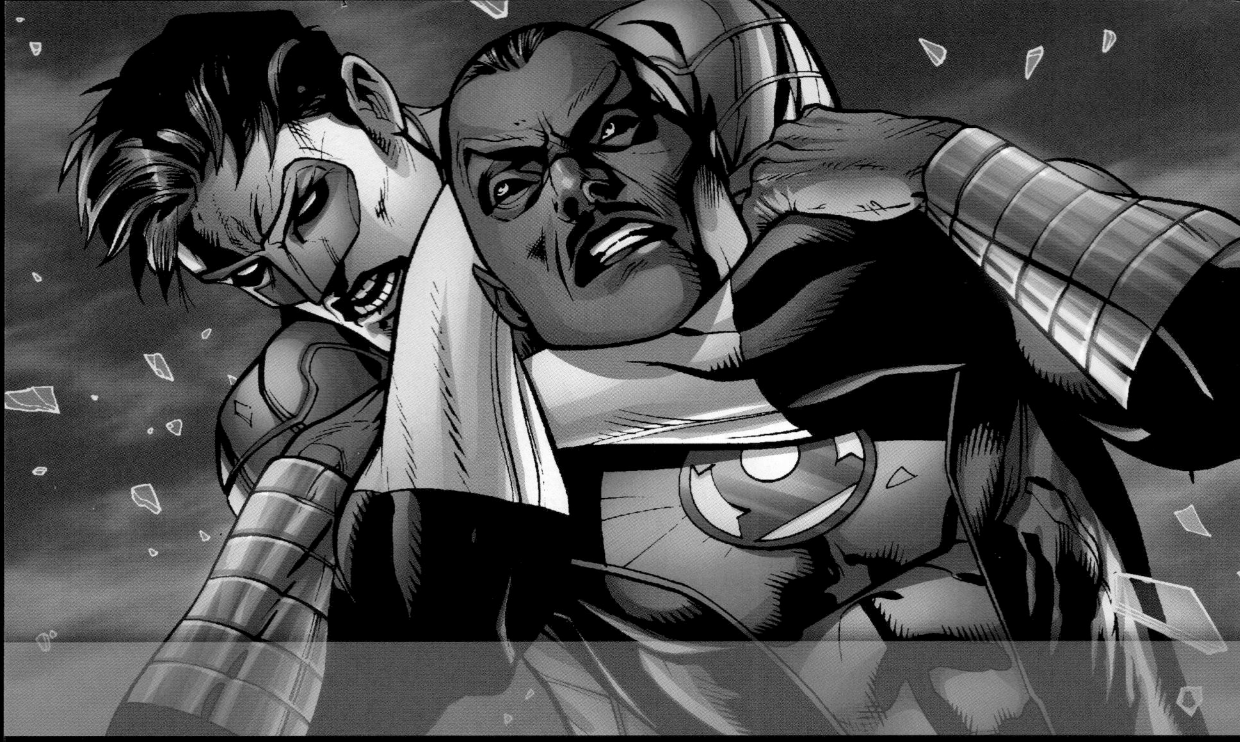

MATT IDELSON BRIAN CUNNINGHAM Editors – Original Series WIL MOSS Associate Editor – Original Series
DARREN SHAN Assistant Editor – Original Series PETER HAMBOUSSI Editor
ROBBIN BROSTERMAN Design Director – Books ROBBIE BIEDERMAN Publication Design

BOB HARRAS VP – Editor-in-Chief

DIANE NELSON President DAN DIDIO and JIM LEE Co-Publishers
GEOFF JOHNS Chief Creative Officer
JOHN ROOD Executive VP – Sales, Marketing and Business Development
AMY GENKINS Senior VP – Business and Legal Affairs NAIRI GARDINER Senior VP – Finance
JEFF BOISON VP – Publishing Operations MARK CHIARELLO VP – Art Direction and Design
JOHN CUNNINGHAM VP – Marketing TERRI CUNNINGHAM VP – Talent Relations and Services
ALISON GILL Senior VP – Manufacturing and Operations
HANK KANALZ Senior VP – Digital JAY KOGAN VP – Business and Legal Affairs, Publishing
JACK MAHAN VP – Business Affairs, Talent NICK NAPOLITANO VP – Manufacturing Administration
SUE POHJA VP – Book Sales COURTNEY SIMMONS Senior VP – Publicity
BOB WAYNE Senior VP – Sales

GREEN LANTERN VOLUME 2: THE REVENGE OF BLACK HAND
Published by DC Comics.

DC Comics, 1700 Broadway, New York, NY 10019
A Warner Bros. Entertainment Company.
Printed by RR Donnelley, Salem, VA, USA. 11/30/12. First Printing.
HC ISBN: 978-1-4012-3766-0
SC ISBN: 978-1-4012-3767-7

SUSTAINABLE FORESTRY INITIATIVE Certified Chain of Custody
At Least 20% Certified Forest Content
www.sfiprogram.org
SFI-01042
APPLIES TO TEXT STOCK ONLY

Library of Congress Cataloging-in-Publication Data

Johns, Geoff, 1973-
Green lantern. Volume 2, The revenge of Black Hand / Geoff Johns, Doug Mahnke.
p. cm.
"Originally published in single magazine form in Green Lantern 7-12, Green Lantern Annual 1."
ISBN 978-1-4012-3766-0
1. Graphic novels. I. Mahnke, Doug. II. Title. III. Title: Revenge of Black Hand.
PN6728.G74J6587 2012
741.5'973—dc23
2012032141

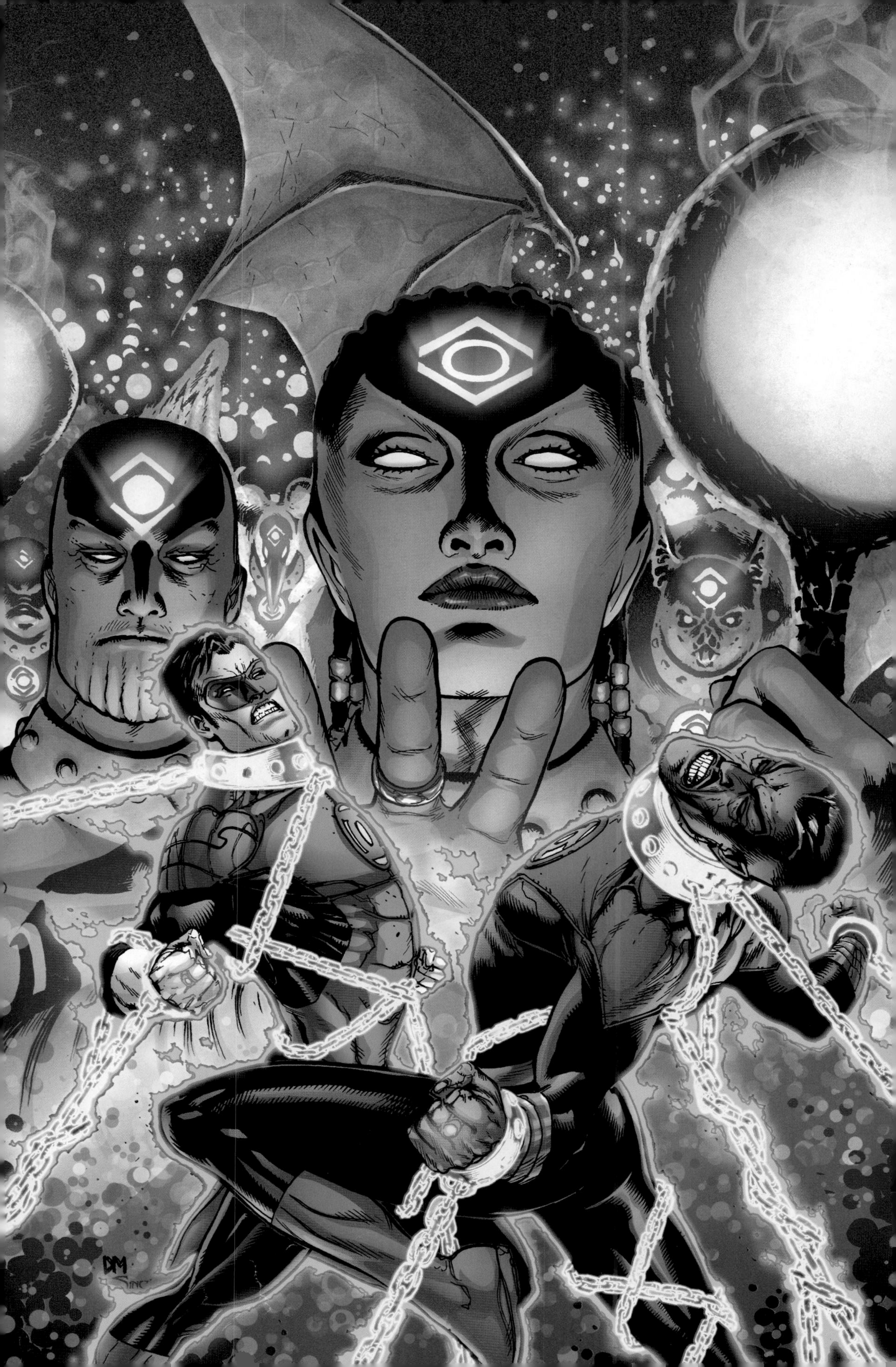

THE SECRET OF THE INDIGO TRIBE part one

GEOFF JOHNS writer DOUG MAHNKE penciller KEITH CHAMPAGNE, CHRISTIAN ALAMY & MARK IRWIN inkers DOUG MAHNKE & ALEX SINCLAIR cover

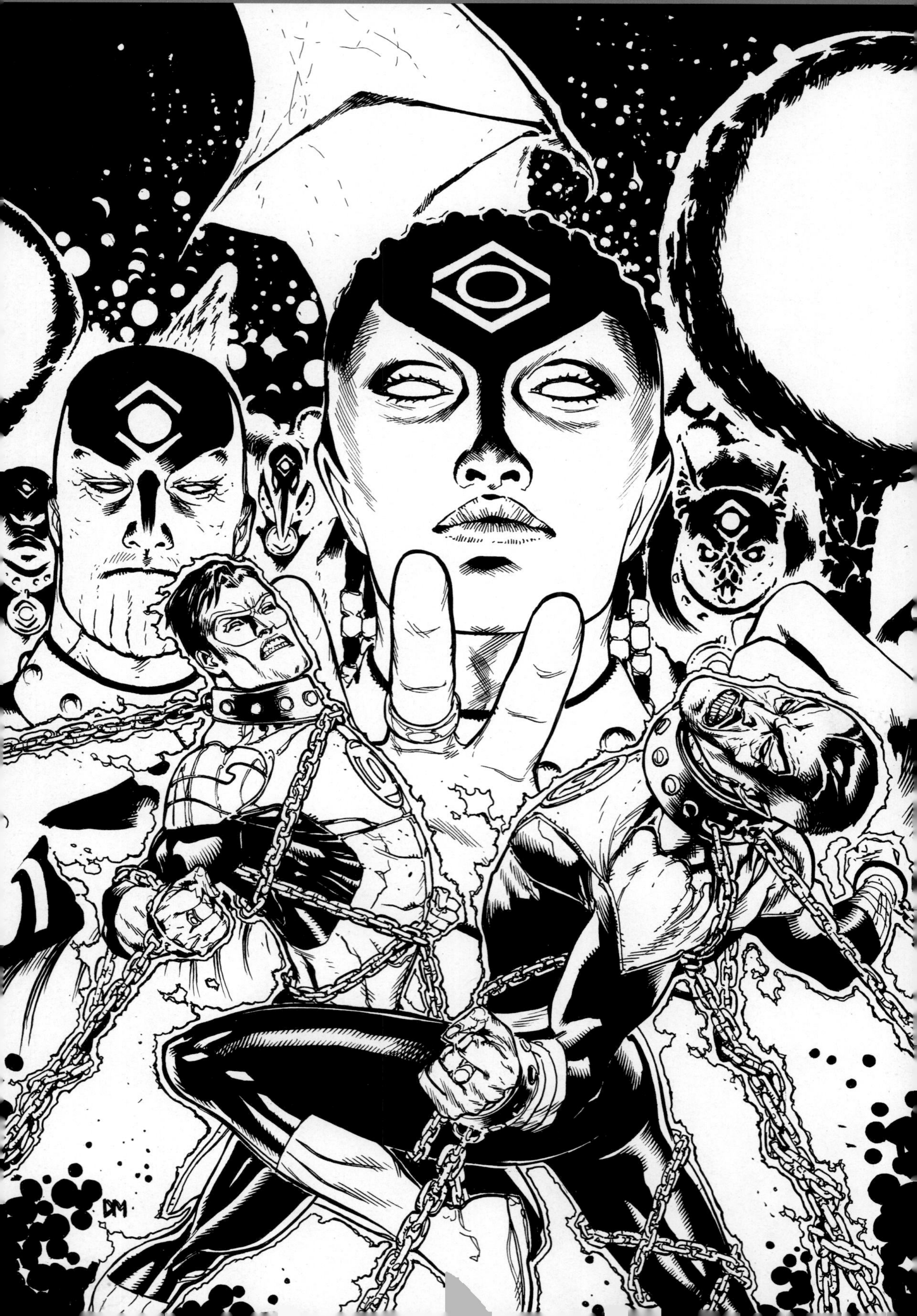

DM

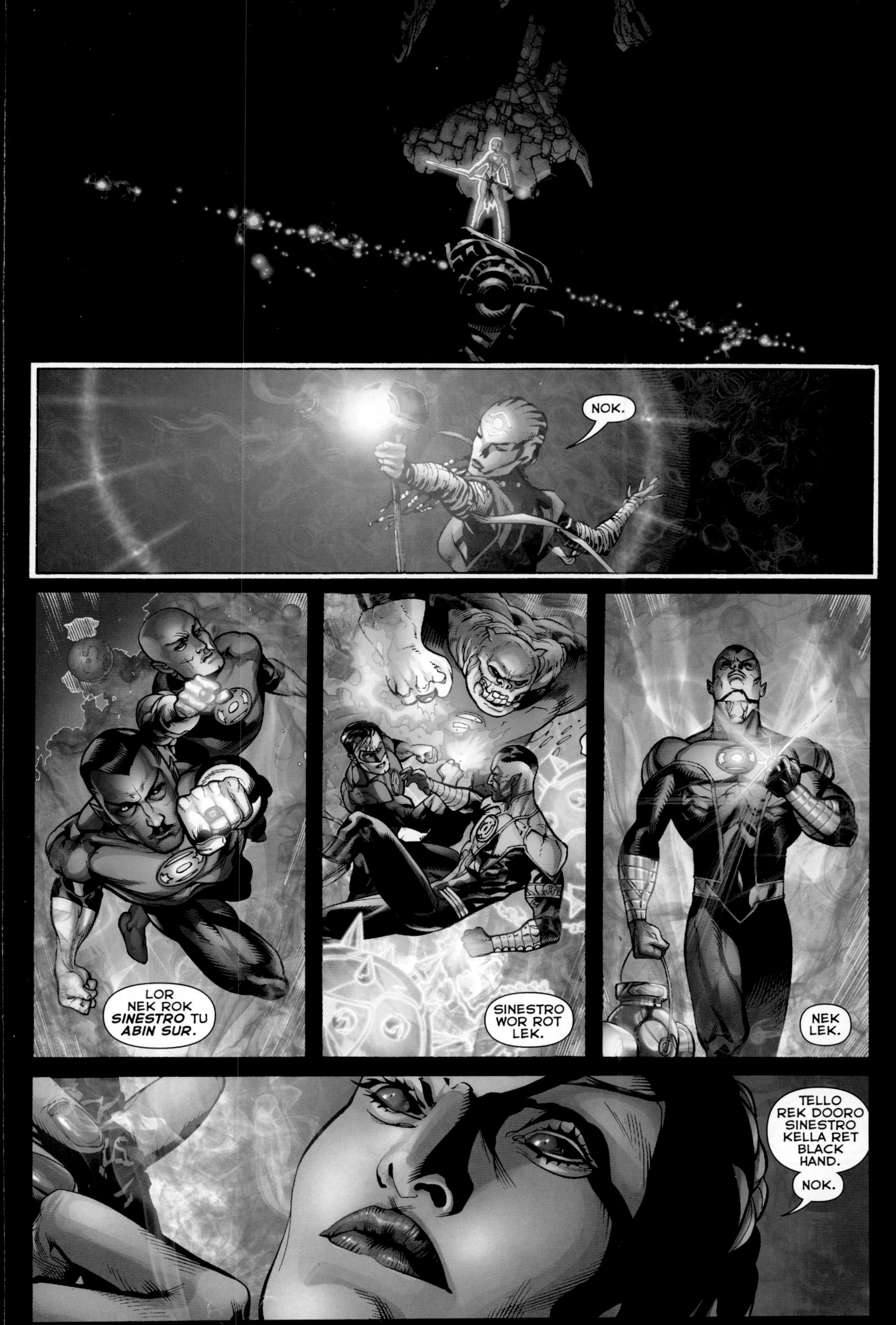
NOK.
LOR NEK ROK *SINESTRO* TU *ABIN SUR.*
SINESTRO WOR ROT LEK.
NEK LEK.
TELLO REK DOORO SINESTRO KELLA RET BLACK HAND.
NOK.

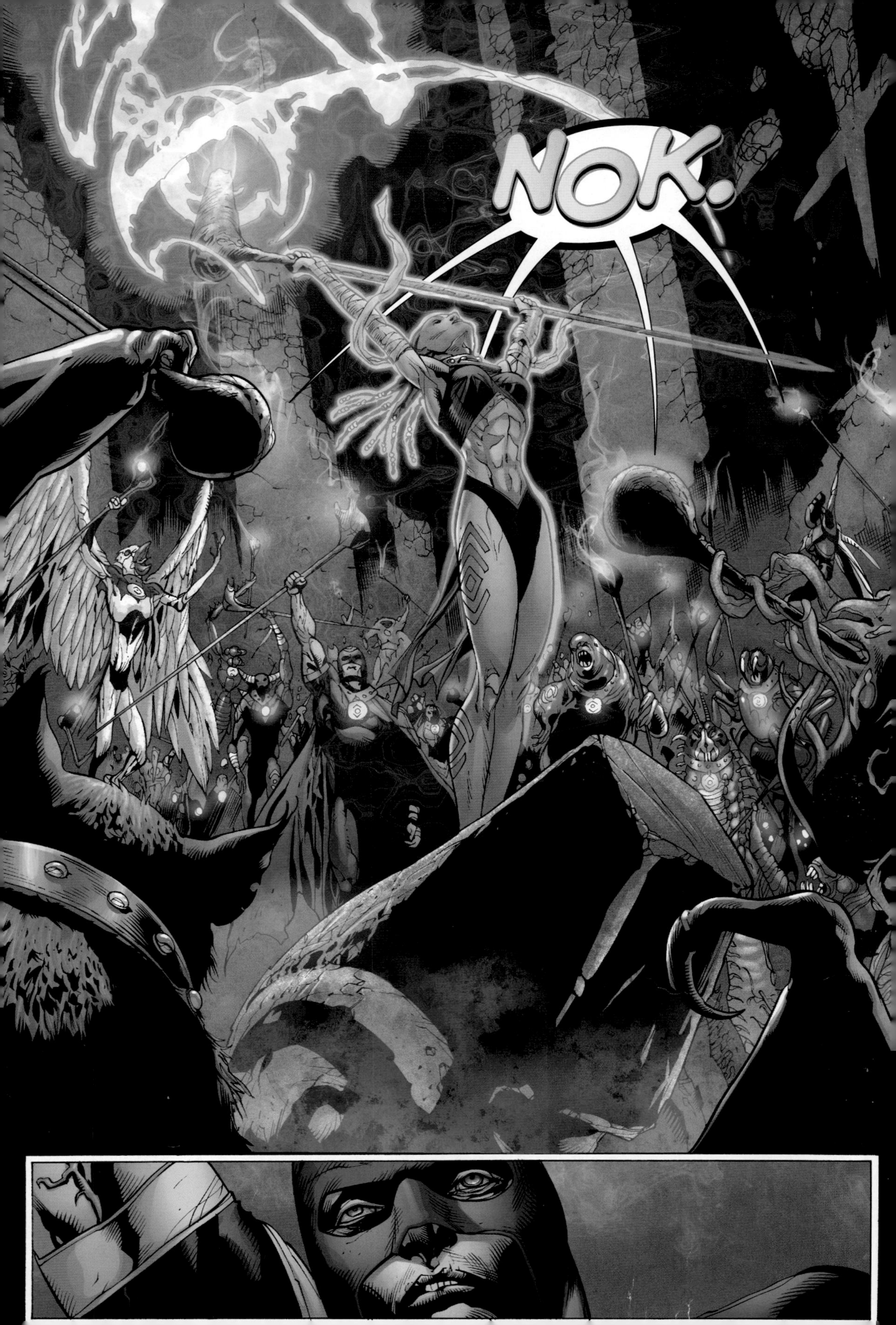
NOK.

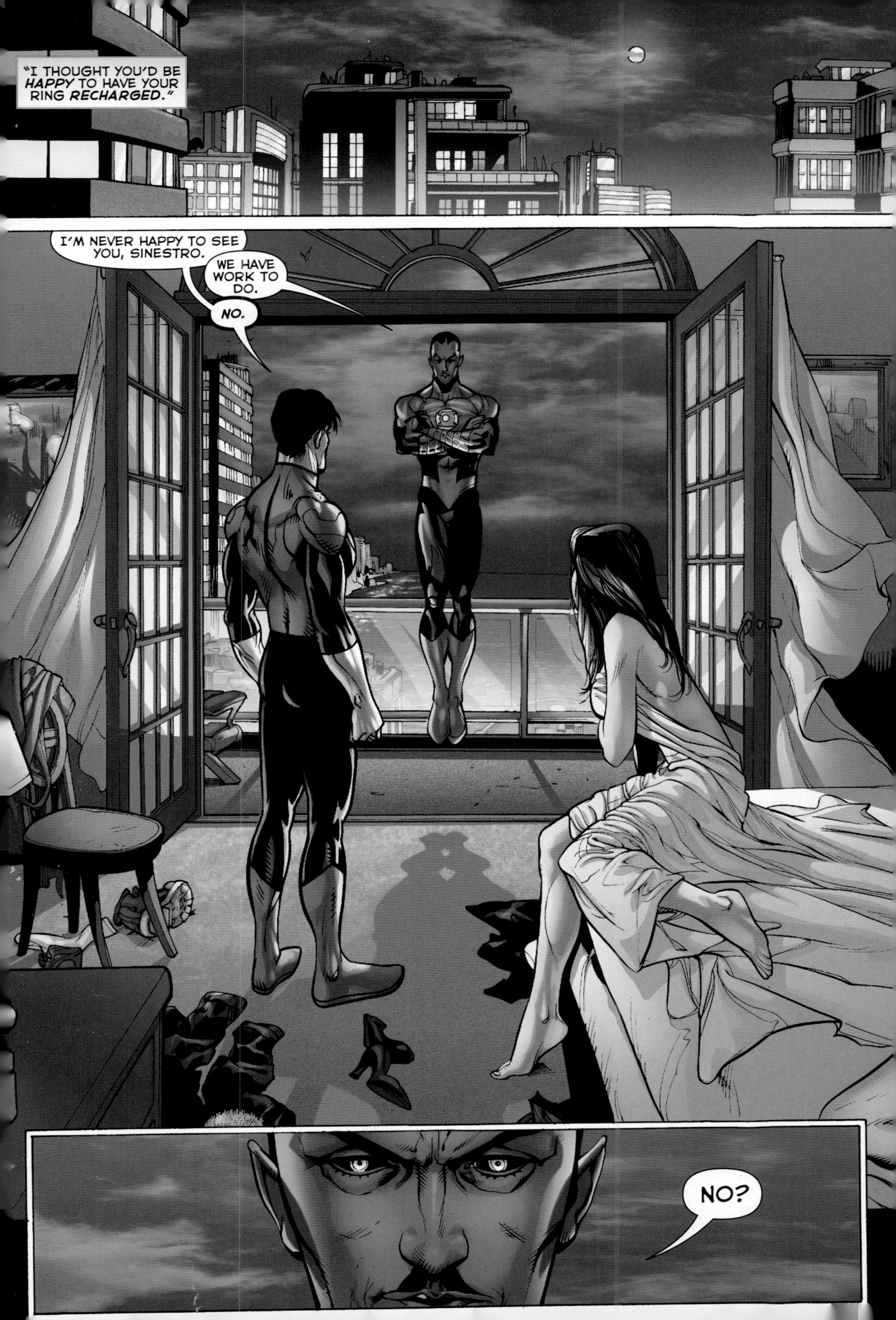
"I THOUGHT YOU'D BE HAPPY TO HAVE YOUR RING RECHARGED."
I'M NEVER HAPPY TO SEE YOU, SINESTRO.
WE HAVE WORK TO DO.
NO.
NO?

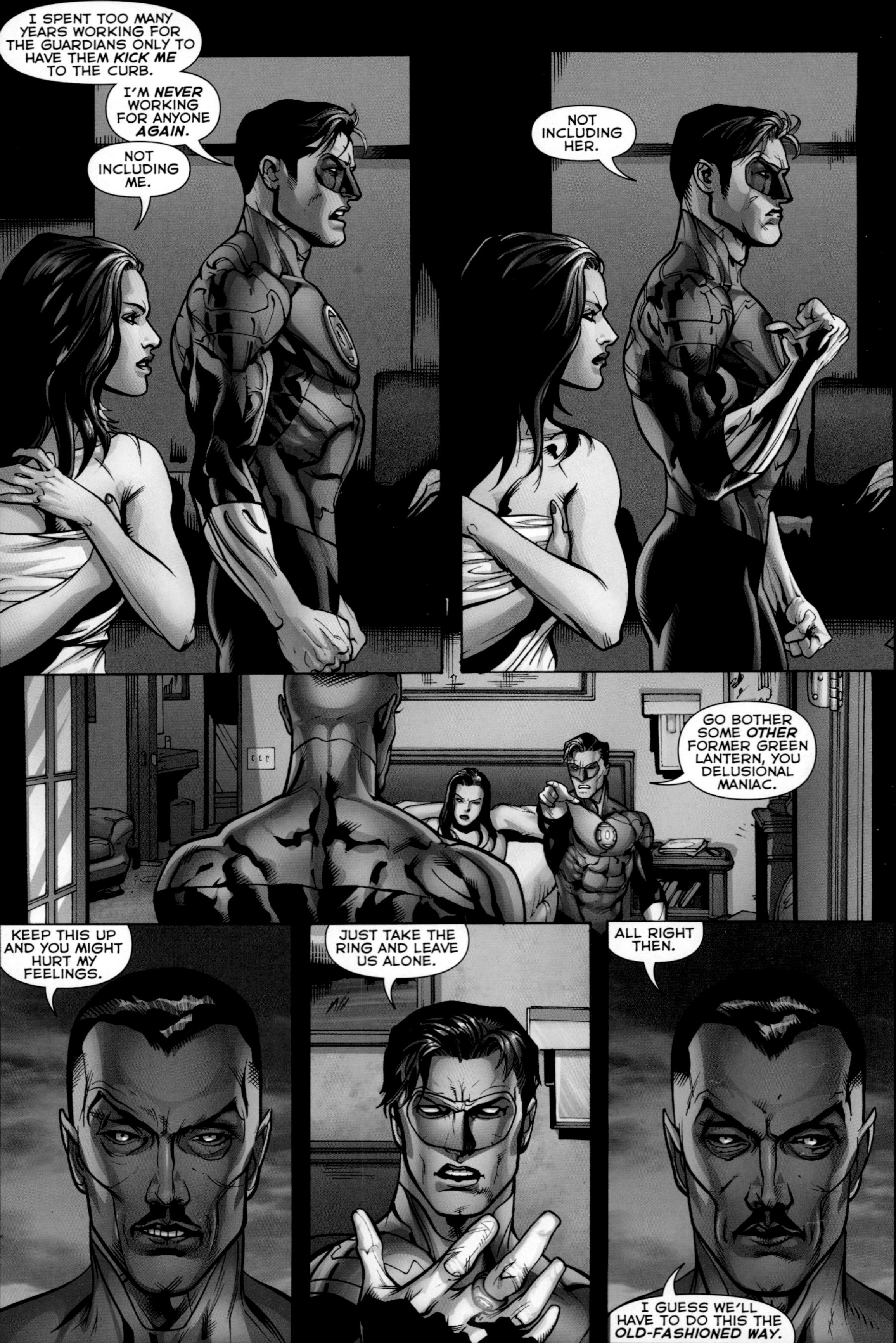
I SPENT TOO MANY YEARS WORKING FOR THE GUARDIANS ONLY TO HAVE THEM KICK ME TO THE CURB.
I'M NEVER WORKING FOR ANYONE AGAIN.
NOT INCLUDING ME.
NOT INCLUDING HER.
GO BOTHER SOME OTHER FORMER GREEN LANTERN, YOU DELUSIONAL MANIAC.
KEEP THIS UP AND YOU MIGHT HURT MY FEELINGS.
JUST TAKE THE RING AND LEAVE US ALONE.
ALL RIGHT THEN.
I GUESS WE'LL HAVE TO DO THIS THE OLD-FASHIONED WAY.

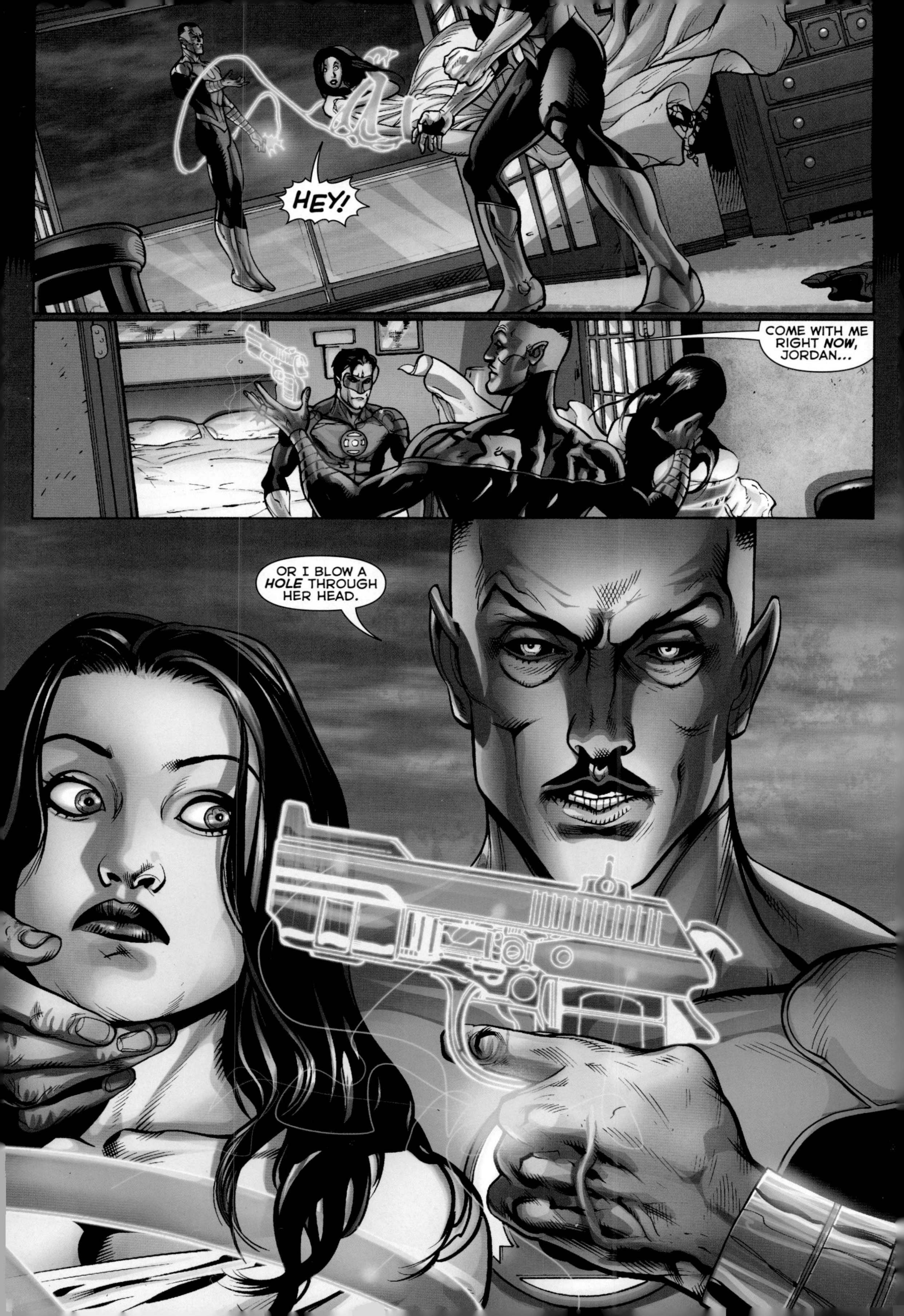

HEY!
COME WITH ME RIGHT NOW, JORDAN...
OR I BLOW A HOLE THROUGH HER HEAD.

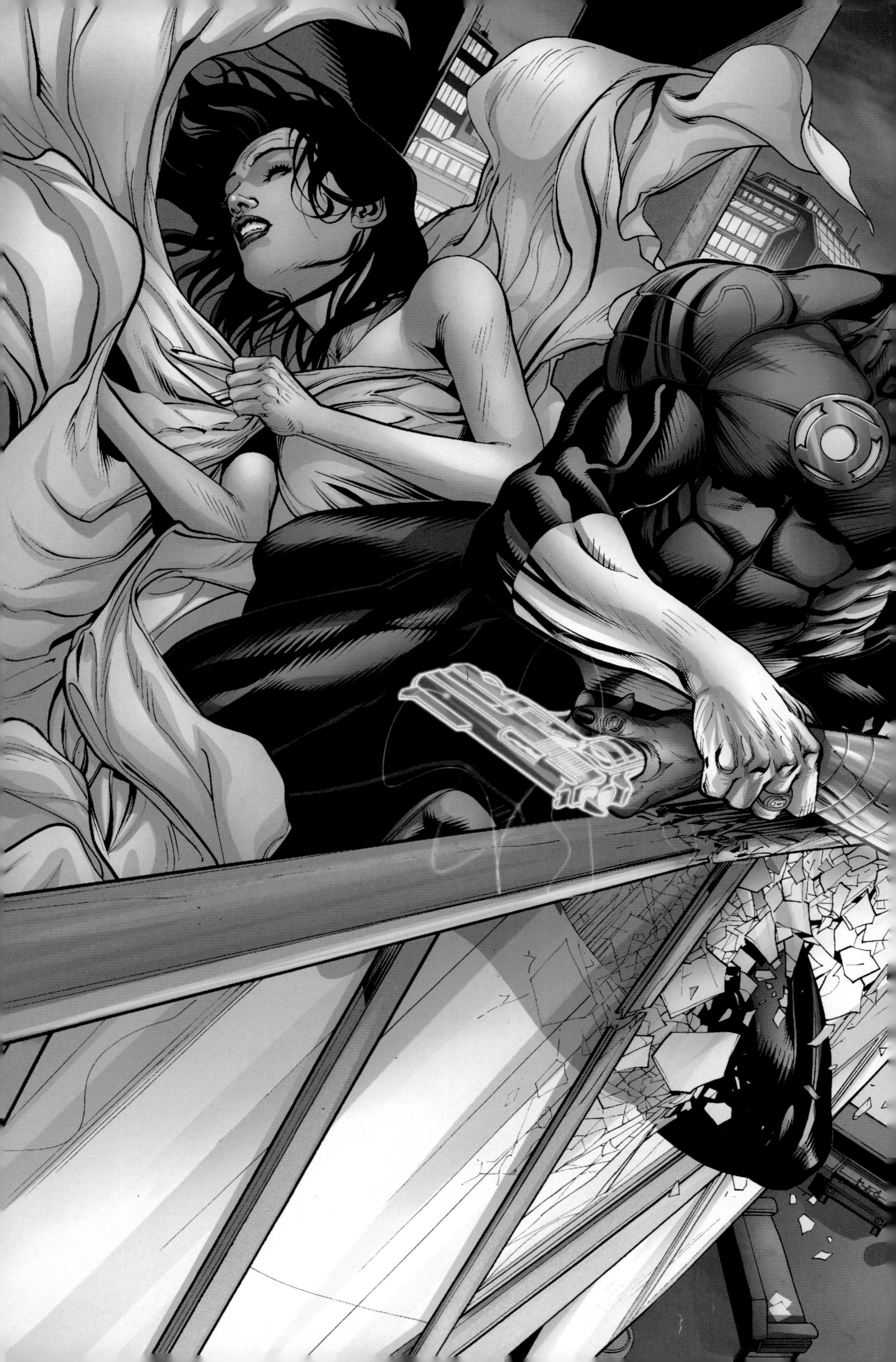

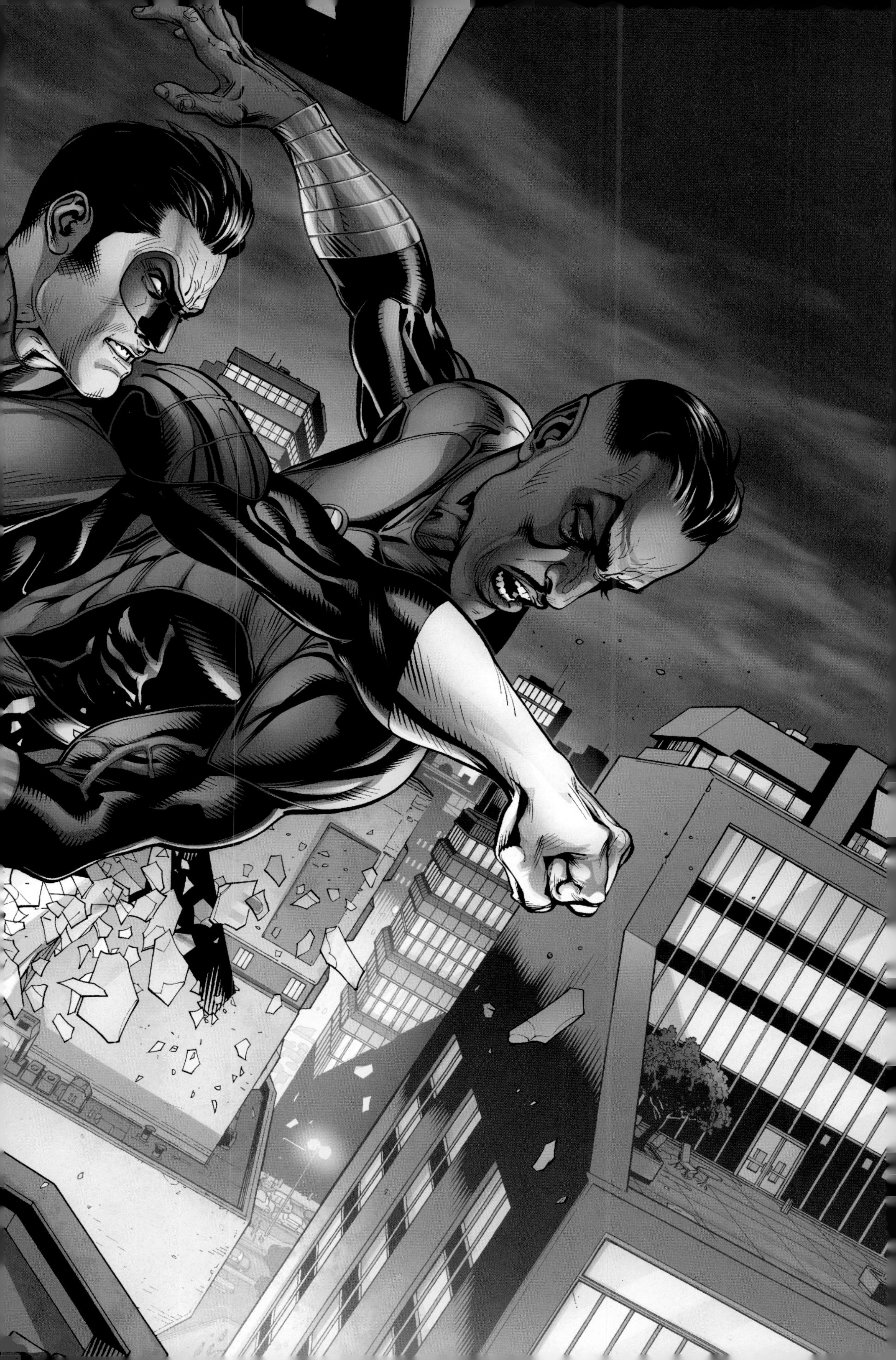

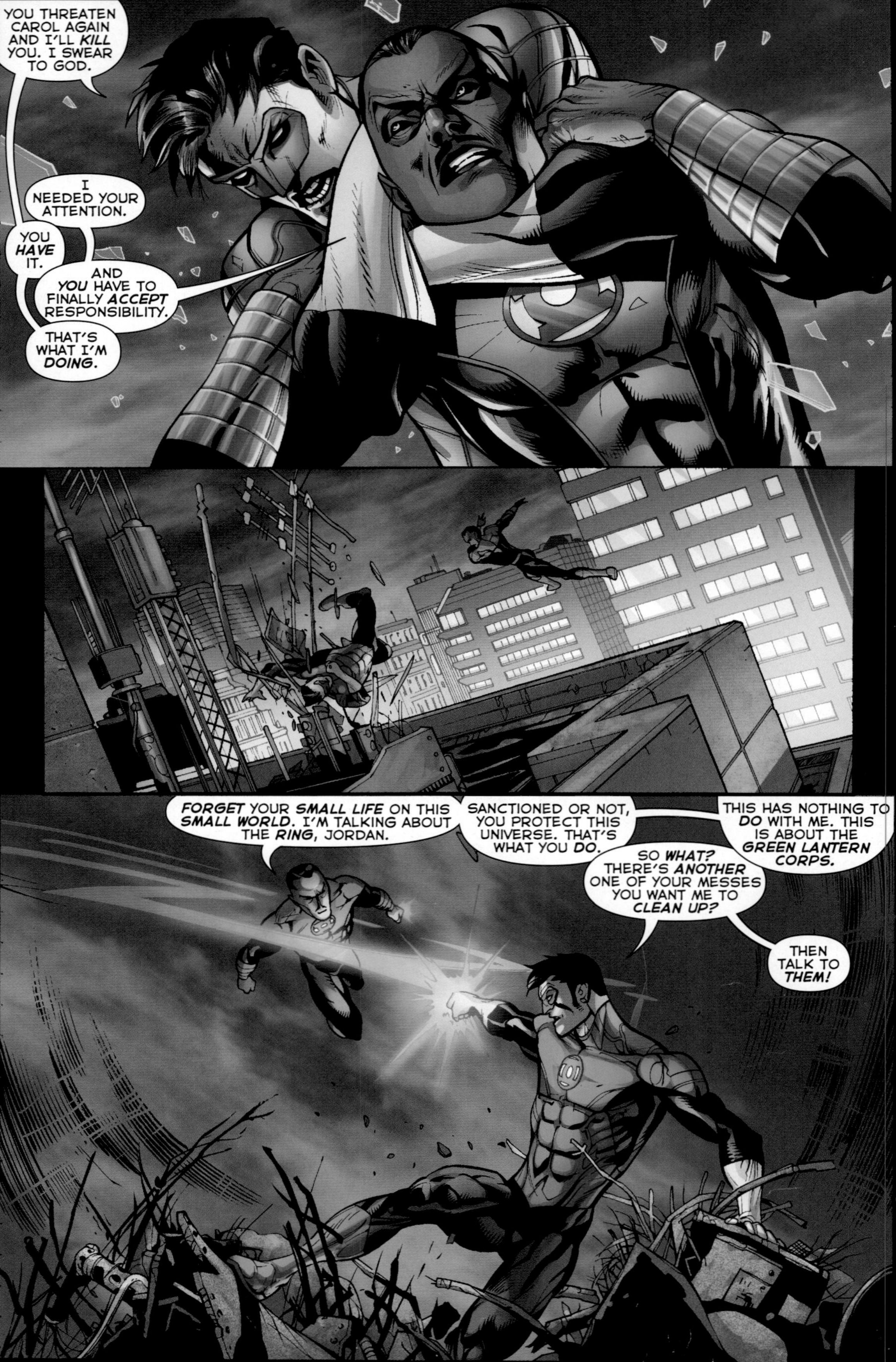
YOU THREATEN CAROL AGAIN AND I'LL *KILL* YOU. I SWEAR TO GOD.
I NEEDED YOUR ATTENTION.
YOU *HAVE* IT.
AND *YOU* HAVE TO FINALLY *ACCEPT* RESPONSIBILITY.
THAT'S WHAT I'M *DOING*.
FORGET YOUR *SMALL LIFE* ON THIS *SMALL WORLD*. I'M TALKING ABOUT THE *RING*, JORDAN.
SANCTIONED OR NOT, YOU PROTECT THIS UNIVERSE. THAT'S WHAT YOU *DO*.
THIS HAS NOTHING TO *DO* WITH ME. THIS IS ABOUT THE *GREEN LANTERN CORPS.*
SO *WHAT?* THERE'S *ANOTHER* ONE OF YOUR MESSES YOU WANT ME TO *CLEAN UP?*
THEN TALK TO *THEM!*

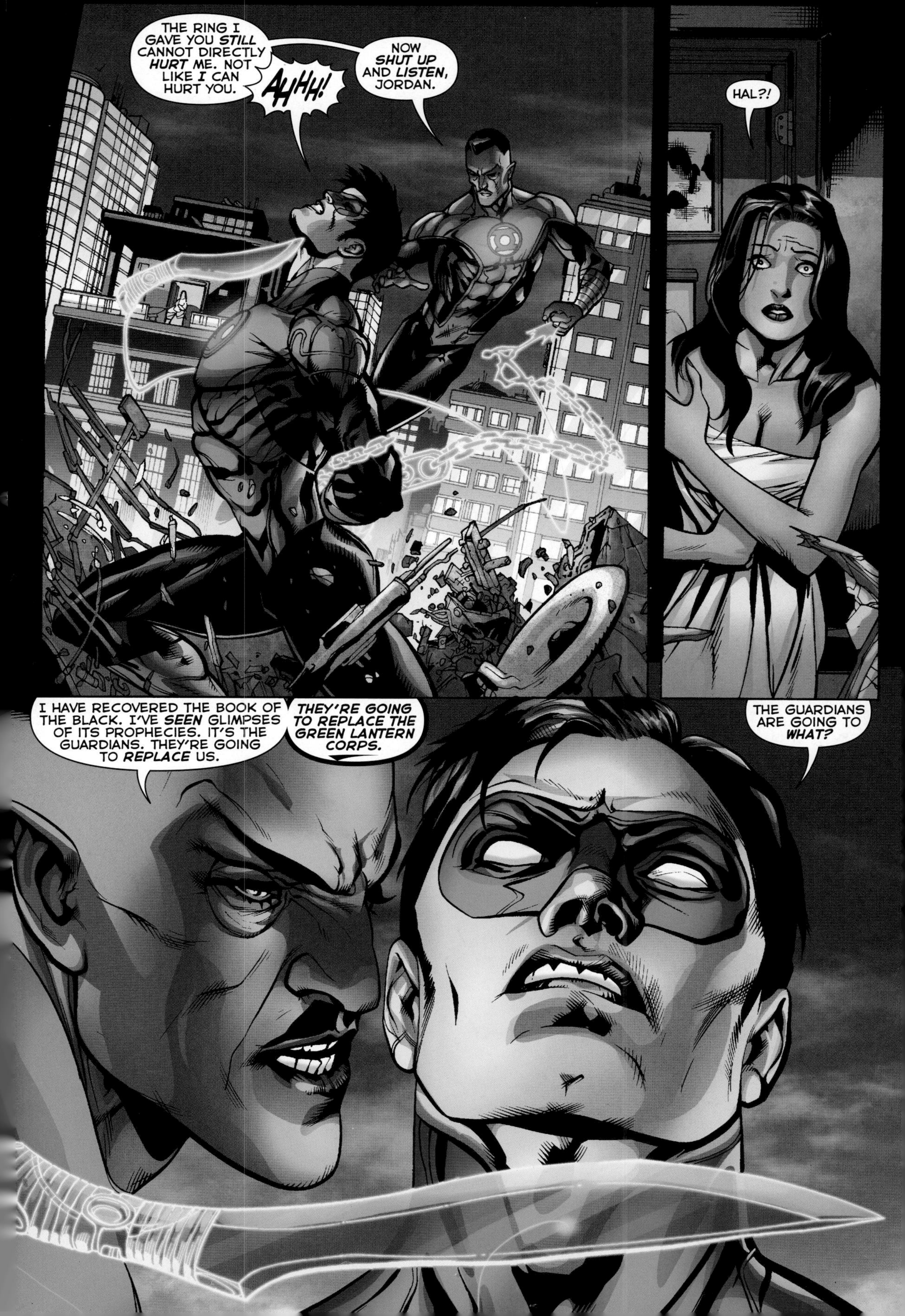

THE RING I GAVE YOU STILL CANNOT DIRECTLY HURT ME. NOT LIKE I CAN HURT YOU.
AHHH!
NOW SHUT UP AND LISTEN, JORDAN.
HAL?!
I HAVE RECOVERED THE BOOK OF THE BLACK. I'VE SEEN GLIMPSES OF ITS PROPHECIES. IT'S THE GUARDIANS. THEY'RE GOING TO REPLACE US.
THEY'RE GOING TO REPLACE THE GREEN LANTERN CORPS.
THE GUARDIANS ARE GOING TO WHAT?

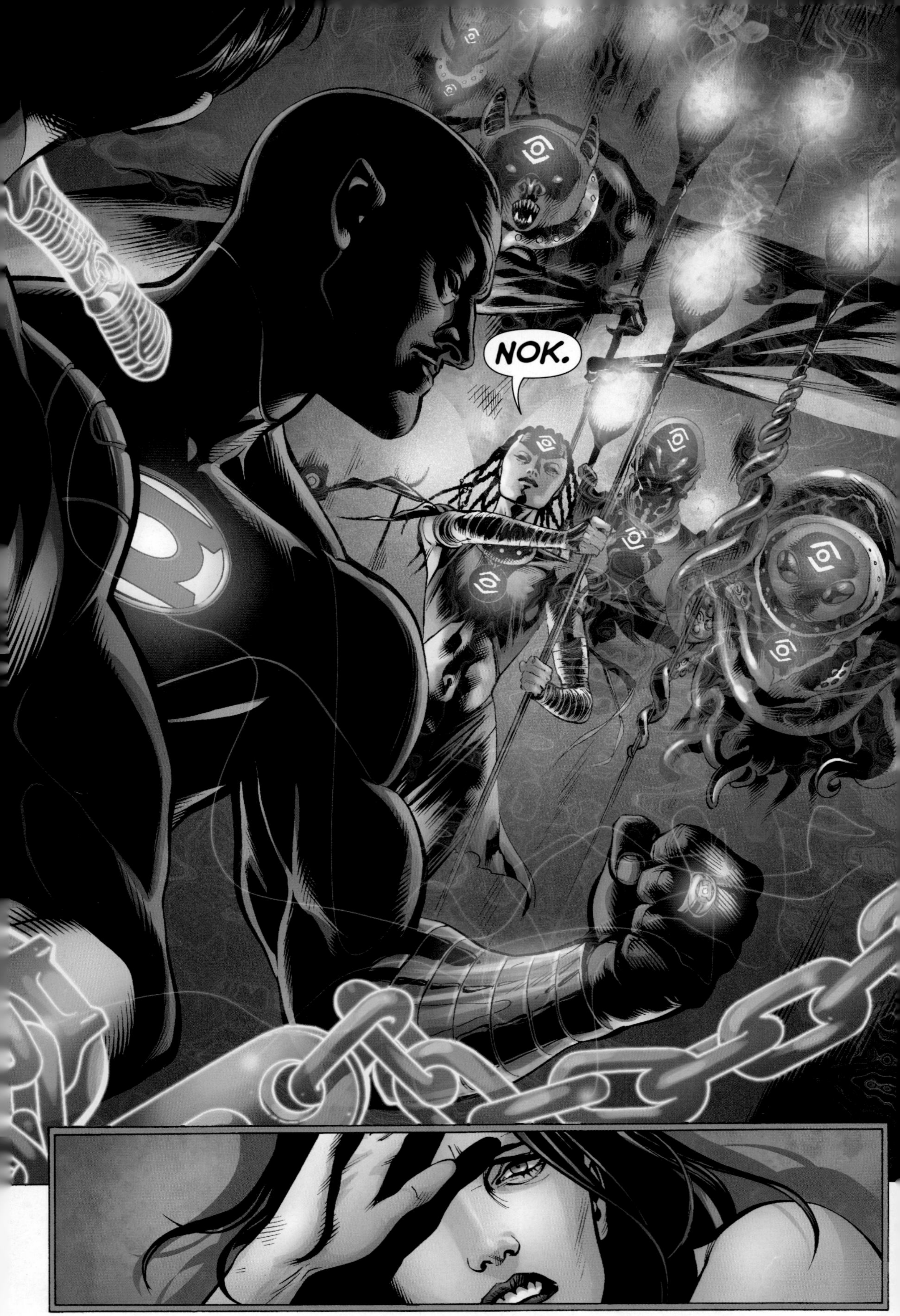
NOK.

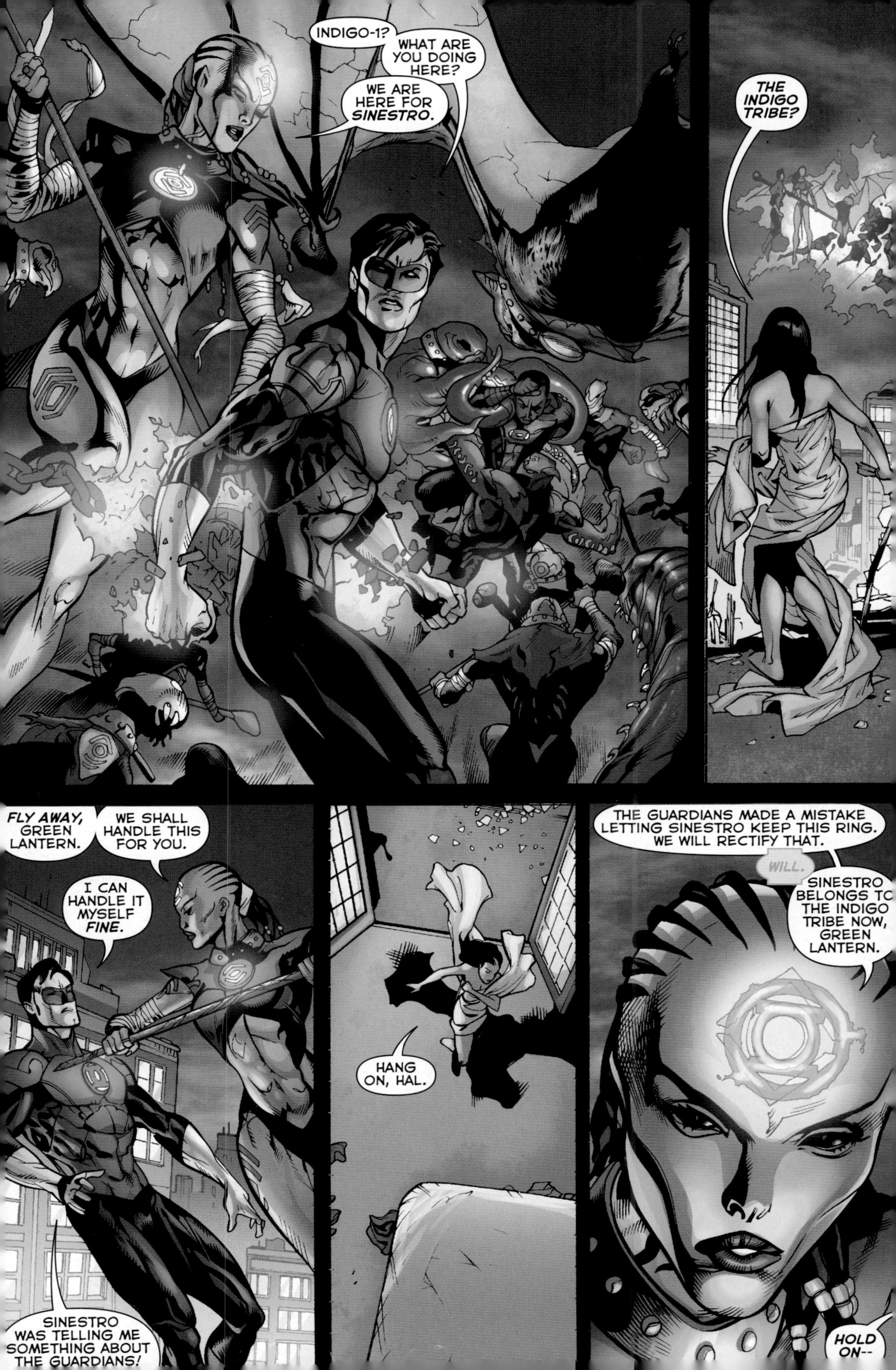
INDIGO-1?
WHAT ARE YOU DOING HERE?
WE ARE HERE FOR *SINESTRO*.
THE INDIGO TRIBE?
FLY AWAY, GREEN LANTERN.
WE SHALL HANDLE THIS FOR YOU.
I CAN HANDLE IT MYSELF *FINE*.
SINESTRO WAS TELLING ME SOMETHING ABOUT THE GUARDIANS!
HANG ON, HAL.
THE GUARDIANS MADE A MISTAKE LETTING SINESTRO KEEP THIS RING. WE WILL RECTIFY THAT.
WILL.
SINESTRO BELONGS TO THE INDIGO TRIBE NOW, GREEN LANTERN.
HOLD ON--

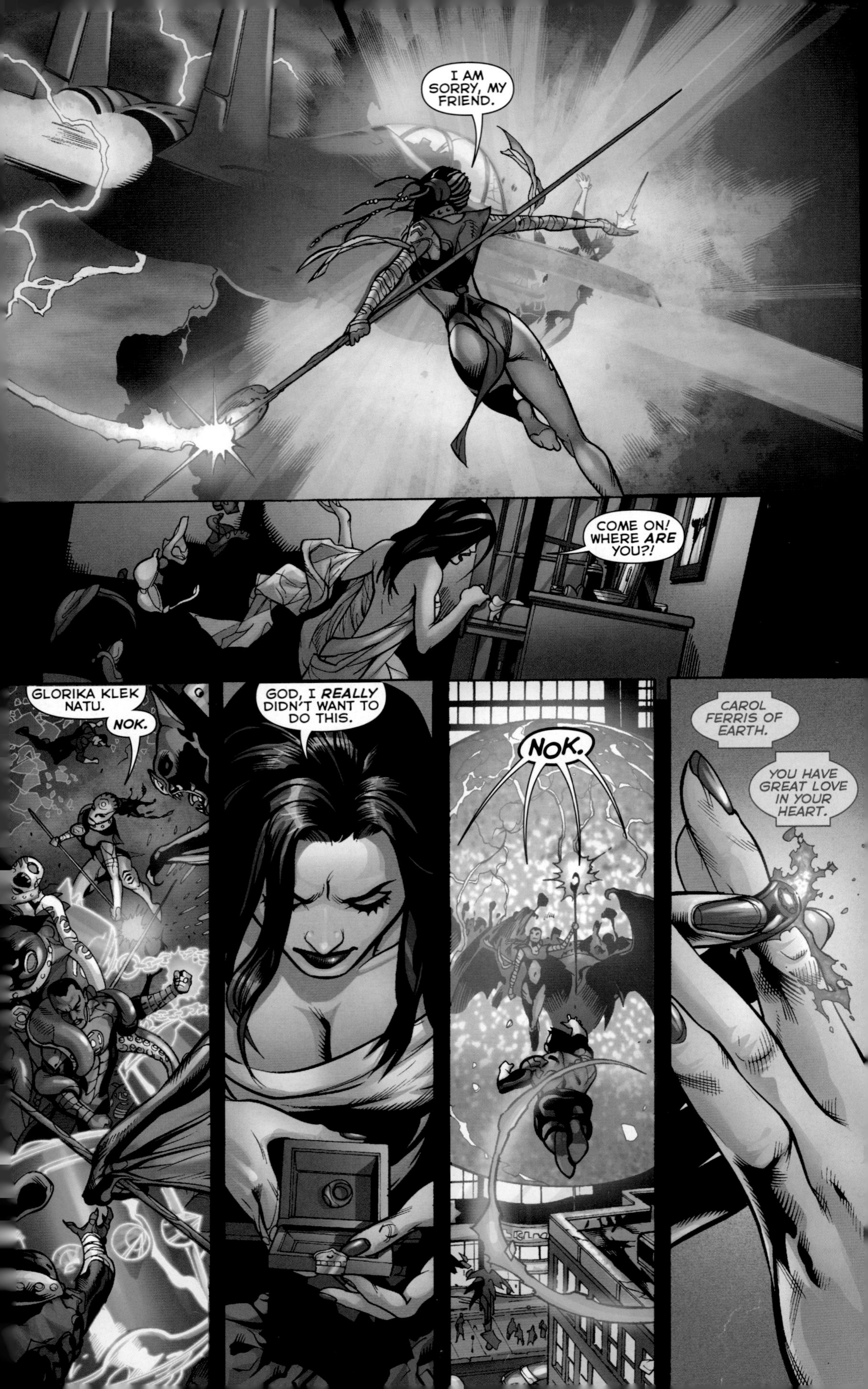
I AM SORRY, MY FRIEND.
COME ON! WHERE *ARE* YOU?!
GLORIKA KLEK NATU.
NOK.
GOD, I *REALLY* DIDN'T WANT TO DO THIS.
NOK.
CAROL FERRIS OF EARTH.
YOU HAVE GREAT LOVE IN YOUR HEART.

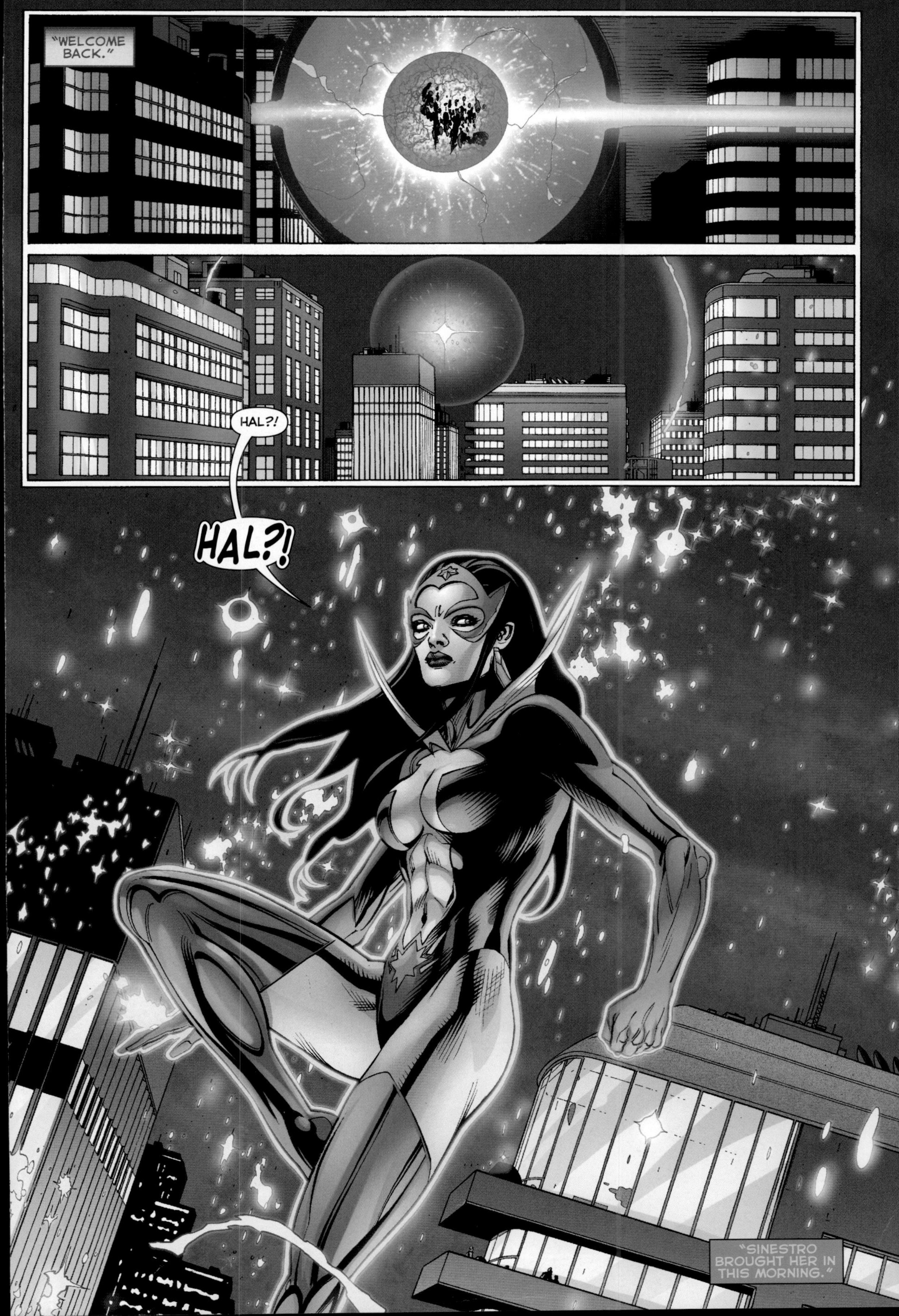
"WELCOME BACK."
HAL?!
HAL?!
"SINESTRO BROUGHT HER IN THIS MORNING."

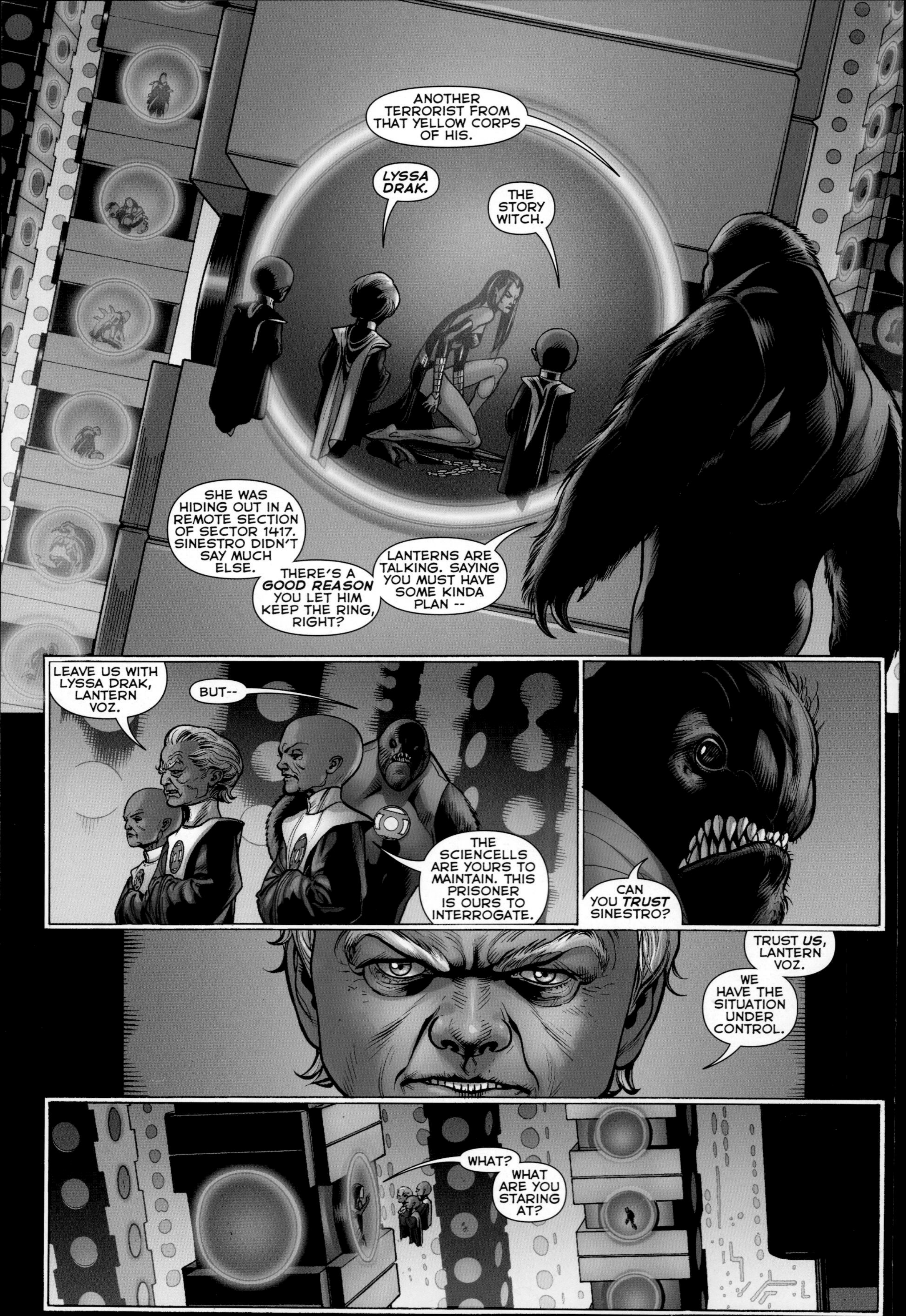
ANOTHER TERRORIST FROM THAT YELLOW CORPS OF HIS.
LYSSA DRAK.
THE STORY WITCH.
SHE WAS HIDING OUT IN A REMOTE SECTION OF SECTOR 1417. SINESTRO DIDN'T SAY MUCH ELSE.
THERE'S A GOOD REASON YOU LET HIM KEEP THE RING, RIGHT?
LANTERNS ARE TALKING. SAYING YOU MUST HAVE SOME KINDA PLAN --
LEAVE US WITH LYSSA DRAK, LANTERN VOZ.
BUT--
THE SCIENCELLS ARE YOURS TO MAINTAIN. THIS PRISONER IS OURS TO INTERROGATE.
CAN YOU TRUST SINESTRO?
TRUST US, LANTERN VOZ.
WE HAVE THE SITUATION UNDER CONTROL.
WHAT?
WHAT ARE YOU STARING AT?

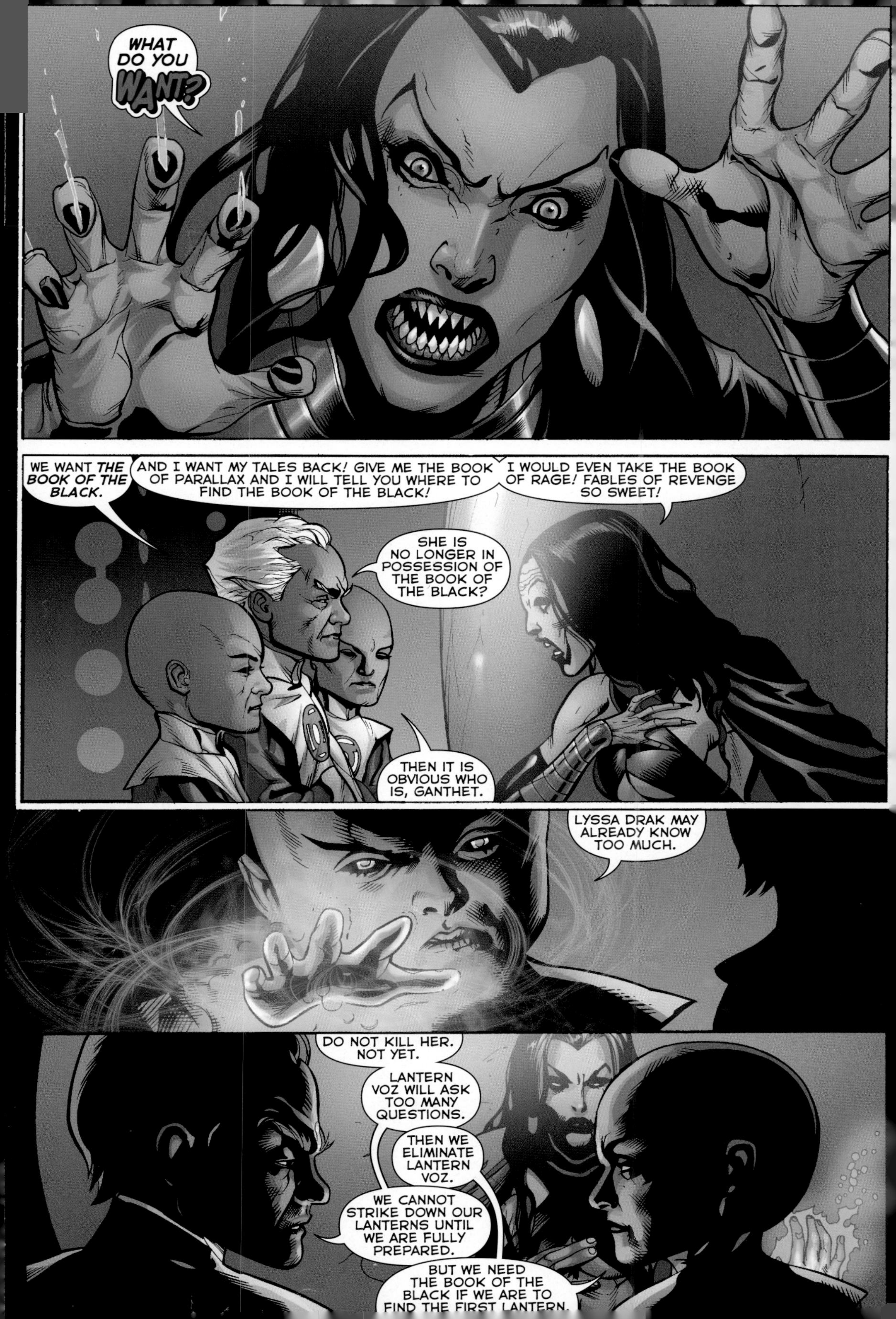
WHAT DO YOU WANT?
WE WANT THE BOOK OF THE BLACK.
AND I WANT MY TALES BACK! GIVE ME THE BOOK OF PARALLAX AND I WILL TELL YOU WHERE TO FIND THE BOOK OF THE BLACK!
I WOULD EVEN TAKE THE BOOK OF RAGE! FABLES OF REVENGE SO SWEET!
SHE IS NO LONGER IN POSSESSION OF THE BOOK OF THE BLACK?
THEN IT IS OBVIOUS WHO IS, GANTHET.
LYSSA DRAK MAY ALREADY KNOW TOO MUCH.
DO NOT KILL HER. NOT YET.
LANTERN VOZ WILL ASK TOO MANY QUESTIONS.
THEN WE ELIMINATE LANTERN VOZ.
WE CANNOT STRIKE DOWN OUR LANTERNS UNTIL WE ARE FULLY PREPARED.
BUT WE NEED THE BOOK OF THE BLACK IF WE ARE TO FIND THE FIRST LANTERN.

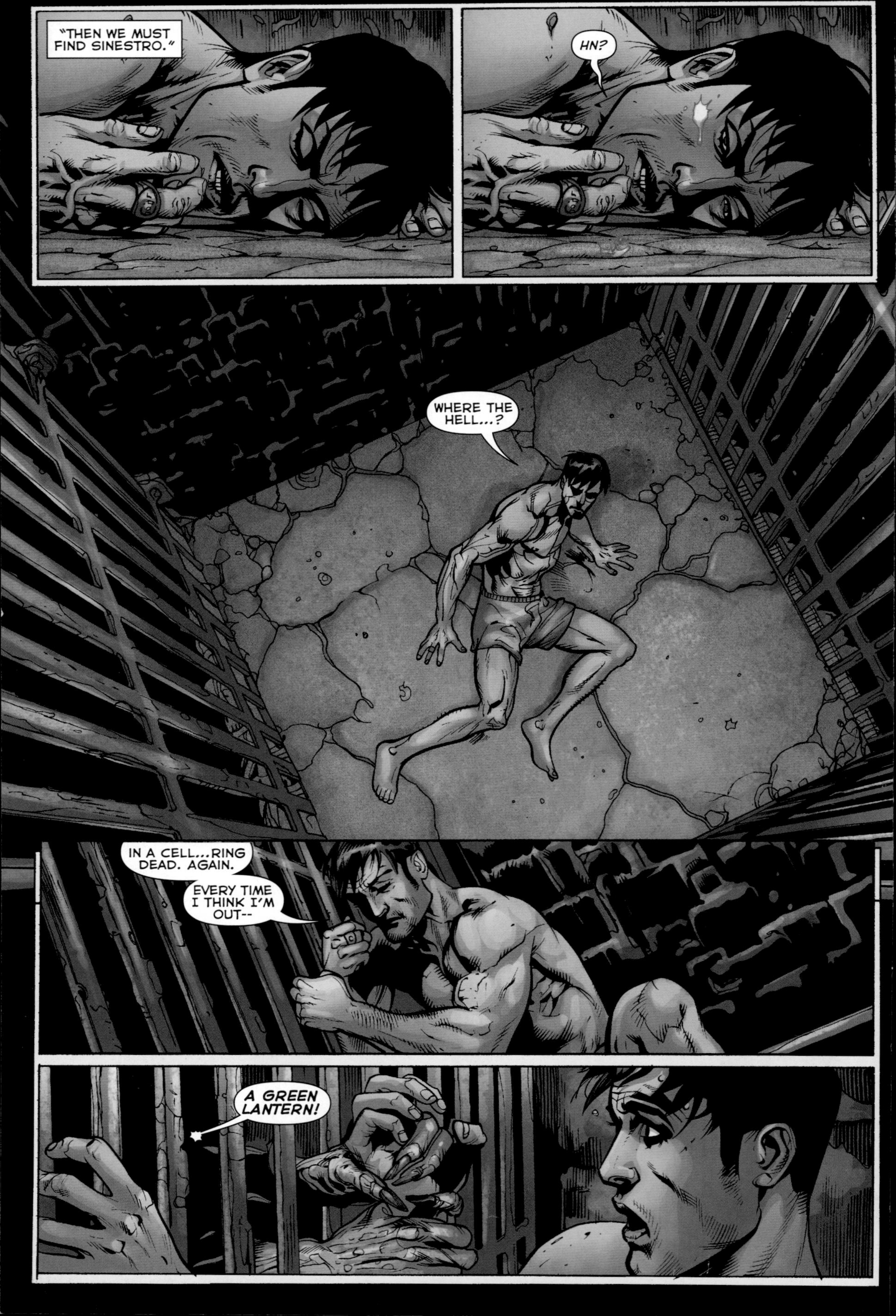

"THEN WE MUST FIND SINESTRO."
HN?
WHERE THE HELL...?
IN A CELL...RING DEAD. AGAIN.
EVERY TIME I THINK I'M OUT--
A GREEN LANTERN!

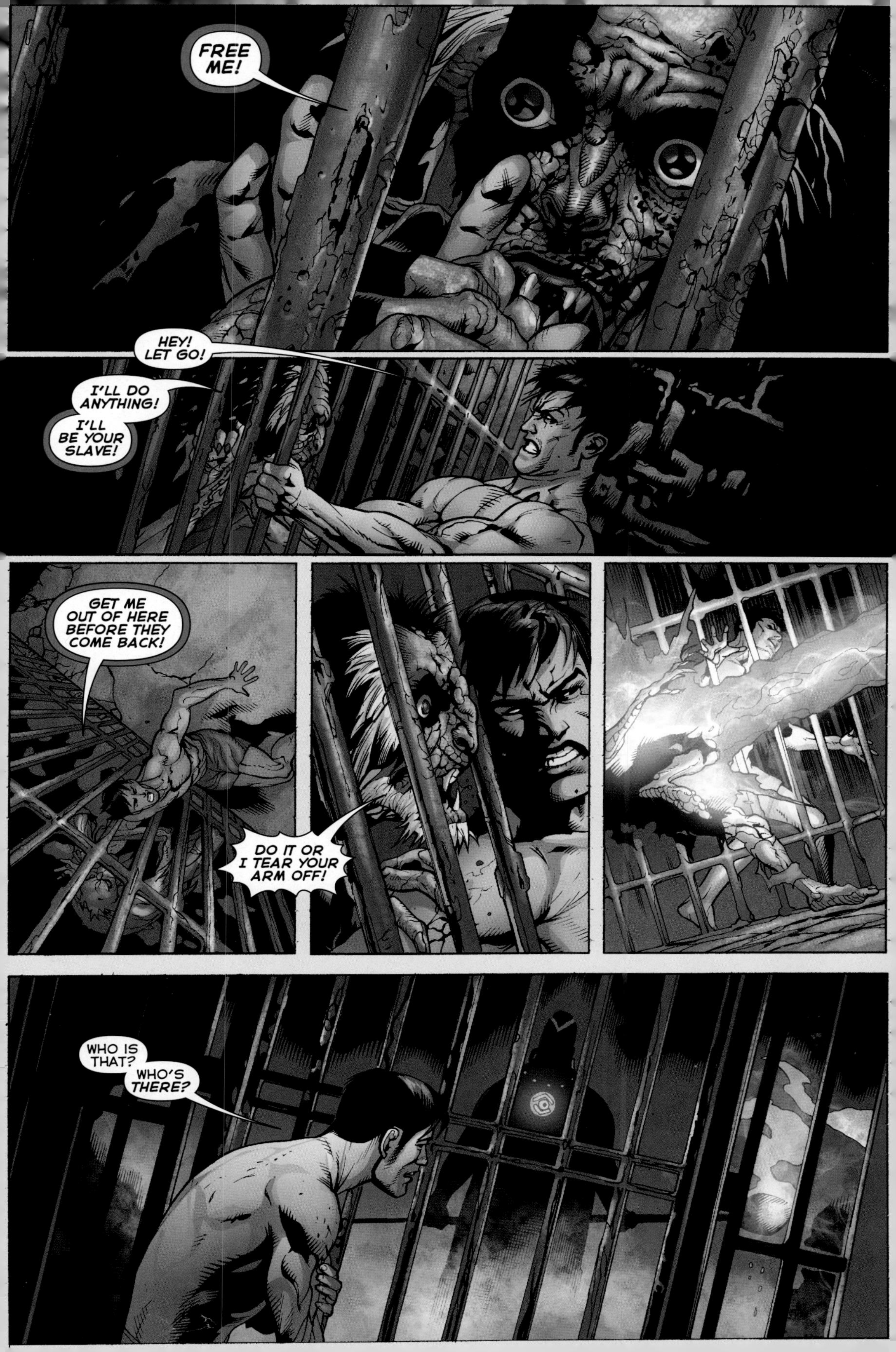
FREE ME!
HEY! LET GO!
I'LL DO ANYTHING!
I'LL BE YOUR SLAVE!
GET ME OUT OF HERE BEFORE THEY COME BACK!
DO IT OR I TEAR YOUR ARM OFF!
WHO IS THAT? WHO'S THERE?

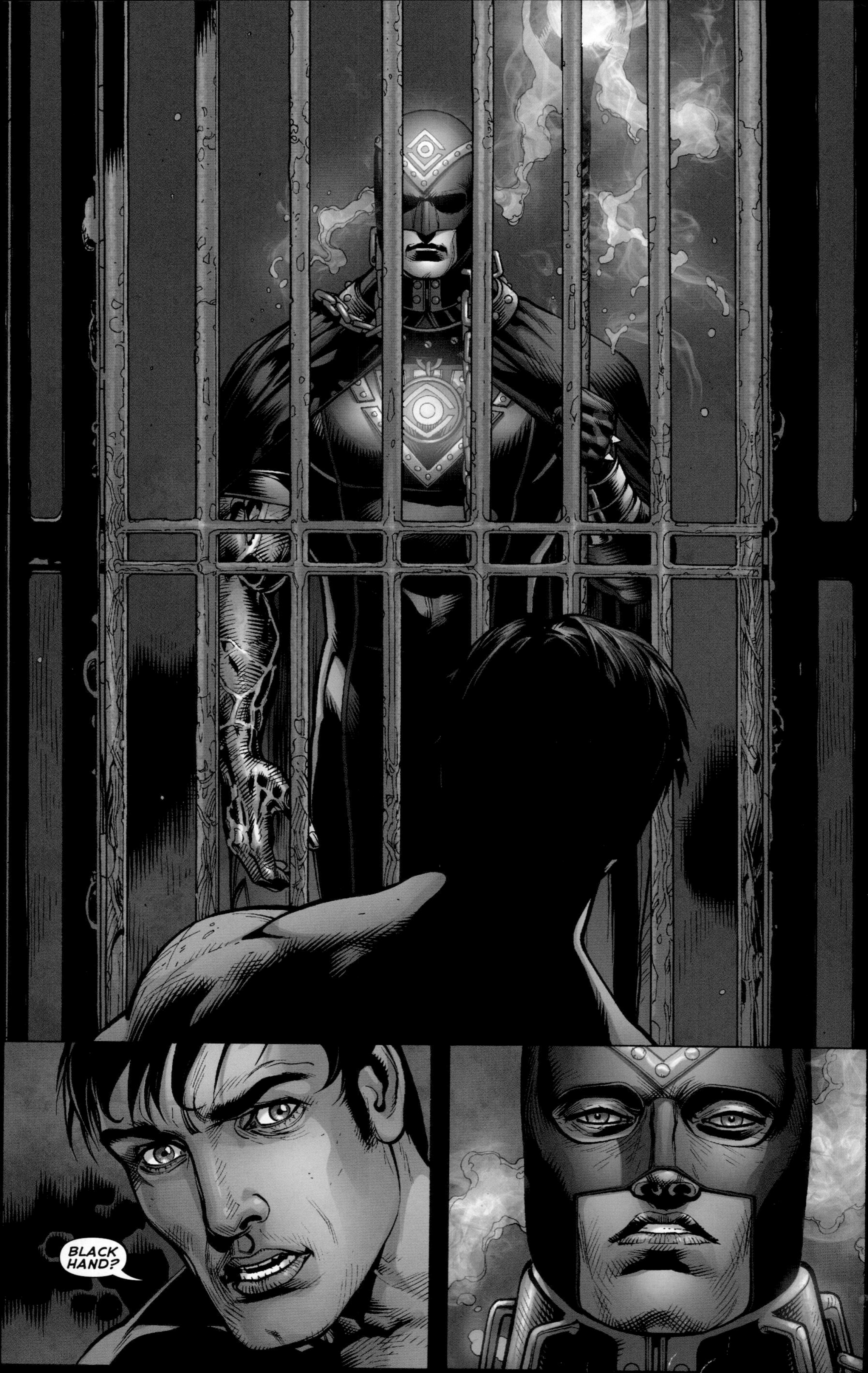
BLACK HAND?

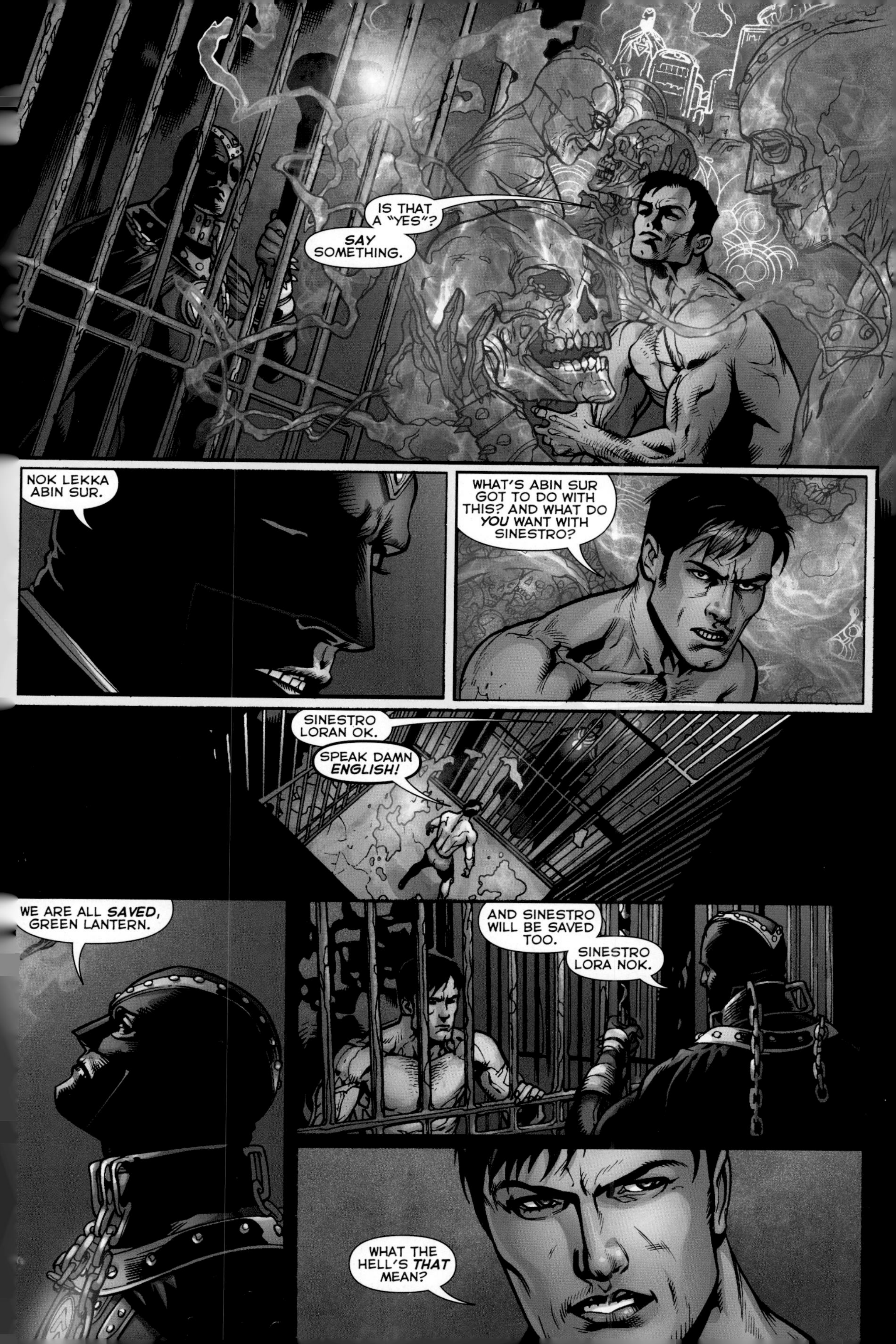
IS THAT A "YES"?
SAY SOMETHING.
NOK LEKKA ABIN SUR.
WHAT'S ABIN SUR GOT TO DO WITH THIS? AND WHAT DO YOU WANT WITH SINESTRO?
SINESTRO LORAN OK.
SPEAK DAMN ENGLISH!
WE ARE ALL SAVED, GREEN LANTERN.
AND SINESTRO WILL BE SAVED TOO.
SINESTRO LORA NOK.
WHAT THE HELL'S THAT MEAN?

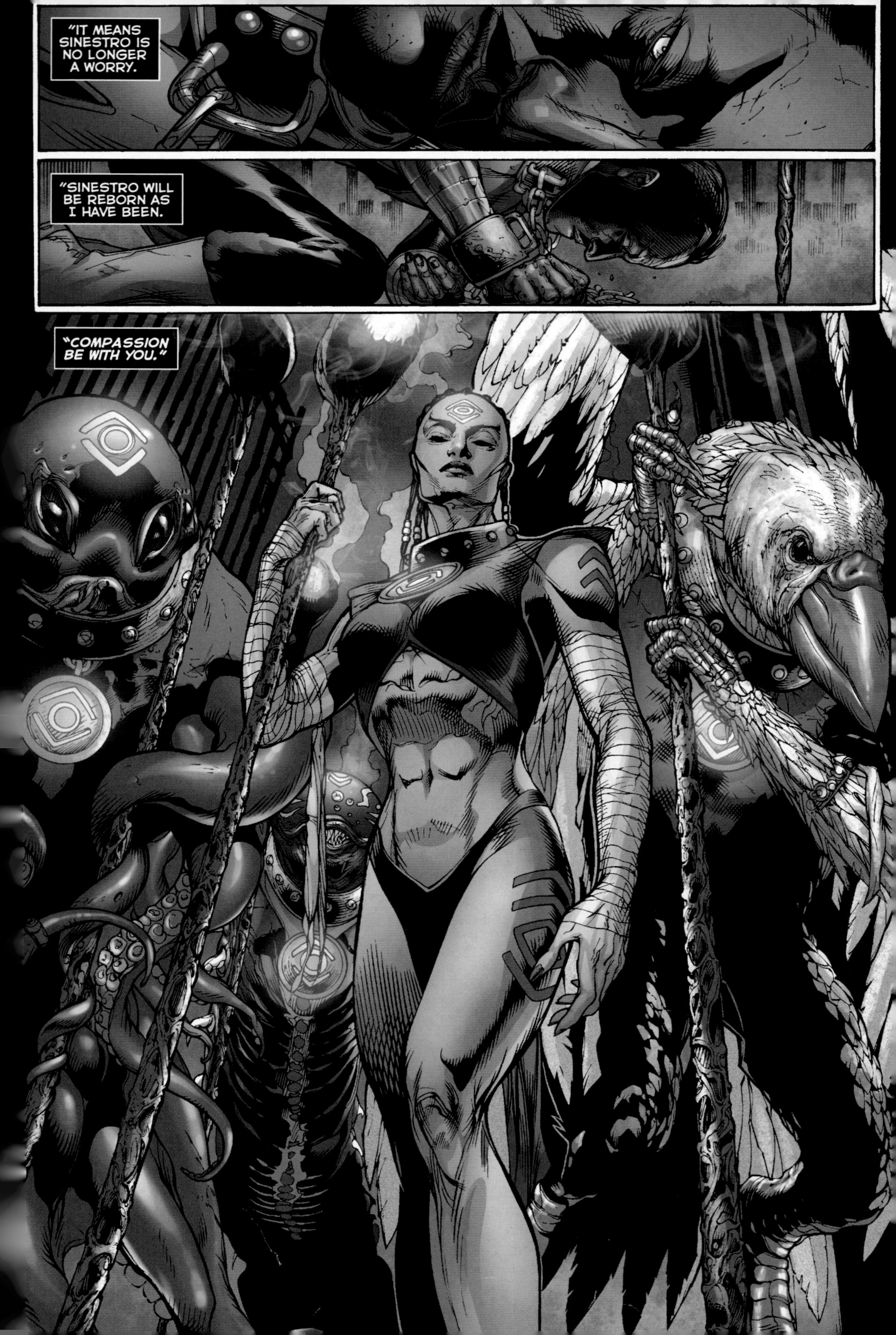
"IT MEANS SINESTRO IS NO LONGER A WORRY.
"SINESTRO WILL BE REBORN AS I HAVE BEEN.
"COMPASSION BE WITH YOU."

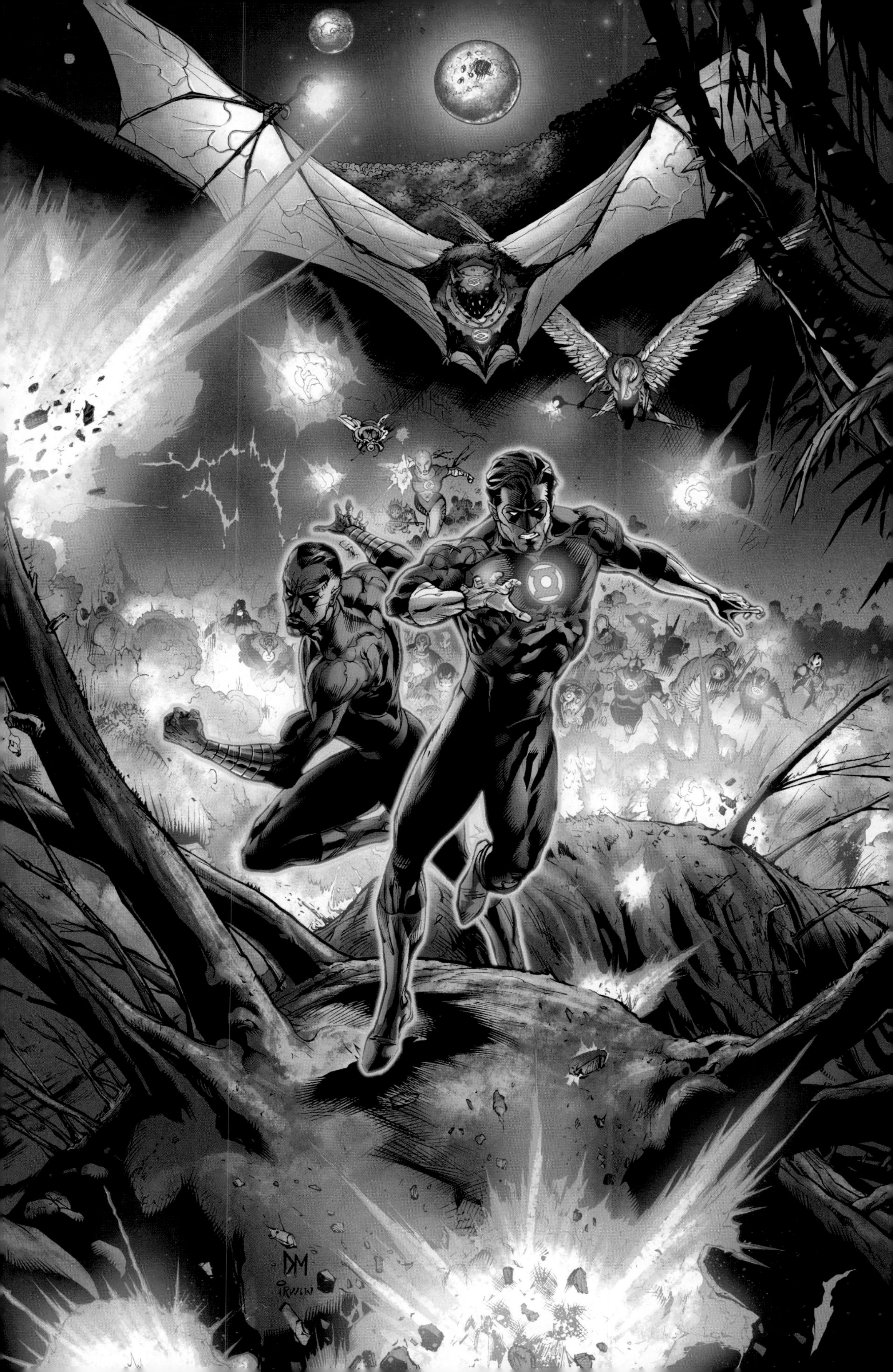

THE SECRET OF THE INDIGO TRIBE part two

GEOFF JOHNS writer **DOUG MAHNKE** penciller KEITH CHAMPAGNE, CHRISTIAN ALAMY, MARK IRWIN & DOUG MAHNKE inkers
DOUG MAHNKE, MARK IRWIN & ALEX SINCLAIR cover

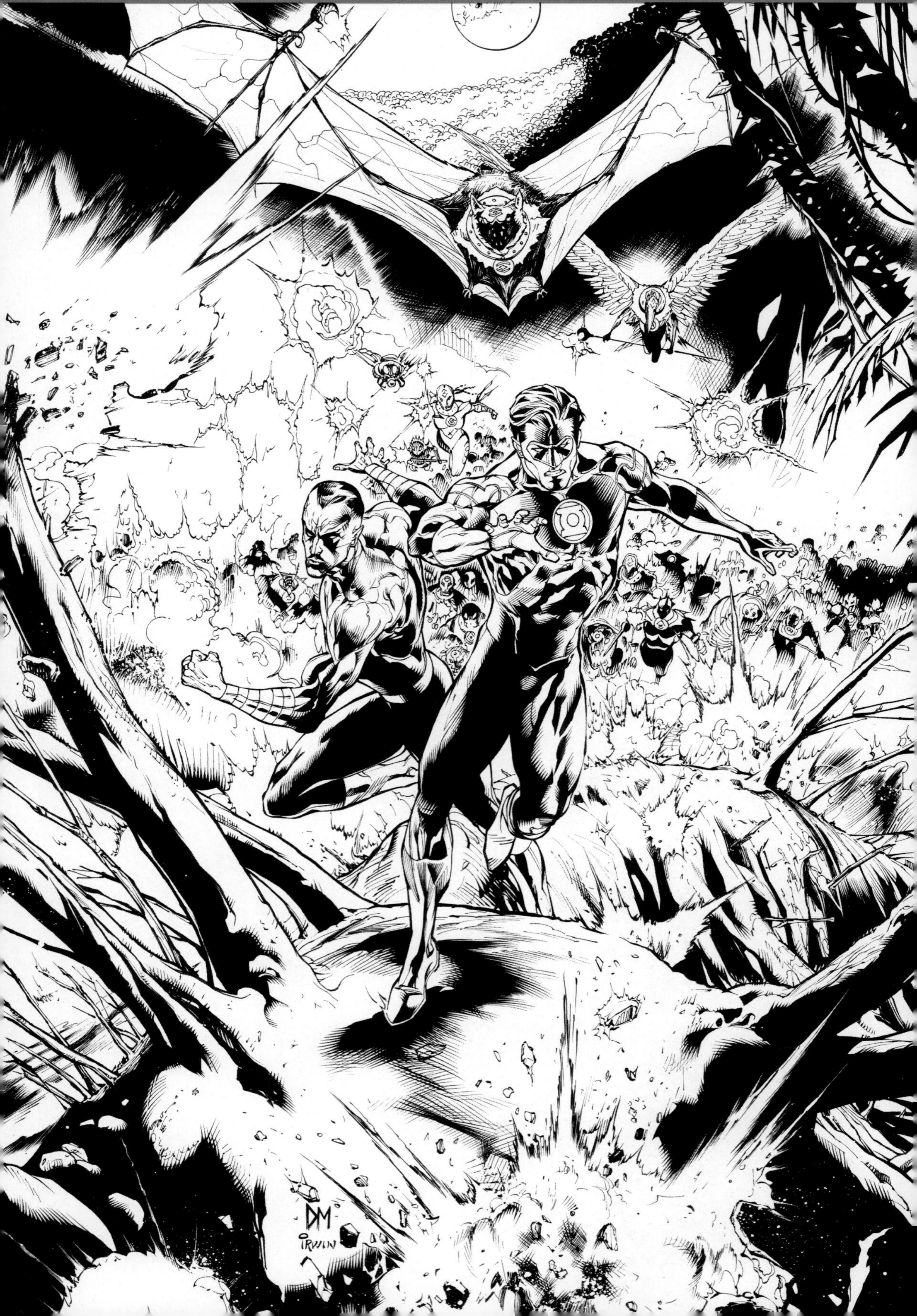

DM
IRWIN

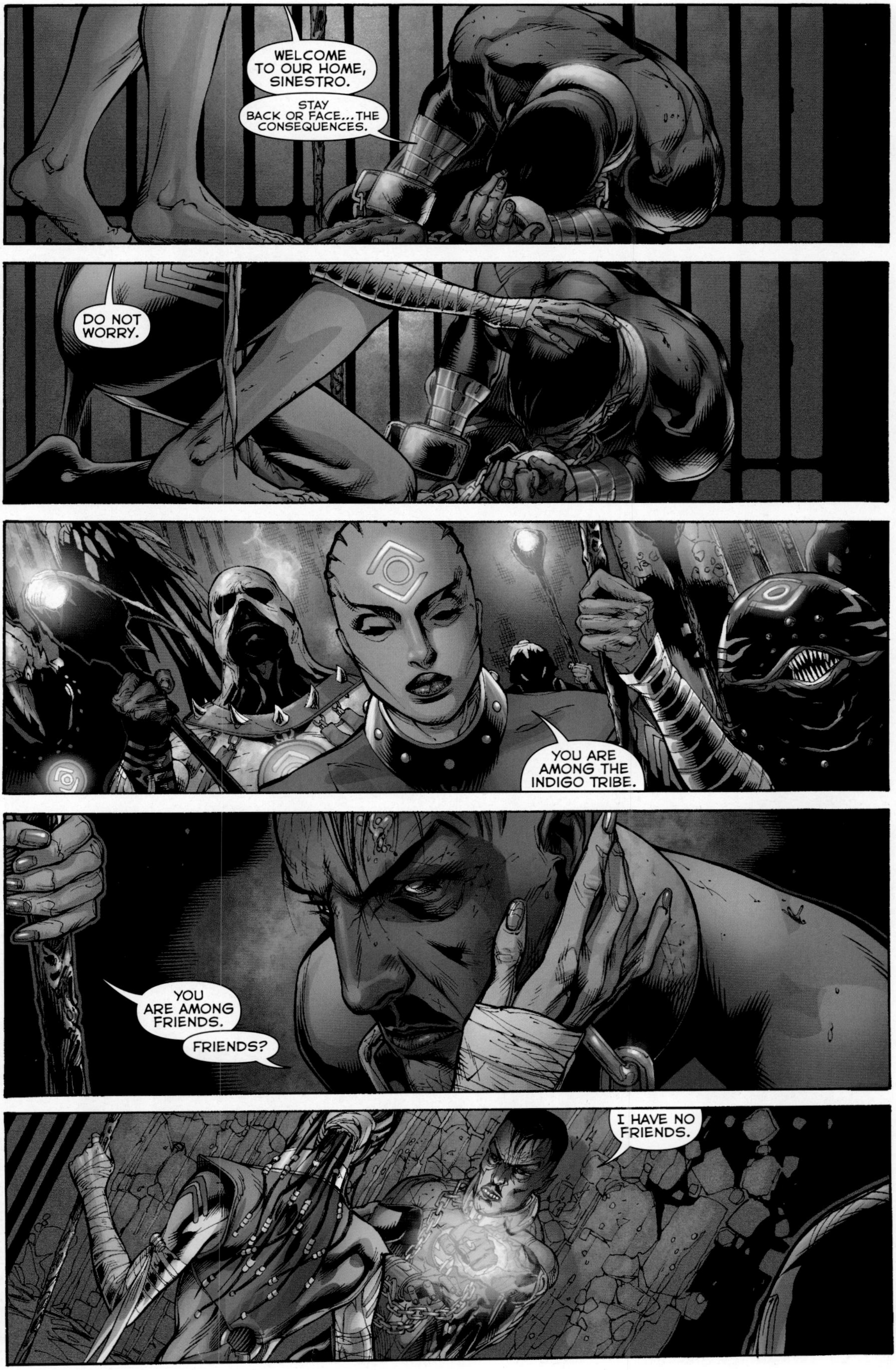
WELCOME TO OUR HOME, SINESTRO.
STAY BACK OR FACE... THE CONSEQUENCES.
DO NOT WORRY.
YOU ARE AMONG THE INDIGO TRIBE.
YOU ARE AMONG FRIENDS.
FRIENDS?
I HAVE NO FRIENDS.

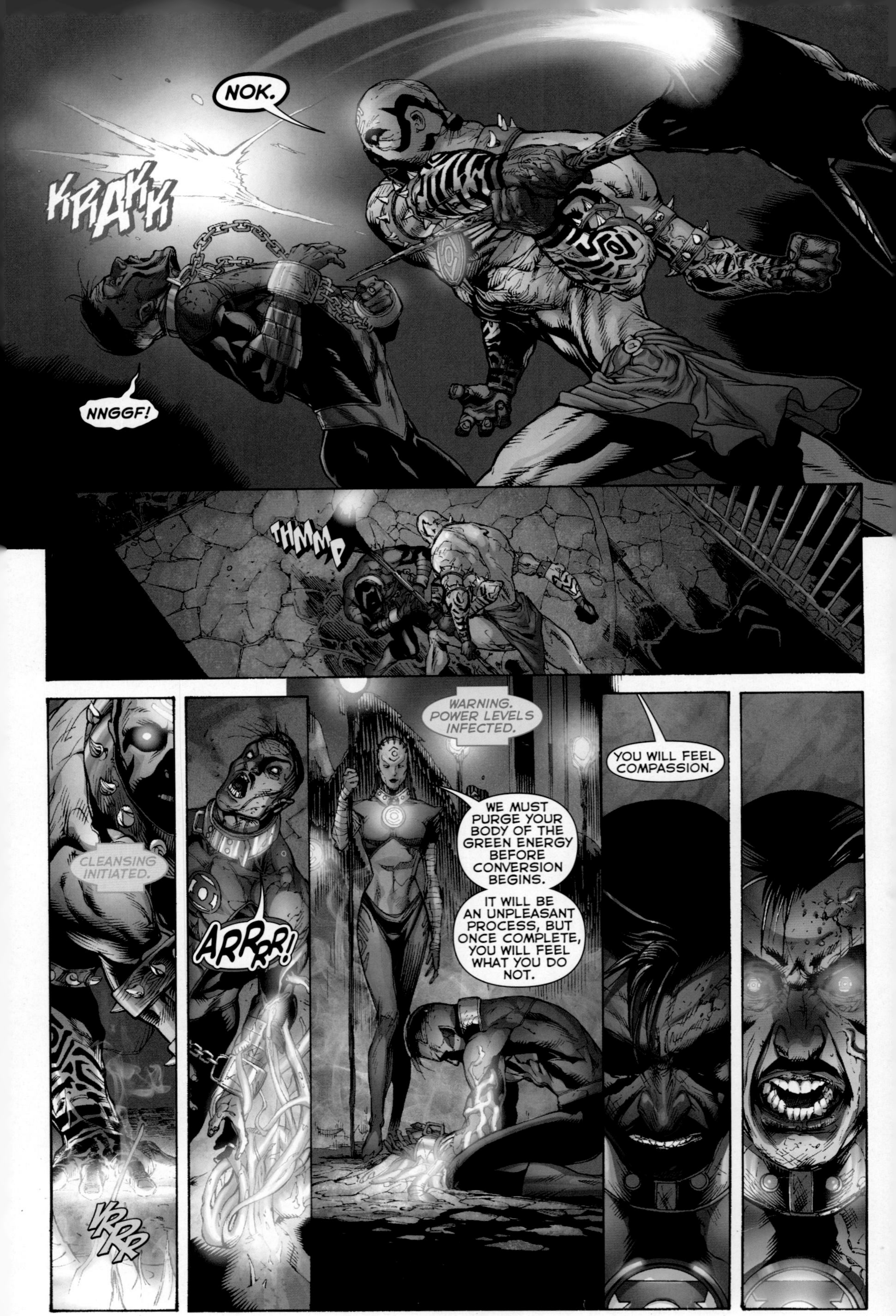
NOK.
KRAKK
NNGGF!
THMMP
CLEANSING INITIATED.
VRRR
ARRRR!
WARNING. POWER LEVELS INFECTED.
WE MUST PURGE YOUR BODY OF THE GREEN ENERGY BEFORE CONVERSION BEGINS.
IT WILL BE AN UNPLEASANT PROCESS, BUT ONCE COMPLETE, YOU WILL FEEL WHAT YOU DO NOT.
YOU WILL FEEL COMPASSION.

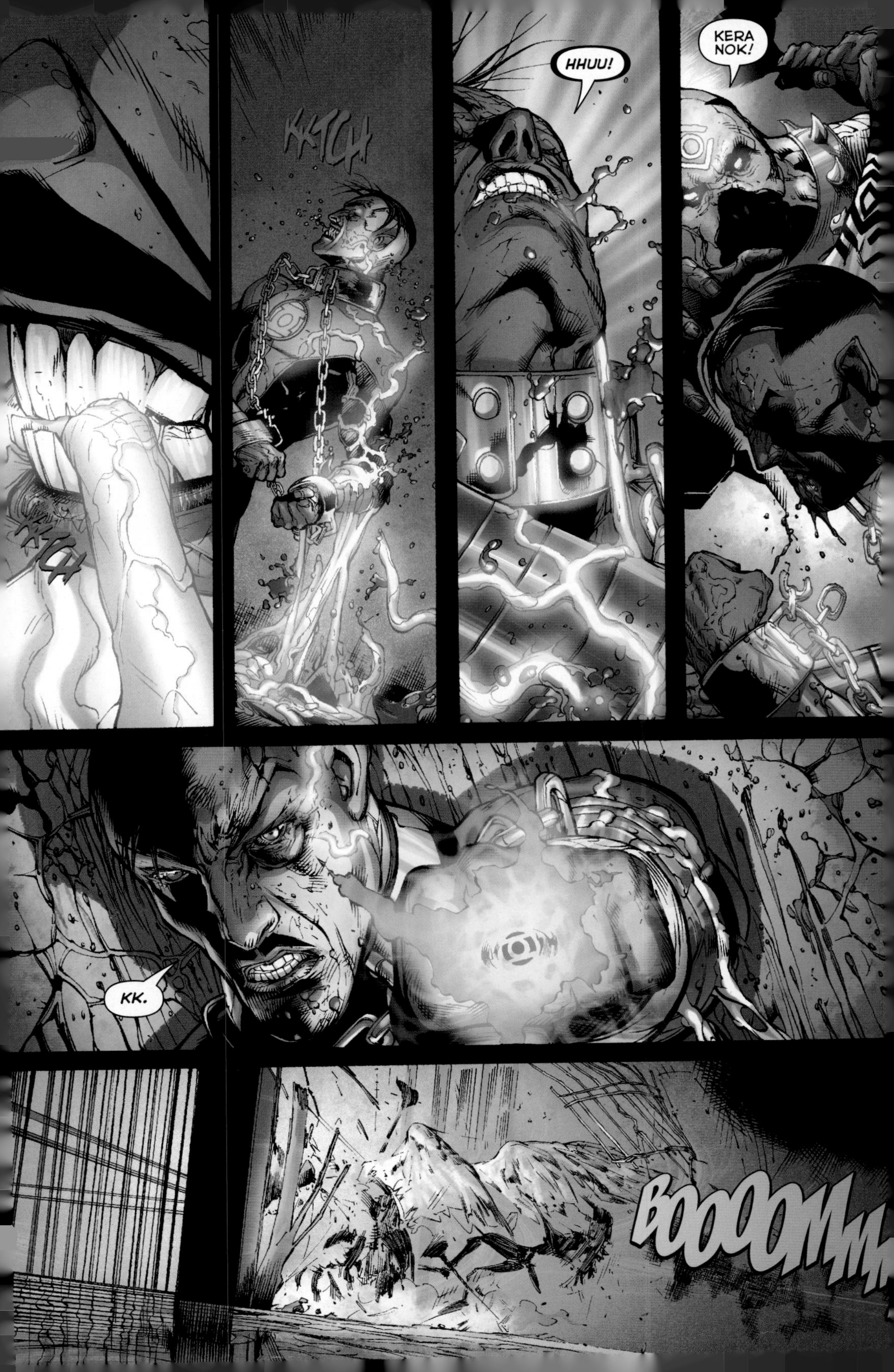

KKTCH
KKTCH
HHUU!
KERA
NOK!
KK.
BOOOOMMM

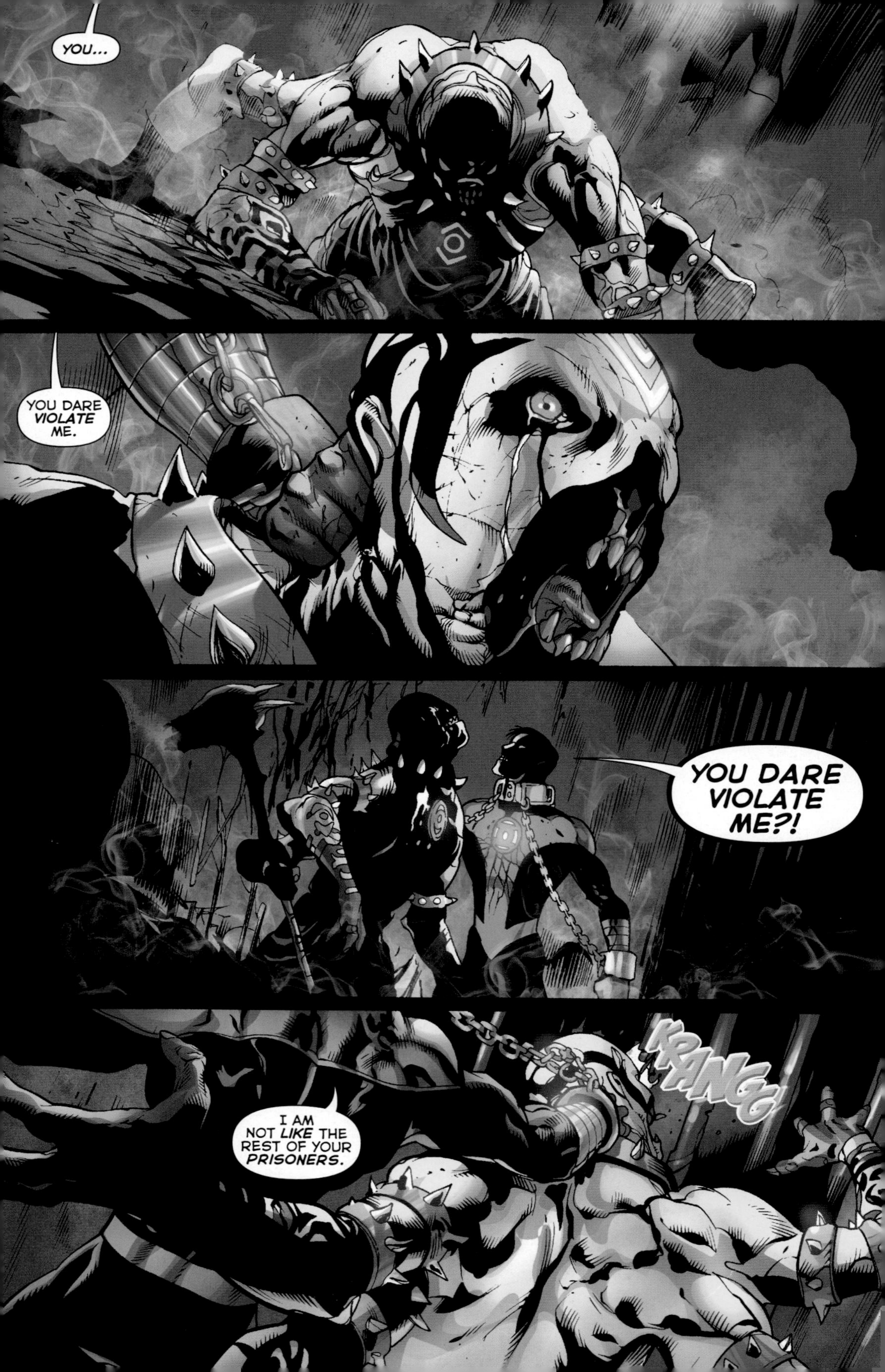
YOU...
YOU DARE *VIOLATE* ME.
YOU DARE VIOLATE ME?!
KRANGG
I AM NOT *LIKE* THE REST OF YOUR *PRISONERS*.

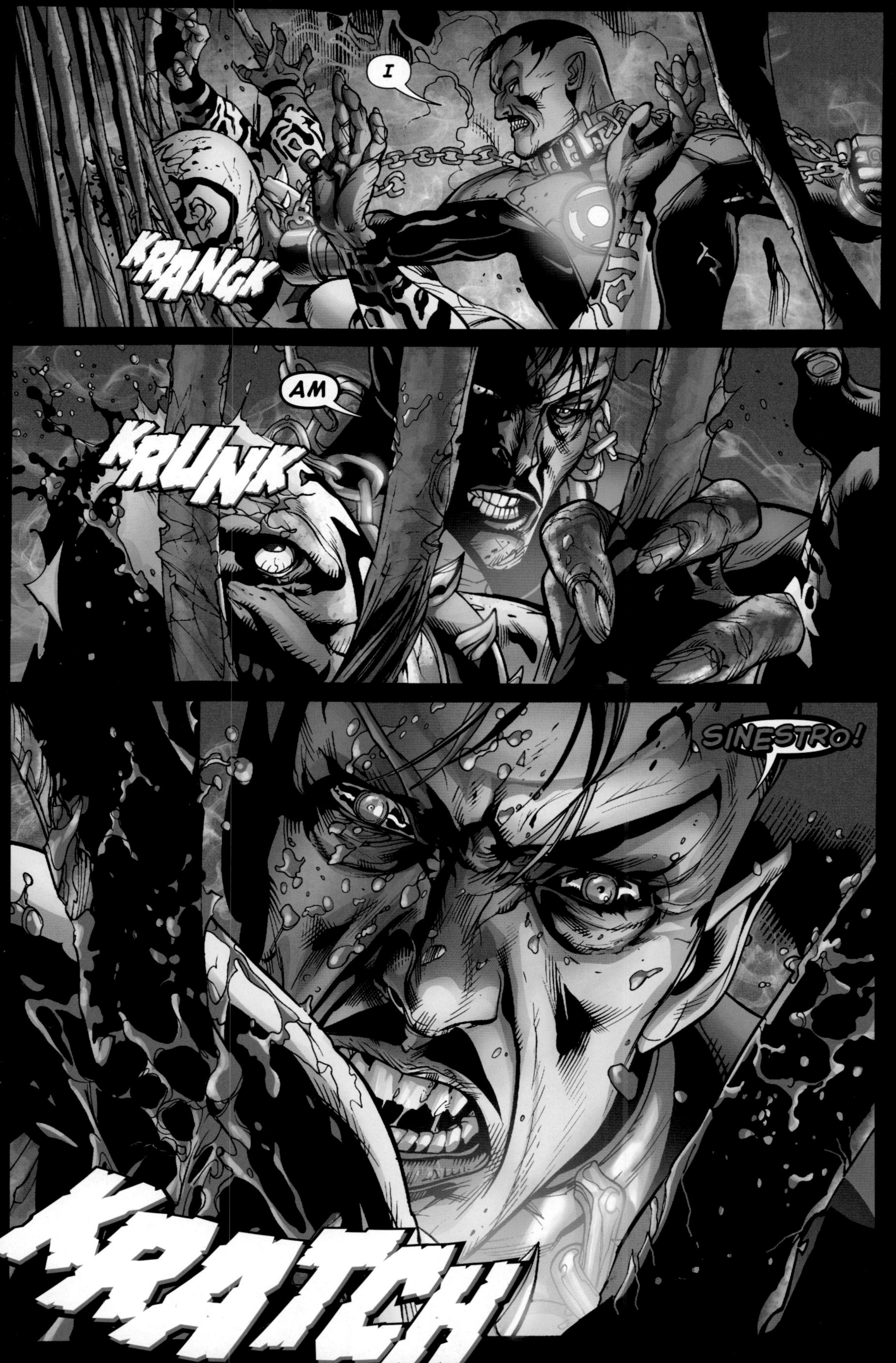

I
KRANCK
AM
KRUNK
SINESTRO!
KRATCH

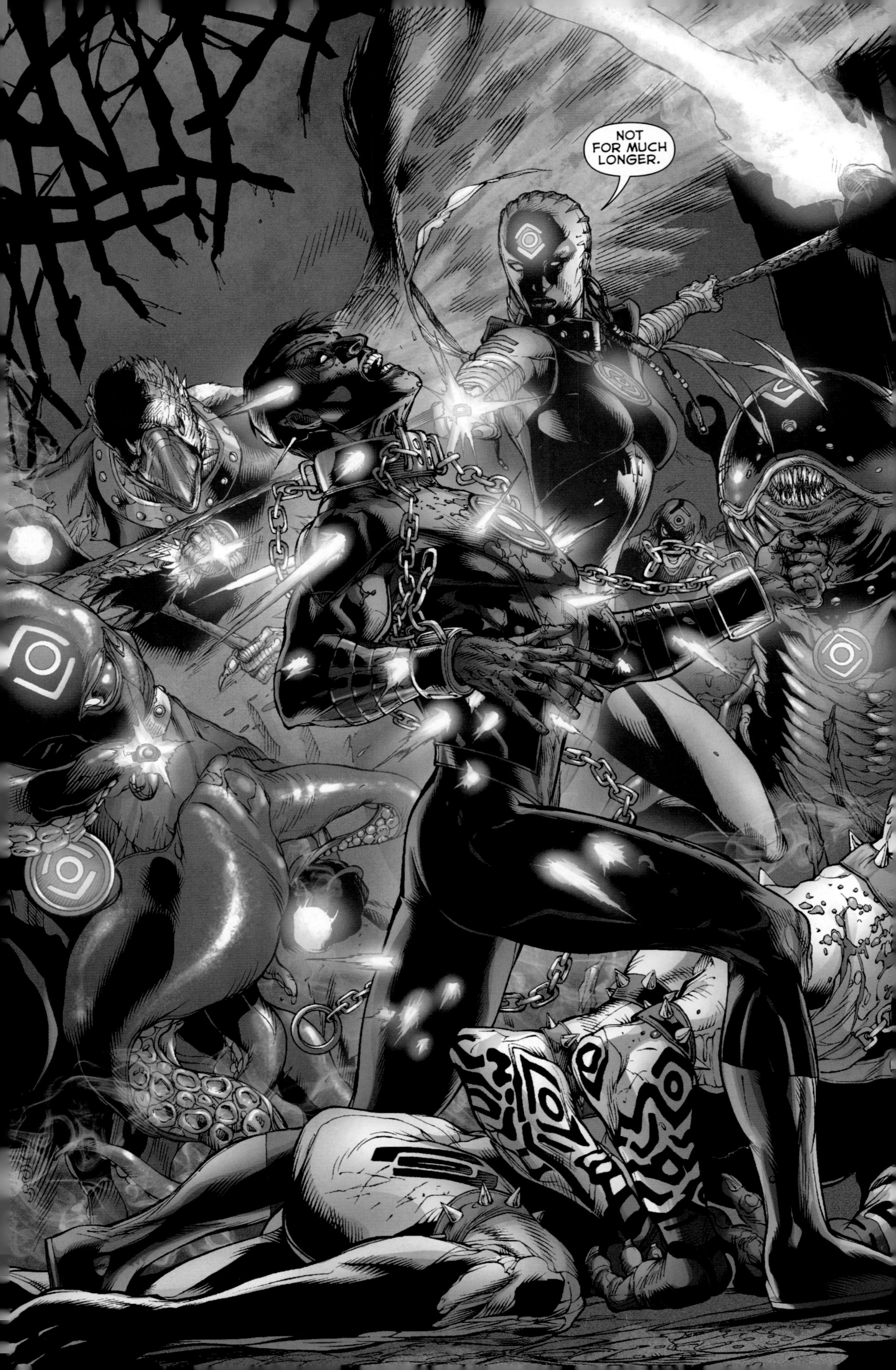
NOT FOR MUCH LONGER.

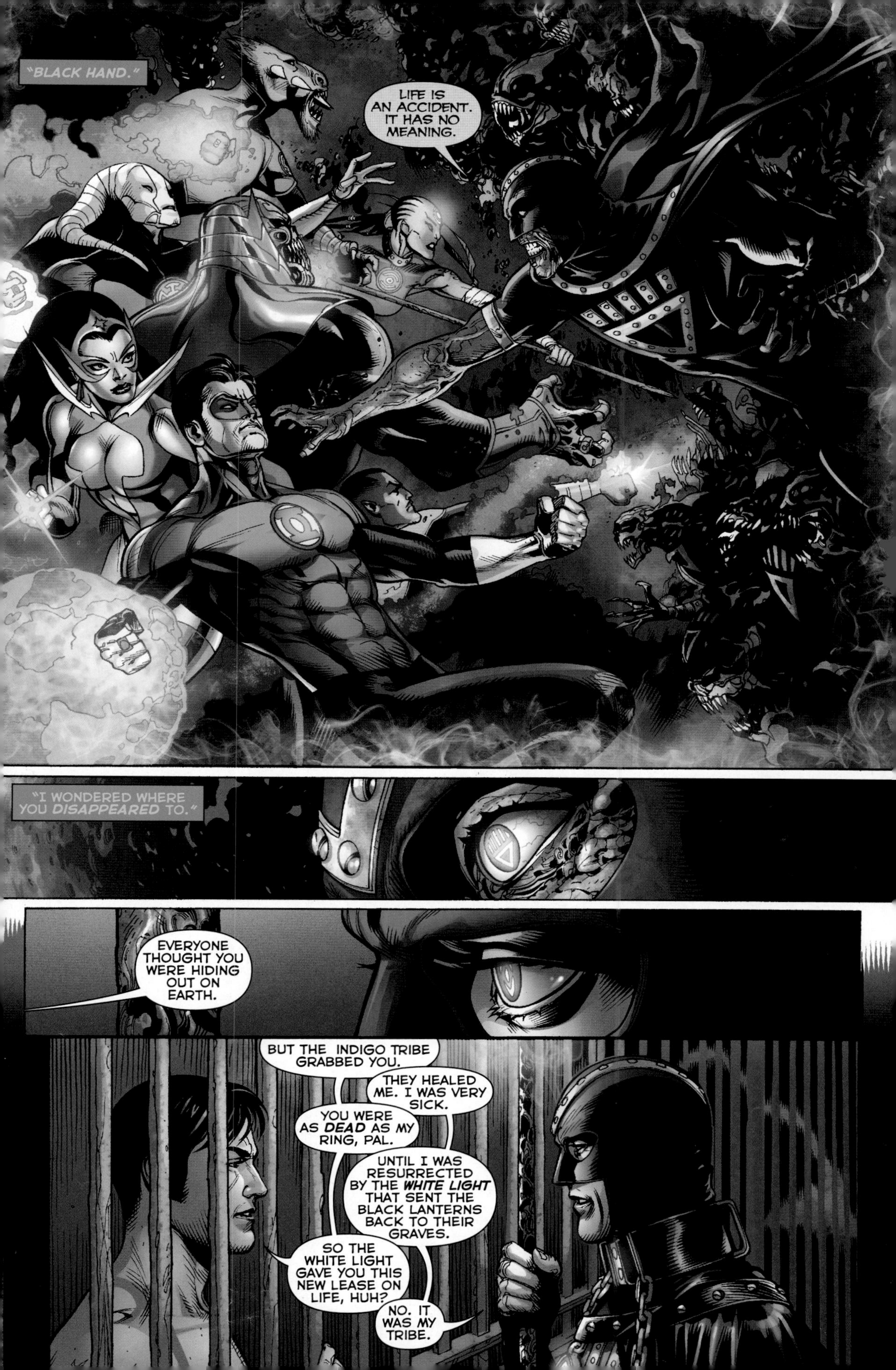
"BLACK HAND."
LIFE IS AN ACCIDENT. IT HAS NO MEANING.
"I WONDERED WHERE YOU DISAPPEARED TO."
EVERYONE THOUGHT YOU WERE HIDING OUT ON EARTH.
BUT THE INDIGO TRIBE GRABBED YOU.
THEY HEALED ME. I WAS VERY SICK.
YOU WERE AS DEAD AS MY RING, PAL.
UNTIL I WAS RESURRECTED BY THE WHITE LIGHT THAT SENT THE BLACK LANTERNS BACK TO THEIR GRAVES.
SO THE WHITE LIGHT GAVE YOU THIS NEW LEASE ON LIFE, HUH?
NO. IT WAS MY TRIBE.

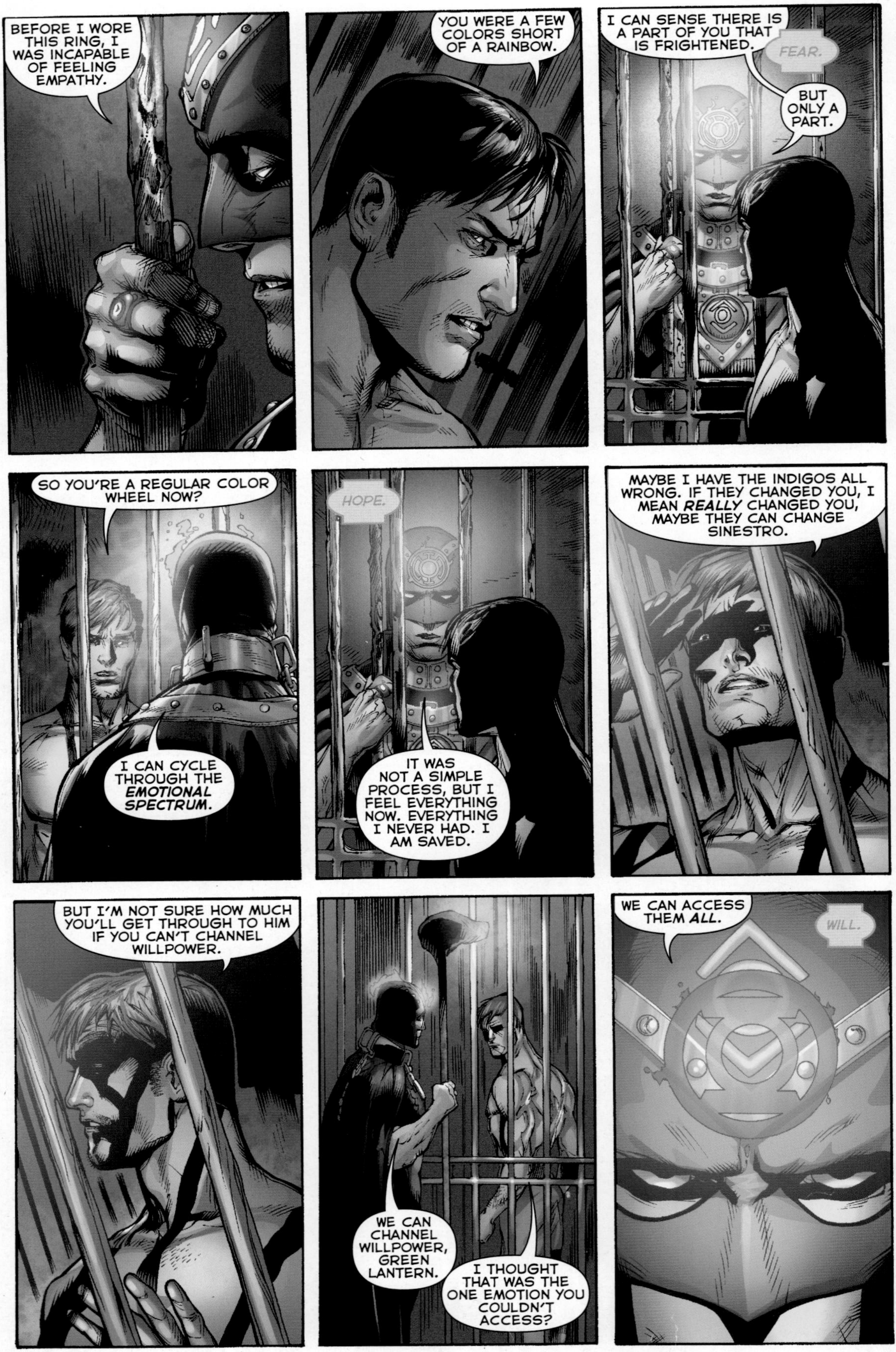
BEFORE I WORE THIS RING, I WAS INCAPABLE OF FEELING EMPATHY.
YOU WERE A FEW COLORS SHORT OF A RAINBOW.
I CAN SENSE THERE IS A PART OF YOU THAT IS FRIGHTENED.
FEAR.
BUT ONLY A PART.
SO YOU'RE A REGULAR COLOR WHEEL NOW?
I CAN CYCLE THROUGH THE EMOTIONAL SPECTRUM.
HOPE.
IT WAS NOT A SIMPLE PROCESS, BUT I FEEL EVERYTHING NOW. EVERYTHING I NEVER HAD. I AM SAVED.
MAYBE I HAVE THE INDIGOS ALL WRONG. IF THEY CHANGED YOU, I MEAN REALLY CHANGED YOU, MAYBE THEY CAN CHANGE SINESTRO.
BUT I'M NOT SURE HOW MUCH YOU'LL GET THROUGH TO HIM IF YOU CAN'T CHANNEL WILLPOWER.
WE CAN CHANNEL WILLPOWER, GREEN LANTERN.
I THOUGHT THAT WAS THE ONE EMOTION YOU COULDN'T ACCESS?
WE CAN ACCESS THEM ALL.
WILL.

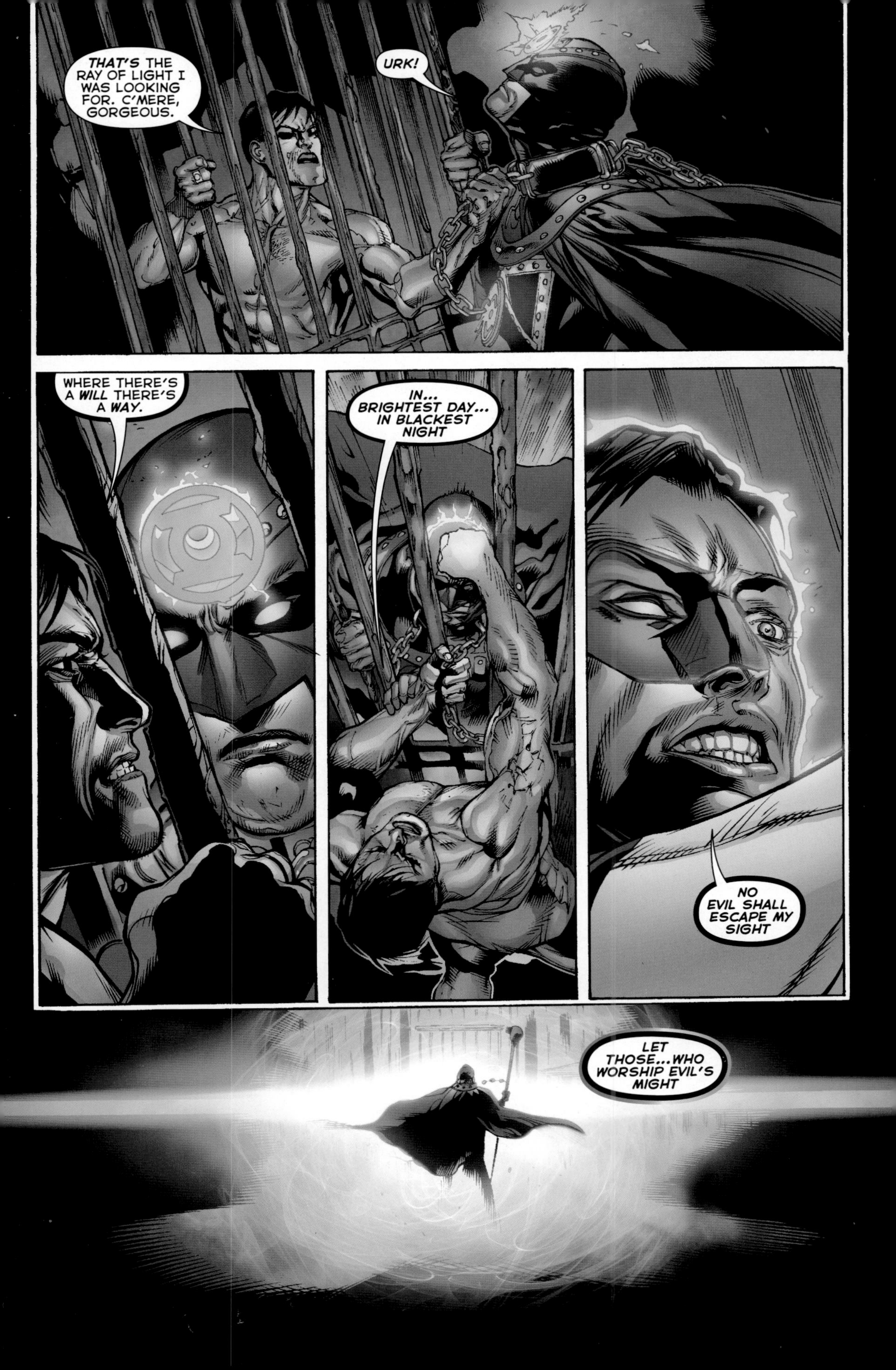
THAT'S THE RAY OF LIGHT I WAS LOOKING FOR. C'MERE, GORGEOUS.
URK!
WHERE THERE'S A WILL THERE'S A WAY.
IN... BRIGHTEST DAY... IN BLACKEST NIGHT
NO EVIL SHALL ESCAPE MY SIGHT
LET THOSE...WHO WORSHIP EVIL'S MIGHT

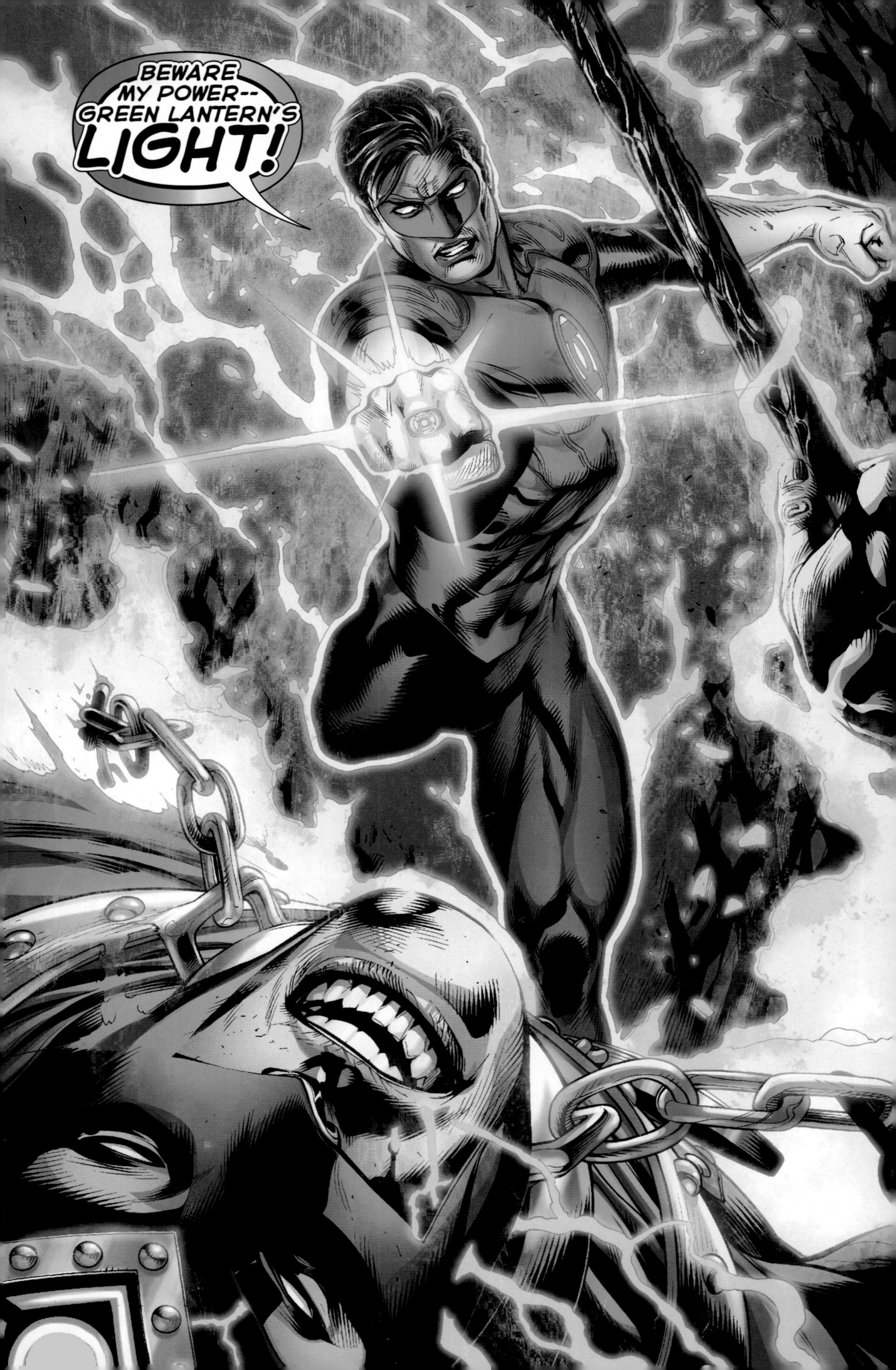
BEWARE MY POWER-- GREEN LANTERN'S LIGHT!

WE'RE GOING TO PLAY A *GAME*, BLACK HAND. IT'S CALLED TAKE ME TO YOUR LEADER BEFORE I SHOVE YOUR STICK WHERE MY LIGHT DOESN'T SH--

FWAAAASH

LERAK KO.

KRUNGG   KRUNGG

NNFF!

KRAAAMMM

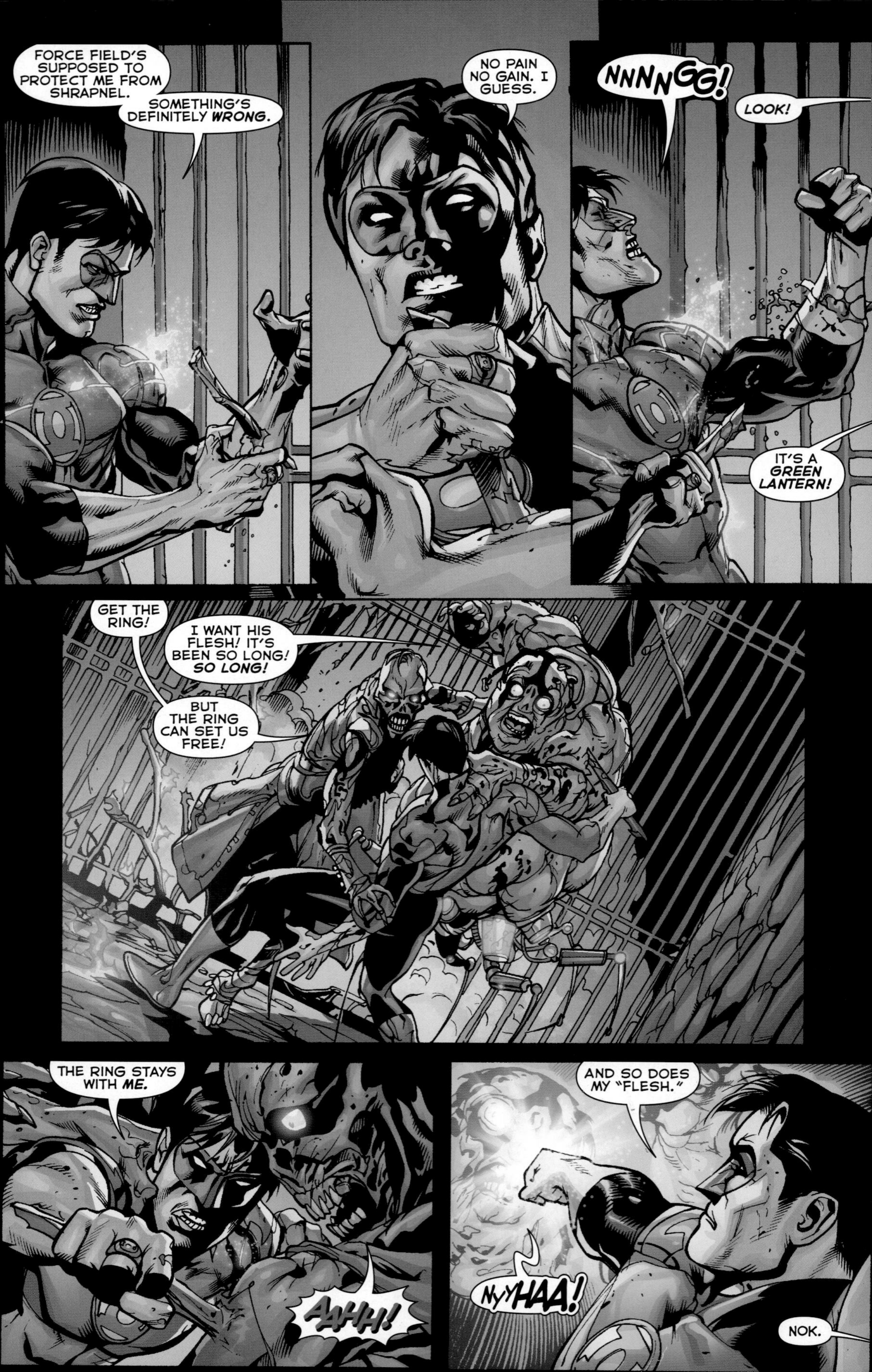

FORCE FIELD'S SUPPOSED TO PROTECT ME FROM SHRAPNEL.
SOMETHING'S DEFINITELY WRONG.
NO PAIN NO GAIN. I GUESS.
NNNNGG!
LOOK!
IT'S A GREEN LANTERN!
GET THE RING!
I WANT HIS FLESH! IT'S BEEN SO LONG! SO LONG!
BUT THE RING CAN SET US FREE!
THE RING STAYS WITH ME.
AAHH!
AND SO DOES MY "FLESH."
NyyHAA!
NOK.

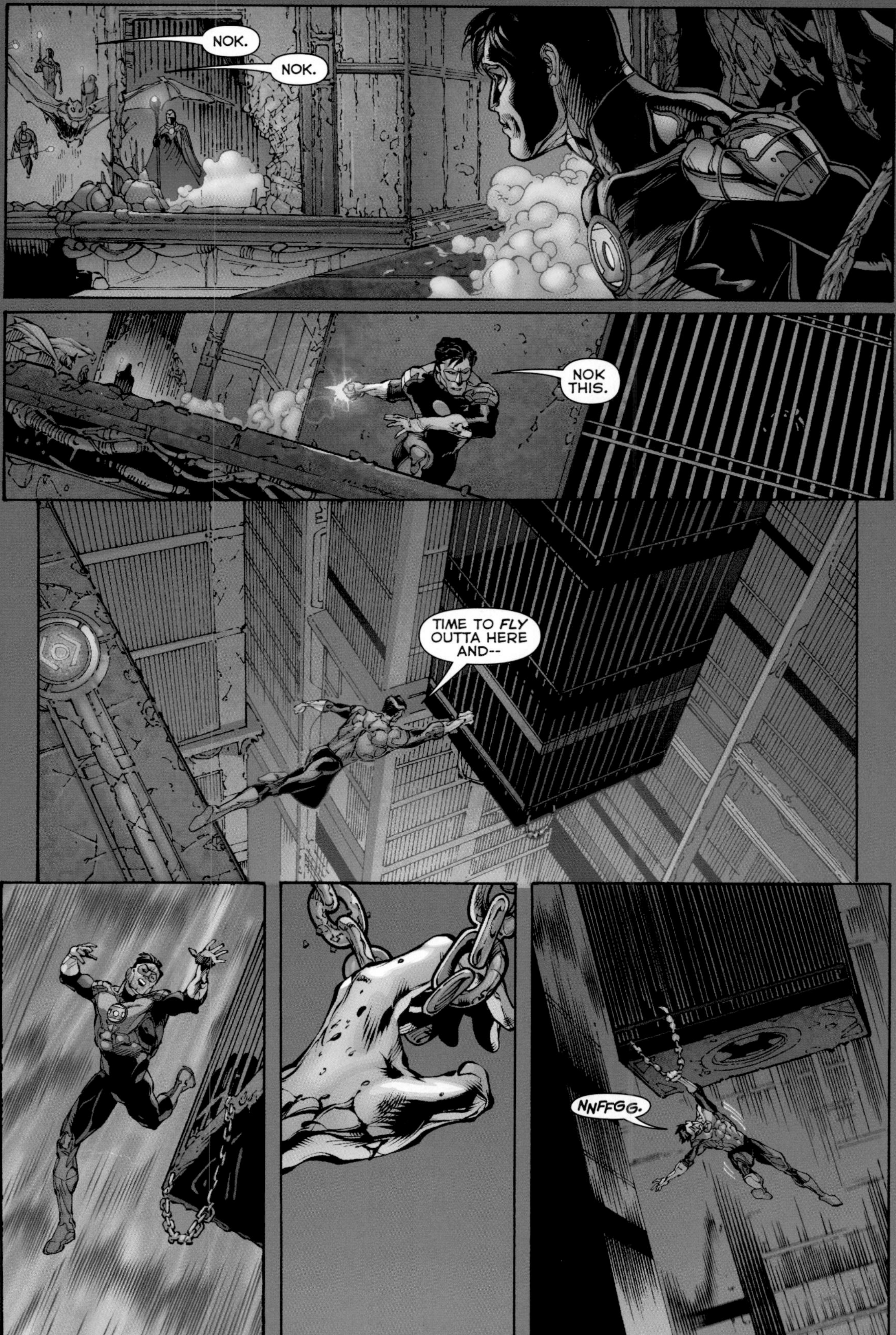
NOK.
NOK.
NOK THIS.
TIME TO FLY OUTTA HERE AND--
NNFFGG.

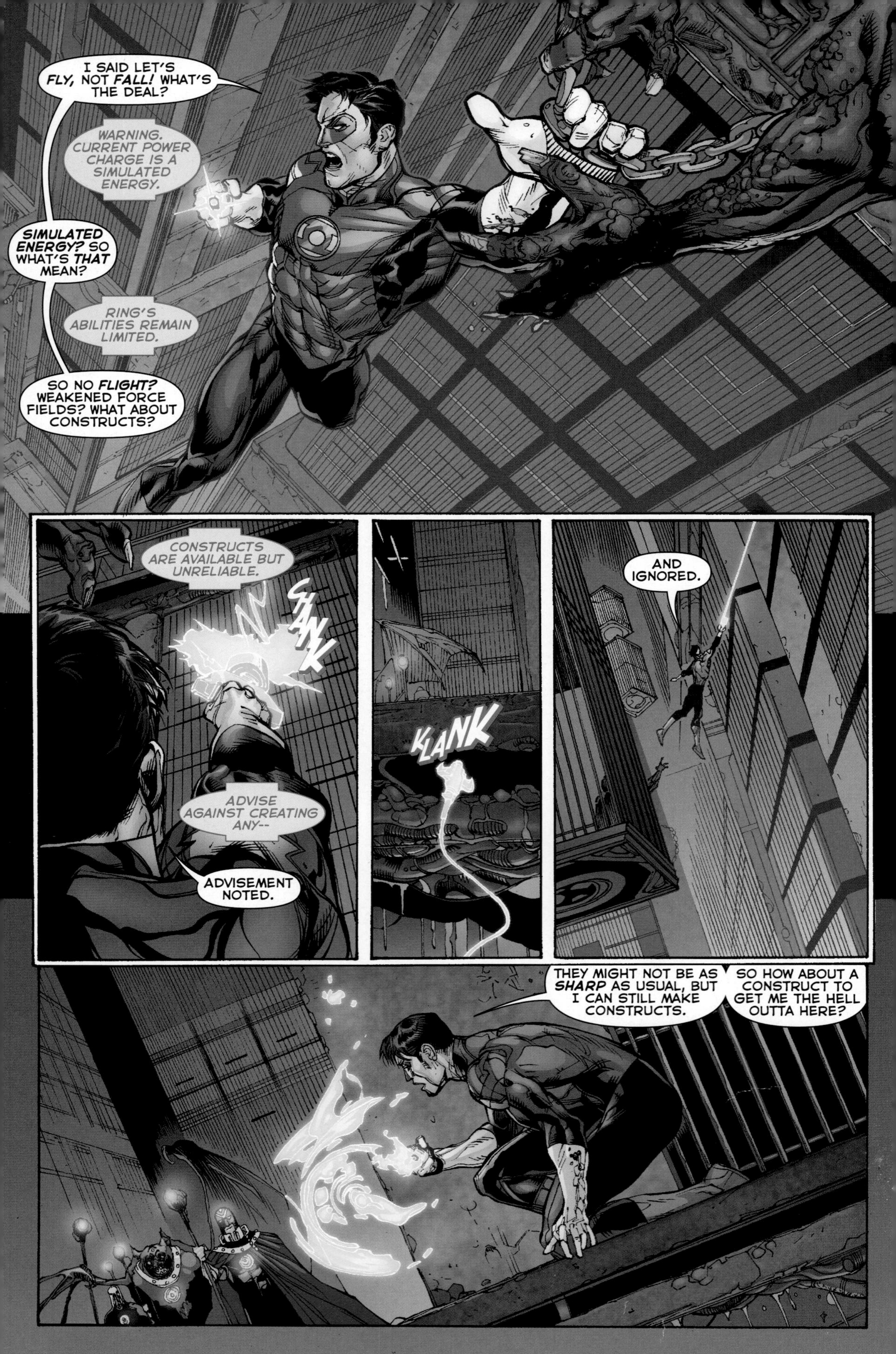

I SAID LET'S FLY, NOT FALL! WHAT'S THE DEAL?
WARNING. CURRENT POWER CHARGE IS A SIMULATED ENERGY.
SIMULATED ENERGY? SO WHAT'S THAT MEAN?
RING'S ABILITIES REMAIN LIMITED.
SO NO FLIGHT? WEAKENED FORCE FIELDS? WHAT ABOUT CONSTRUCTS?
CONSTRUCTS ARE AVAILABLE BUT UNRELIABLE.
CHANK
ADVISE AGAINST CREATING ANY--
ADVISEMENT NOTED.
KLANK
AND IGNORED.
THEY MIGHT NOT BE AS SHARP AS USUAL, BUT I CAN STILL MAKE CONSTRUCTS.
SO HOW ABOUT A CONSTRUCT TO GET ME THE HELL OUTTA HERE?

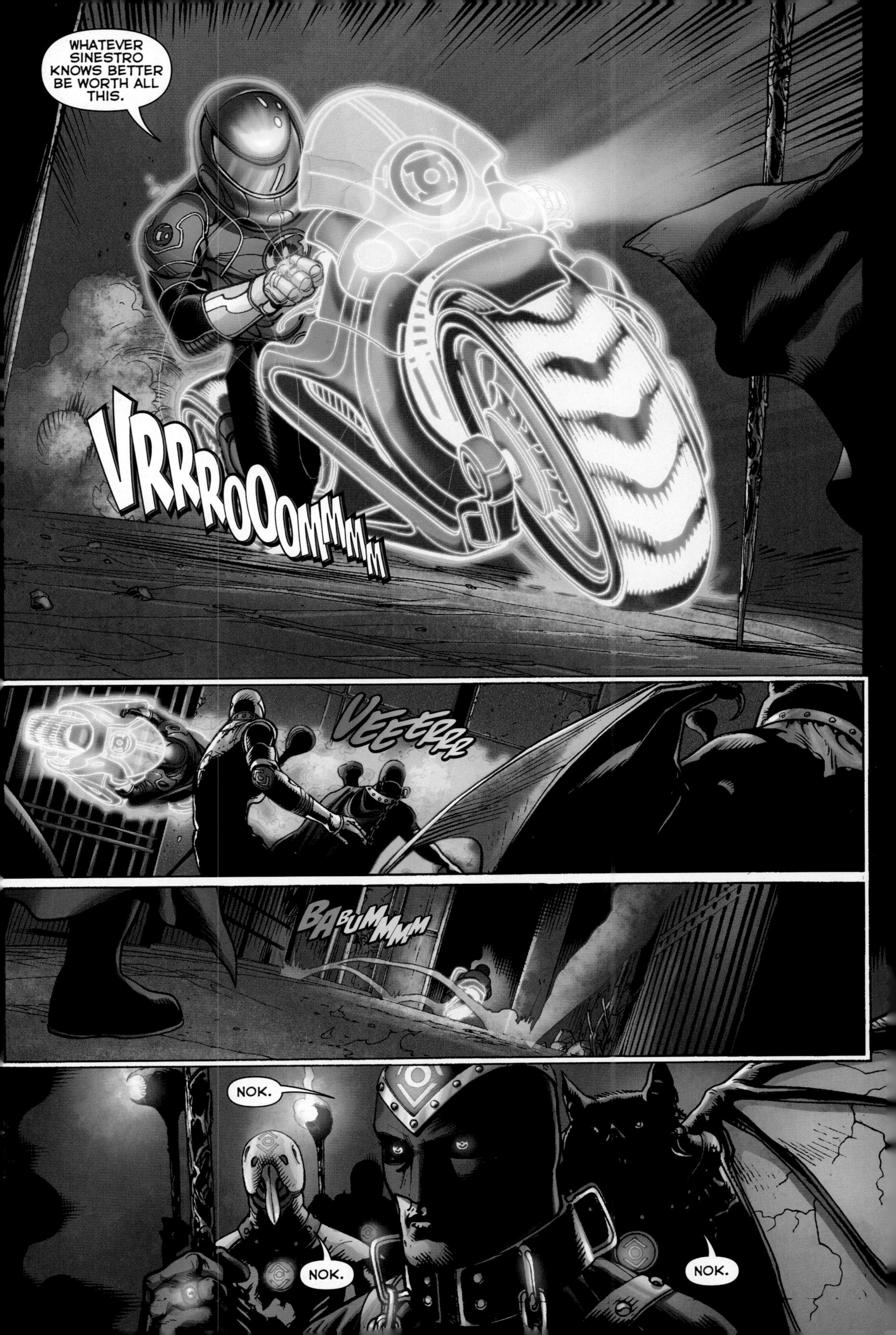

WHATEVER SINESTRO KNOWS BETTER BE WORTH ALL THIS.
VRRROOOMMMM
VEEERRR
BABUMMMM
NOK.
NOK.
NOK.

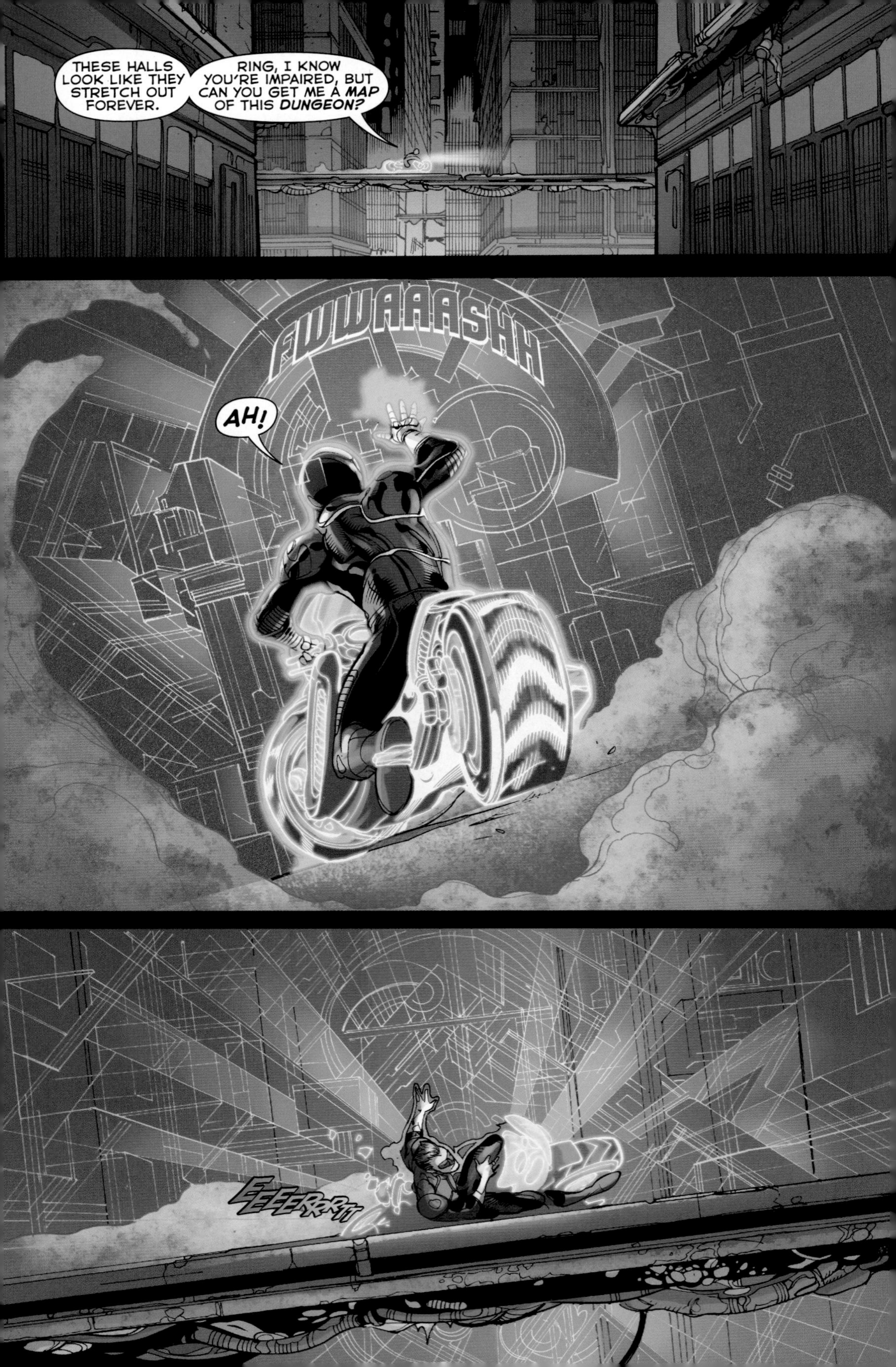
THESE HALLS LOOK LIKE THEY STRETCH OUT FOREVER.
RING, I KNOW YOU'RE IMPAIRED, BUT CAN YOU GET ME A MAP OF THIS DUNGEON?
FWWAAASHH
AH!
EEEERRRTT

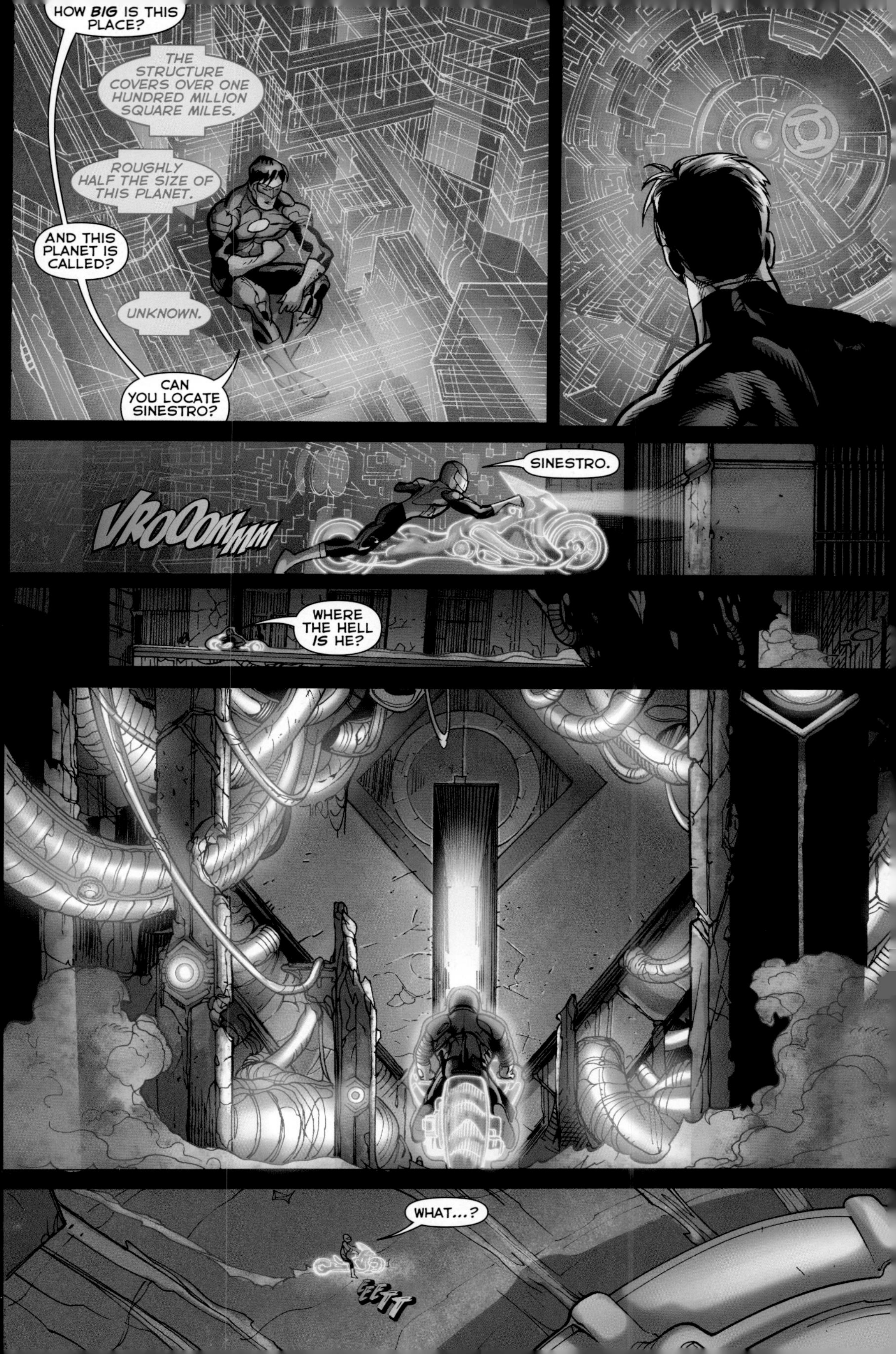
HOW BIG IS THIS PLACE?
THE STRUCTURE COVERS OVER ONE HUNDRED MILLION SQUARE MILES.
ROUGHLY HALF THE SIZE OF THIS PLANET.
AND THIS PLANET IS CALLED?
UNKNOWN.
CAN YOU LOCATE SINESTRO?
SINESTRO.
VROOOMMM
WHERE THE HELL IS HE?
WHAT...?
EEEITT

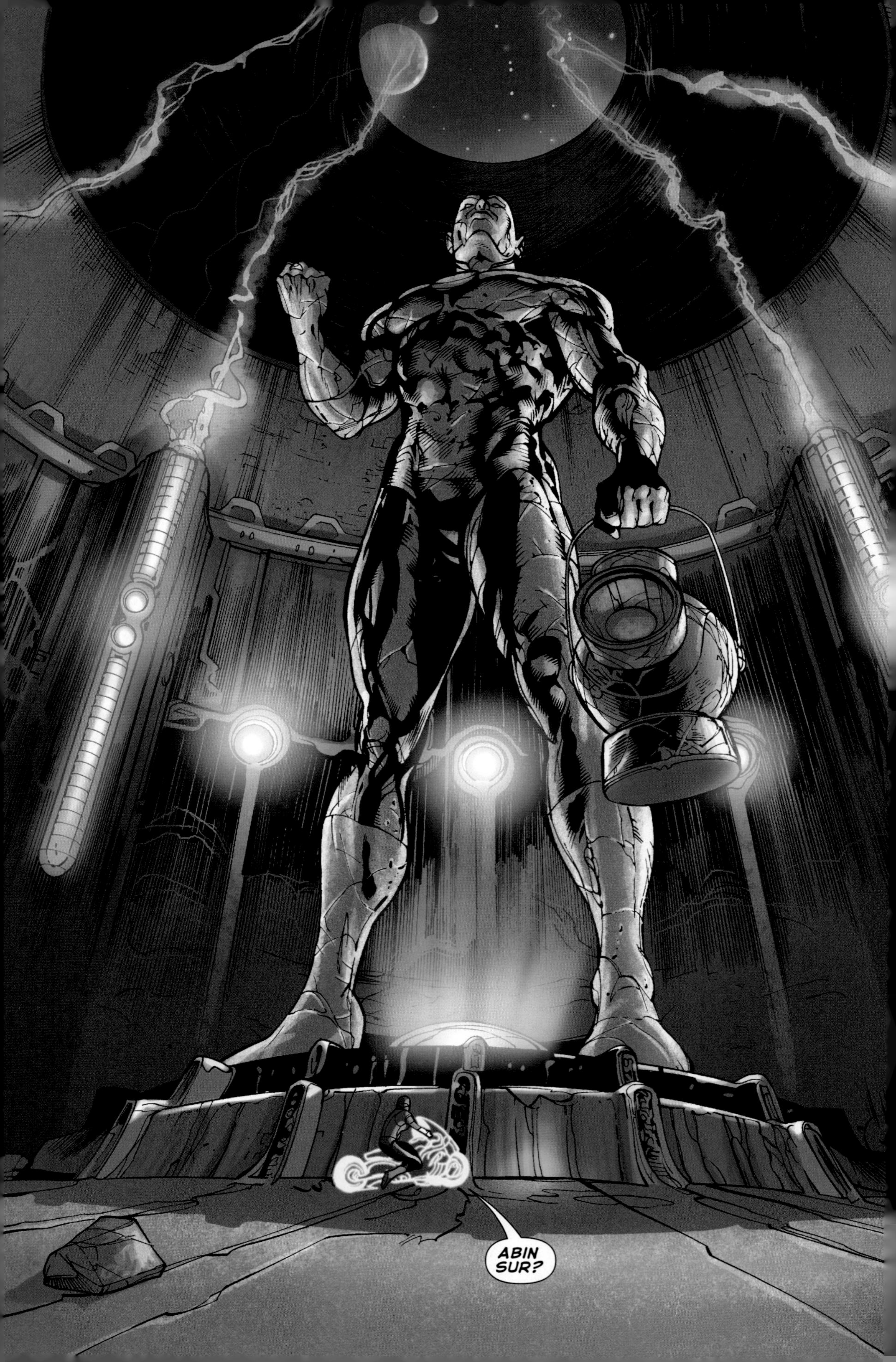
ABIN SUR?

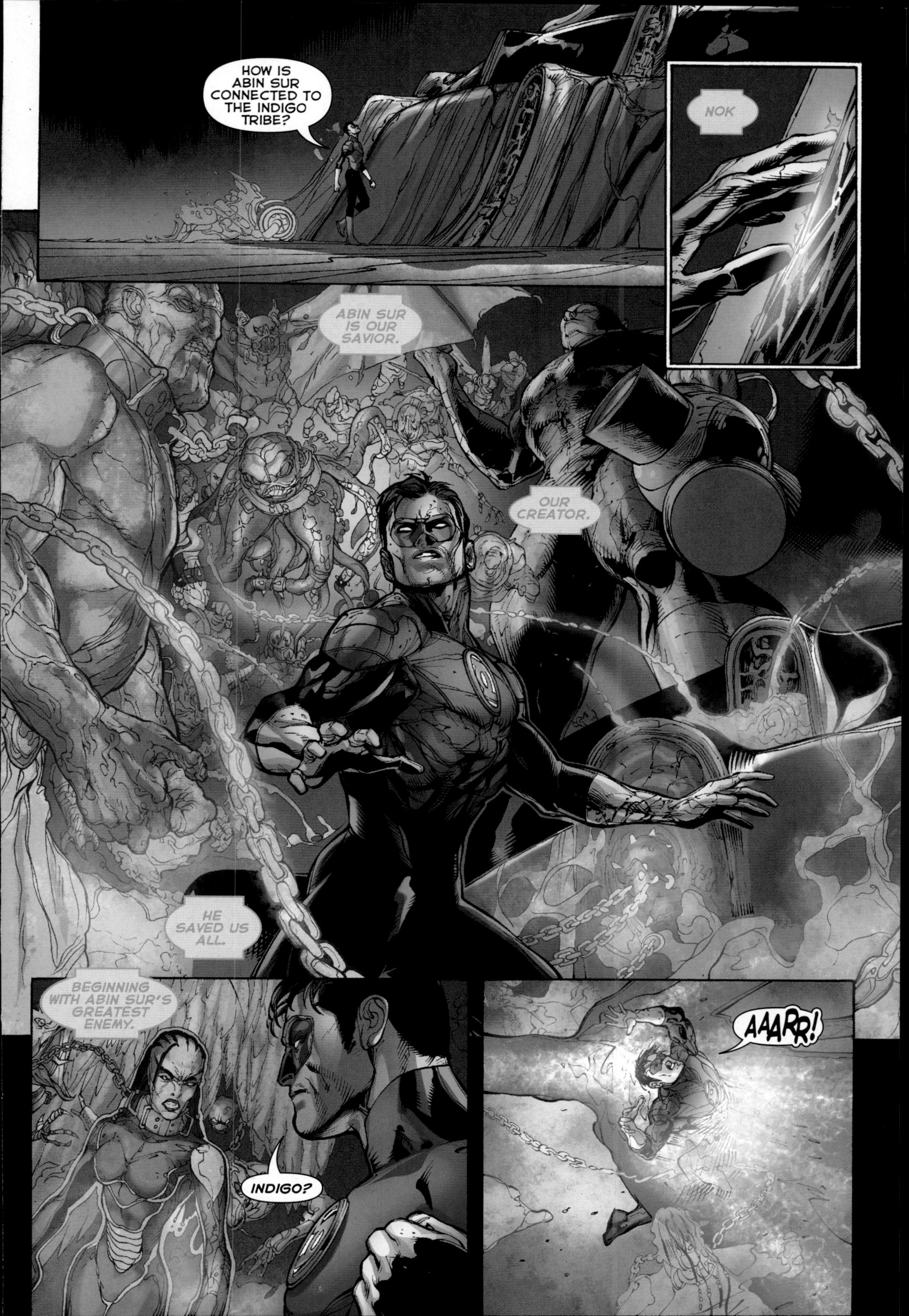
HOW IS ABIN SUR CONNECTED TO THE INDIGO TRIBE?
NOK
ABIN SUR IS OUR SAVIOR.
OUR CREATOR.
HE SAVED US ALL.
BEGINNING WITH ABIN SUR'S GREATEST ENEMY.
INDIGO?
AAARR!

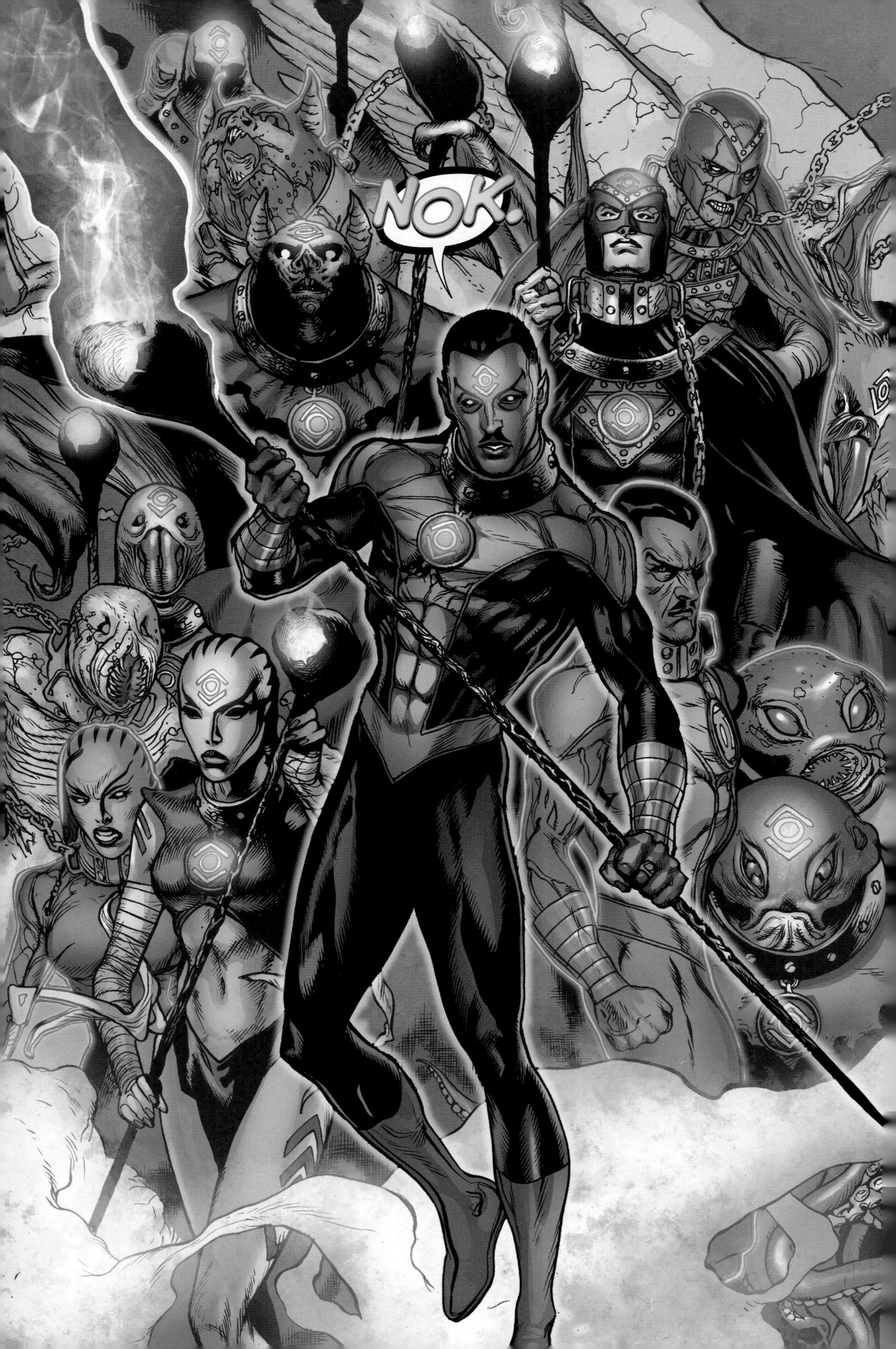
NOK.

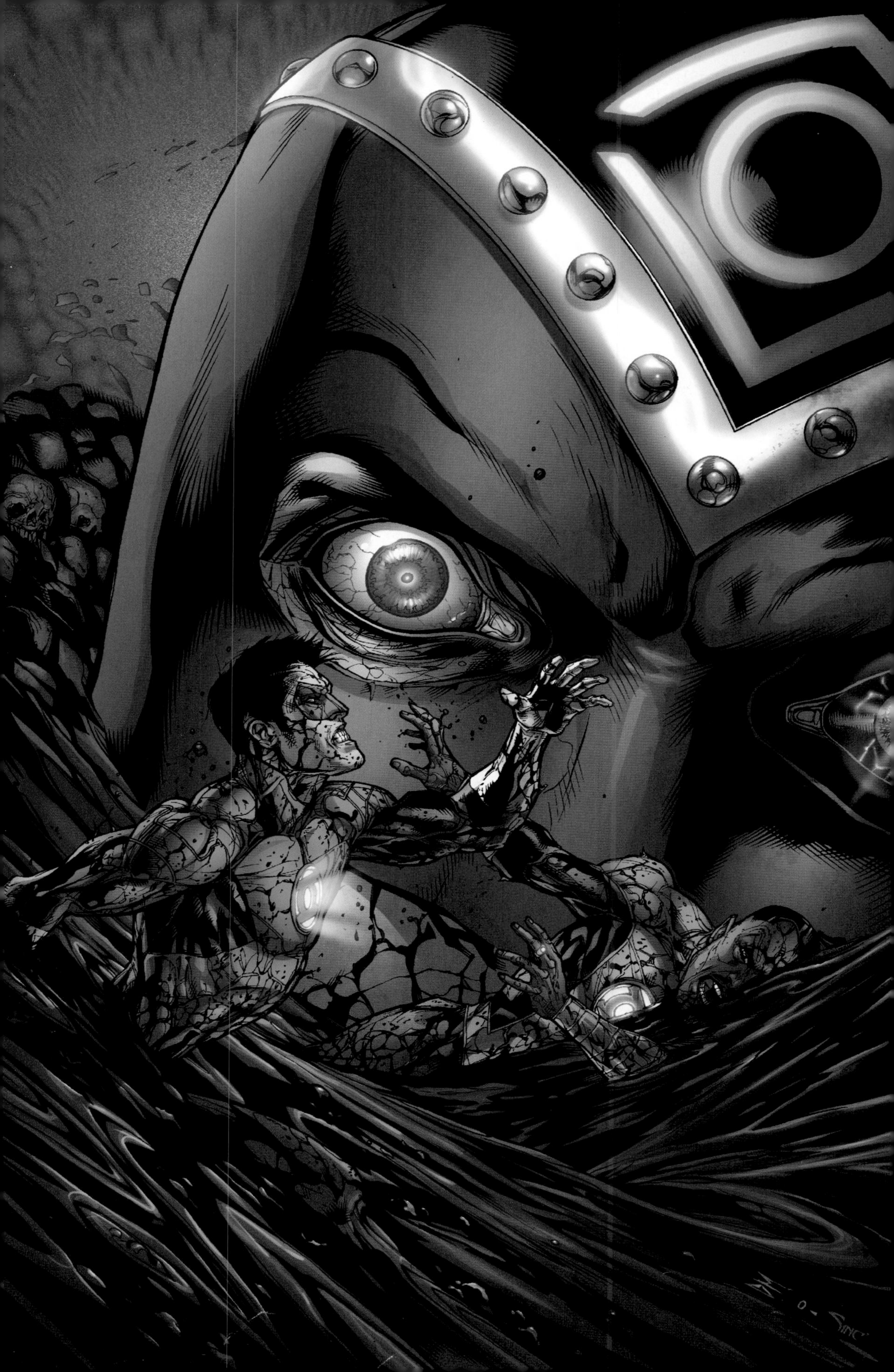

THE SECRET OF THE INDIGO TRIBE part three

GEOFF JOHNS writer **DOUG MAHNKE** penciller KEITH CHAMPAGNE, CHRISTIAN ALAMY, MARK IRWIN & TOM NGUYEN inkers

DOUG MAHNKE, MARK IRWIN & ALEX SINCLAIR cover

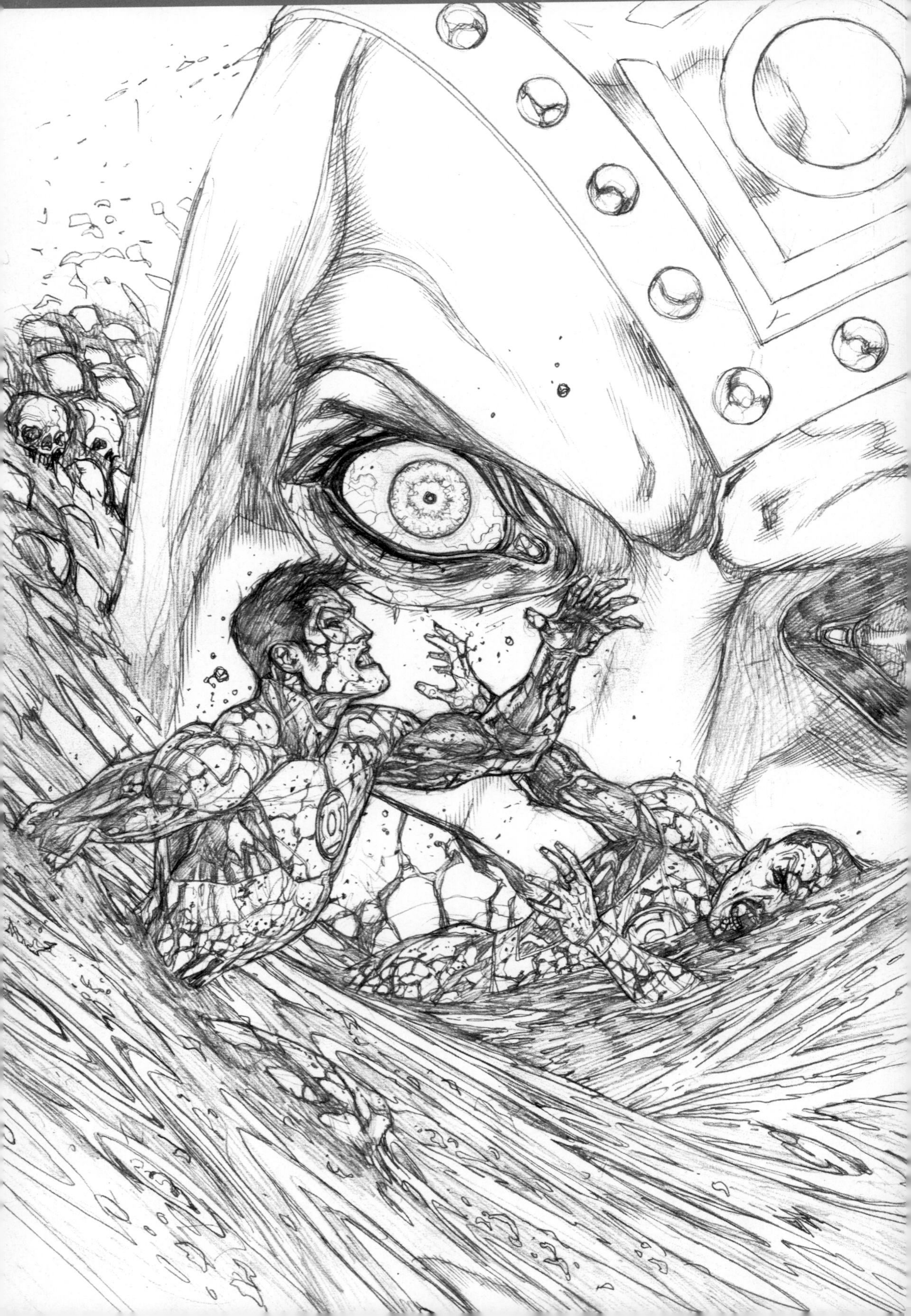

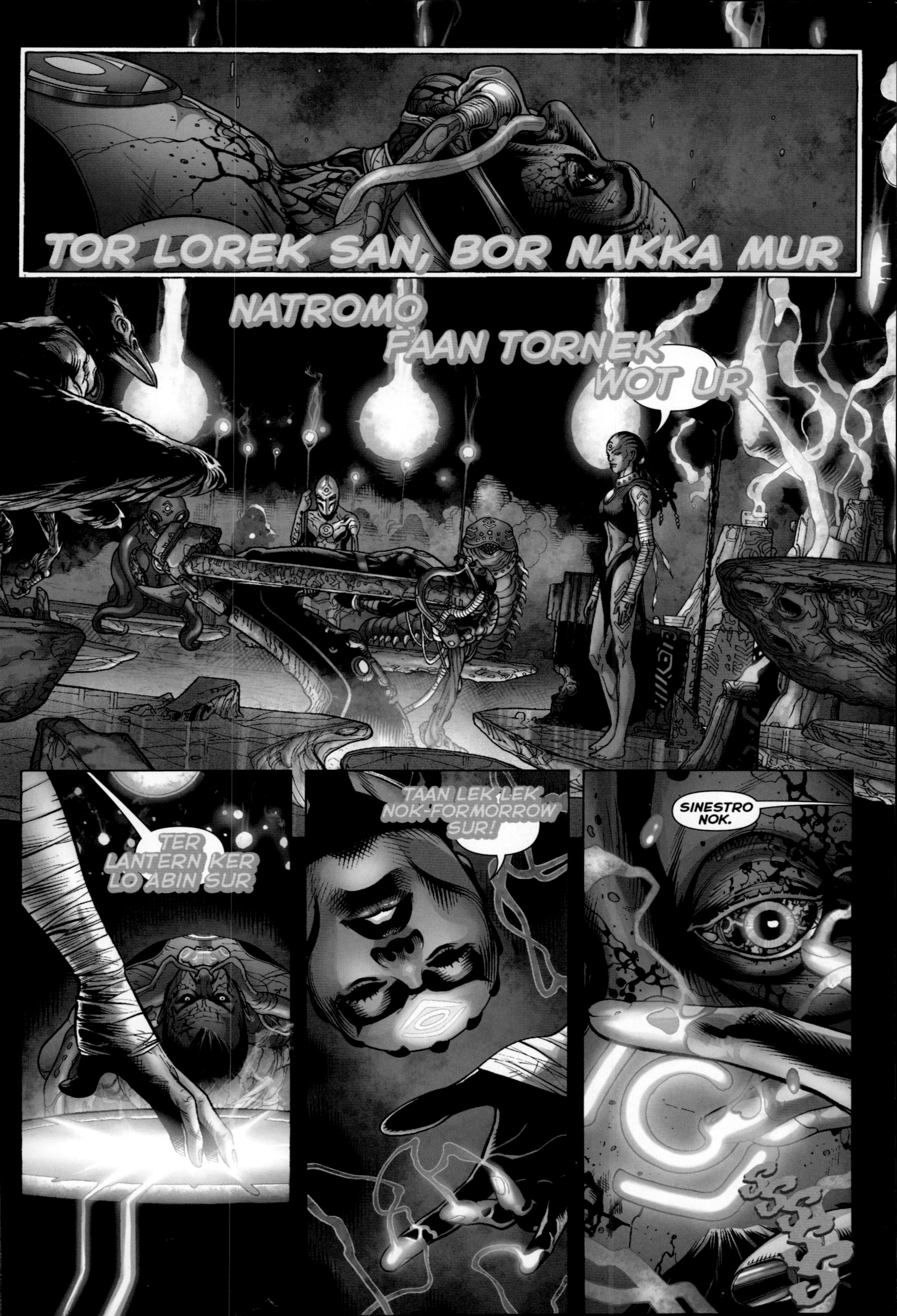
TOR LOREK SAN, BOR NAKKA MUR
NATROMO FAAN TORNEK WOT UR
TER LANTERN KER LO ABIN SUR
TAAN LEK LEK NOK-FORMORROW SUR!
SINESTRO NOK.

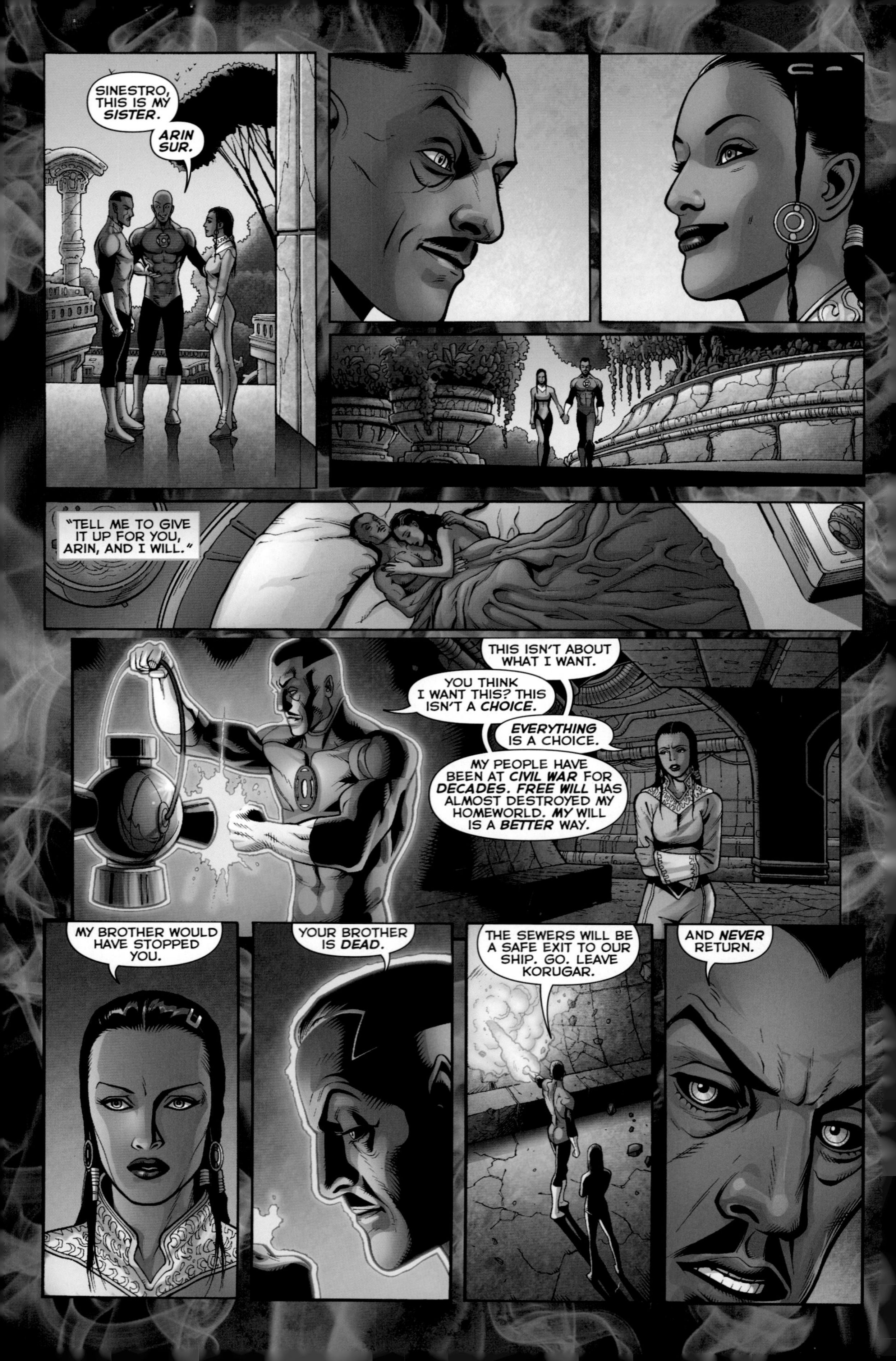

SINESTRO, THIS IS MY SISTER.
ARIN SUR.
"TELL ME TO GIVE IT UP FOR YOU, ARIN, AND I WILL."
THIS ISN'T ABOUT WHAT I WANT.
YOU THINK I WANT THIS? THIS ISN'T A CHOICE.
EVERYTHING IS A CHOICE.
MY PEOPLE HAVE BEEN AT CIVIL WAR FOR DECADES. FREE WILL HAS ALMOST DESTROYED MY HOMEWORLD. MY WILL IS A BETTER WAY.
MY BROTHER WOULD HAVE STOPPED YOU.
YOUR BROTHER IS DEAD.
THE SEWERS WILL BE A SAFE EXIT TO OUR SHIP. GO. LEAVE KORUGAR.
AND NEVER RETURN.

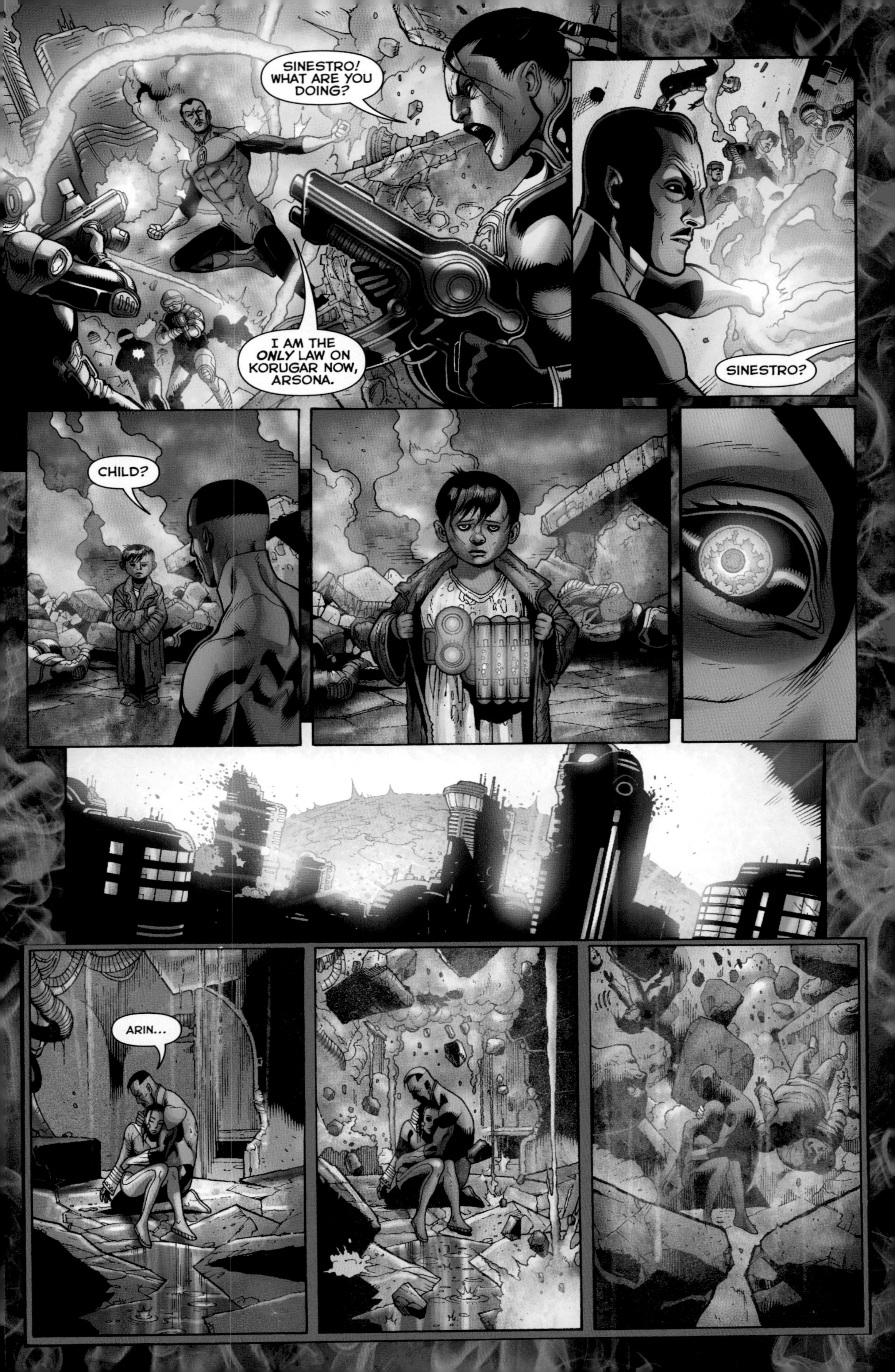
SINESTRO! WHAT ARE YOU DOING?
I AM THE ONLY LAW ON KORUGAR NOW, ARSONA.
SINESTRO?
CHILD?
ARIN...

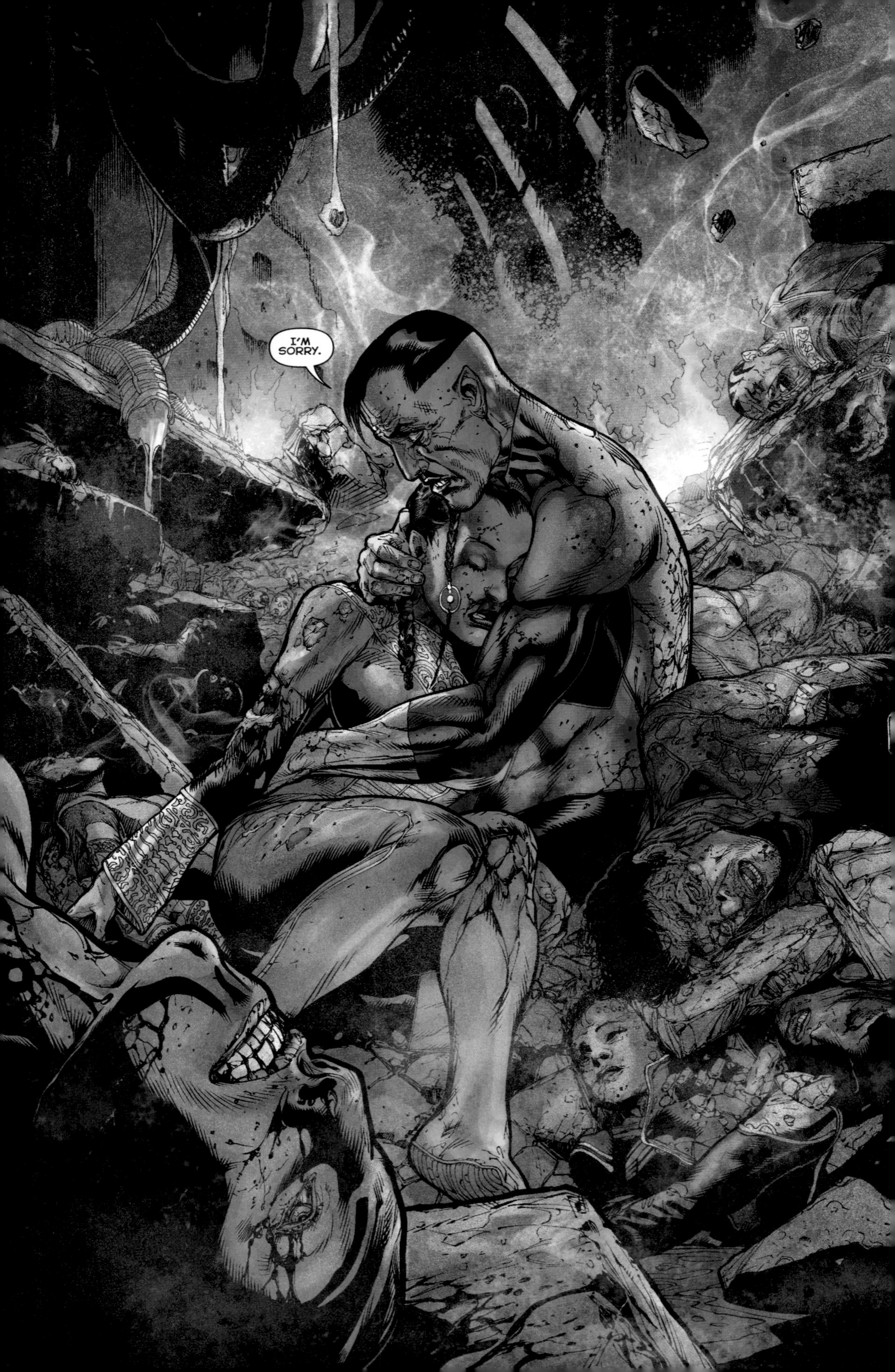
I'M SORRY.

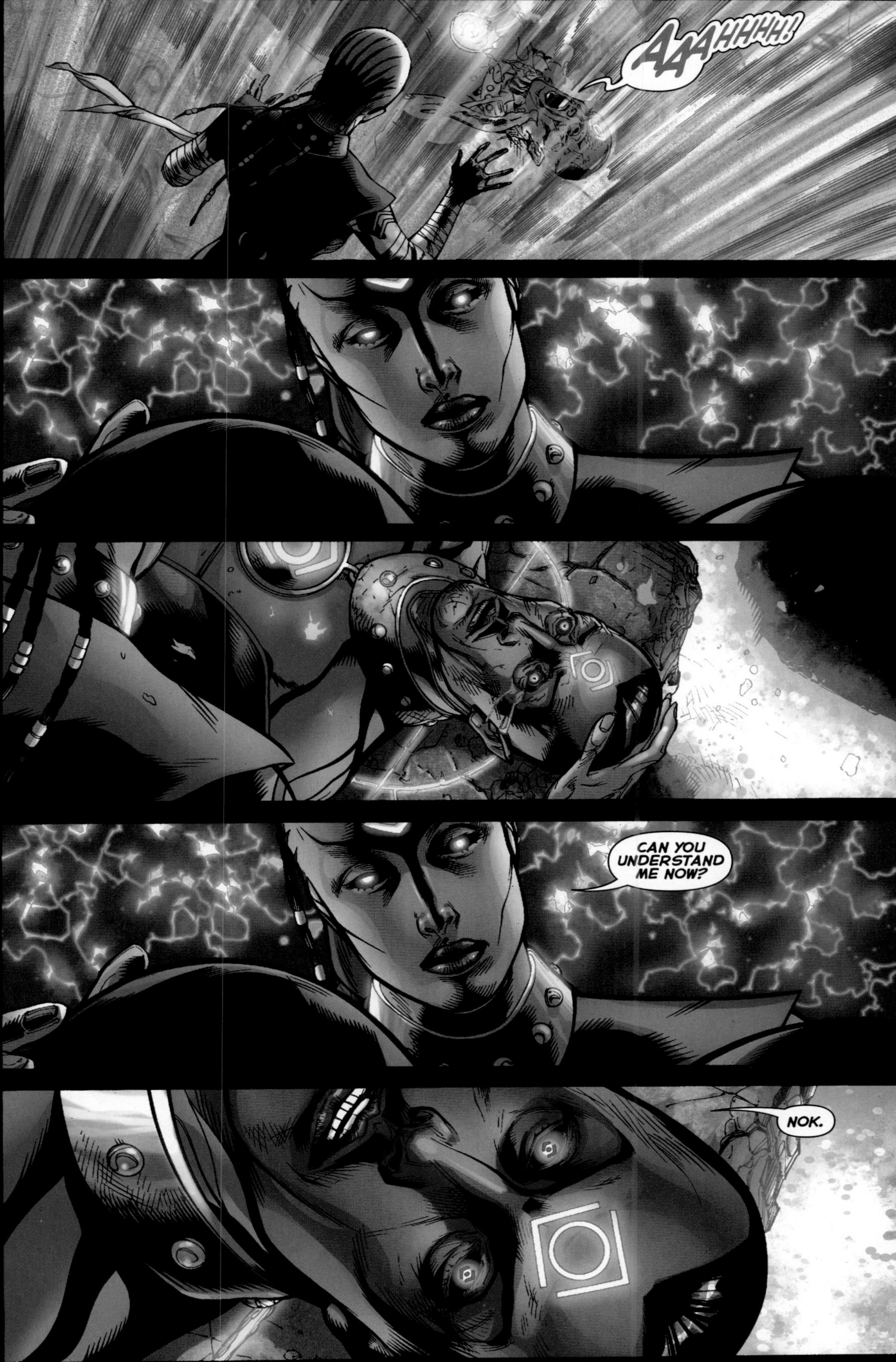
AAAHHHH!
CAN YOU UNDERSTAND ME NOW?
NOK.

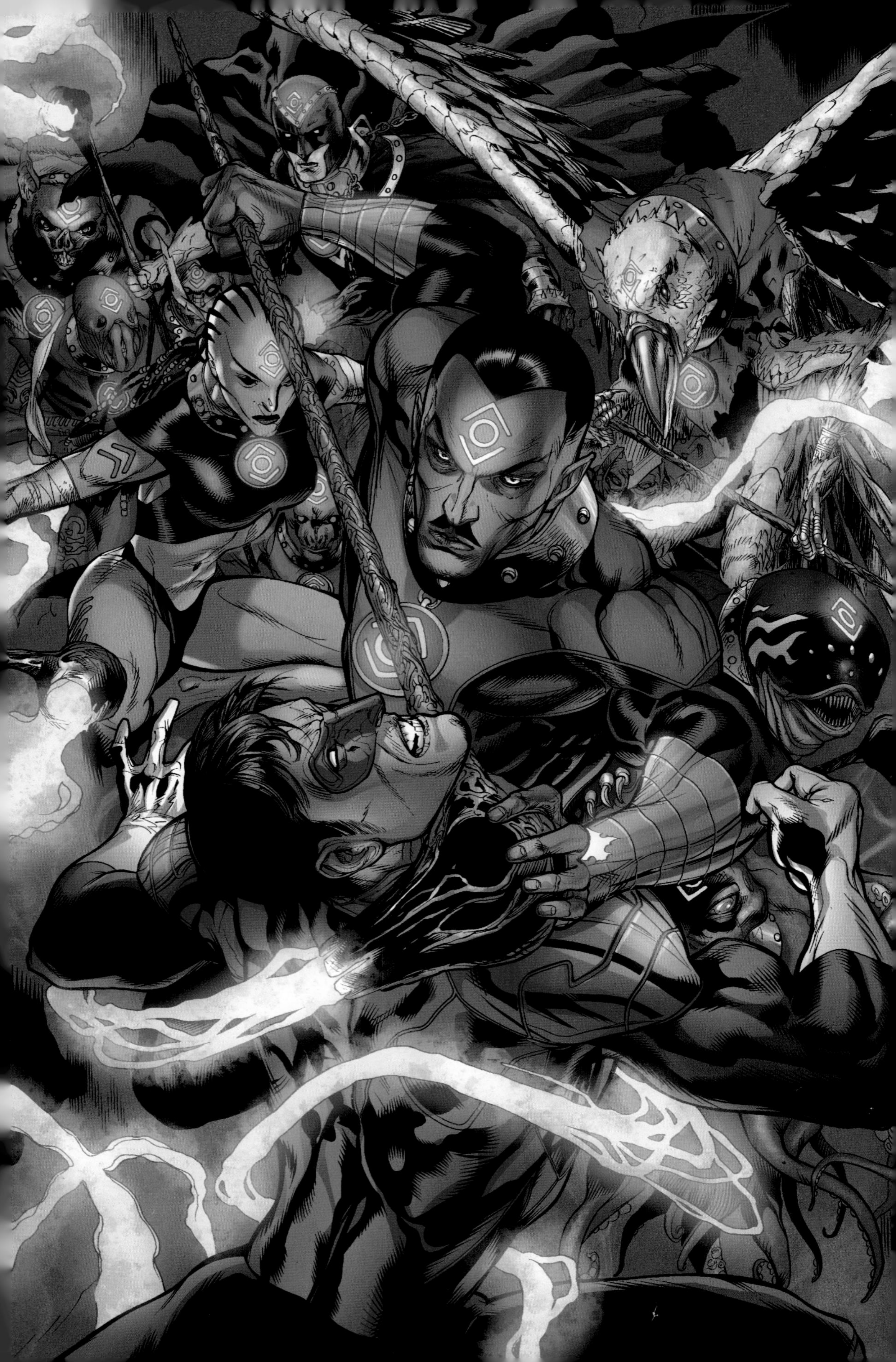

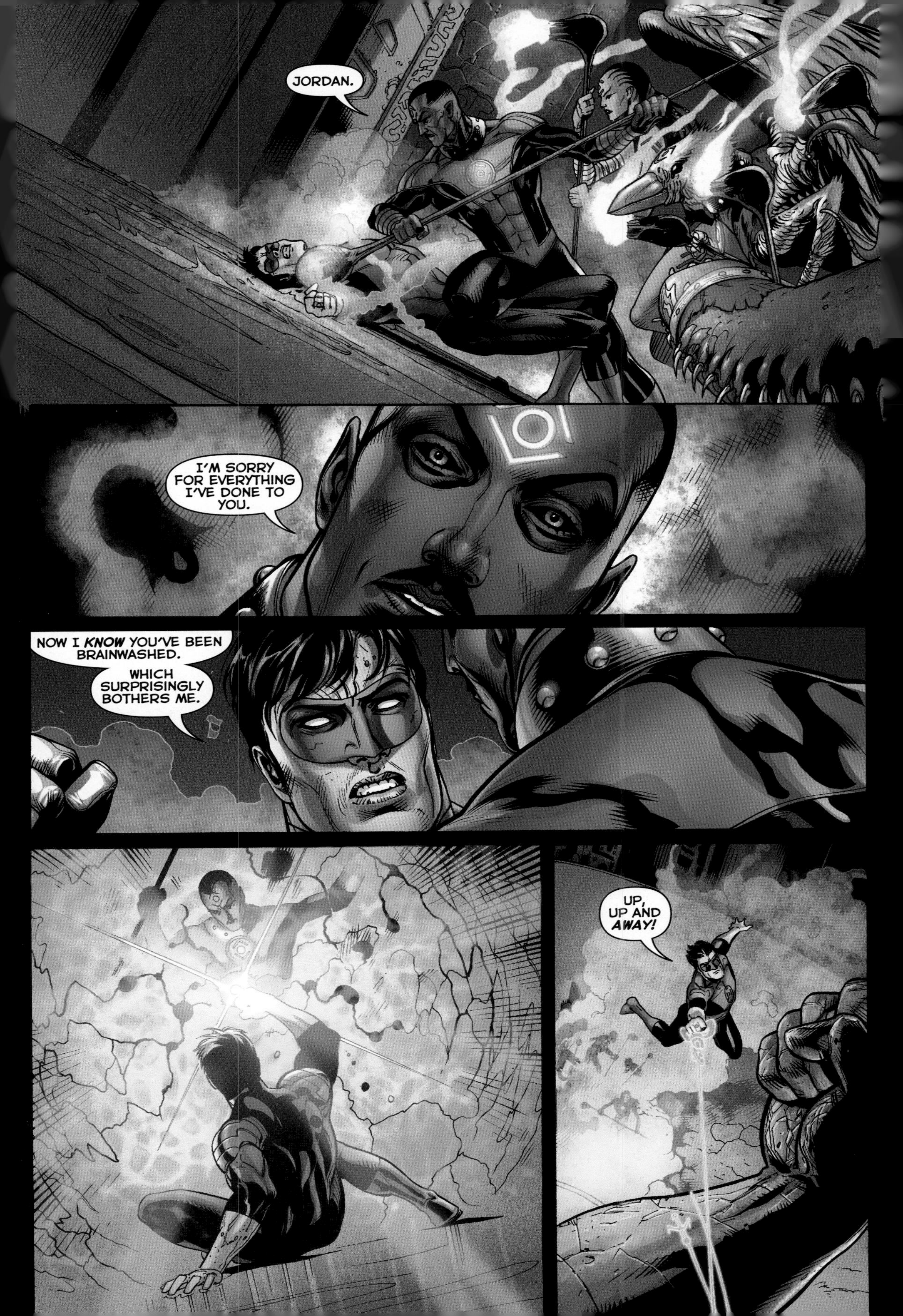
JORDAN.
I'M SORRY FOR EVERYTHING I'VE DONE TO YOU.
NOW I *KNOW* YOU'VE BEEN BRAINWASHED.
WHICH SURPRISINGLY BOTHERS ME.
UP, UP AND *AWAY!*

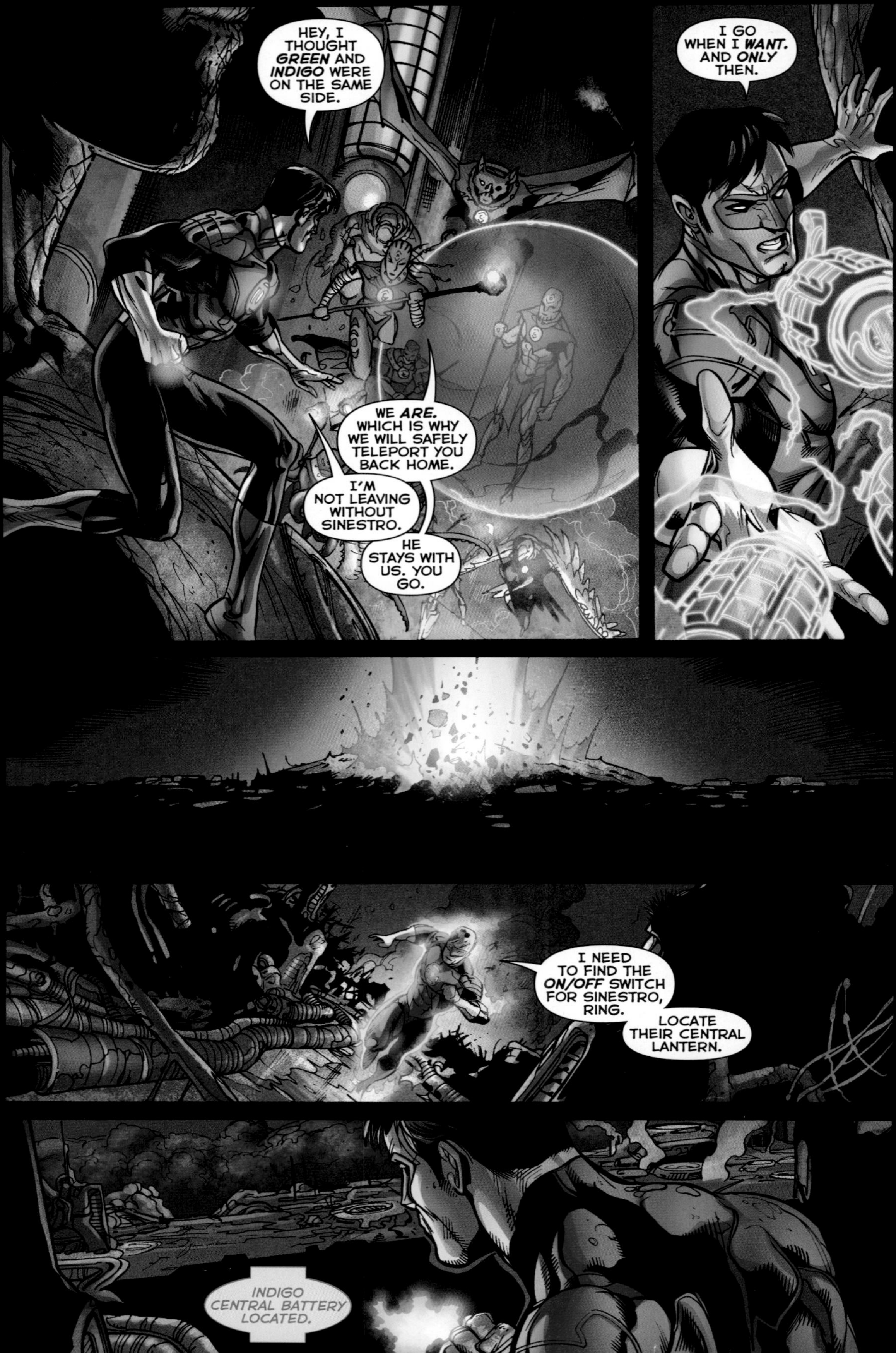
HEY, I THOUGHT GREEN AND INDIGO WERE ON THE SAME SIDE.
WE ARE. WHICH IS WHY WE WILL SAFELY TELEPORT YOU BACK HOME.
I'M NOT LEAVING WITHOUT SINESTRO.
HE STAYS WITH US. YOU GO.
I GO WHEN I WANT. AND ONLY THEN.
I NEED TO FIND THE ON/OFF SWITCH FOR SINESTRO, RING.
LOCATE THEIR CENTRAL LANTERN.
INDIGO CENTRAL BATTERY LOCATED.

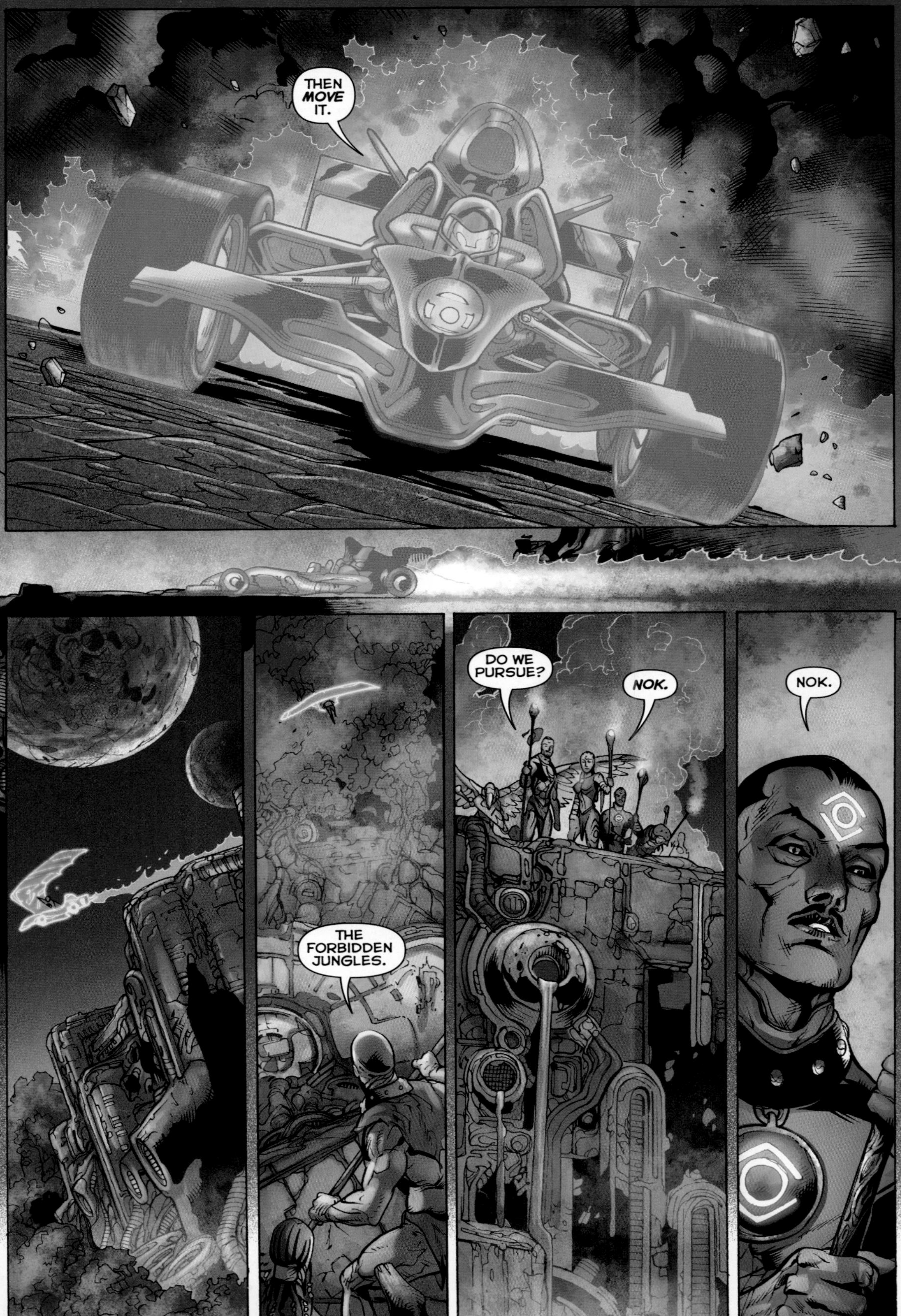
THEN MOVE IT.
THE FORBIDDEN JUNGLES.
DO WE PURSUE?
NOK.
NOK.

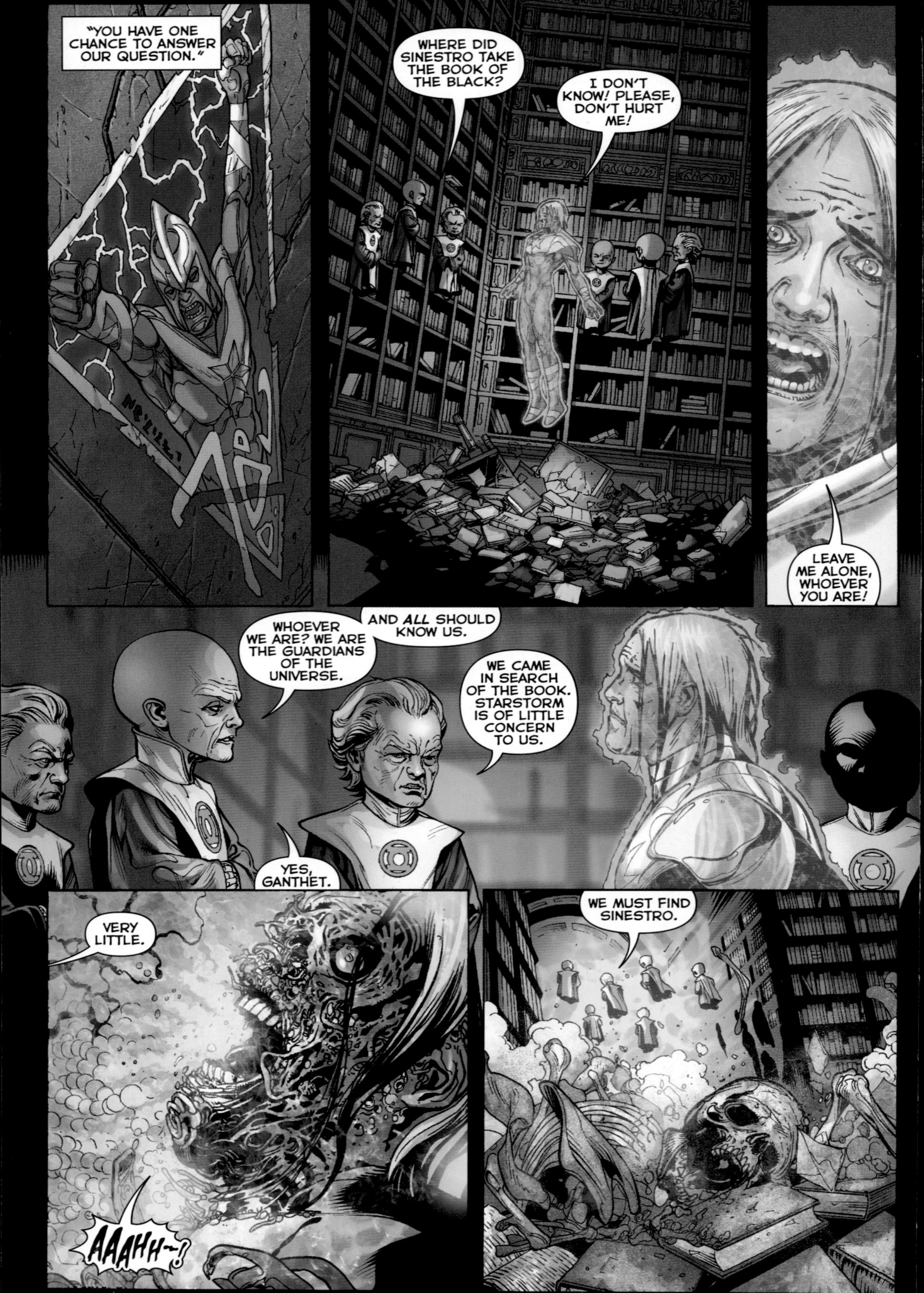
"YOU HAVE ONE CHANCE TO ANSWER OUR QUESTION."
WHERE DID SINESTRO TAKE THE BOOK OF THE BLACK?
I DON'T KNOW! PLEASE, DON'T HURT ME!
LEAVE ME ALONE, WHOEVER YOU ARE!
WHOEVER WE ARE? WE ARE THE GUARDIANS OF THE UNIVERSE.
AND ALL SHOULD KNOW US.
WE CAME IN SEARCH OF THE BOOK. STARSTORM IS OF LITTLE CONCERN TO US.
YES, GANTHET.
VERY LITTLE.
AAAHH--!
WE MUST FIND SINESTRO.

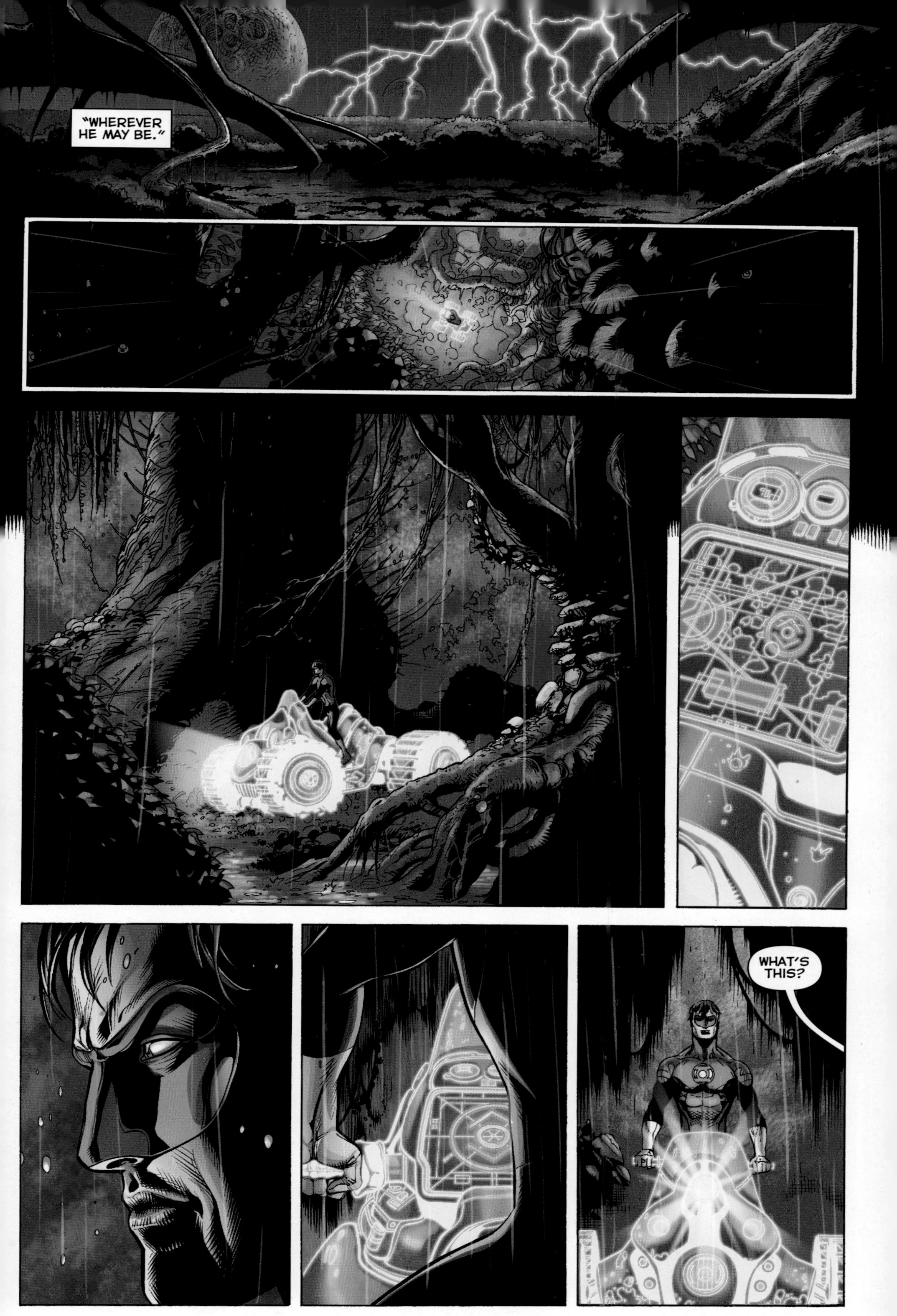
"WHEREVER HE MAY BE."
WHAT'S THIS?

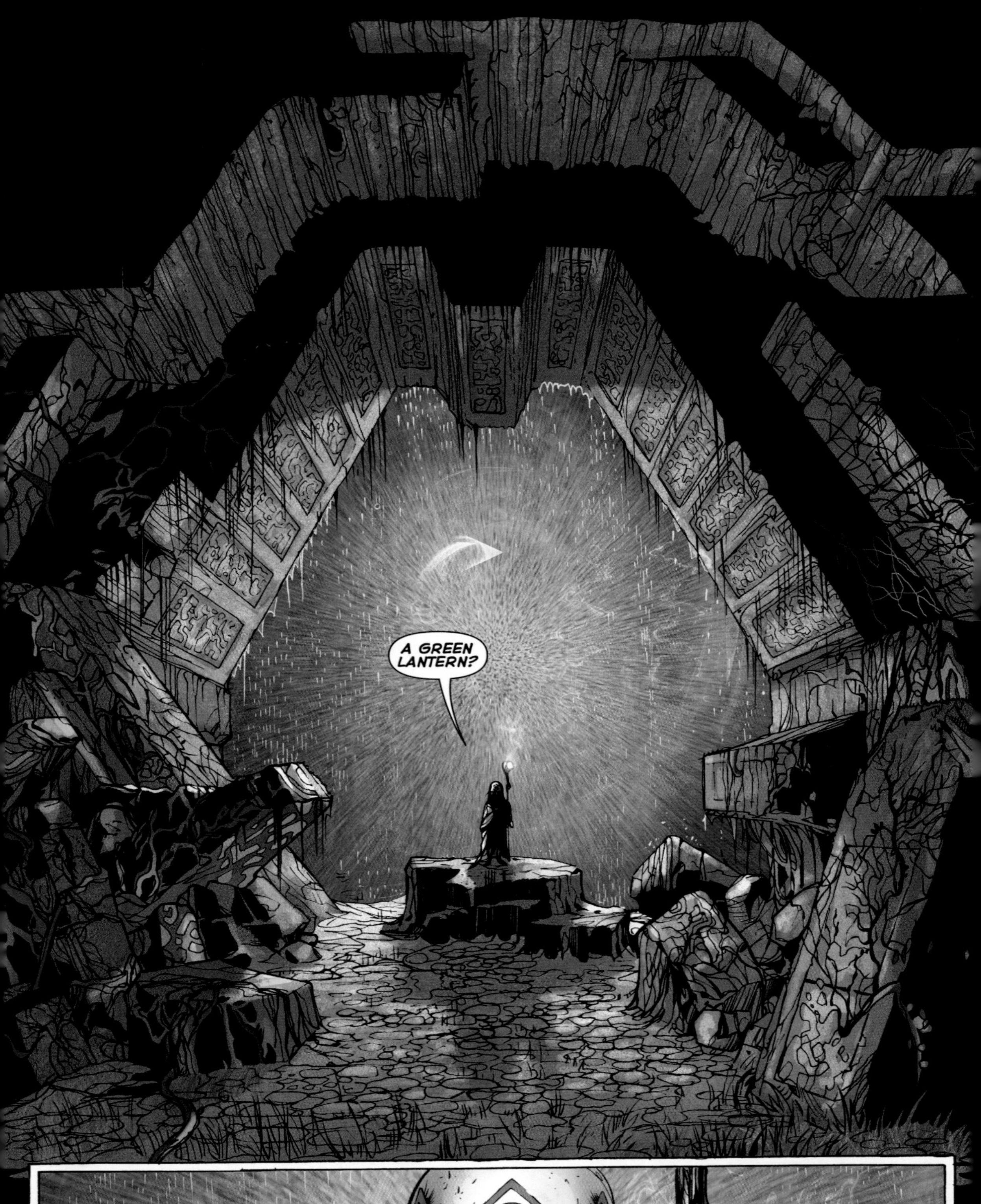
A GREEN LANTERN?

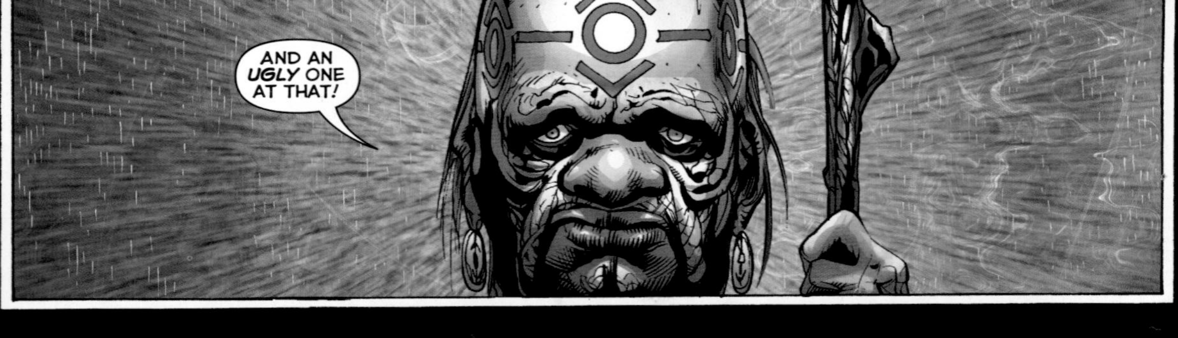
AND AN UGLY ONE AT THAT!

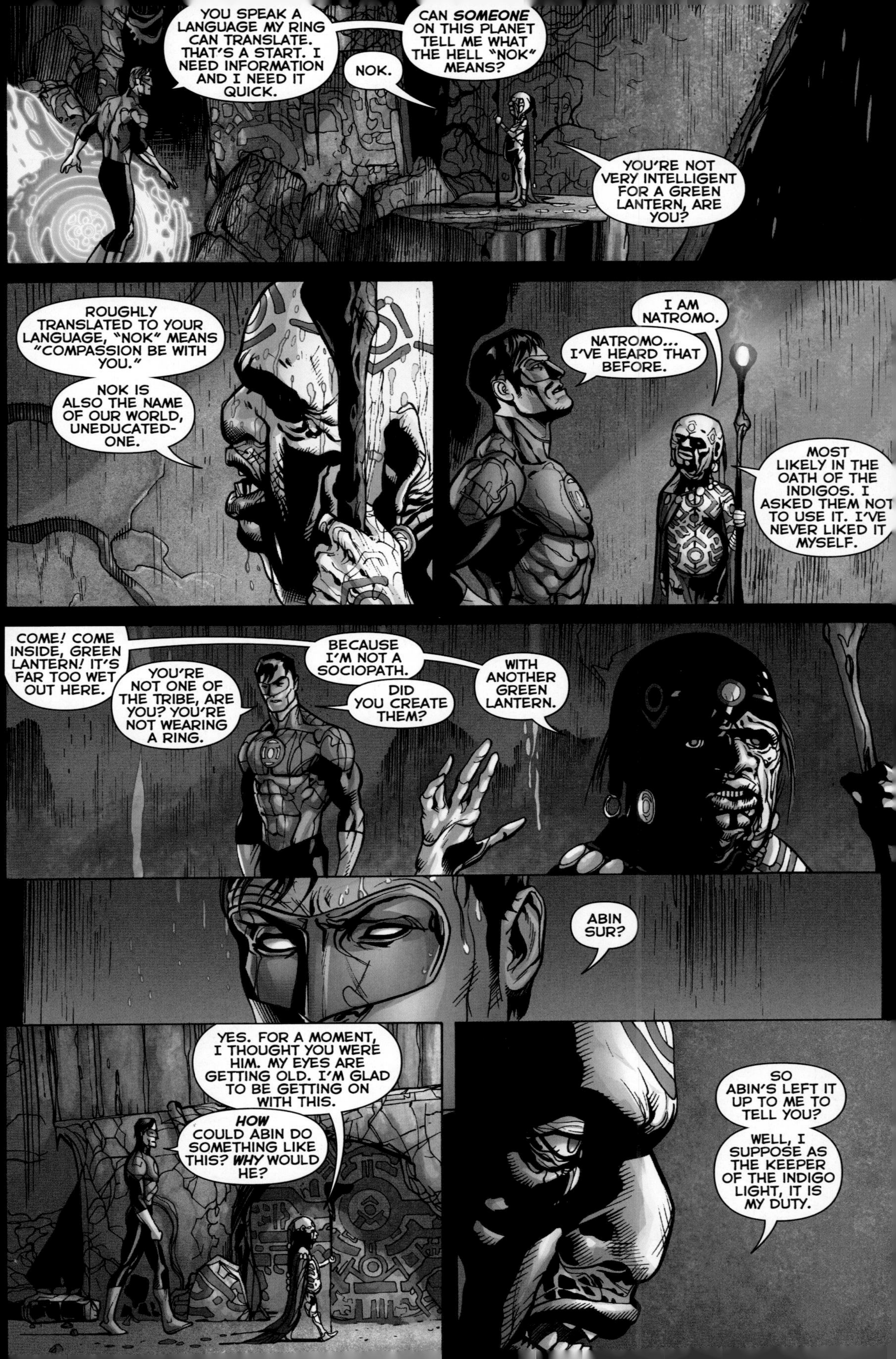
YOU SPEAK A LANGUAGE MY RING CAN TRANSLATE. THAT'S A START. I NEED INFORMATION AND I NEED IT QUICK.
CAN *SOMEONE* ON THIS PLANET TELL ME WHAT THE HELL "NOK" MEANS?
NOK.
YOU'RE NOT VERY INTELLIGENT FOR A GREEN LANTERN, ARE YOU?
ROUGHLY TRANSLATED TO YOUR LANGUAGE, "NOK" MEANS "COMPASSION BE WITH YOU."
NOK IS ALSO THE NAME OF OUR WORLD, UNEDUCATED-ONE.
I AM NATROMO.
NATROMO... I'VE HEARD THAT BEFORE.
MOST LIKELY IN THE OATH OF THE INDIGOS. I ASKED THEM NOT TO USE IT. I'VE NEVER LIKED IT MYSELF.
COME! COME INSIDE, GREEN LANTERN! IT'S FAR TOO WET OUT HERE.
YOU'RE NOT ONE OF THE TRIBE, ARE YOU? YOU'RE NOT WEARING A RING.
BECAUSE I'M NOT A SOCIOPATH.
DID YOU CREATE THEM?
WITH ANOTHER GREEN LANTERN.
ABIN SUR?
YES. FOR A MOMENT, I THOUGHT YOU WERE HIM. MY EYES ARE GETTING OLD. I'M GLAD TO BE GETTING ON WITH THIS.
HOW COULD ABIN DO SOMETHING LIKE THIS? *WHY* WOULD HE?
SO ABIN'S LEFT IT UP TO ME TO TELL YOU?
WELL, I SUPPOSE AS THE KEEPER OF THE INDIGO LIGHT, IT IS MY DUTY.

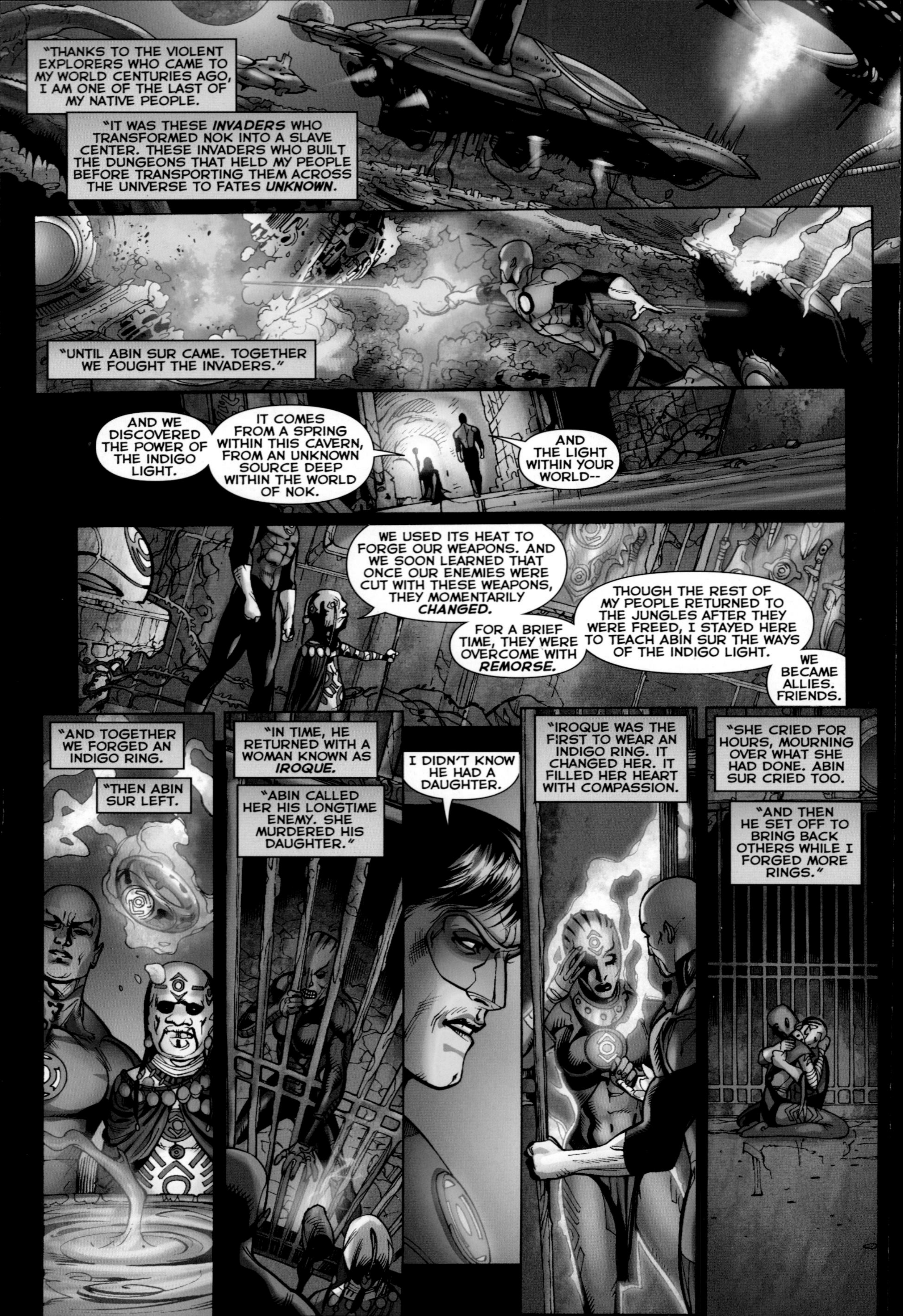
"THANKS TO THE VIOLENT EXPLORERS WHO CAME TO MY WORLD CENTURIES AGO, I AM ONE OF THE LAST OF MY NATIVE PEOPLE.
"IT WAS THESE *INVADERS* WHO TRANSFORMED NOK INTO A SLAVE CENTER. THESE INVADERS WHO BUILT THE DUNGEONS THAT HELD MY PEOPLE BEFORE TRANSPORTING THEM ACROSS THE UNIVERSE TO FATES *UNKNOWN*.
"UNTIL ABIN SUR CAME. TOGETHER WE FOUGHT THE INVADERS."
AND WE DISCOVERED THE POWER OF THE INDIGO LIGHT.
IT COMES FROM A SPRING WITHIN THIS CAVERN, FROM AN UNKNOWN SOURCE DEEP WITHIN THE WORLD OF NOK.
AND THE LIGHT WITHIN YOUR WORLD--
WE USED ITS HEAT TO FORGE OUR WEAPONS. AND WE SOON LEARNED THAT ONCE OUR ENEMIES WERE CUT WITH THESE WEAPONS, THEY MOMENTARILY *CHANGED.*
FOR A BRIEF TIME, THEY WERE OVERCOME WITH *REMORSE.*
THOUGH THE REST OF MY PEOPLE RETURNED TO THE JUNGLES AFTER THEY WERE FREED, I STAYED HERE TO TEACH ABIN SUR THE WAYS OF THE INDIGO LIGHT.
WE BECAME ALLIES. FRIENDS.
"AND TOGETHER WE FORGED AN INDIGO RING.
"THEN ABIN SUR LEFT.
"IN TIME, HE RETURNED WITH A WOMAN KNOWN AS *IROQUE.*
"ABIN CALLED HER HIS LONGTIME ENEMY. SHE MURDERED HIS DAUGHTER."
I DIDN'T KNOW HE HAD A DAUGHTER.
"IROQUE WAS THE FIRST TO WEAR AN INDIGO RING. IT CHANGED HER. IT FILLED HER HEART WITH COMPASSION.
"SHE CRIED FOR HOURS, MOURNING OVER WHAT SHE HAD DONE. ABIN SUR CRIED TOO.
"AND THEN HE SET OFF TO BRING BACK OTHERS WHILE I FORGED MORE RINGS."

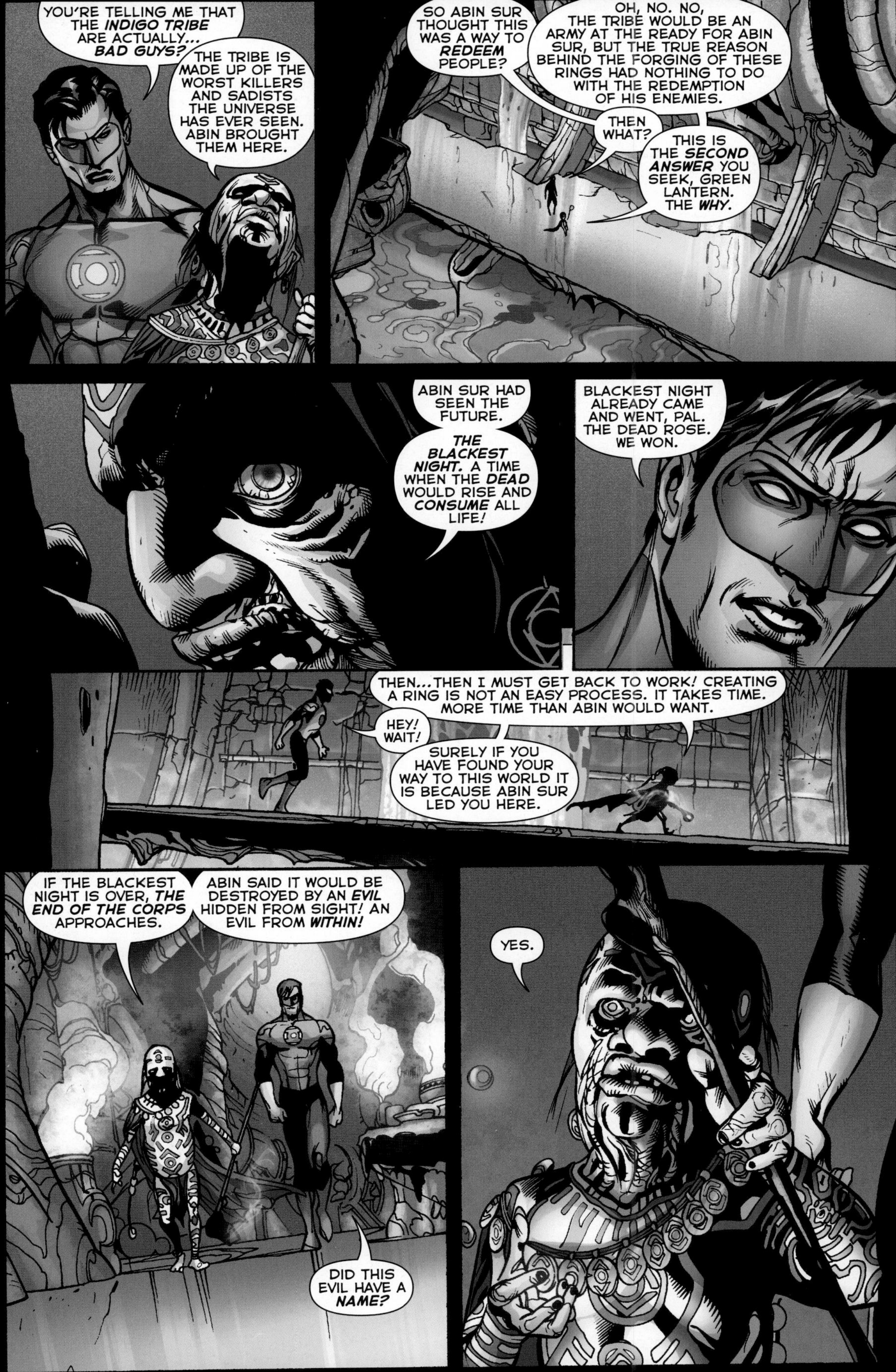
YOU'RE TELLING ME THAT THE INDIGO TRIBE ARE ACTUALLY... BAD GUYS?
THE TRIBE IS MADE UP OF THE WORST KILLERS AND SADISTS THE UNIVERSE HAS EVER SEEN. ABIN BROUGHT THEM HERE.
SO ABIN SUR THOUGHT THIS WAS A WAY TO REDEEM PEOPLE?
OH, NO. NO, THE TRIBE WOULD BE AN ARMY AT THE READY FOR ABIN SUR, BUT THE TRUE REASON BEHIND THE FORGING OF THESE RINGS HAD NOTHING TO DO WITH THE REDEMPTION OF HIS ENEMIES.
THEN WHAT?
THIS IS THE SECOND ANSWER YOU SEEK, GREEN LANTERN. THE WHY.
ABIN SUR HAD SEEN THE FUTURE.
THE BLACKEST NIGHT. A TIME WHEN THE DEAD WOULD RISE AND CONSUME ALL LIFE!
BLACKEST NIGHT ALREADY CAME AND WENT, PAL. THE DEAD ROSE. WE WON.
THEN...THEN I MUST GET BACK TO WORK! CREATING A RING IS NOT AN EASY PROCESS. IT TAKES TIME. MORE TIME THAN ABIN WOULD WANT.
HEY! WAIT!
SURELY IF YOU HAVE FOUND YOUR WAY TO THIS WORLD IT IS BECAUSE ABIN SUR LED YOU HERE.
IF THE BLACKEST NIGHT IS OVER, THE END OF THE CORPS APPROACHES.
ABIN SAID IT WOULD BE DESTROYED BY AN EVIL HIDDEN FROM SIGHT! AN EVIL FROM WITHIN!
DID THIS EVIL HAVE A NAME?
YES.

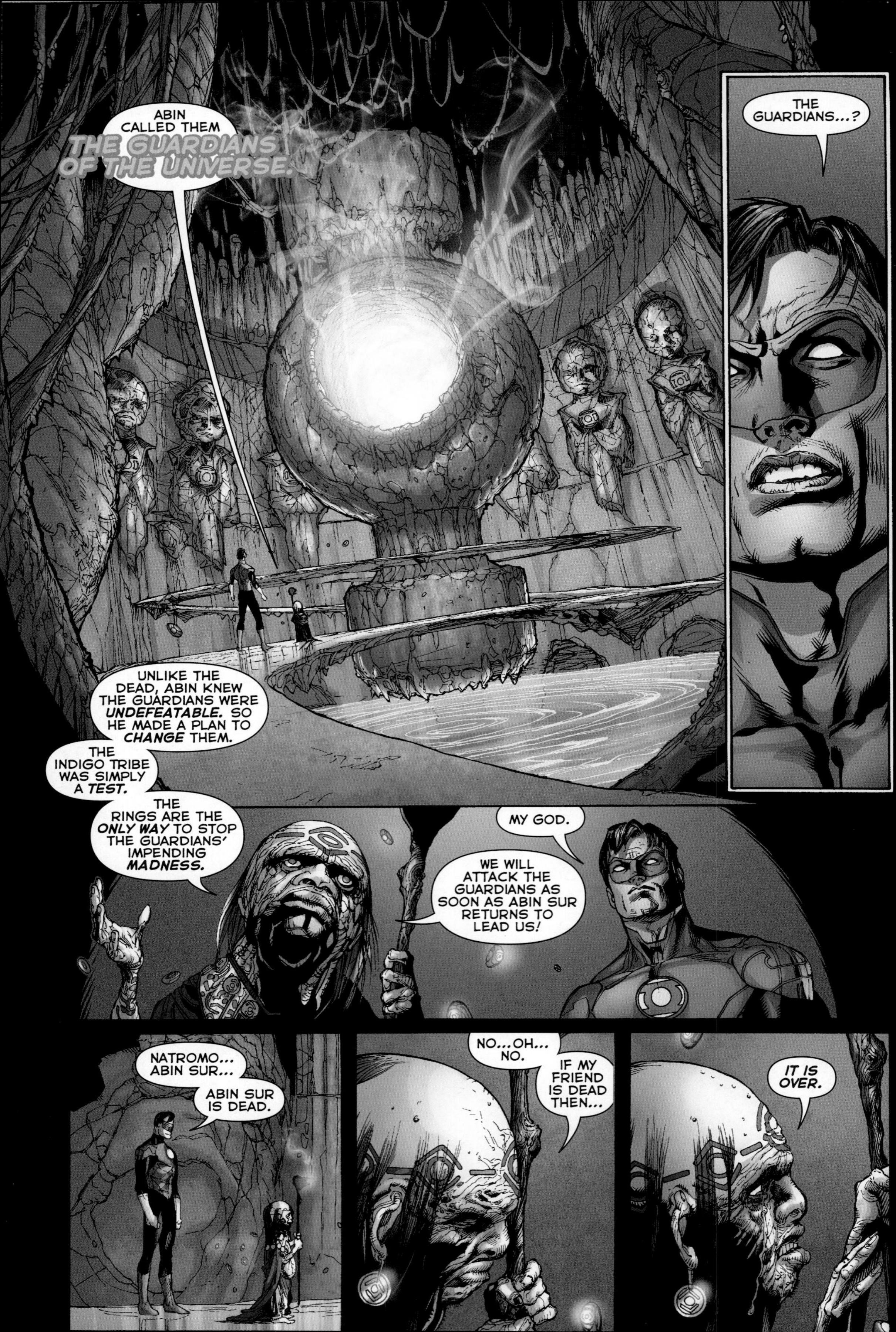
ABIN CALLED THEM THE GUARDIANS OF THE UNIVERSE.
THE GUARDIANS...?
UNLIKE THE DEAD, ABIN KNEW THE GUARDIANS WERE UNDEFEATABLE. SO HE MADE A PLAN TO CHANGE THEM.
THE INDIGO TRIBE WAS SIMPLY A TEST.
THE RINGS ARE THE ONLY WAY TO STOP THE GUARDIANS' IMPENDING MADNESS.
MY GOD.
WE WILL ATTACK THE GUARDIANS AS SOON AS ABIN SUR RETURNS TO LEAD US!
NATROMO... ABIN SUR...
ABIN SUR IS DEAD.
NO...OH... NO.
IF MY FRIEND IS DEAD THEN...
IT IS OVER.

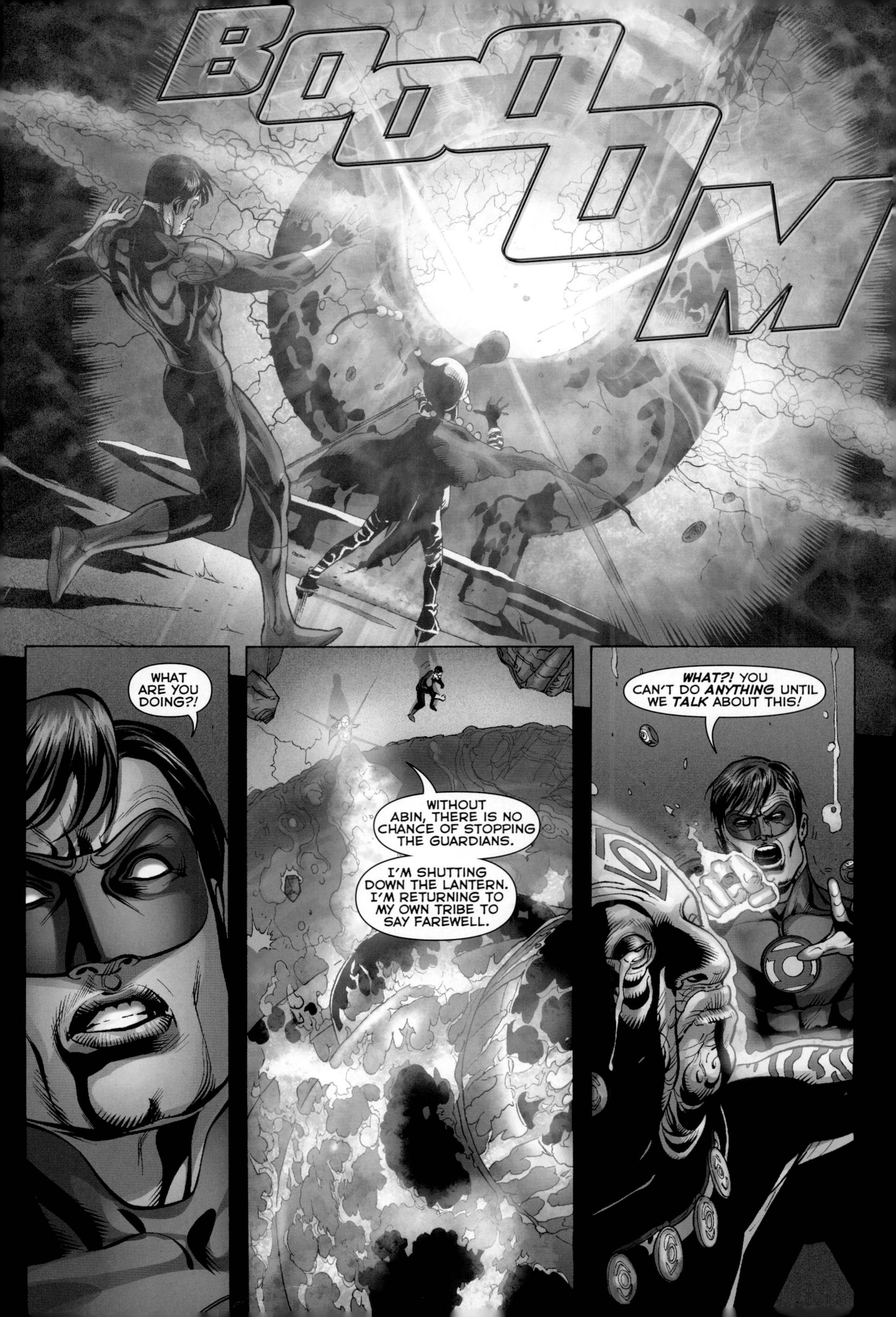
BOOOOM
WHAT ARE YOU DOING?!
WITHOUT ABIN, THERE IS NO CHANCE OF STOPPING THE GUARDIANS.
I'M SHUTTING DOWN THE LANTERN. I'M RETURNING TO MY OWN TRIBE TO SAY FAREWELL.
WHAT?! YOU CAN'T DO ANYTHING UNTIL WE TALK ABOUT THIS!

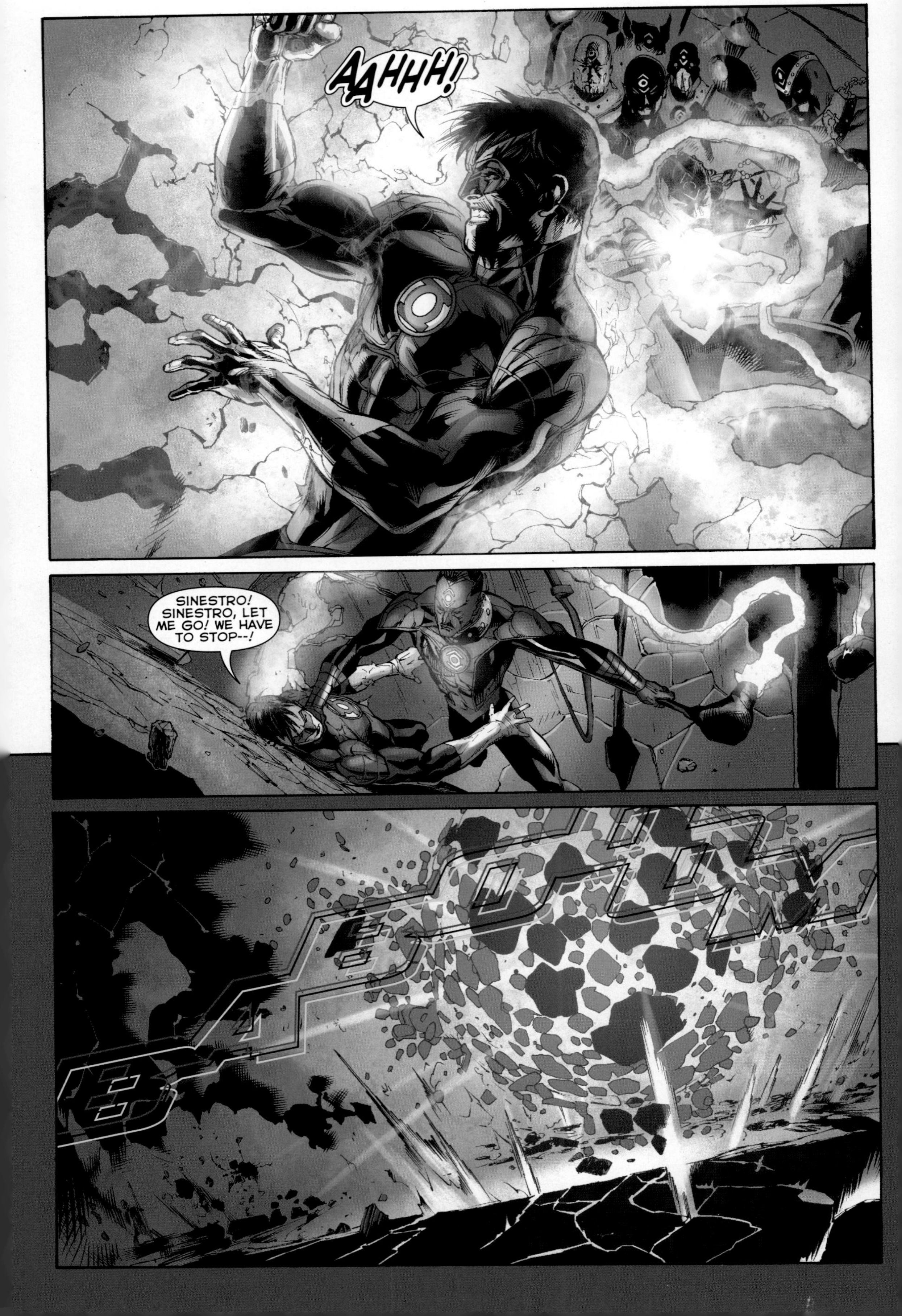
AAHHH!
SINESTRO! SINESTRO, LET ME GO! WE HAVE TO STOP--!

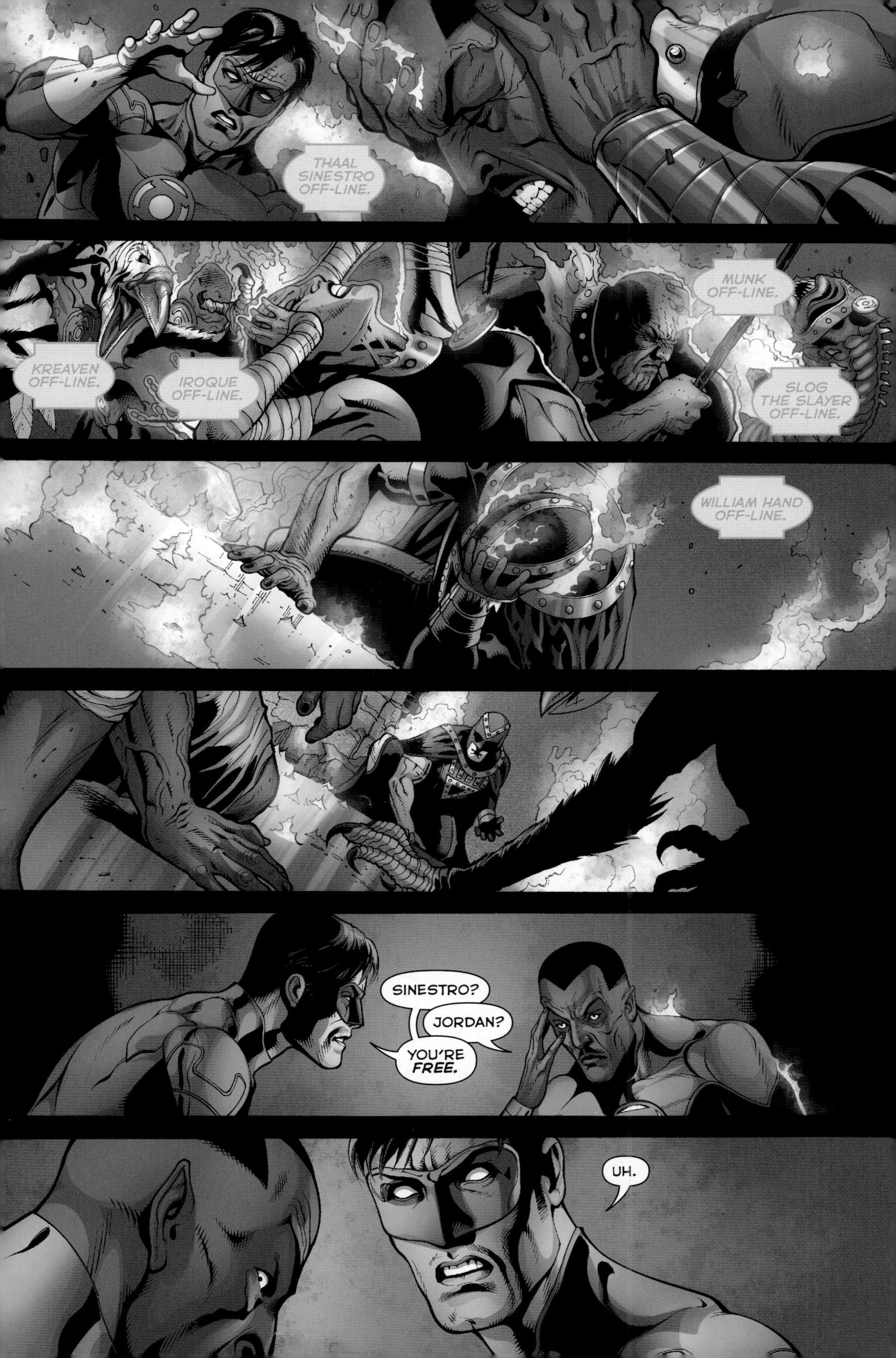
THAAL SINESTRO OFF-LINE.
KREAVEN OFF-LINE.
IROQUE OFF-LINE.
MUNK OFF-LINE.
SLOG THE SLAYER OFF-LINE.
WILLIAM HAND OFF-LINE.
SINESTRO?
JORDAN?
YOU'RE FREE.
UH.

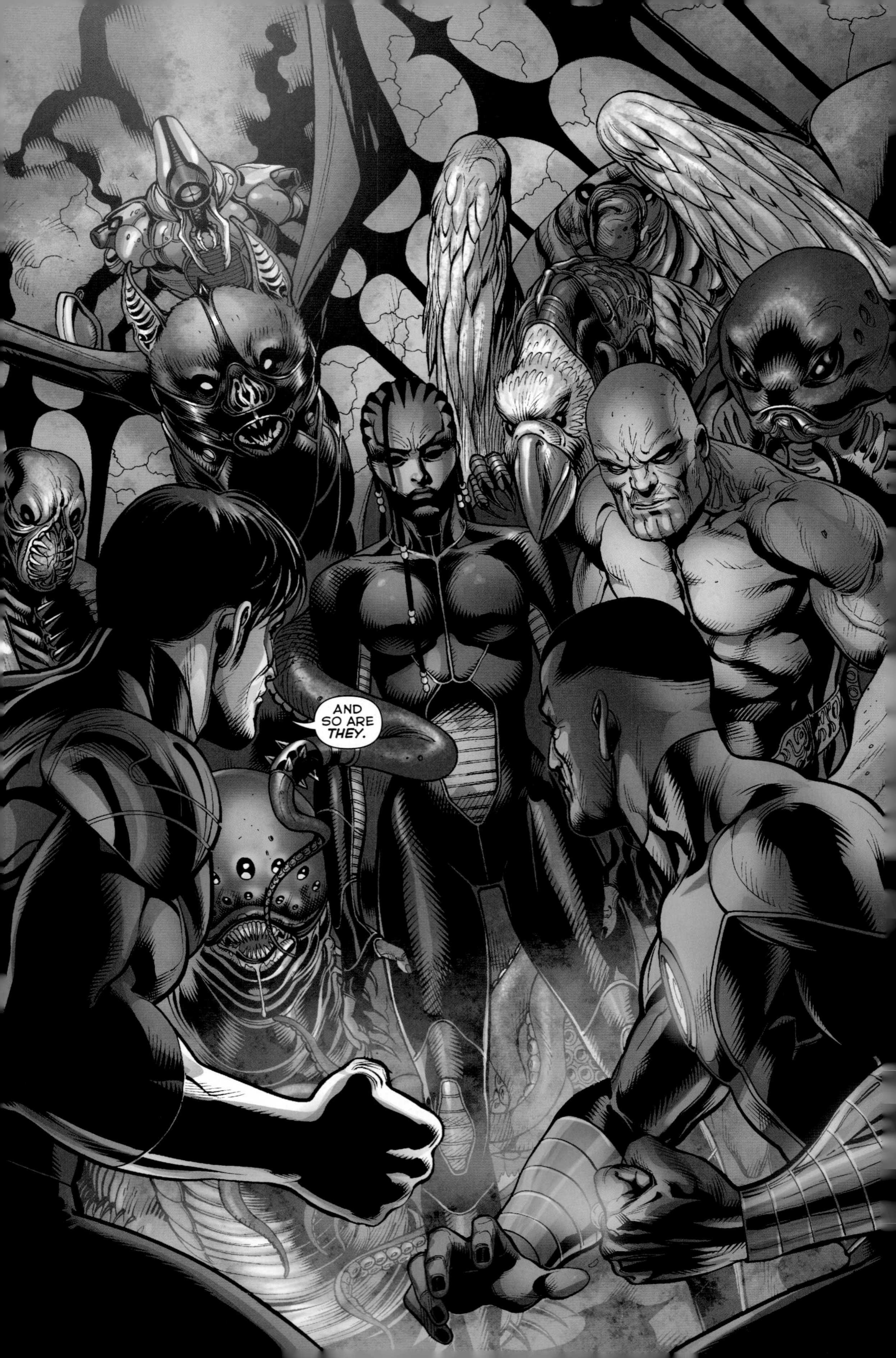
AND SO ARE *THEY.*

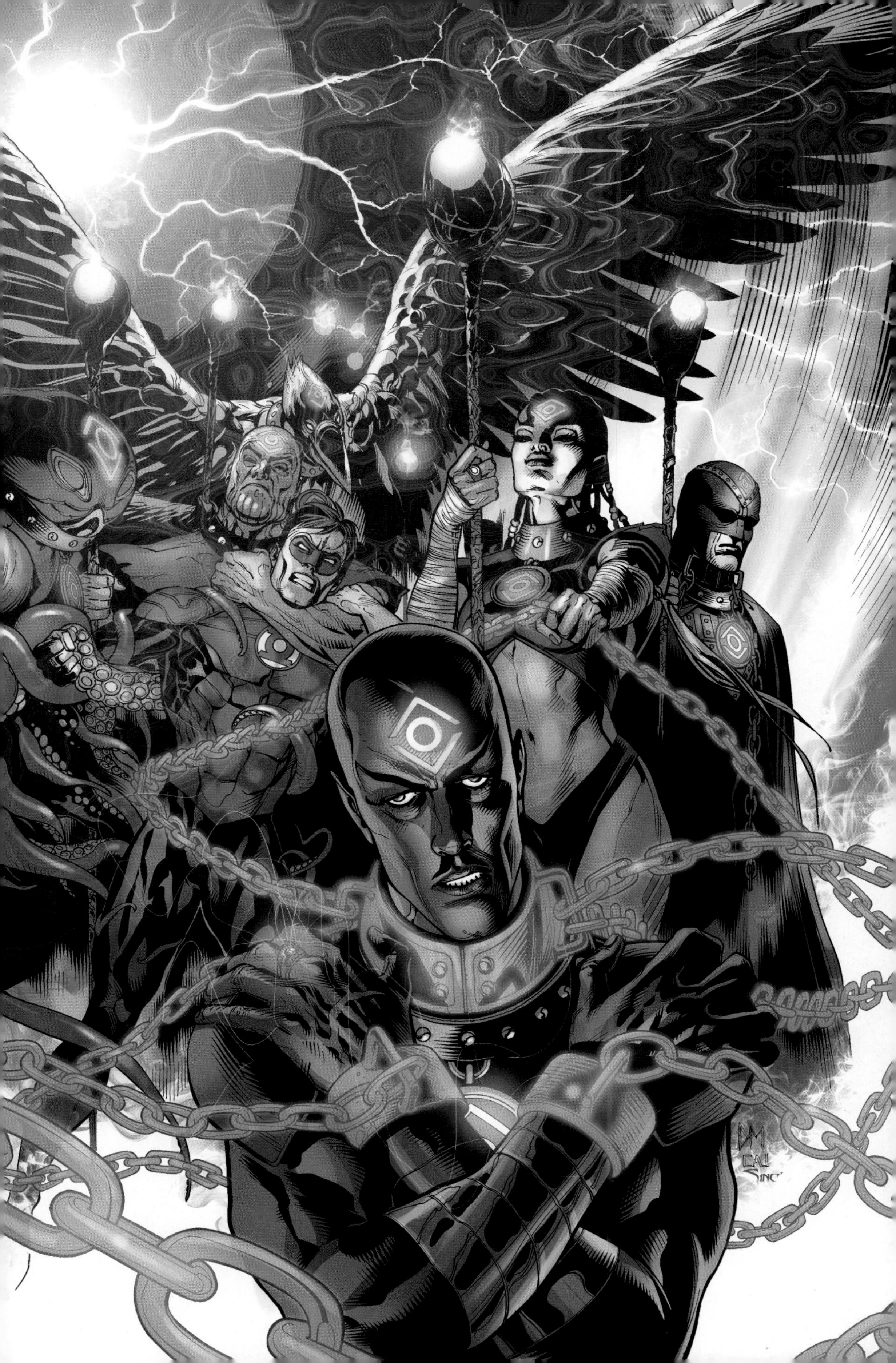

THE SECRET OF THE INDIGO TRIBE conclusion

GEOFF JOHNS writer **DOUG MAHNKE** penciller KEITH CHAMPAGNE, CHRISTIAN ALAMY, MARK IRWIN & TOM NGUYEN inkers

DOUG MAHNKE, CHRISTIAN ALAMY & ALEX SINCLAIR cover

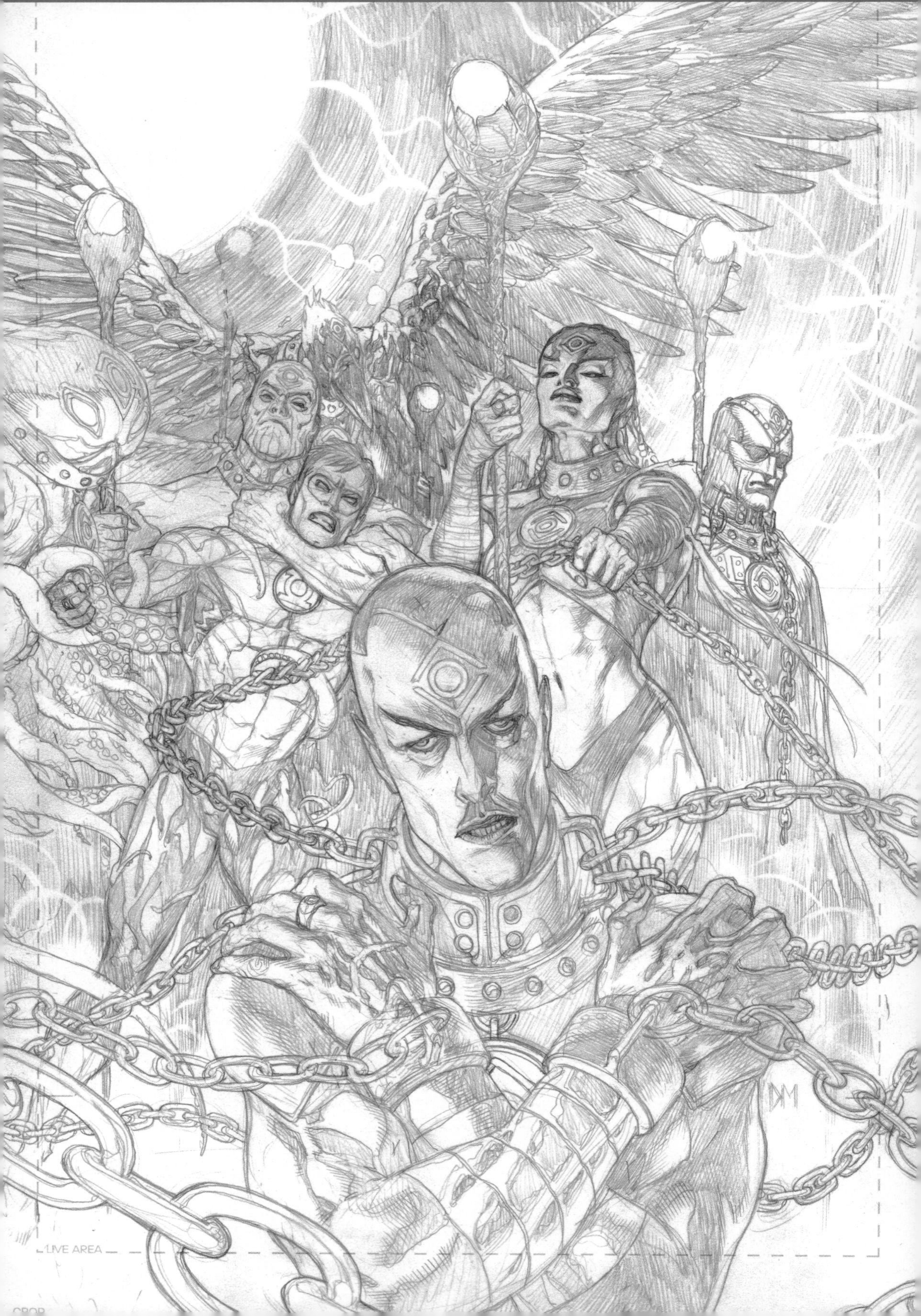
LIVE AREA

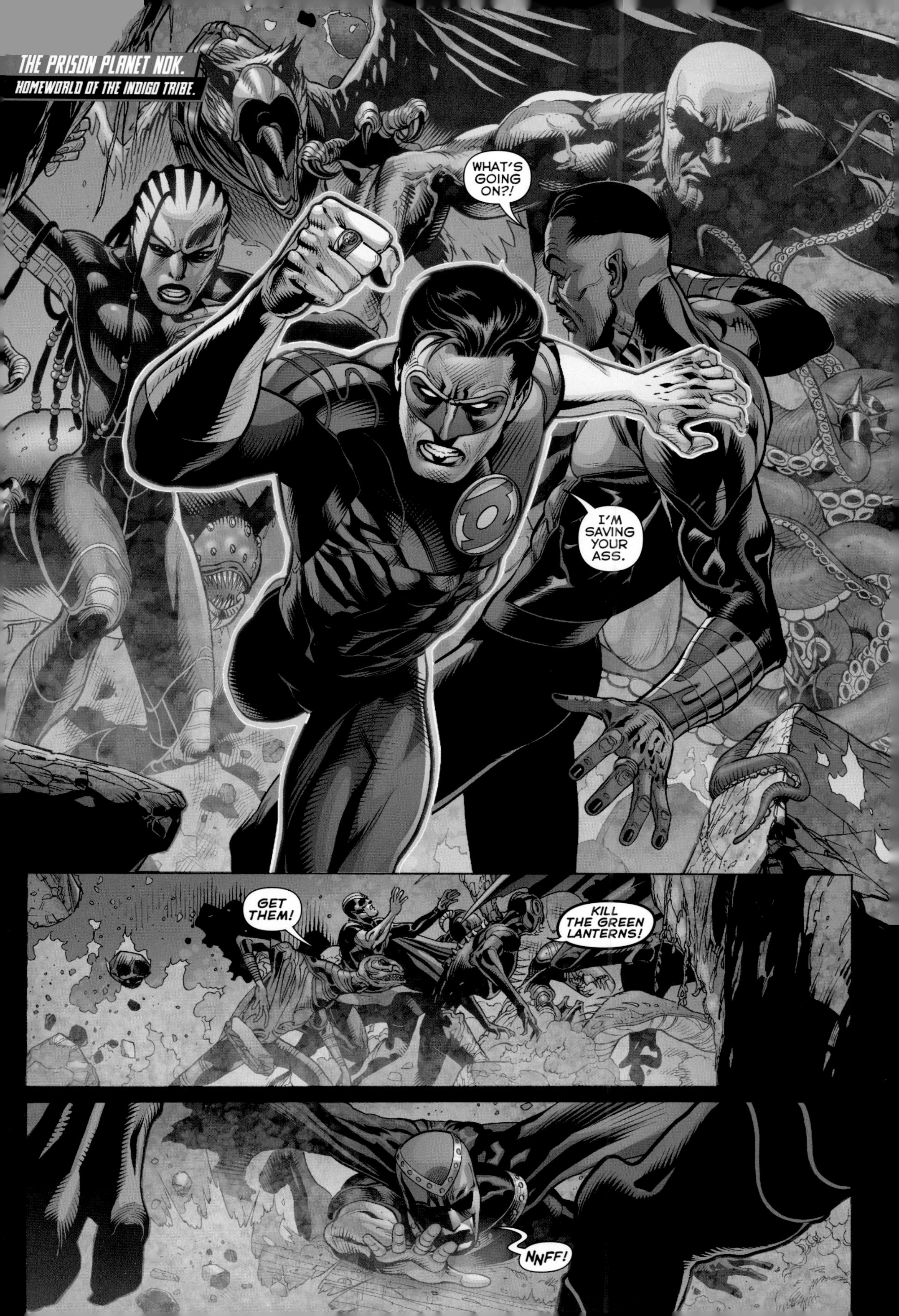
THE PRISON PLANET NOK.
HOMEWORLD OF THE INDIGO TRIBE.
WHAT'S GOING ON?!
I'M SAVING YOUR ASS.
GET THEM!
KILL THE GREEN LANTERNS!
NNFF!

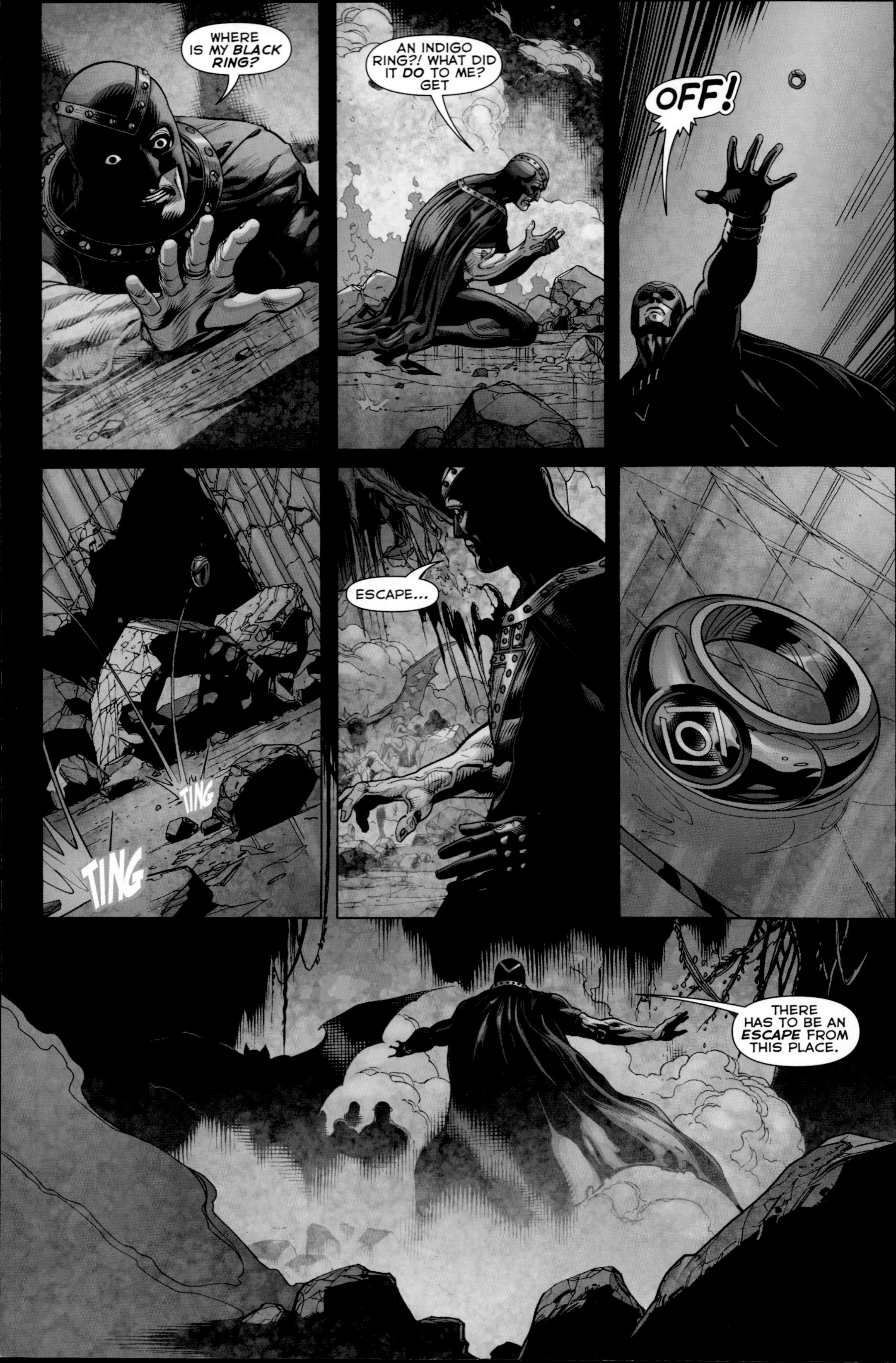
WHERE IS MY BLACK RING?
AN INDIGO RING?! WHAT DID IT DO TO ME? GET
OFF!
TING
TING
ESCAPE...
THERE HAS TO BE AN ESCAPE FROM THIS PLACE.

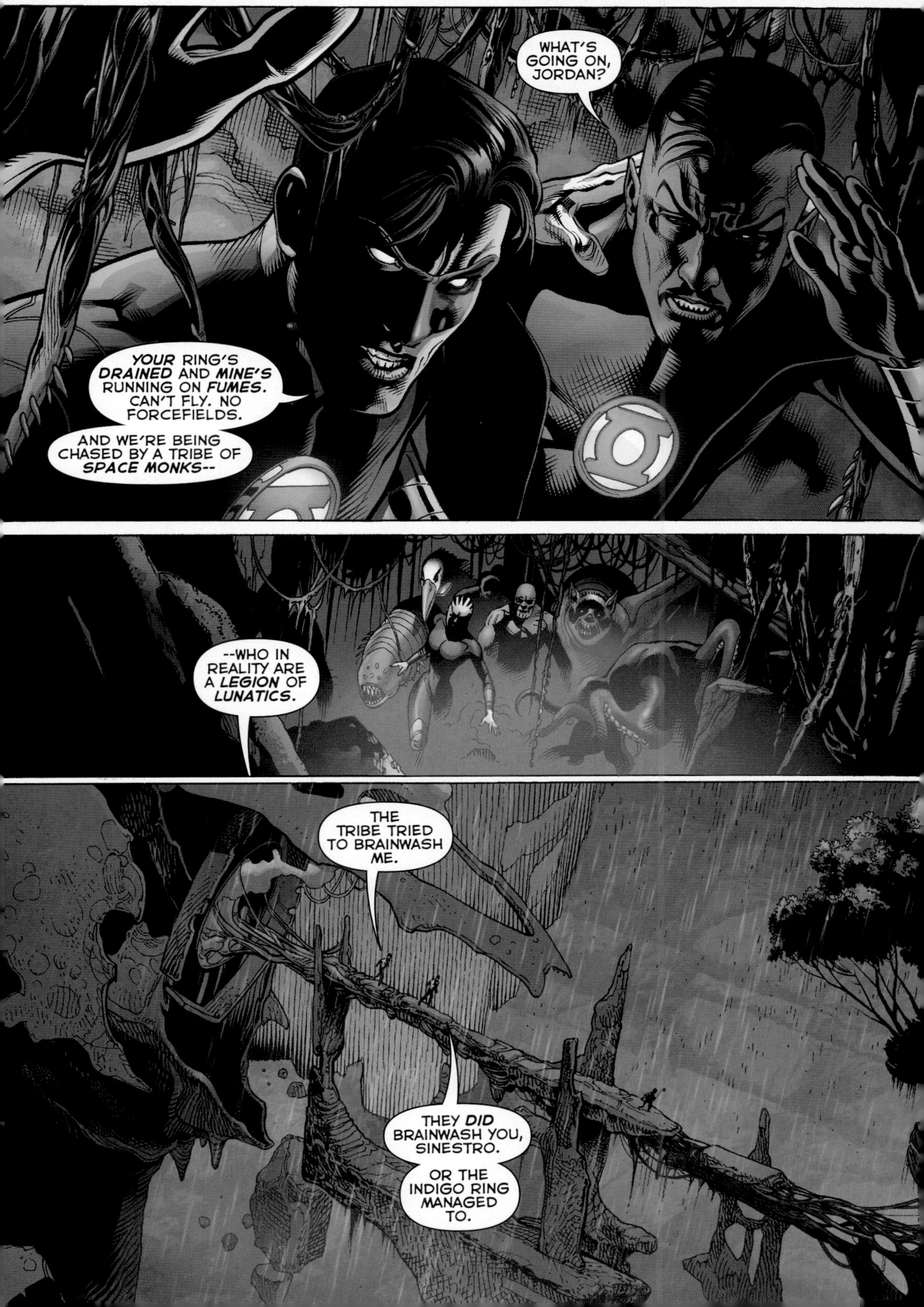

WHAT'S GOING ON, JORDAN?
YOUR RING'S DRAINED AND MINE'S RUNNING ON FUMES. CAN'T FLY. NO FORCEFIELDS.
AND WE'RE BEING CHASED BY A TRIBE OF SPACE MONKS--
--WHO IN REALITY ARE A LEGION OF LUNATICS.
THE TRIBE TRIED TO BRAINWASH ME.
THEY DID BRAINWASH YOU, SINESTRO.
OR THE INDIGO RING MANAGED TO.

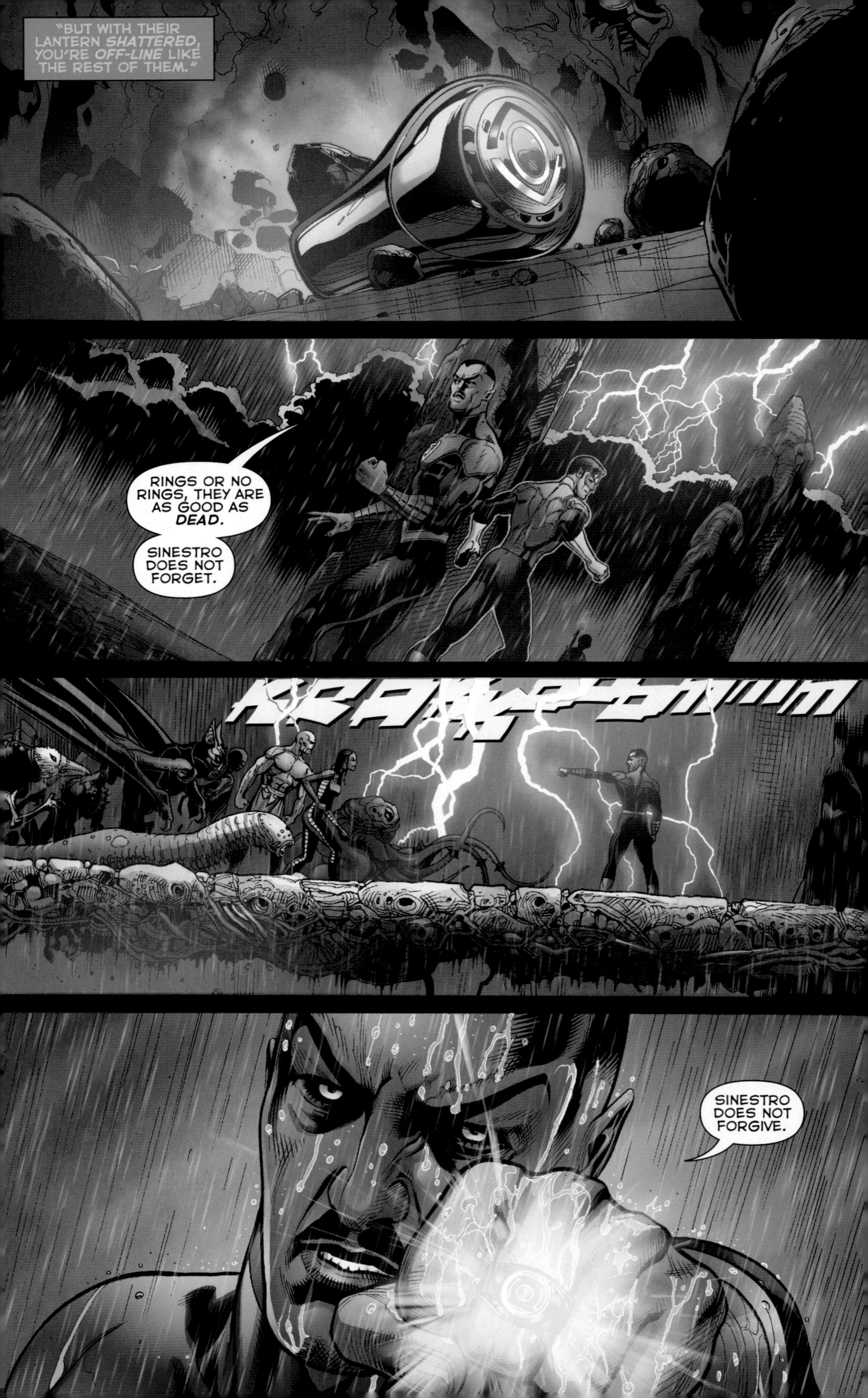
"BUT WITH THEIR LANTERN *SHATTERED*, YOU'RE *OFF-LINE* LIKE THE REST OF THEM."
RINGS OR NO RINGS, THEY ARE AS GOOD AS ***DEAD***.
SINESTRO DOES NOT FORGET.
SINESTRO DOES NOT FORGIVE.

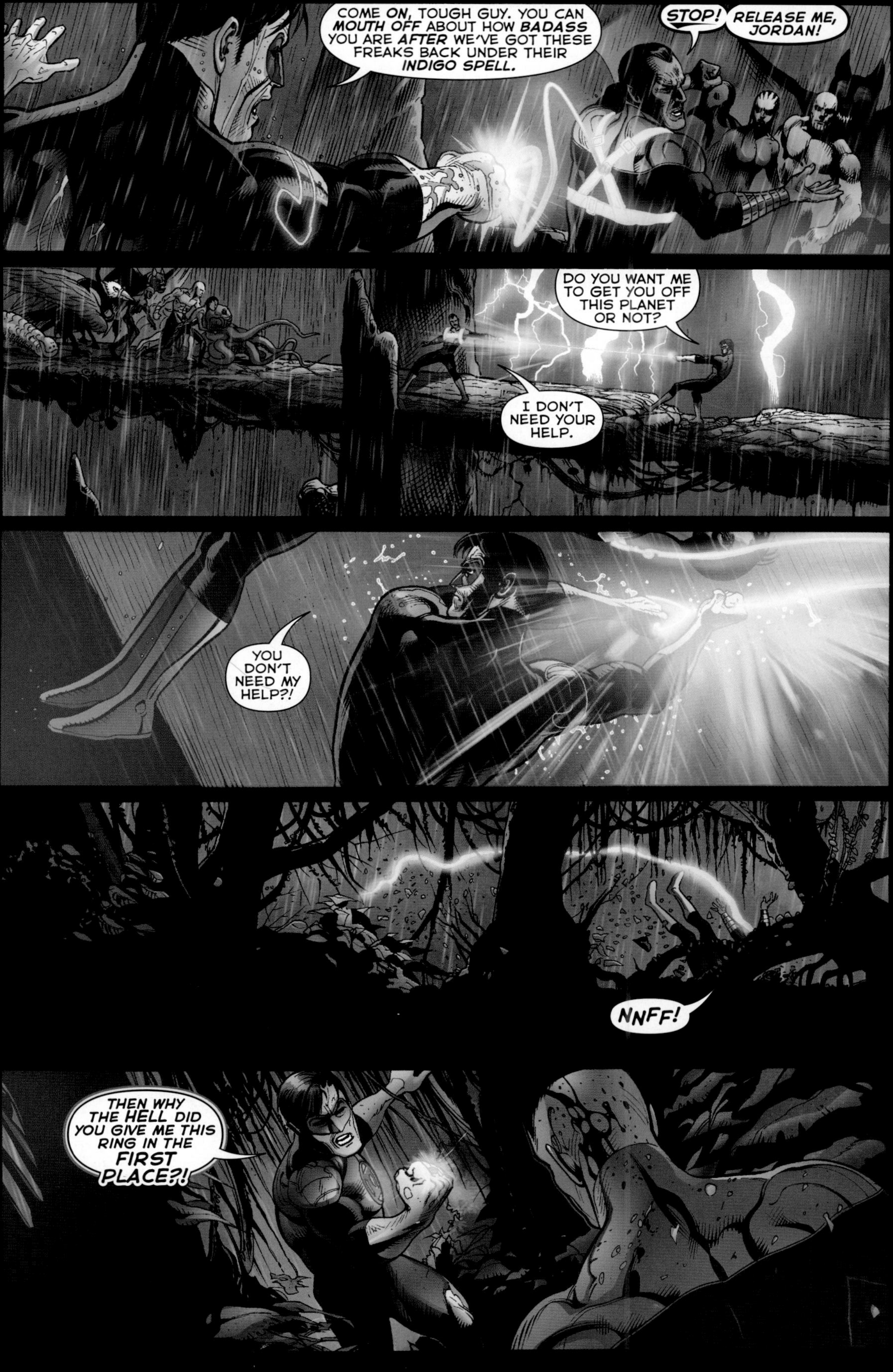
COME ON, TOUGH GUY. YOU CAN MOUTH OFF ABOUT HOW BADASS YOU ARE AFTER WE'VE GOT THESE FREAKS BACK UNDER THEIR INDIGO SPELL.
STOP!
RELEASE ME, JORDAN!
DO YOU WANT ME TO GET YOU OFF THIS PLANET OR NOT?
I DON'T NEED YOUR HELP.
YOU DON'T NEED MY HELP?!
NNFF!
THEN WHY THE HELL DID YOU GIVE ME THIS RING IN THE FIRST PLACE?!

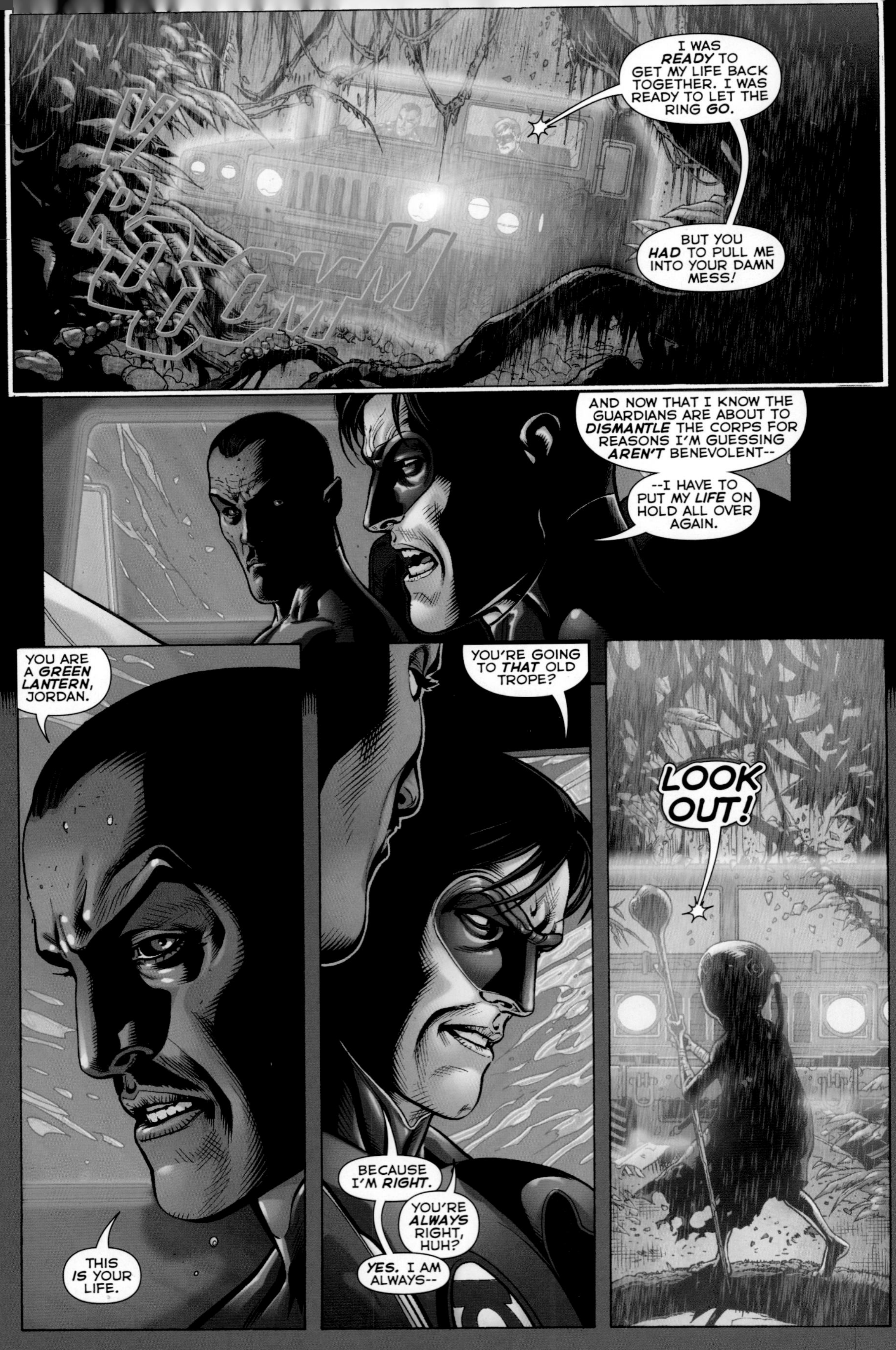
VRRROOOMM
I WAS READY TO GET MY LIFE BACK TOGETHER. I WAS READY TO LET THE RING GO.
BUT YOU HAD TO PULL ME INTO YOUR DAMN MESS!
AND NOW THAT I KNOW THE GUARDIANS ARE ABOUT TO DISMANTLE THE CORPS FOR REASONS I'M GUESSING AREN'T BENEVOLENT--
--I HAVE TO PUT MY LIFE ON HOLD ALL OVER AGAIN.
YOU ARE A GREEN LANTERN, JORDAN.
THIS IS YOUR LIFE.
YOU'RE GOING TO THAT OLD TROPE?
BECAUSE I'M RIGHT.
YOU'RE ALWAYS RIGHT, HUH?
YES. I AM ALWAYS--
LOOK OUT!

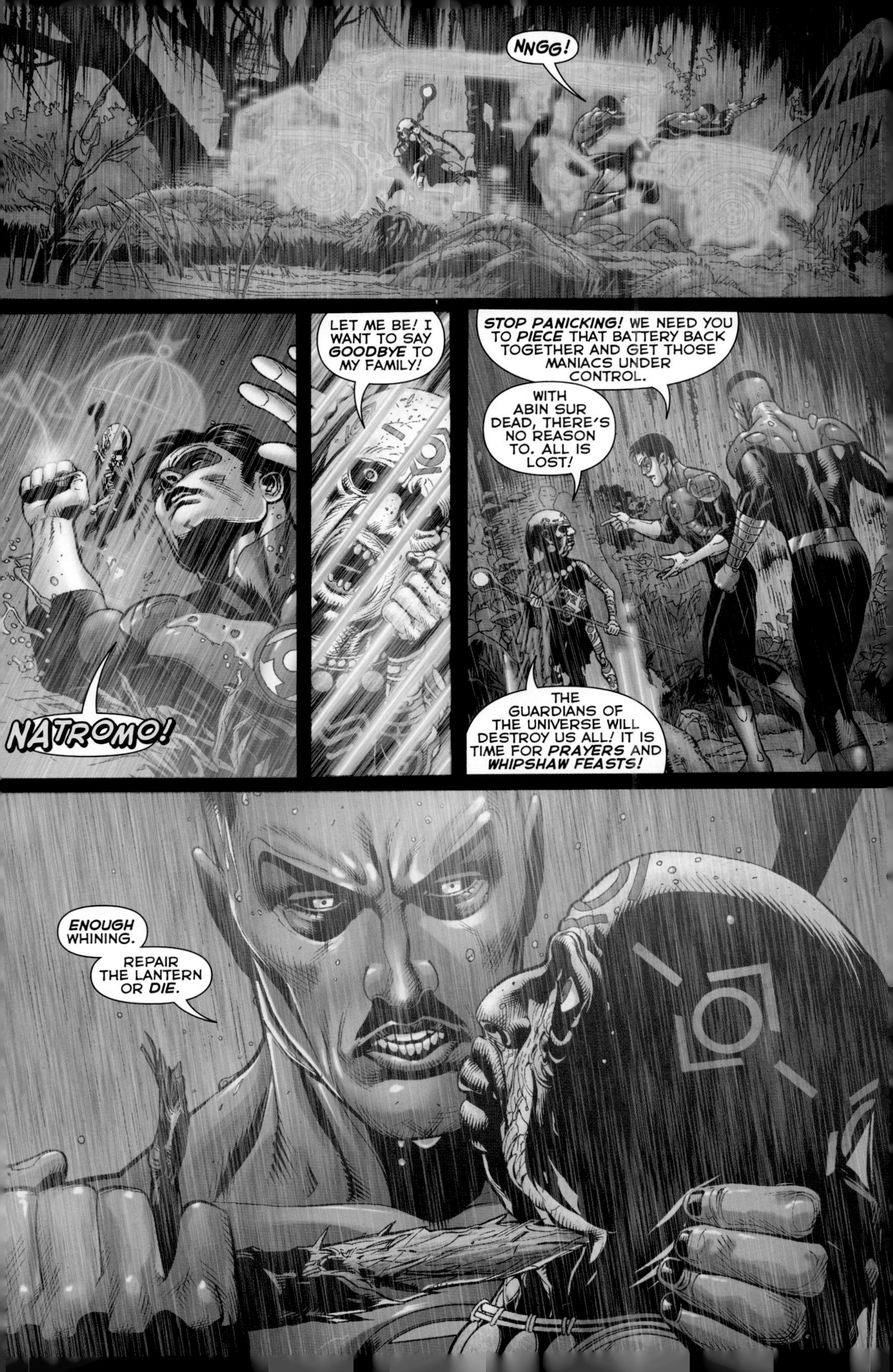
NNGG!
NATROMO!
LET ME BE! I WANT TO SAY GOODBYE TO MY FAMILY!
STOP PANICKING! WE NEED YOU TO PIECE THAT BATTERY BACK TOGETHER AND GET THOSE MANIACS UNDER CONTROL.
WITH ABIN SUR DEAD, THERE'S NO REASON TO. ALL IS LOST!
THE GUARDIANS OF THE UNIVERSE WILL DESTROY US ALL! IT IS TIME FOR PRAYERS AND WHIPSHAW FEASTS!
ENOUGH WHINING.
REPAIR THE LANTERN OR DIE.

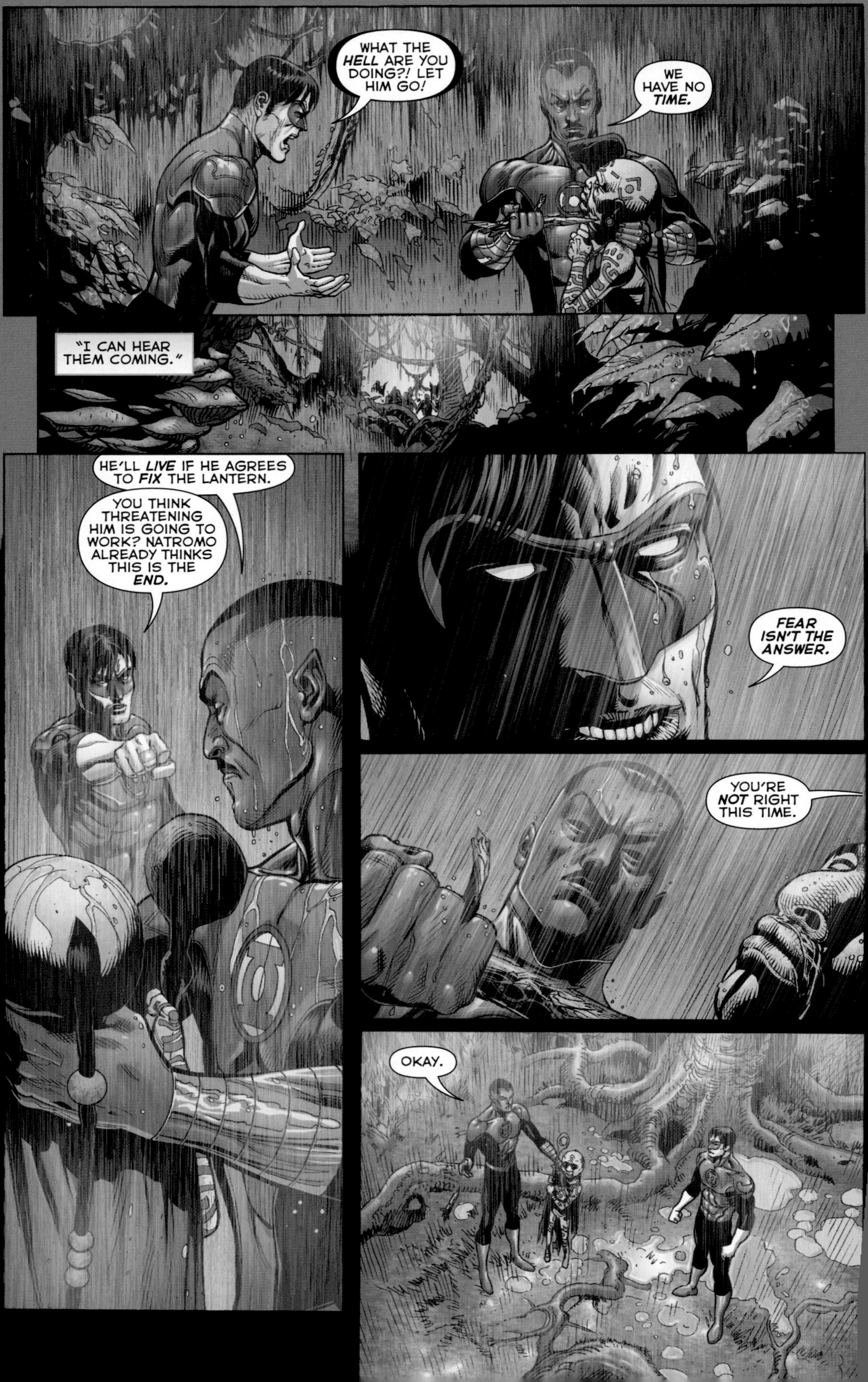
WHAT THE *HELL* ARE YOU DOING?! LET HIM GO!
WE HAVE NO *TIME.*
"I CAN HEAR THEM COMING."
HE'LL *LIVE* IF HE AGREES TO *FIX* THE LANTERN.
YOU THINK THREATENING HIM IS GOING TO WORK? NATROMO ALREADY THINKS THIS IS THE *END.*
FEAR ISN'T THE ANSWER.
YOU'RE *NOT* RIGHT THIS TIME.
OKAY.

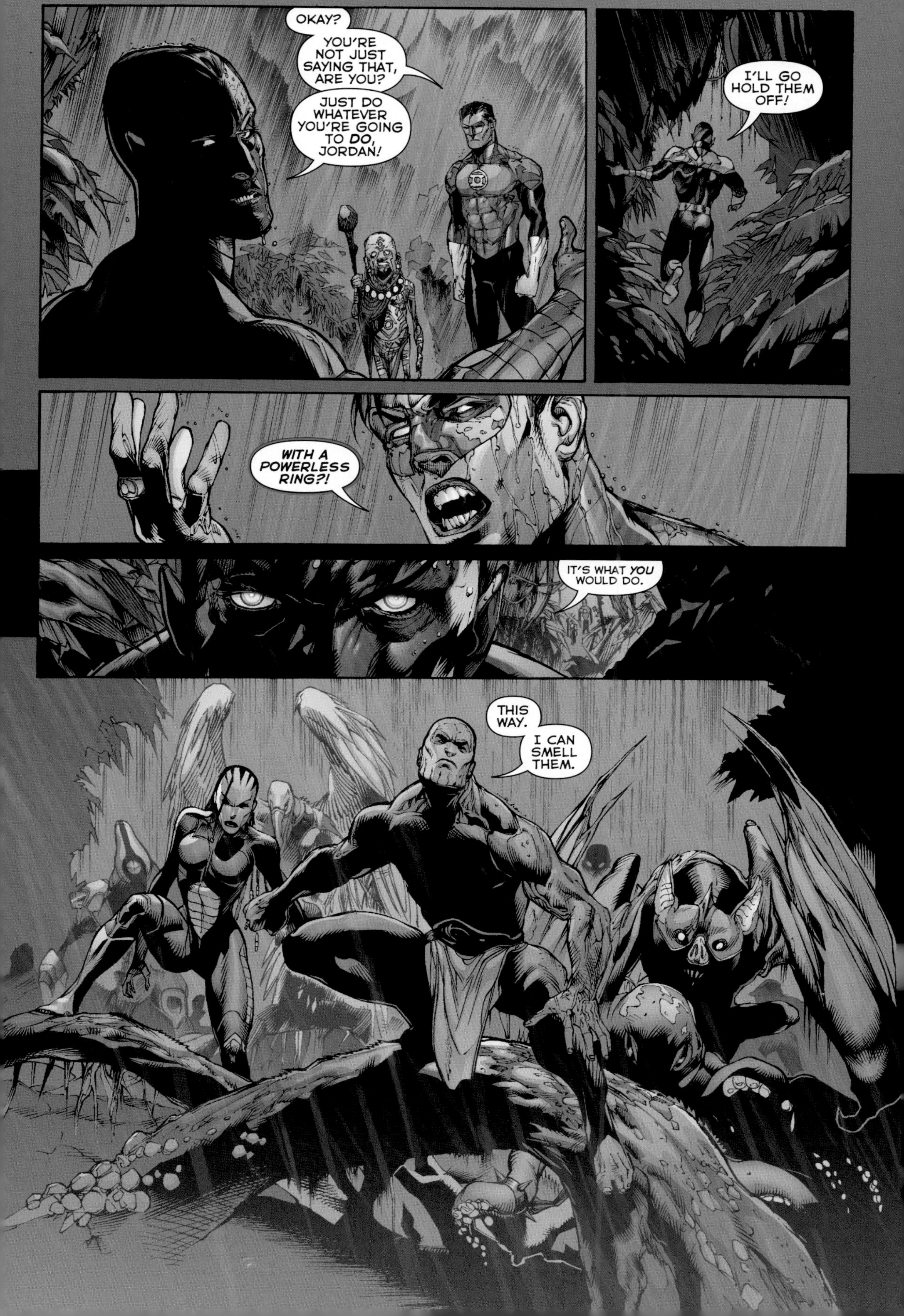
OKAY?
YOU'RE NOT JUST SAYING THAT, ARE YOU?
JUST DO WHATEVER YOU'RE GOING TO DO, JORDAN!
I'LL GO HOLD THEM OFF!
WITH A POWERLESS RING?!
IT'S WHAT YOU WOULD DO.
THIS WAY.
I CAN SMELL THEM.

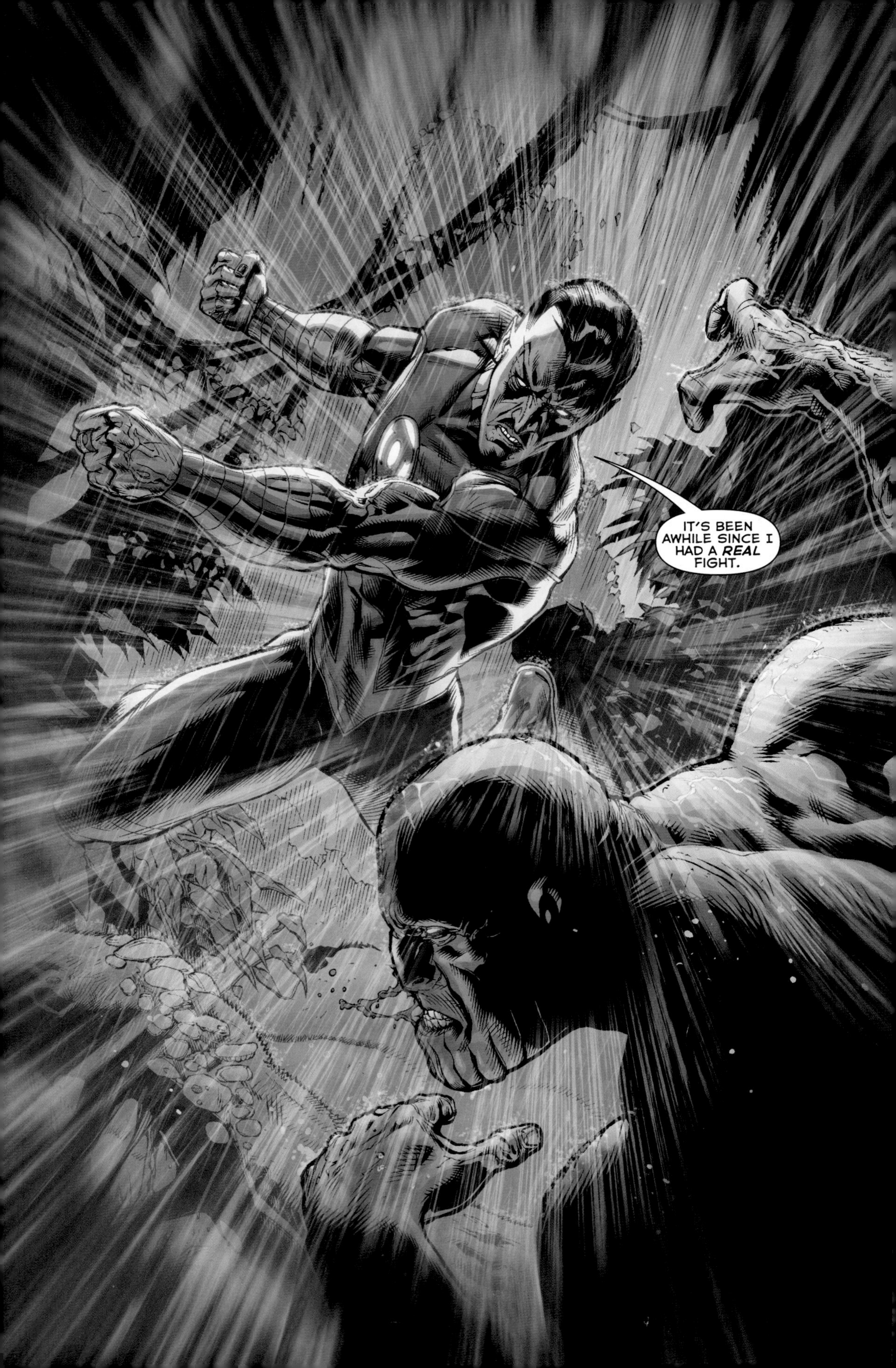
IT'S BEEN AWHILE SINCE I HAD A *REAL* FIGHT.

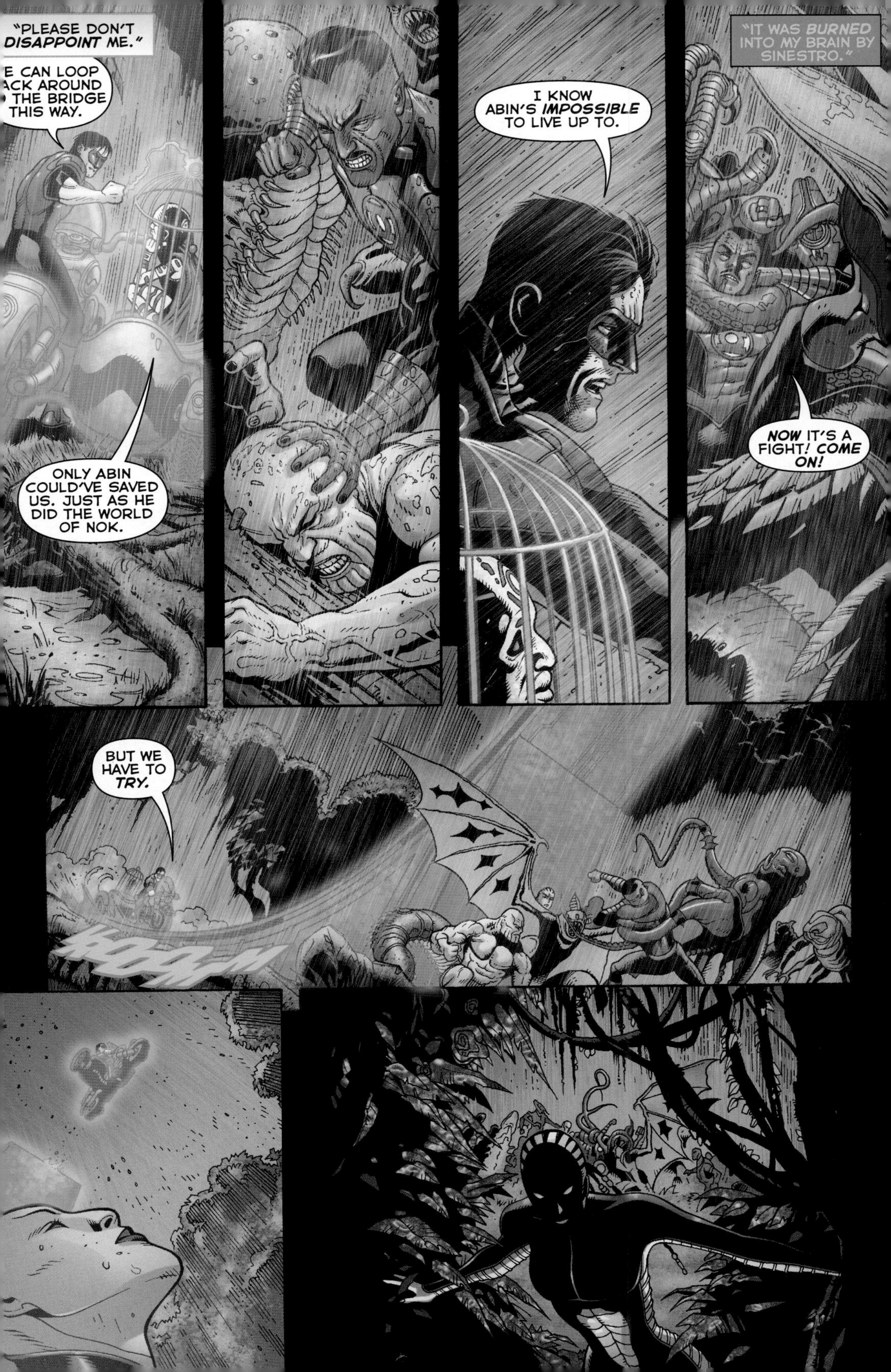
"PLEASE DON'T *DISAPPOINT* ME."
E CAN LOOP ACK AROUND THE BRIDGE THIS WAY.
ONLY ABIN COULD'VE SAVED US. JUST AS HE DID THE WORLD OF NOK.
I KNOW ABIN'S *IMPOSSIBLE* TO LIVE UP TO.
"IT WAS *BURNED* INTO MY BRAIN BY SINESTRO."
NOW IT'S A FIGHT! *COME ON!*
BUT WE HAVE TO *TRY.*

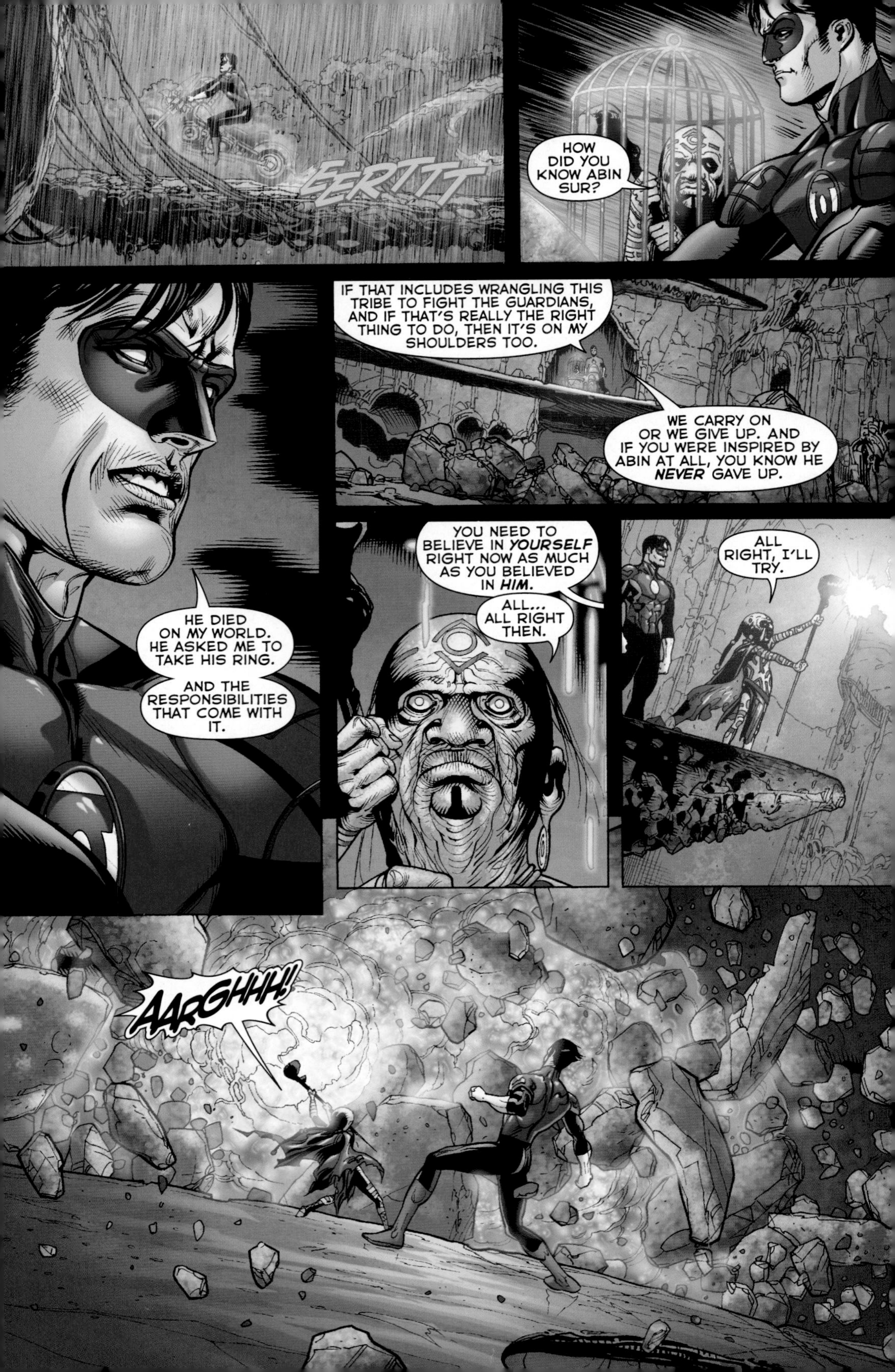
EERTTT
HOW DID YOU KNOW ABIN SUR?
HE DIED ON MY WORLD. HE ASKED ME TO TAKE HIS RING.
AND THE RESPONSIBILITIES THAT COME WITH IT.
IF THAT INCLUDES WRANGLING THIS TRIBE TO FIGHT THE GUARDIANS, AND IF THAT'S REALLY THE RIGHT THING TO DO, THEN IT'S ON MY SHOULDERS TOO.
WE CARRY ON OR WE GIVE UP. AND IF YOU WERE INSPIRED BY ABIN AT ALL, YOU KNOW HE NEVER GAVE UP.
YOU NEED TO BELIEVE IN YOURSELF RIGHT NOW AS MUCH AS YOU BELIEVED IN HIM.
ALL... ALL RIGHT THEN.
ALL RIGHT, I'LL TRY.
AARGHHH!

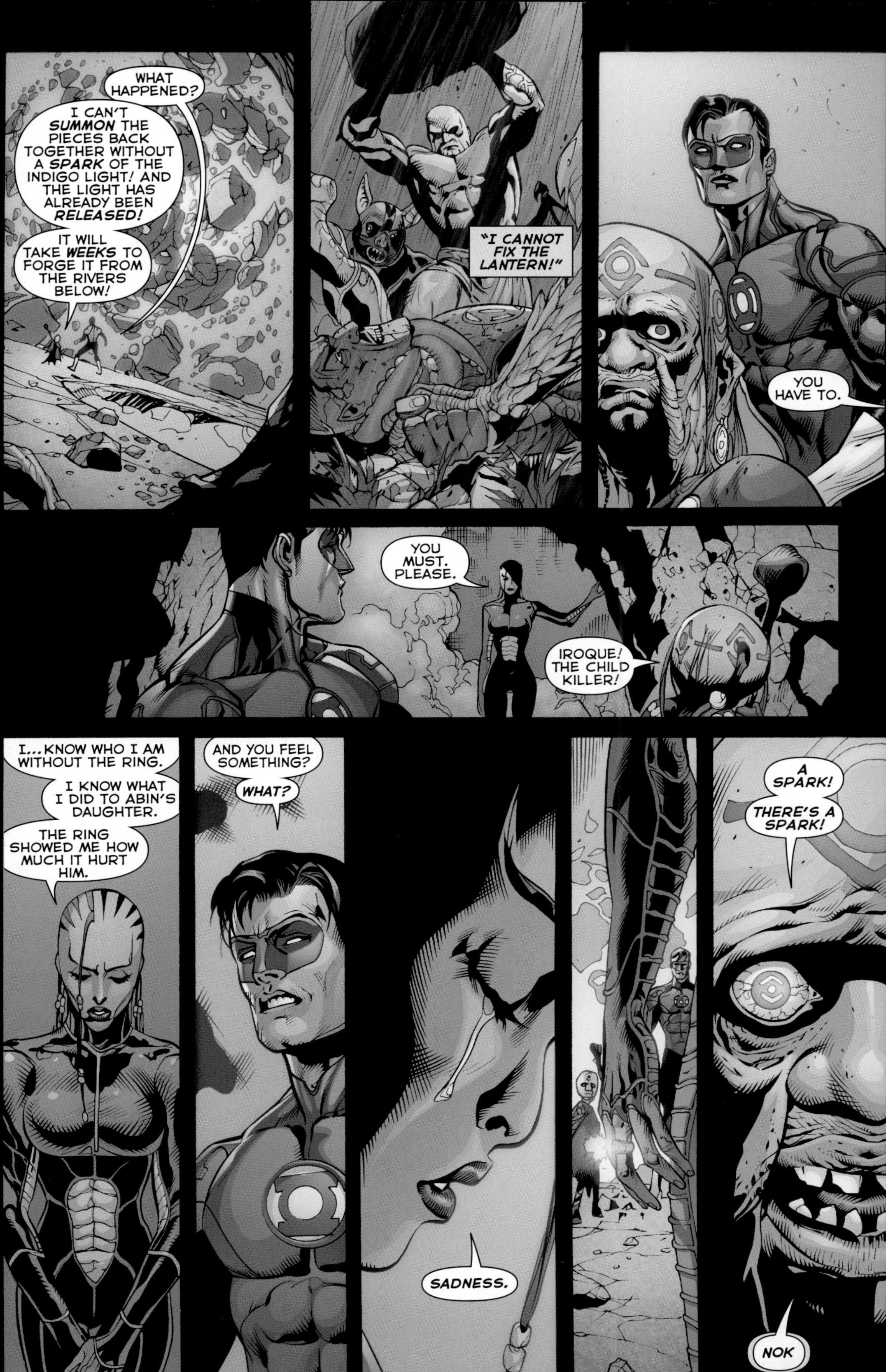
WHAT HAPPENED?
I CAN'T SUMMON THE PIECES BACK TOGETHER WITHOUT A SPARK OF THE INDIGO LIGHT! AND THE LIGHT HAS ALREADY BEEN RELEASED!
IT WILL TAKE WEEKS TO FORGE IT FROM THE RIVERS BELOW!
"I CANNOT FIX THE LANTERN!"
YOU HAVE TO.
YOU MUST. PLEASE.
IROQUE! THE CHILD KILLER!
I...KNOW WHO I AM WITHOUT THE RING.
I KNOW WHAT I DID TO ABIN'S DAUGHTER.
THE RING SHOWED ME HOW MUCH IT HURT HIM.
AND YOU FEEL SOMETHING?
WHAT?
SADNESS.
A SPARK!
THERE'S A SPARK!
NOK

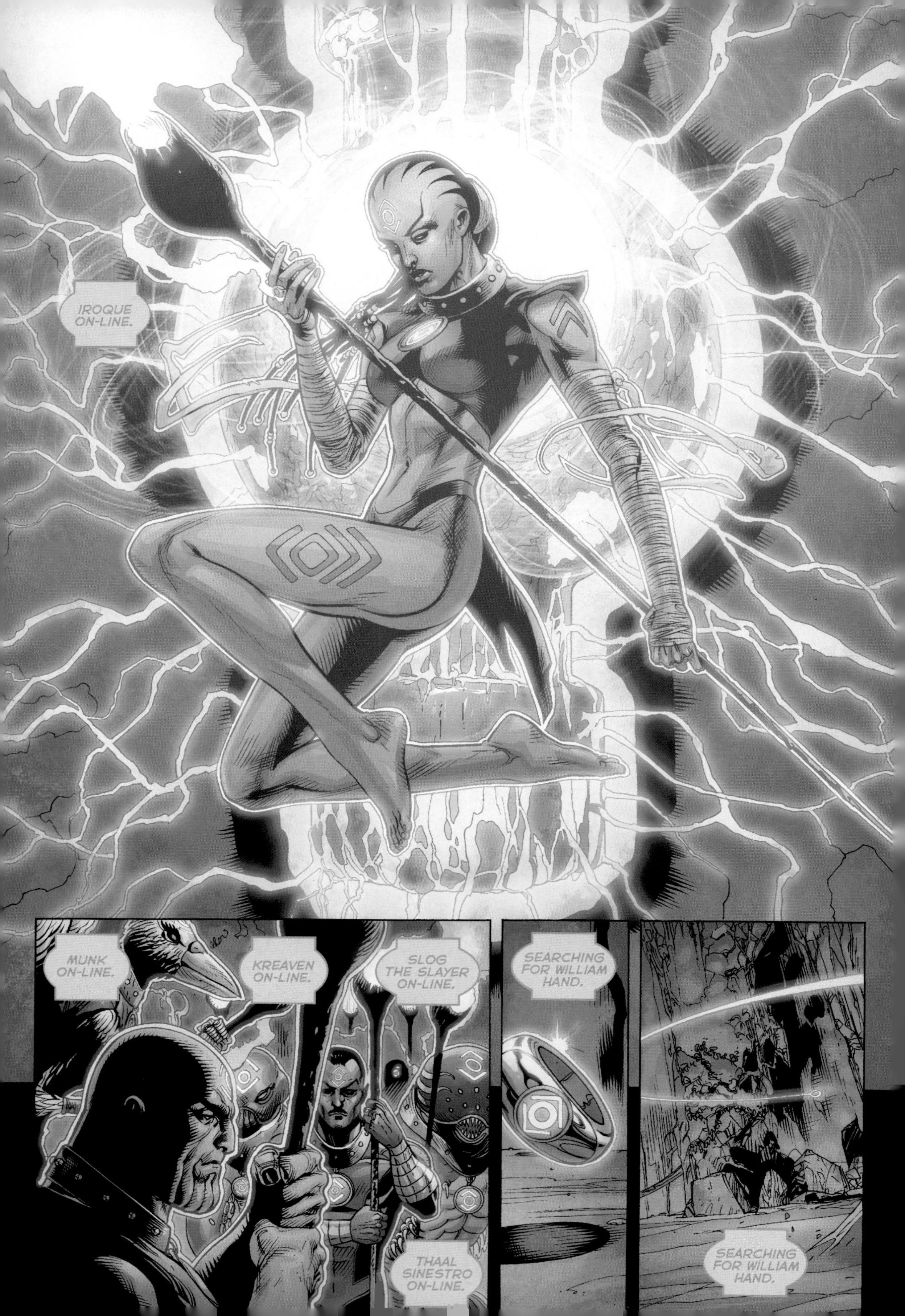
IROQUE ON-LINE.
MUNK ON-LINE.
KREAVEN ON-LINE.
SLOG THE SLAYER ON-LINE.
THAAL SINESTRO ON-LINE.
SEARCHING FOR WILLIAM HAND.
SEARCHING FOR WILLIAM HAND.

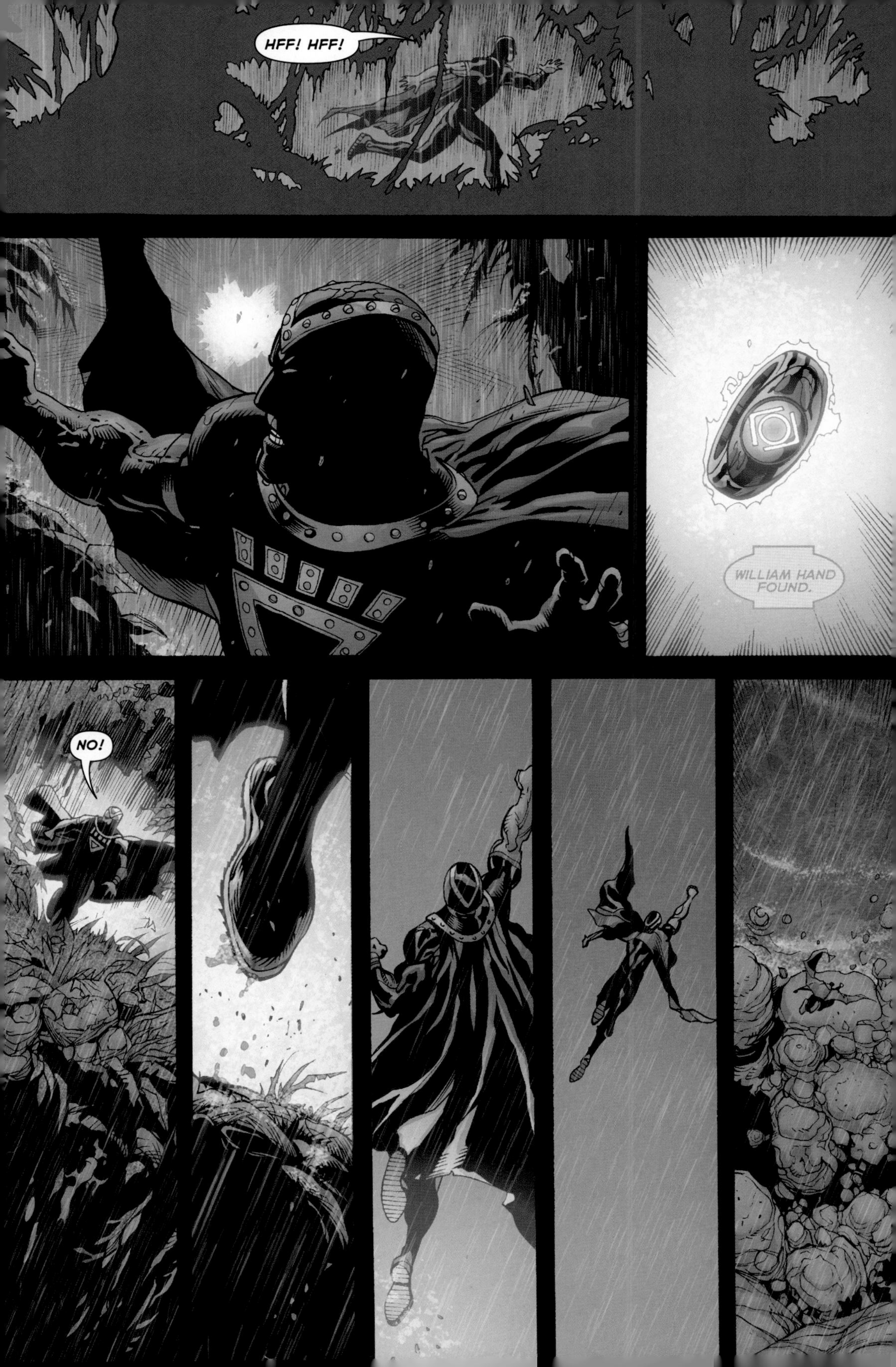
HFF! HFF!
WILLIAM HAND FOUND.
NO!

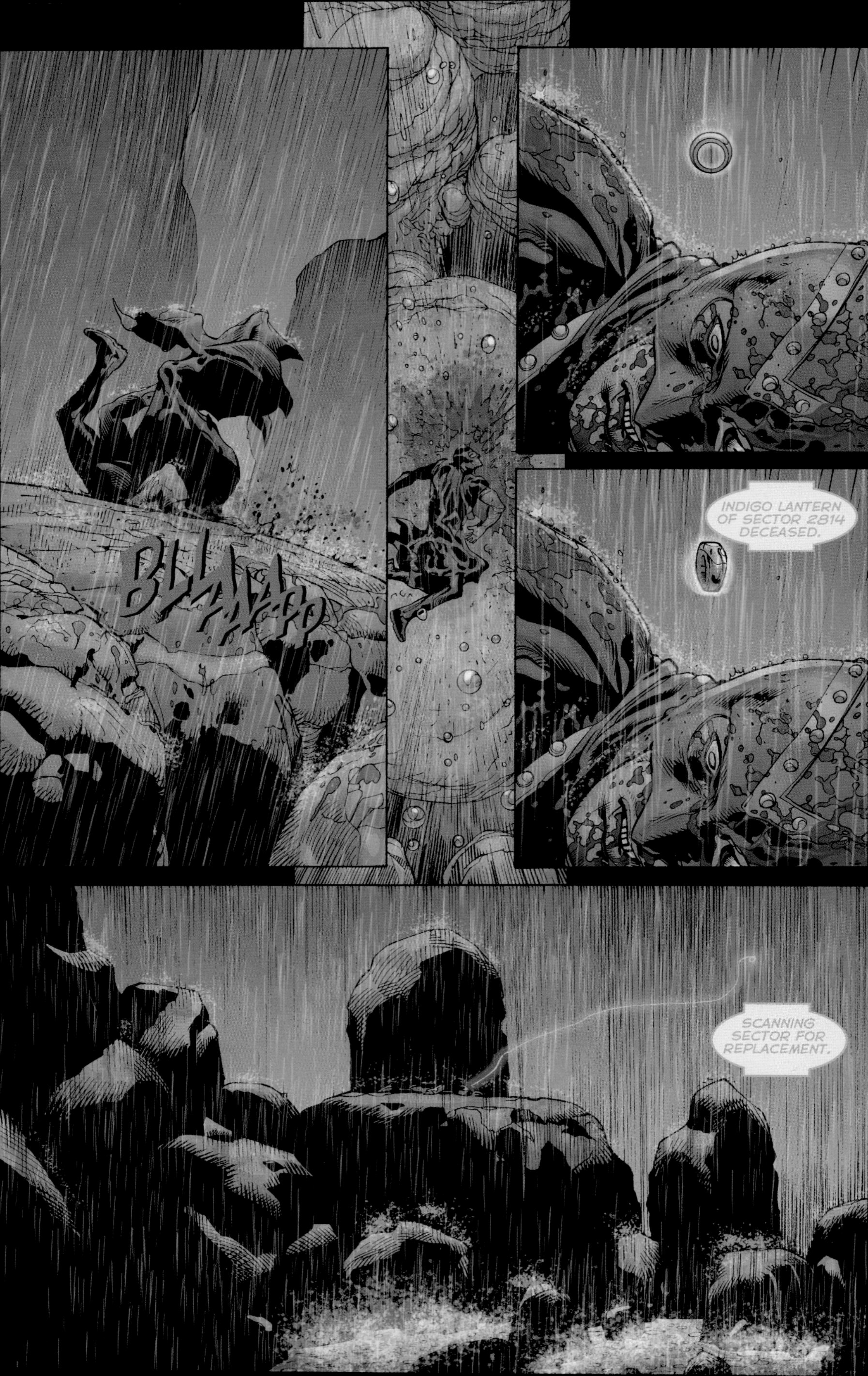
BLAM
INDIGO LANTERN OF SECTOR 2814 DECEASED.
SCANNING SECTOR FOR REPLACEMENT.

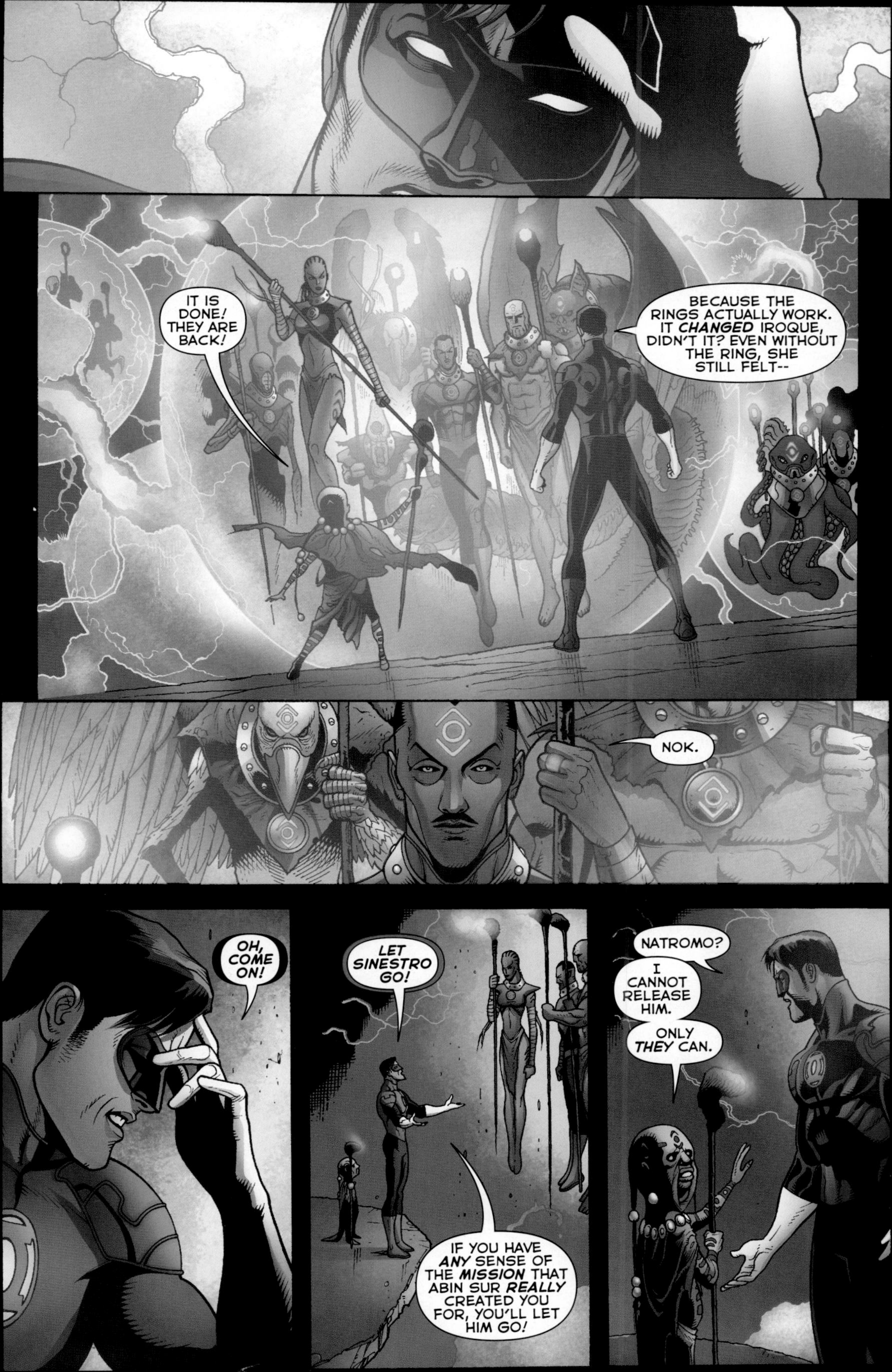
IT IS DONE! THEY ARE BACK!
BECAUSE THE RINGS ACTUALLY WORK. IT CHANGED IROQUE, DIDN'T IT? EVEN WITHOUT THE RING, SHE STILL FELT--
NOK.
OH, COME ON!
LET SINESTRO GO!
IF YOU HAVE ANY SENSE OF THE MISSION THAT ABIN SUR REALLY CREATED YOU FOR, YOU'LL LET HIM GO!
NATROMO?
I CANNOT RELEASE HIM.
ONLY THEY CAN.

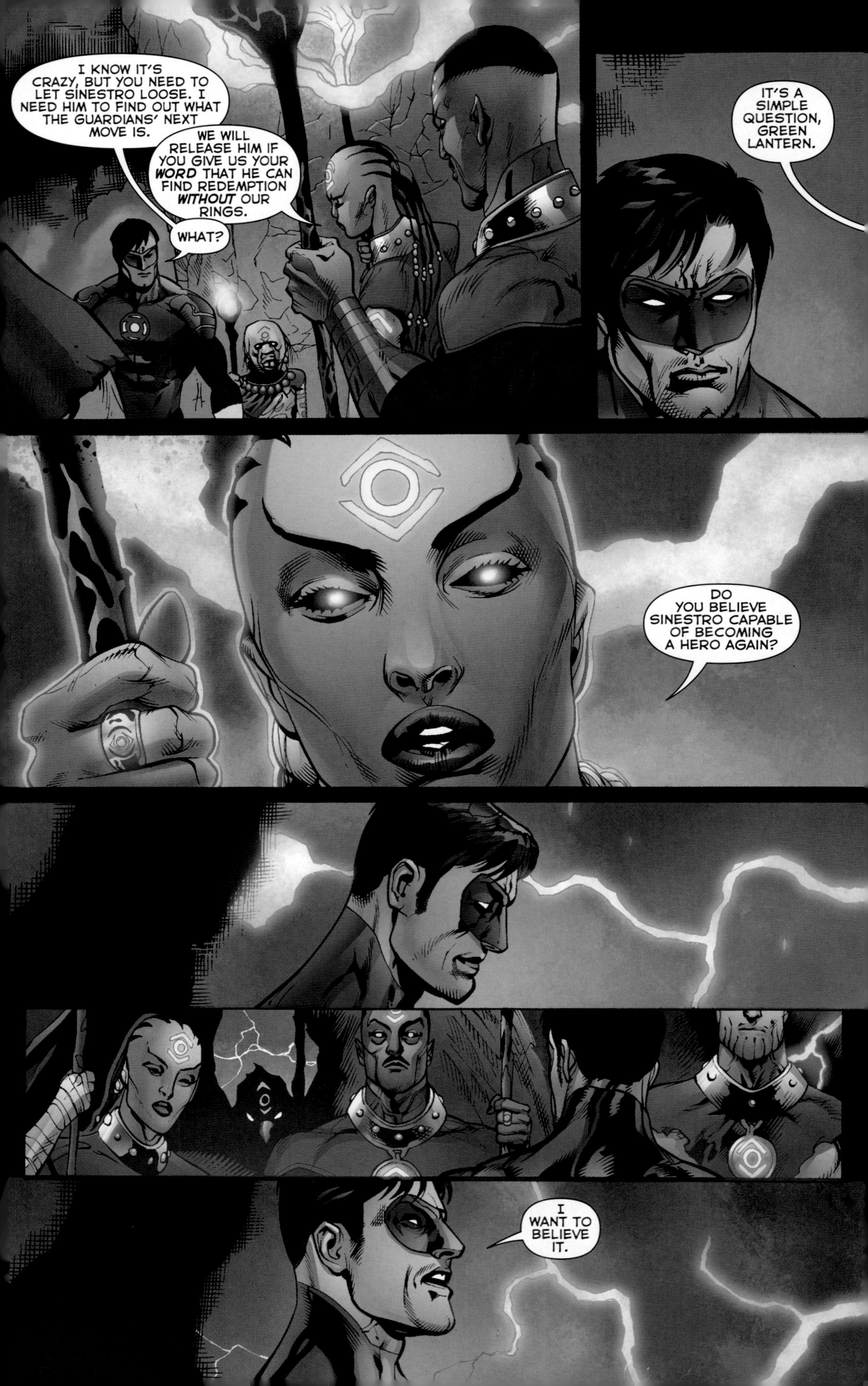
I KNOW IT'S CRAZY, BUT YOU NEED TO LET SINESTRO LOOSE. I NEED HIM TO FIND OUT WHAT THE GUARDIANS' NEXT MOVE IS.
WE WILL RELEASE HIM IF YOU GIVE US YOUR **WORD** THAT HE CAN FIND REDEMPTION ***WITHOUT*** OUR RINGS.
WHAT?
IT'S A SIMPLE QUESTION, GREEN LANTERN.
DO YOU BELIEVE SINESTRO CAPABLE OF BECOMING A HERO AGAIN?
I WANT TO BELIEVE IT.

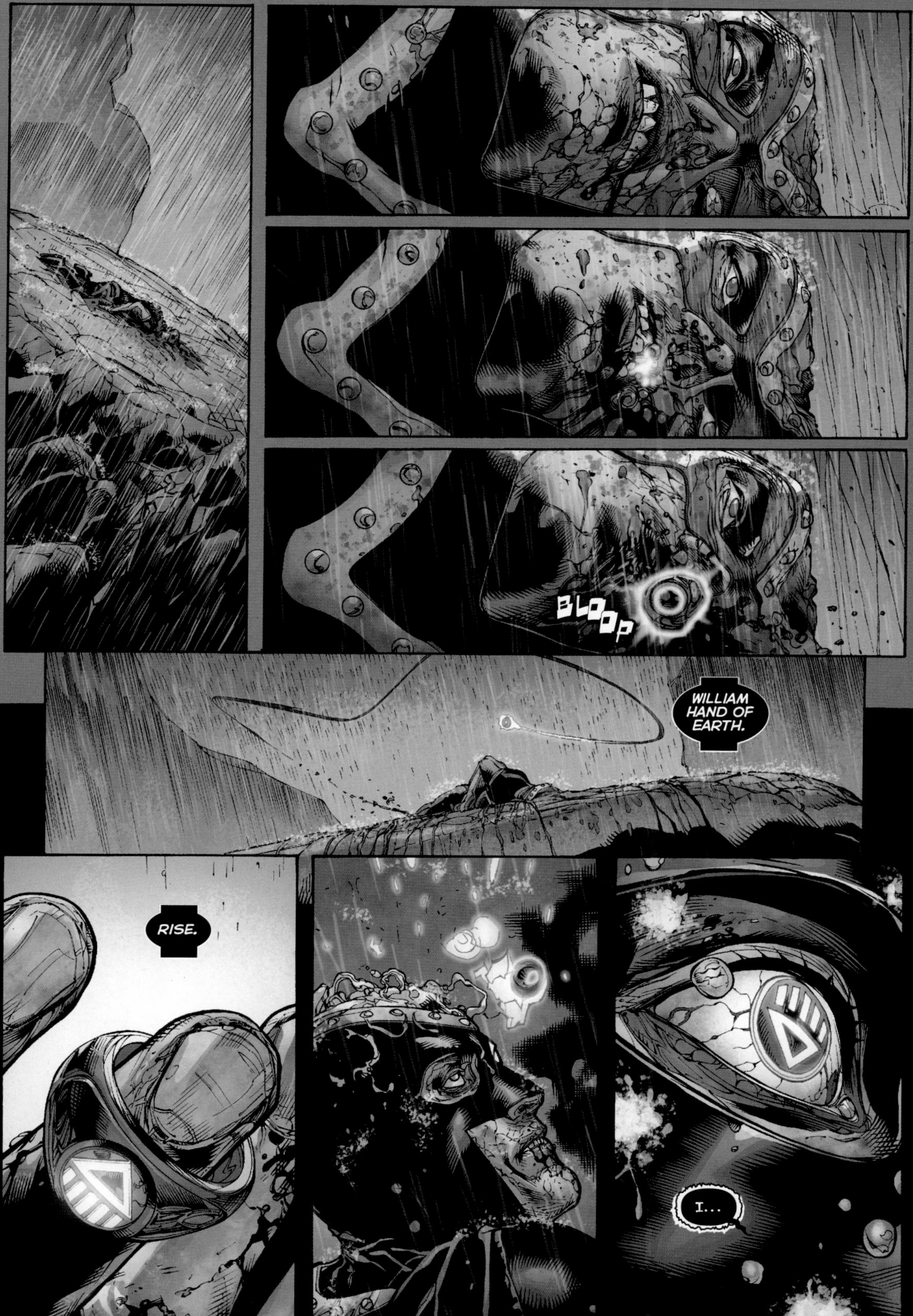
BLOOP
WILLIAM HAND OF EARTH.
RISE.
I...

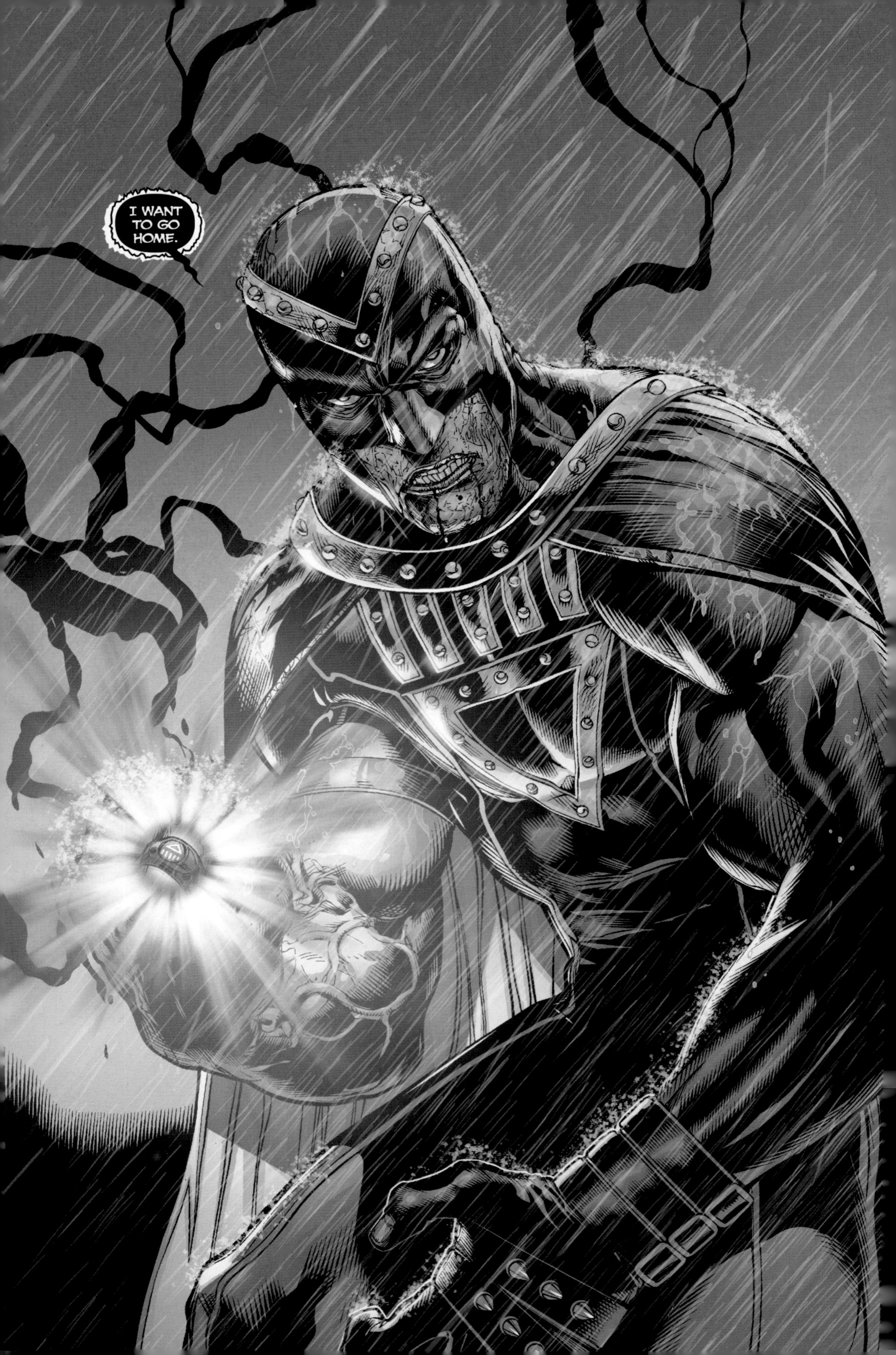
I WANT TO GO HOME.

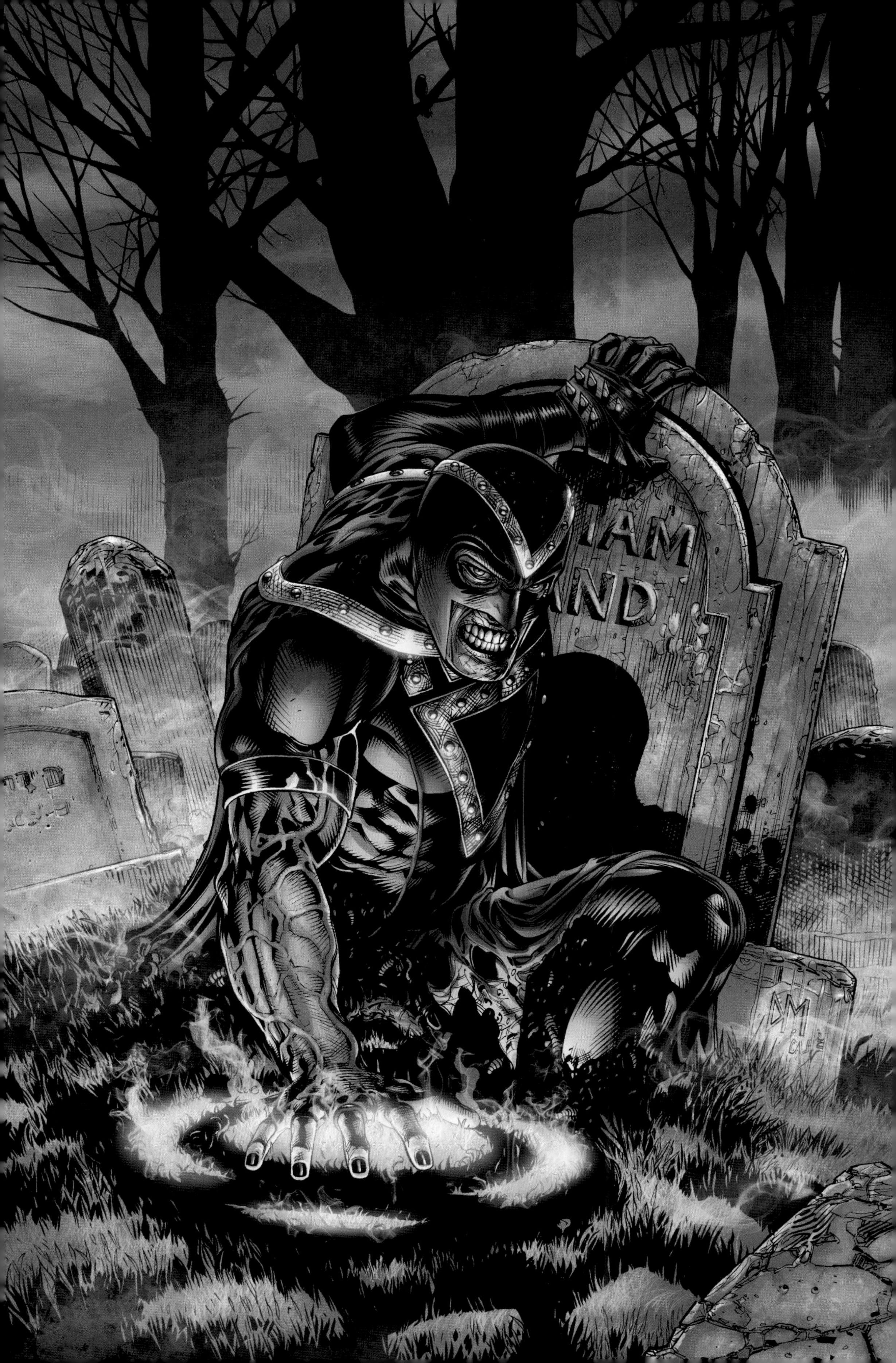

THE REVENGE OF BLACK HAND part one

GEOFF JOHNS writer **DOUG MAHNKE** penciller KEITH CHAMPAGNE, CHRISTIAN ALAMY, MARK IRWIN, TOM NGUYEN & DOUG MAHNKE inkers
DOUG MAHNKE, CHRISTIAN ALAMY & ALEX SINCLAIR cover

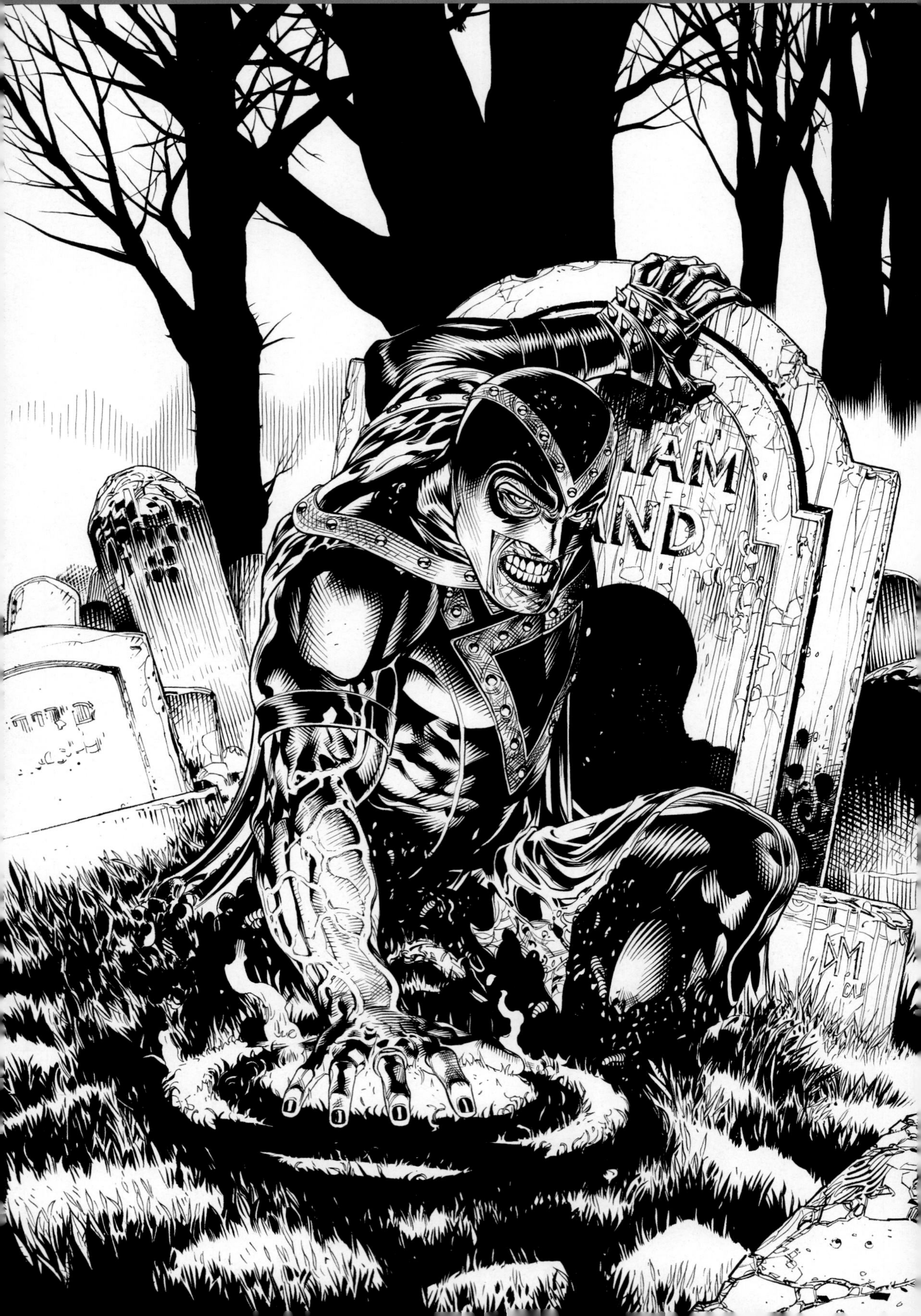

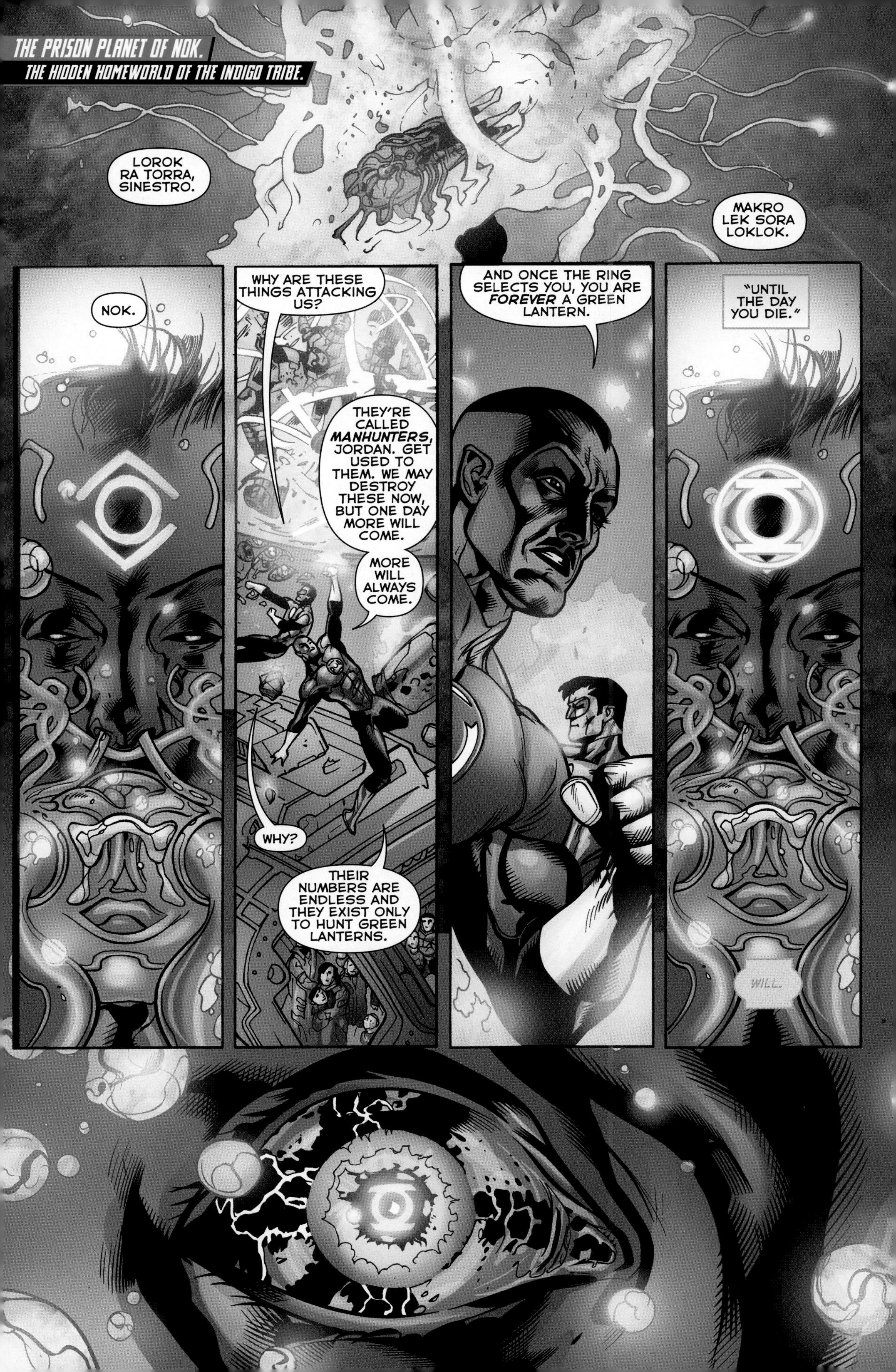
THE PRISON PLANET OF NOK.
THE HIDDEN HOMEWORLD OF THE INDIGO TRIBE.
LOROK RA TORRA, SINESTRO.
MAKRO LEK SORA LOKLOK.
NOK.
WHY ARE THESE THINGS ATTACKING US?
THEY'RE CALLED MANHUNTERS, JORDAN. GET USED TO THEM. WE MAY DESTROY THESE NOW, BUT ONE DAY MORE WILL COME.
MORE WILL ALWAYS COME.
WHY?
THEIR NUMBERS ARE ENDLESS AND THEY EXIST ONLY TO HUNT GREEN LANTERNS.
AND ONCE THE RING SELECTS YOU, YOU ARE FOREVER A GREEN LANTERN.
"UNTIL THE DAY YOU DIE."
WILL.

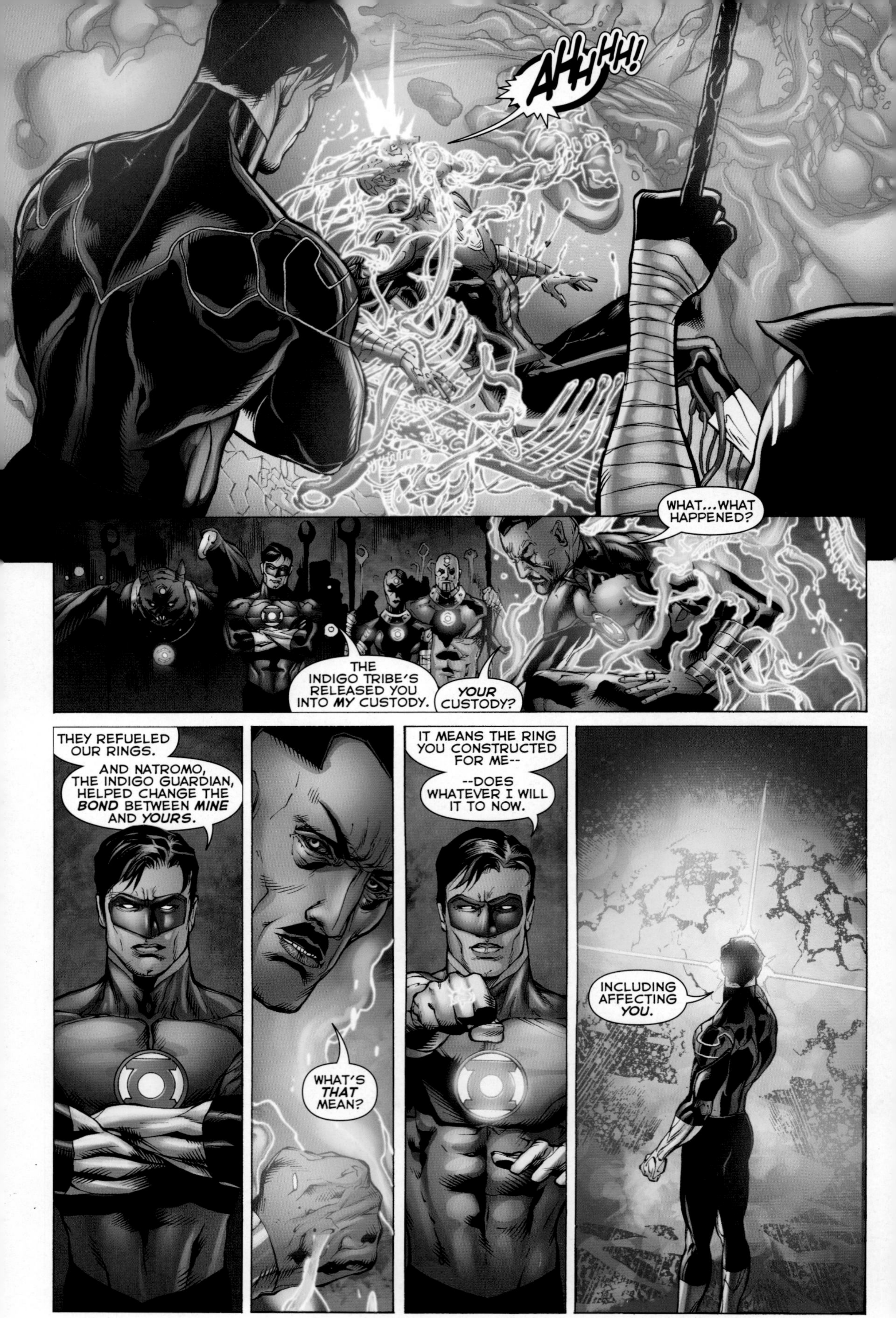
AHHHH!
WHAT...WHAT HAPPENED?
THE INDIGO TRIBE'S RELEASED YOU INTO *MY* CUSTODY.
YOUR CUSTODY?
THEY REFUELED OUR RINGS.
AND NATROMO, THE INDIGO GUARDIAN, HELPED CHANGE THE *BOND* BETWEEN *MINE* AND *YOURS*.
WHAT'S *THAT* MEAN?
IT MEANS THE RING YOU CONSTRUCTED FOR ME--
--DOES WHATEVER I WILL IT TO NOW.
INCLUDING AFFECTING *YOU*.

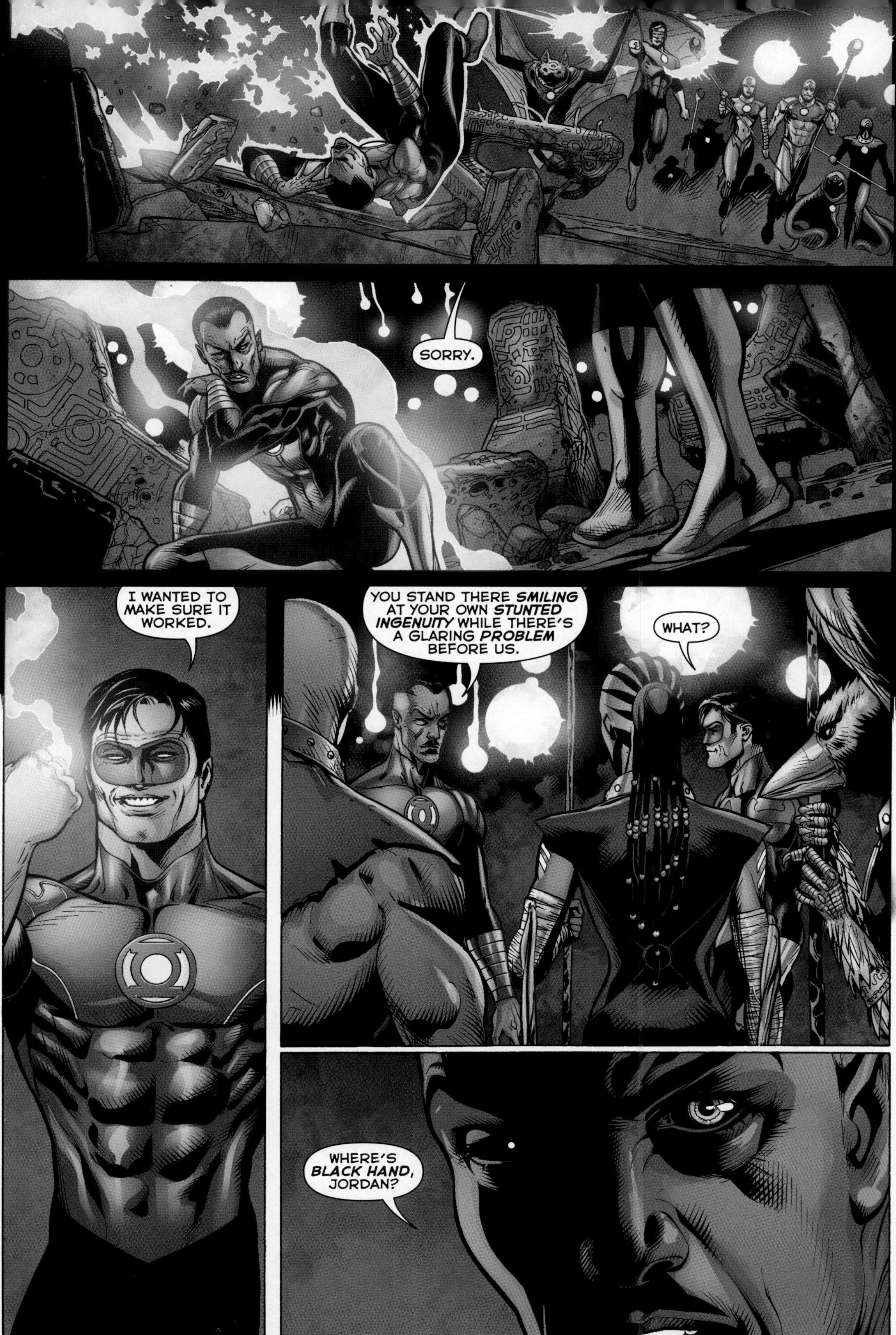
SORRY.
I WANTED TO MAKE SURE IT WORKED.
YOU STAND THERE *SMILING* AT YOUR OWN *STUNTED INGENUITY* WHILE THERE'S A GLARING *PROBLEM* BEFORE US.
WHAT?
WHERE'S *BLACK HAND*, JORDAN?

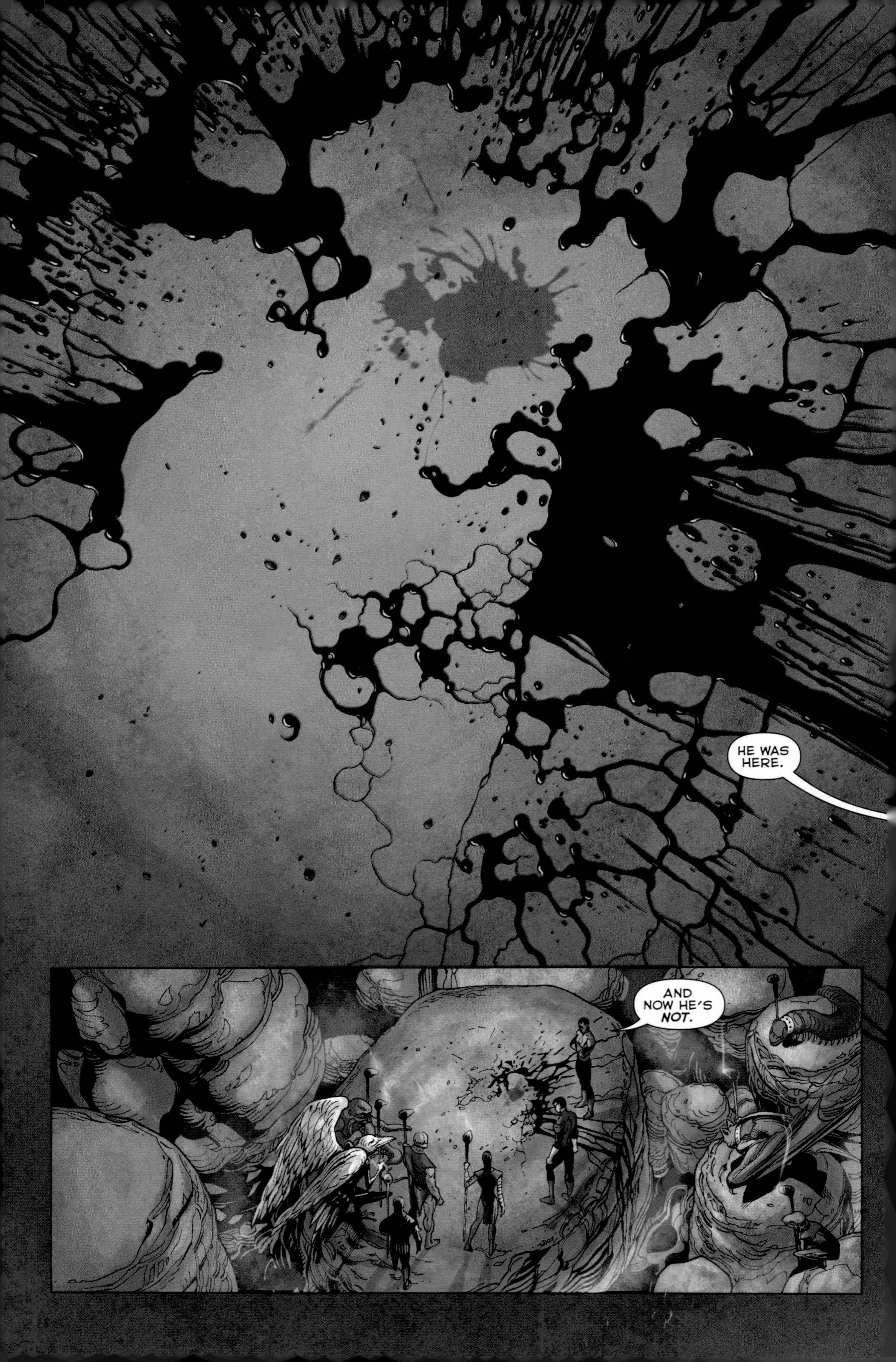

HE WAS HERE.
AND NOW HE'S *NOT*.

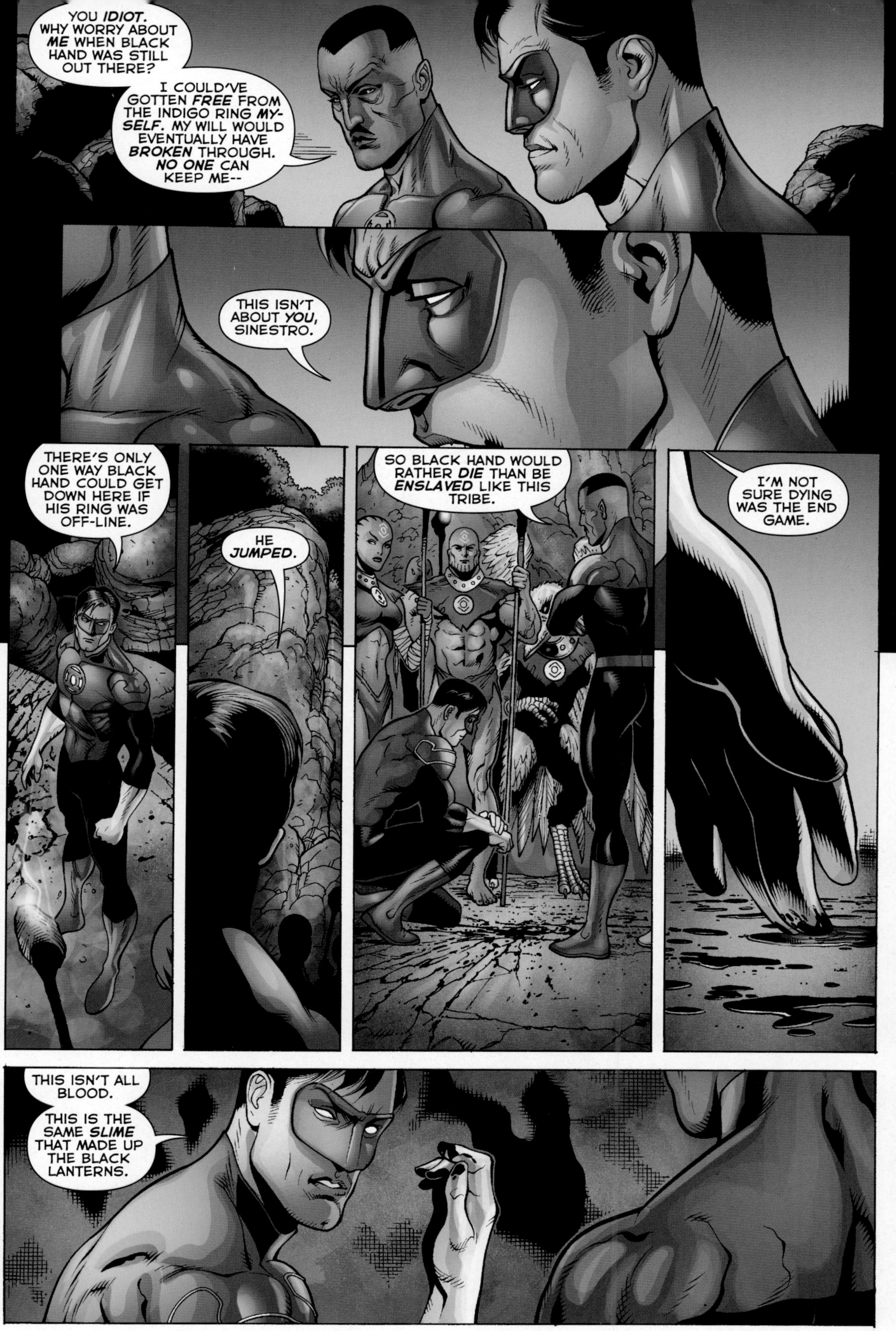
YOU *IDIOT*. WHY WORRY ABOUT *ME* WHEN BLACK HAND WAS STILL OUT THERE?
I COULD'VE GOTTEN *FREE* FROM THE INDIGO RING *MY-SELF*. MY WILL WOULD EVENTUALLY HAVE *BROKEN* THROUGH. *NO ONE* CAN KEEP ME--
THIS ISN'T ABOUT *YOU*, SINESTRO.
THERE'S ONLY ONE WAY BLACK HAND COULD GET DOWN HERE IF HIS RING WAS OFF-LINE.
HE *JUMPED*.
SO BLACK HAND WOULD RATHER *DIE* THAN BE *ENSLAVED* LIKE THIS TRIBE.
I'M NOT SURE DYING WAS THE END GAME.
THIS ISN'T ALL BLOOD.
THIS IS THE SAME *SLIME* THAT MADE UP THE BLACK LANTERNS.

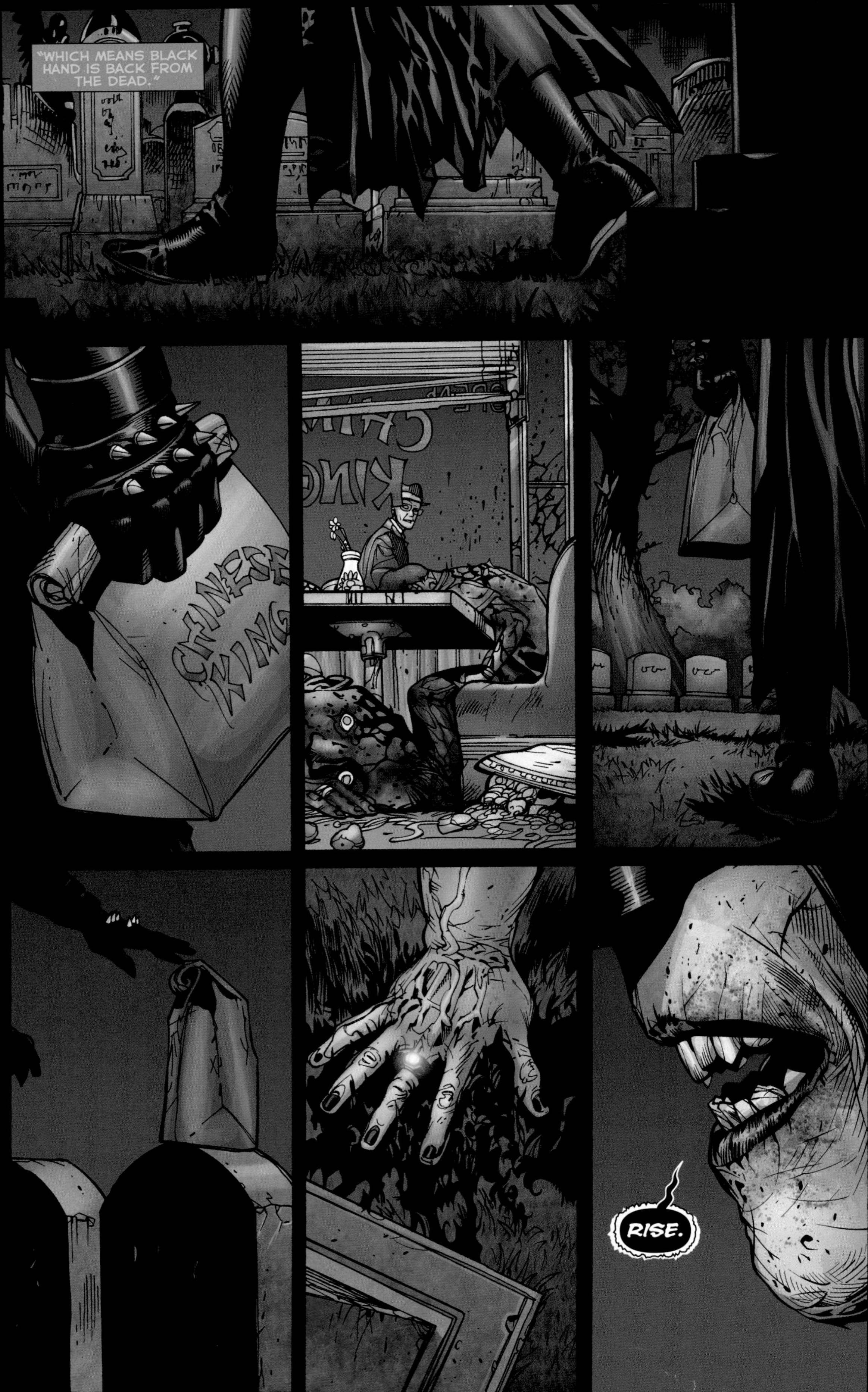
"WHICH MEANS BLACK HAND IS BACK FROM THE DEAD."
CHINESE KING
RISE.

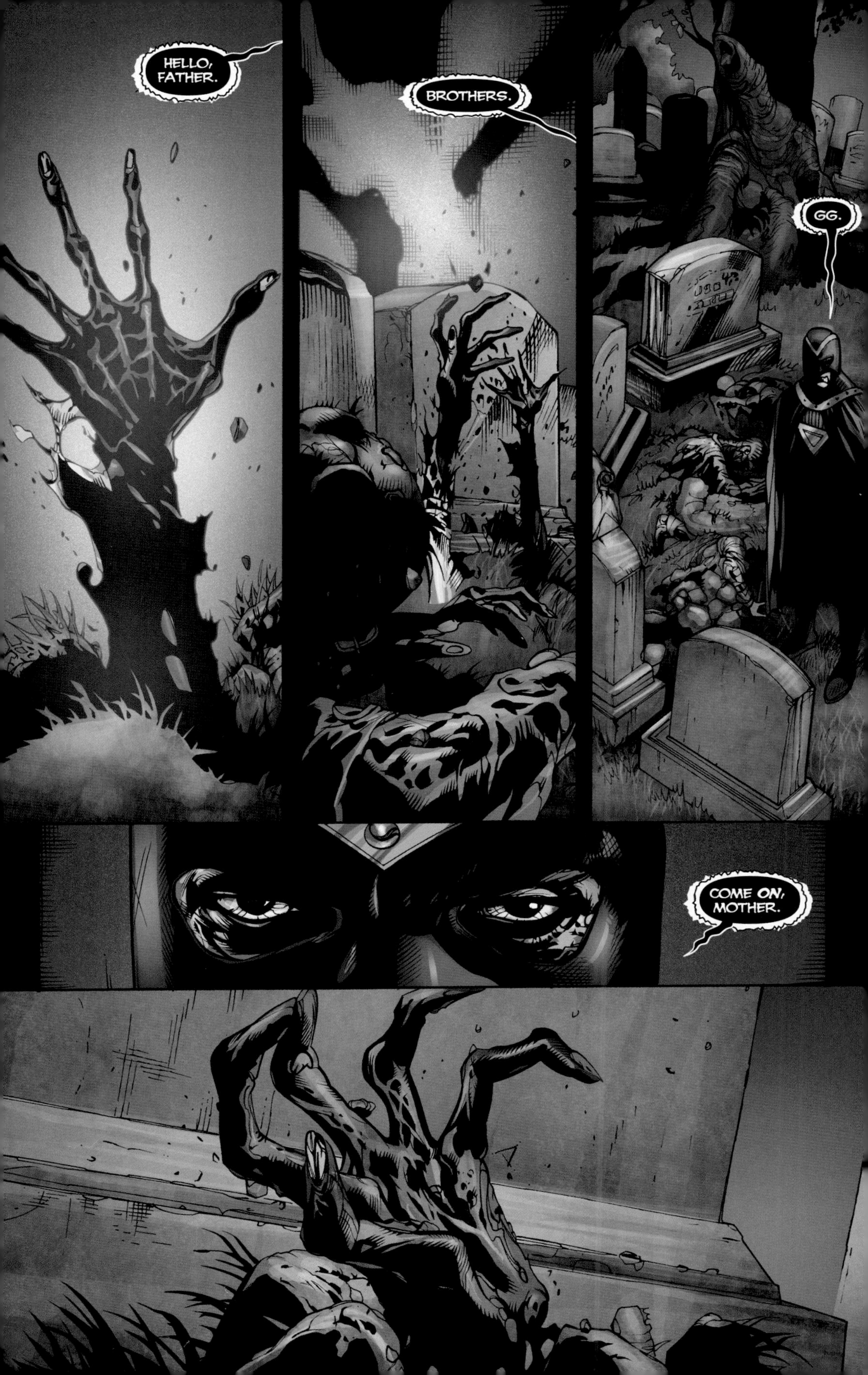
HELLO, FATHER.
BROTHERS.
GG.
COME ON, MOTHER.

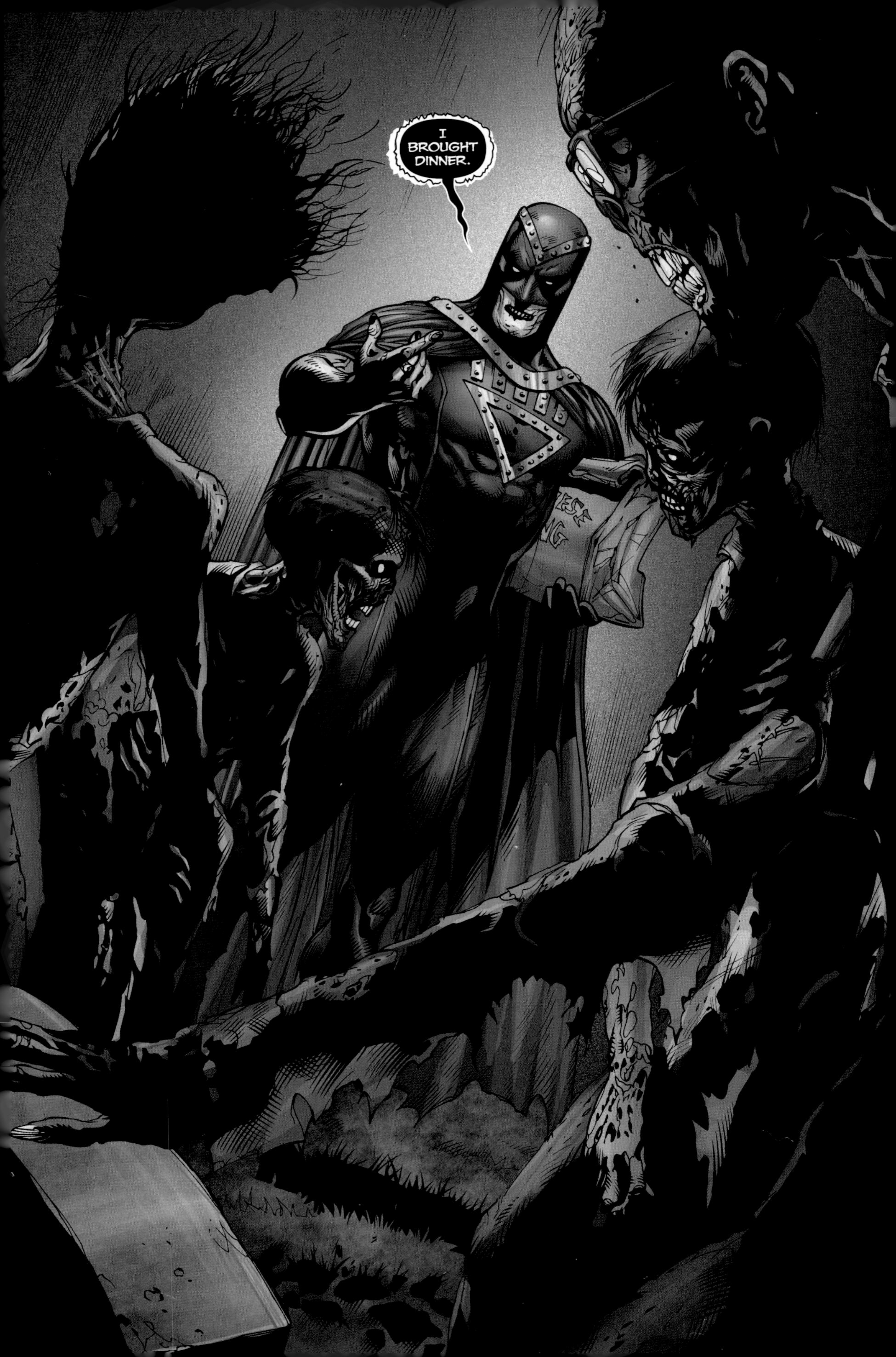
I BROUGHT DINNER.

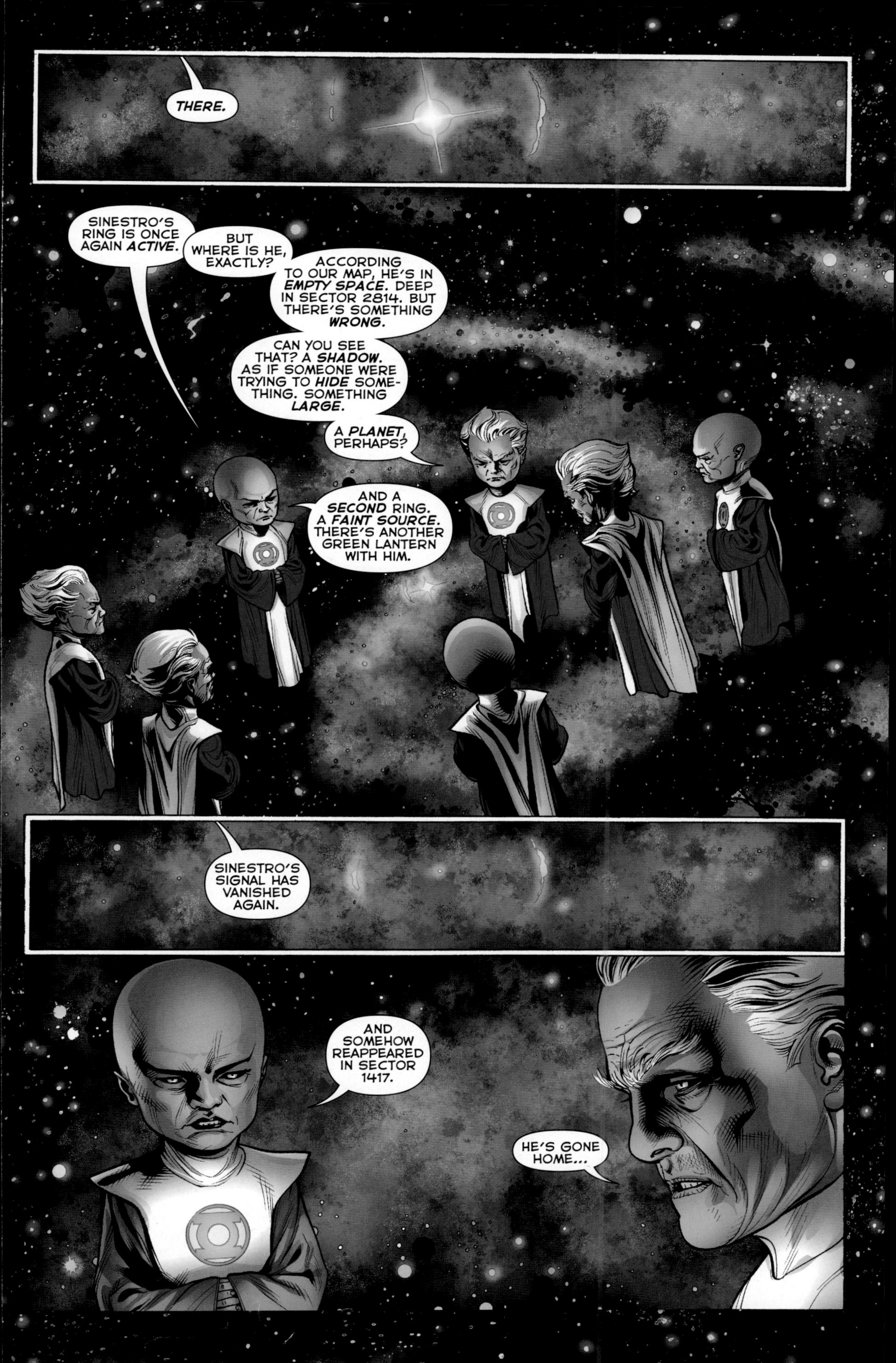
THERE.
SINESTRO'S RING IS ONCE AGAIN ACTIVE.
BUT WHERE IS HE, EXACTLY?
ACCORDING TO OUR MAP, HE'S IN EMPTY SPACE. DEEP IN SECTOR 2814. BUT THERE'S SOMETHING WRONG.
CAN YOU SEE THAT? A SHADOW. AS IF SOMEONE WERE TRYING TO HIDE SOME-THING. SOMETHING LARGE.
A PLANET, PERHAPS?
AND A SECOND RING. A FAINT SOURCE. THERE'S ANOTHER GREEN LANTERN WITH HIM.
SINESTRO'S SIGNAL HAS VANISHED AGAIN.
AND SOMEHOW REAPPEARED IN SECTOR 1417.
HE'S GONE HOME...

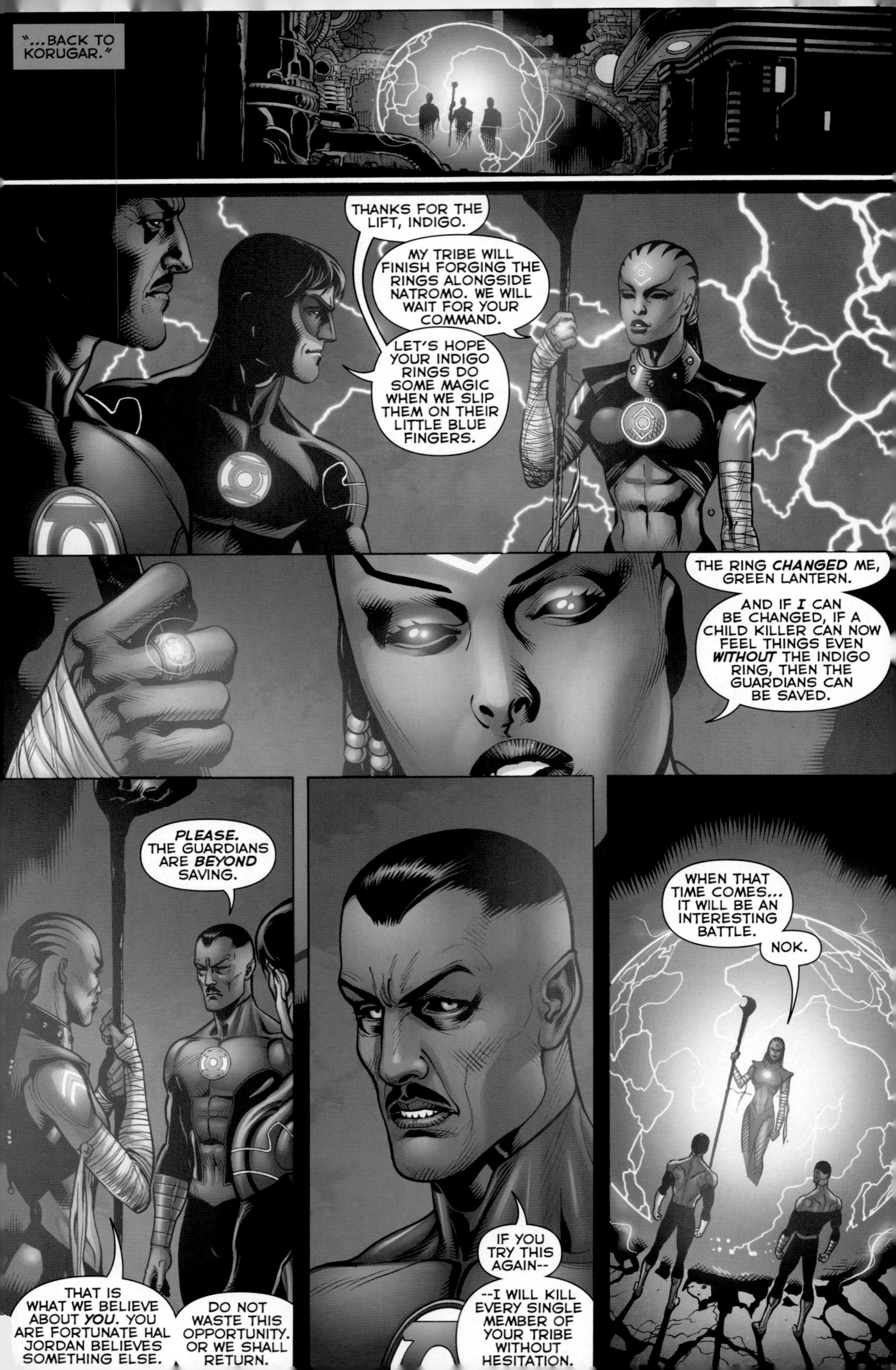
"...BACK TO KORUGAR."
THANKS FOR THE LIFT, INDIGO.
MY TRIBE WILL FINISH FORGING THE RINGS ALONGSIDE NATROMO. WE WILL WAIT FOR YOUR COMMAND.
LET'S HOPE YOUR INDIGO RINGS DO SOME MAGIC WHEN WE SLIP THEM ON THEIR LITTLE BLUE FINGERS.
THE RING *CHANGED* ME, GREEN LANTERN.
AND IF *I* CAN BE CHANGED, IF A CHILD KILLER CAN NOW FEEL THINGS EVEN *WITHOUT* THE INDIGO RING, THEN THE GUARDIANS CAN BE SAVED.
PLEASE. THE GUARDIANS ARE *BEYOND* SAVING.
THAT IS WHAT WE BELIEVE ABOUT *YOU*. YOU ARE FORTUNATE HAL JORDAN BELIEVES SOMETHING ELSE.
DO NOT WASTE THIS OPPORTUNITY. OR WE SHALL RETURN.
IF YOU TRY THIS AGAIN--
--I WILL KILL EVERY SINGLE MEMBER OF YOUR TRIBE WITHOUT HESITATION.
WHEN THAT TIME COMES... IT WILL BE AN INTERESTING BATTLE.
NOK.

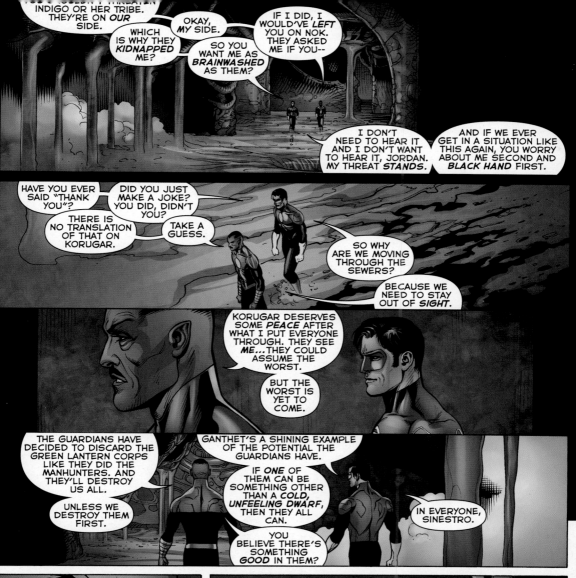

INDIGO OR HER TRIBE. THEY'RE ON *OUR* SIDE.

WHICH IS WHY THEY *KIDNAPPED* ME?

OKAY, *MY* SIDE.

SO YOU WANT ME AS *BRAINWASHED* AS THEM?

IF I DID, I WOULD'VE *LEFT* YOU ON NOK. THEY ASKED ME IF YOU--

I DON'T NEED TO HEAR IT AND I DON'T WANT TO HEAR IT, JORDAN. MY THREAT *STANDS*.

AND IF WE EVER GET IN A SITUATION LIKE THIS AGAIN, YOU WORRY ABOUT ME SECOND AND *BLACK HAND* FIRST.

HAVE YOU EVER SAID "THANK YOU"?

DID YOU JUST MAKE A JOKE? YOU DID, DIDN'T YOU?

THERE IS NO TRANSLATION OF THAT ON KORUGAR.

TAKE A GUESS.

SO WHY ARE WE MOVING THROUGH THE SEWERS?

BECAUSE WE NEED TO STAY OUT OF *SIGHT*.

KORUGAR DESERVES SOME *PEACE* AFTER WHAT I PUT EVERYONE THROUGH. THEY SEE *ME*...THEY COULD ASSUME THE WORST.

BUT THE WORST IS YET TO COME.

THE GUARDIANS HAVE DECIDED TO DISCARD THE GREEN LANTERN CORPS LIKE THEY DID THE MANHUNTERS. AND THEY'LL DESTROY US ALL.

UNLESS WE DESTROY THEM FIRST.

GANTHET'S A SHINING EXAMPLE OF THE POTENTIAL THE GUARDIANS HAVE.

IF *ONE* OF THEM CAN BE SOMETHING OTHER THAN A *COLD, UNFEELING DWARF*, THEN THEY ALL CAN.

YOU BELIEVE THERE'S SOMETHING *GOOD* IN THEM?

IN EVERYONE, SINESTRO.

EVEN *BLACK HAND?*

WELL...

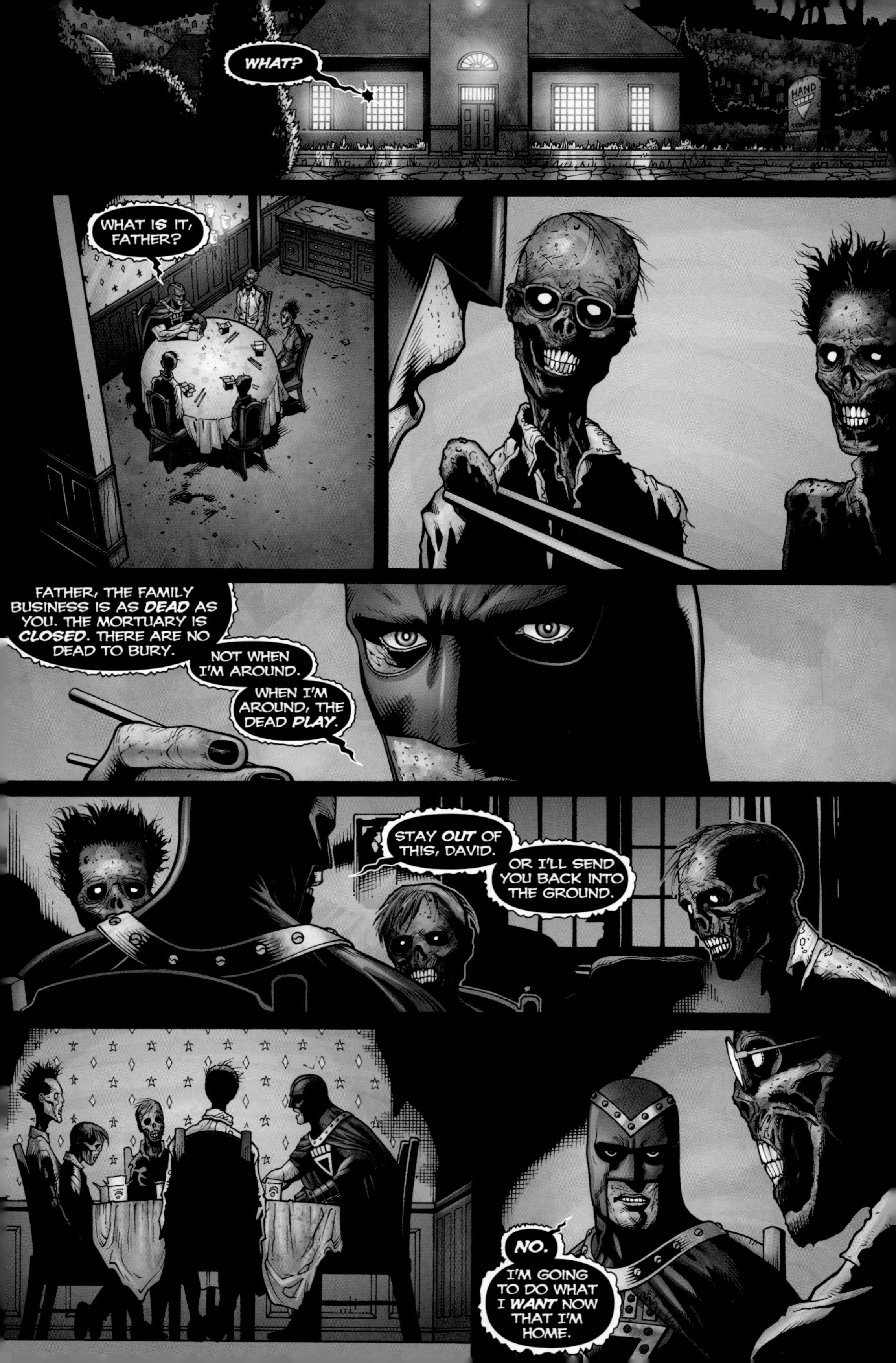
WHAT?
WHAT IS IT, FATHER?
FATHER, THE FAMILY BUSINESS IS AS DEAD AS YOU. THE MORTUARY IS CLOSED. THERE ARE NO DEAD TO BURY.
NOT WHEN I'M AROUND.
WHEN I'M AROUND, THE DEAD PLAY.
STAY OUT OF THIS, DAVID.
OR I'LL SEND YOU BACK INTO THE GROUND.
NO.
I'M GOING TO DO WHAT I WANT NOW THAT I'M HOME.

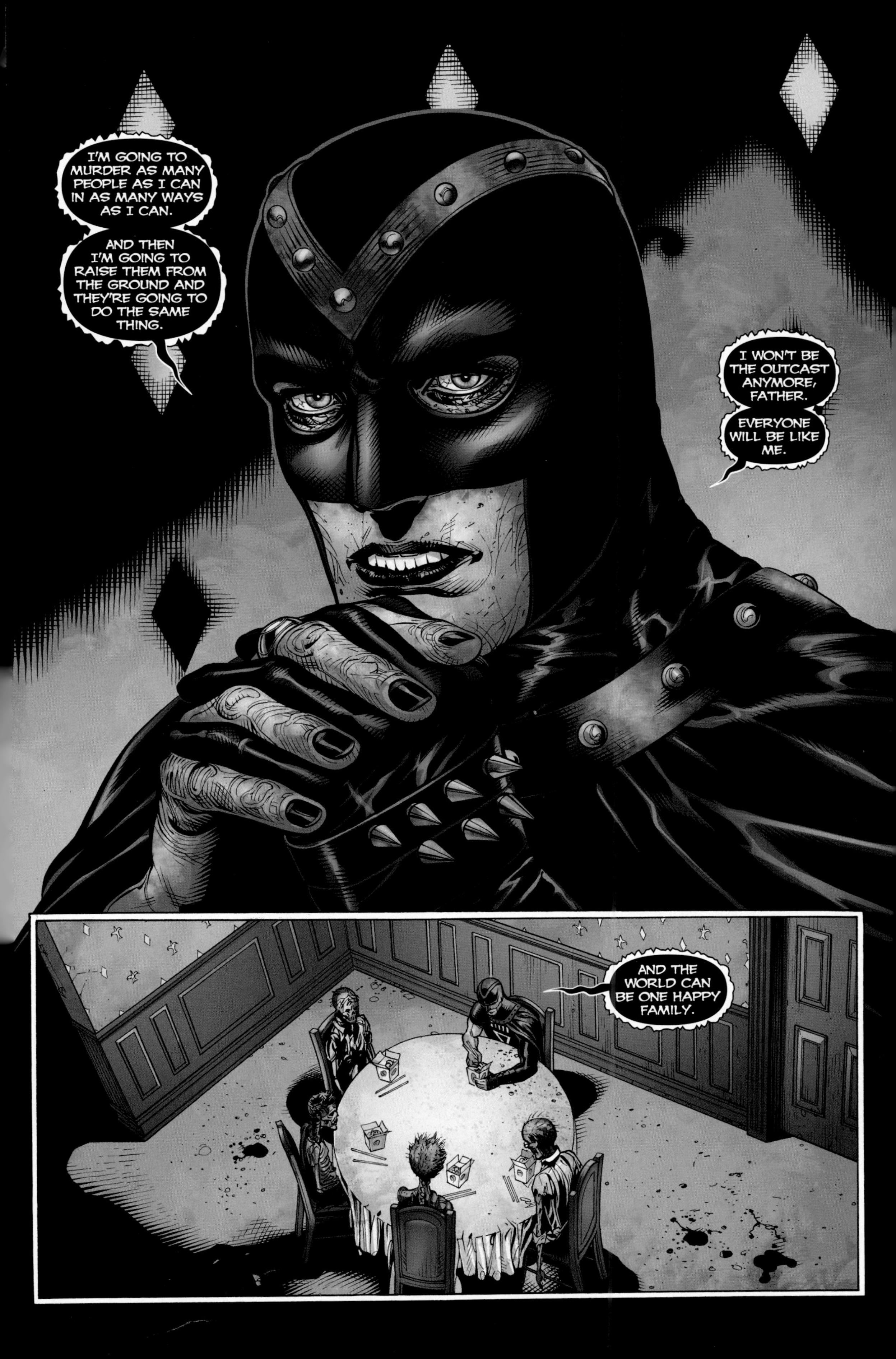

I'M GOING TO MURDER AS MANY PEOPLE AS I CAN IN AS MANY WAYS AS I CAN.
AND THEN I'M GOING TO RAISE THEM FROM THE GROUND AND THEY'RE GOING TO DO THE SAME THING.
I WON'T BE THE OUTCAST ANYMORE, FATHER.
EVERYONE WILL BE LIKE ME.
AND THE WORLD CAN BE ONE HAPPY FAMILY.

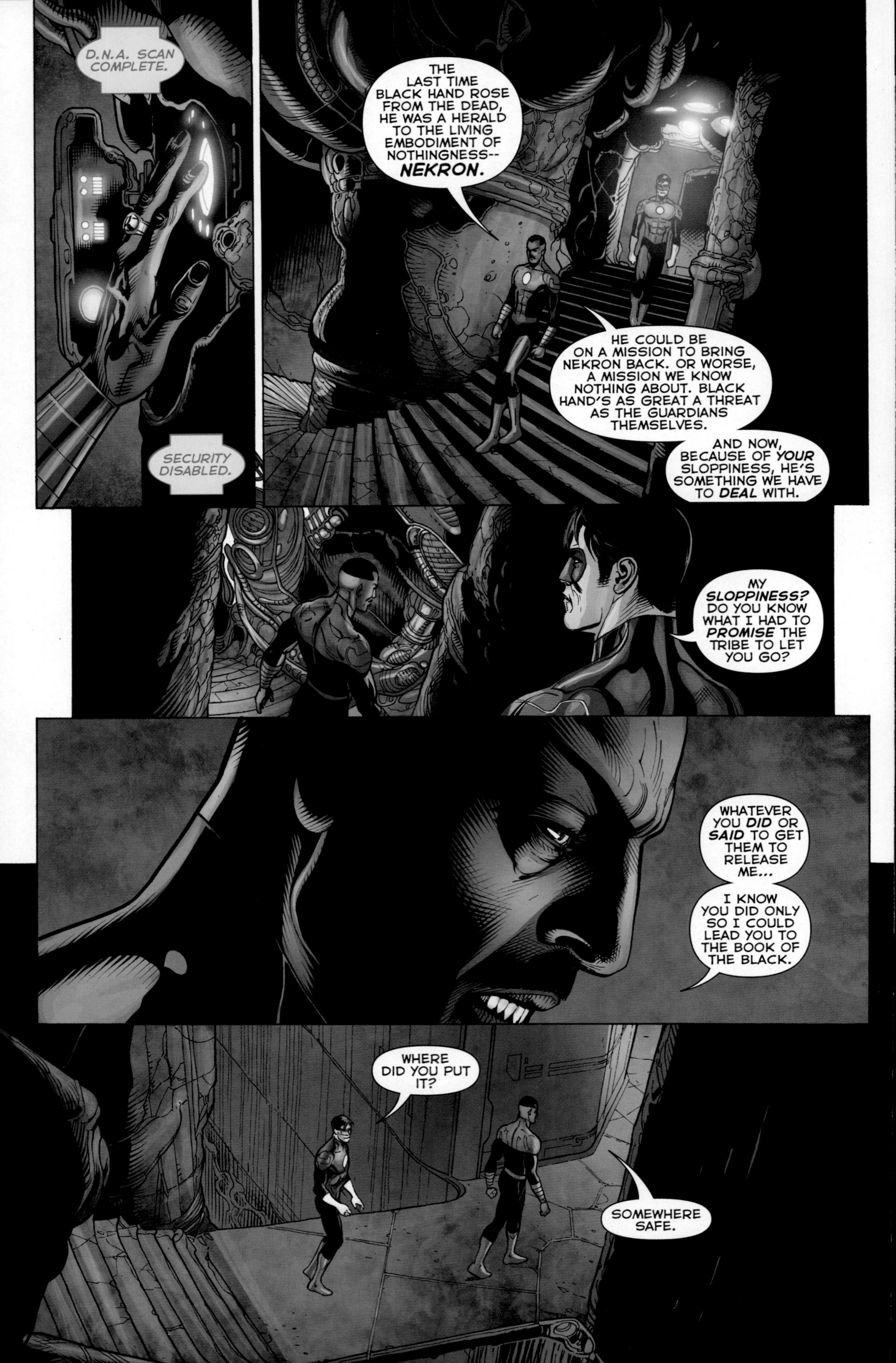
D.N.A. SCAN COMPLETE.
SECURITY DISABLED.
THE LAST TIME BLACK HAND ROSE FROM THE DEAD, HE WAS A HERALD TO THE LIVING EMBODIMENT OF NOTHINGNESS-- NEKRON.
HE COULD BE ON A MISSION TO BRING NEKRON BACK. OR WORSE, A MISSION WE KNOW NOTHING ABOUT. BLACK HAND'S AS GREAT A THREAT AS THE GUARDIANS THEMSELVES.
AND NOW, BECAUSE OF YOUR SLOPPINESS, HE'S SOMETHING WE HAVE TO DEAL WITH.
MY SLOPPINESS? DO YOU KNOW WHAT I HAD TO PROMISE THE TRIBE TO LET YOU GO?
WHATEVER YOU DID OR SAID TO GET THEM TO RELEASE ME...
I KNOW YOU DID ONLY SO I COULD LEAD YOU TO THE BOOK OF THE BLACK.
WHERE DID YOU PUT IT?
SOMEWHERE SAFE.

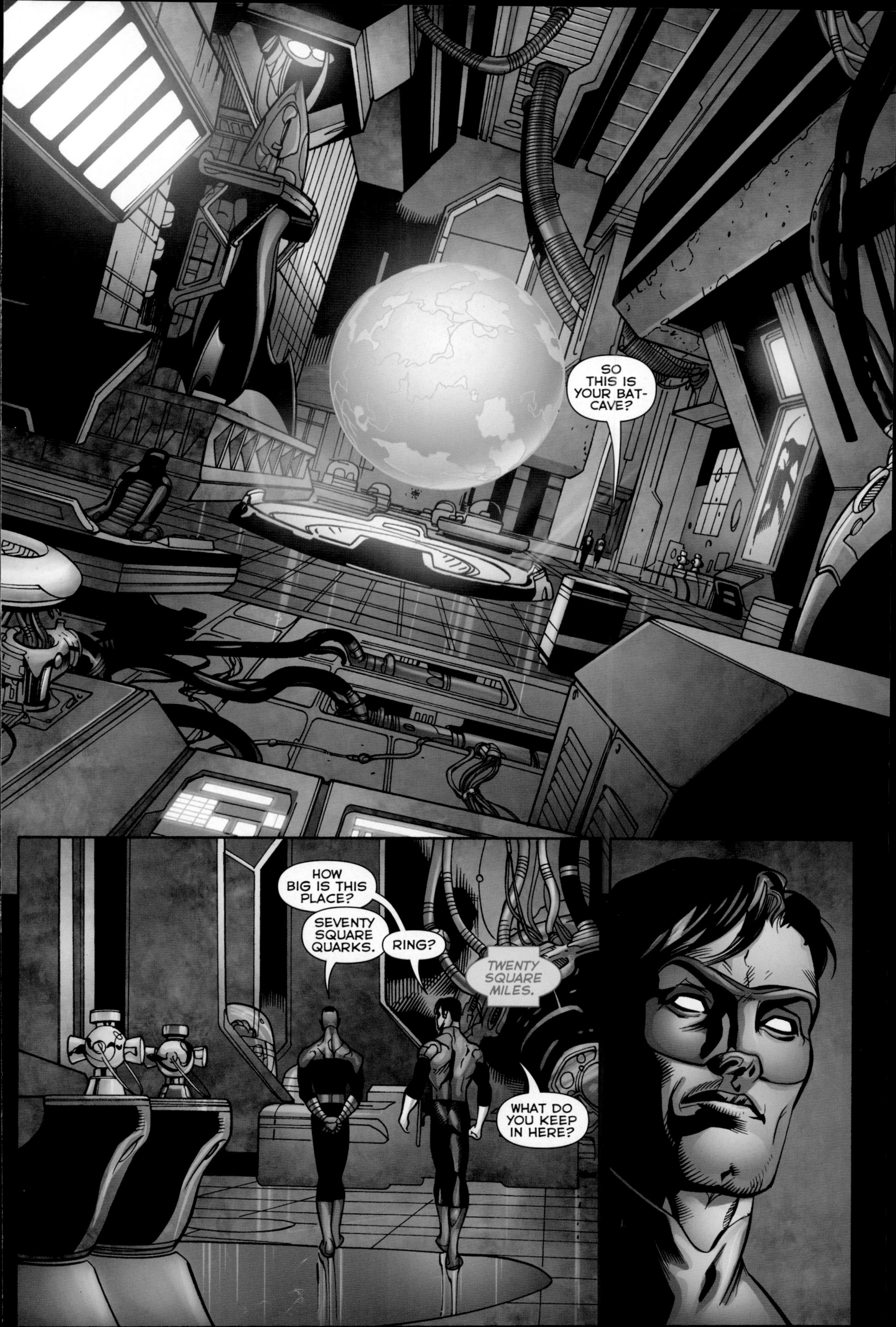
SO THIS IS YOUR BAT-CAVE?
HOW BIG IS THIS PLACE?
SEVENTY SQUARE QUARKS.
RING?
TWENTY SQUARE MILES.
WHAT DO YOU KEEP IN HERE?

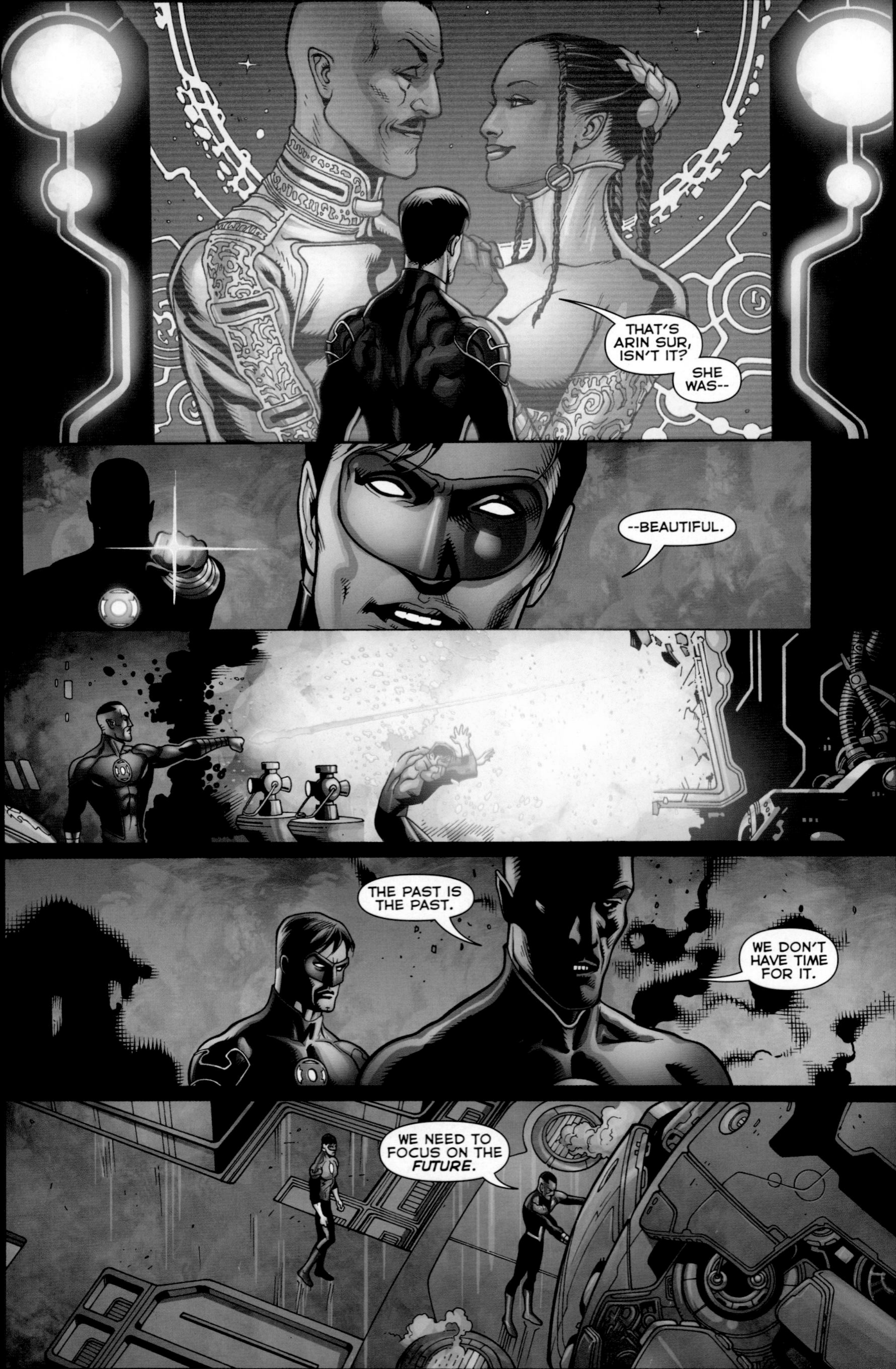
THAT'S ARIN SUR, ISN'T IT?
SHE WAS--
--BEAUTIFUL.
THE PAST IS THE PAST.
WE DON'T HAVE TIME FOR IT.
WE NEED TO FOCUS ON THE *FUTURE*.

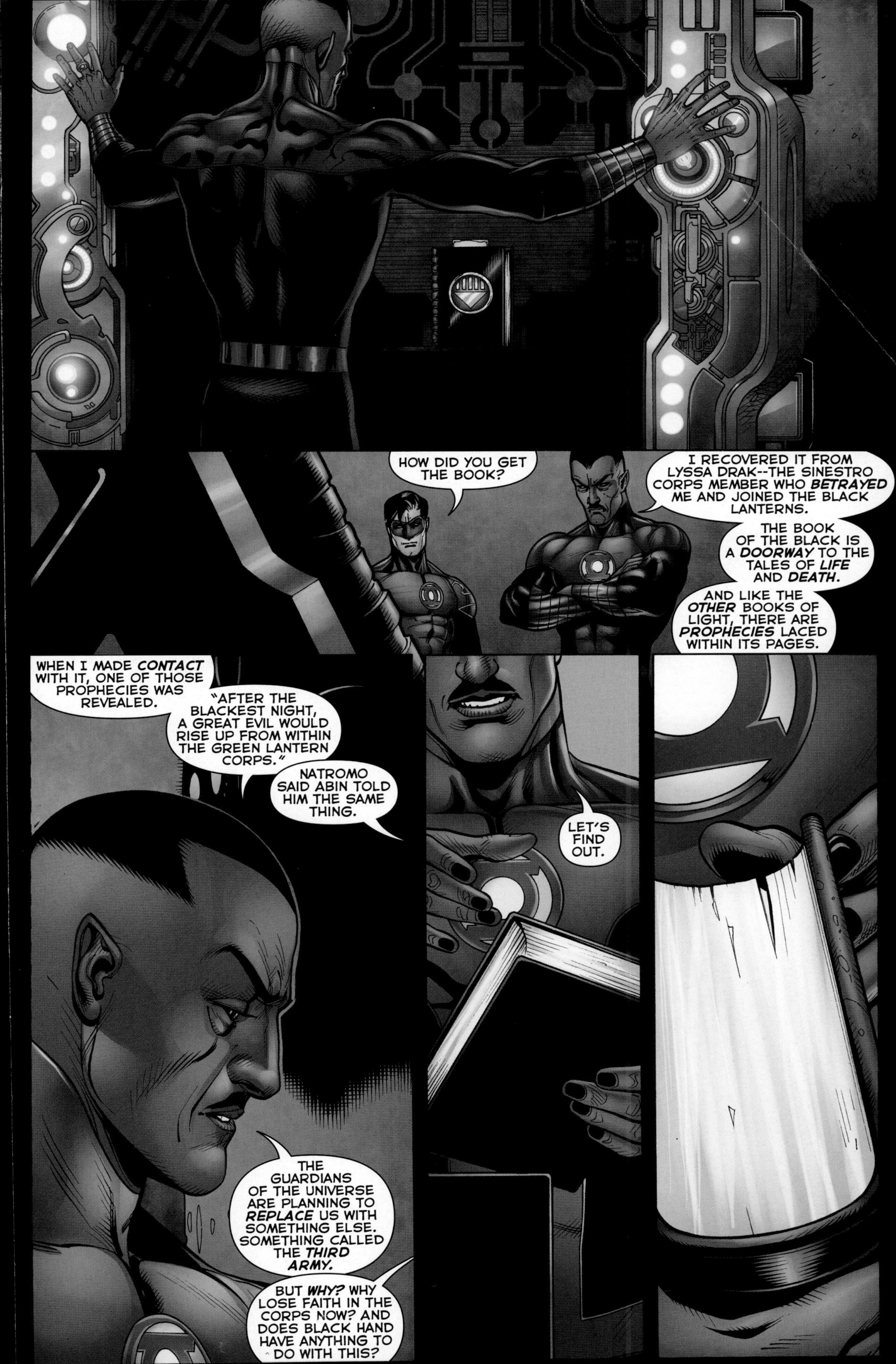
HOW DID YOU GET THE BOOK?
I RECOVERED IT FROM LYSSA DRAK--THE SINESTRO CORPS MEMBER WHO *BETRAYED* ME AND JOINED THE BLACK LANTERNS.
THE BOOK OF THE BLACK IS A *DOORWAY* TO THE TALES OF *LIFE* AND *DEATH*.
AND LIKE THE *OTHER* BOOKS OF LIGHT, THERE ARE *PROPHECIES* LACED WITHIN ITS PAGES.
WHEN I MADE *CONTACT* WITH IT, ONE OF THOSE PROPHECIES WAS REVEALED.
"AFTER THE BLACKEST NIGHT, A GREAT EVIL WOULD RISE UP FROM WITHIN THE GREEN LANTERN CORPS."
NATROMO SAID ABIN TOLD HIM THE SAME THING.
THE GUARDIANS OF THE UNIVERSE ARE PLANNING TO *REPLACE* US WITH SOMETHING ELSE. SOMETHING CALLED THE *THIRD ARMY.*
BUT *WHY?* WHY LOSE FAITH IN THE CORPS NOW? AND DOES BLACK HAND HAVE ANYTHING TO DO WITH THIS?
LET'S FIND OUT.

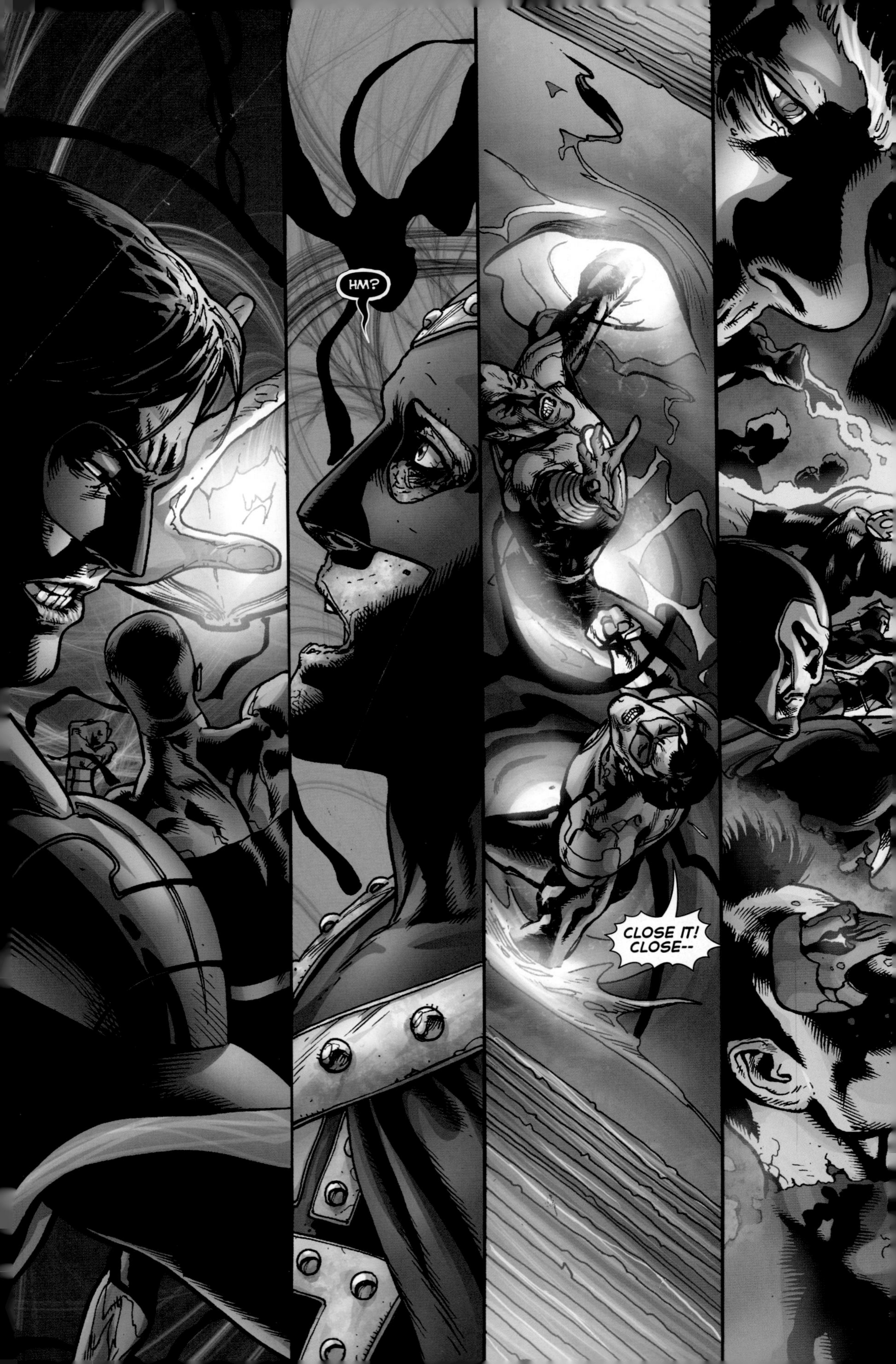
HM?
CLOSE IT! CLOSE--

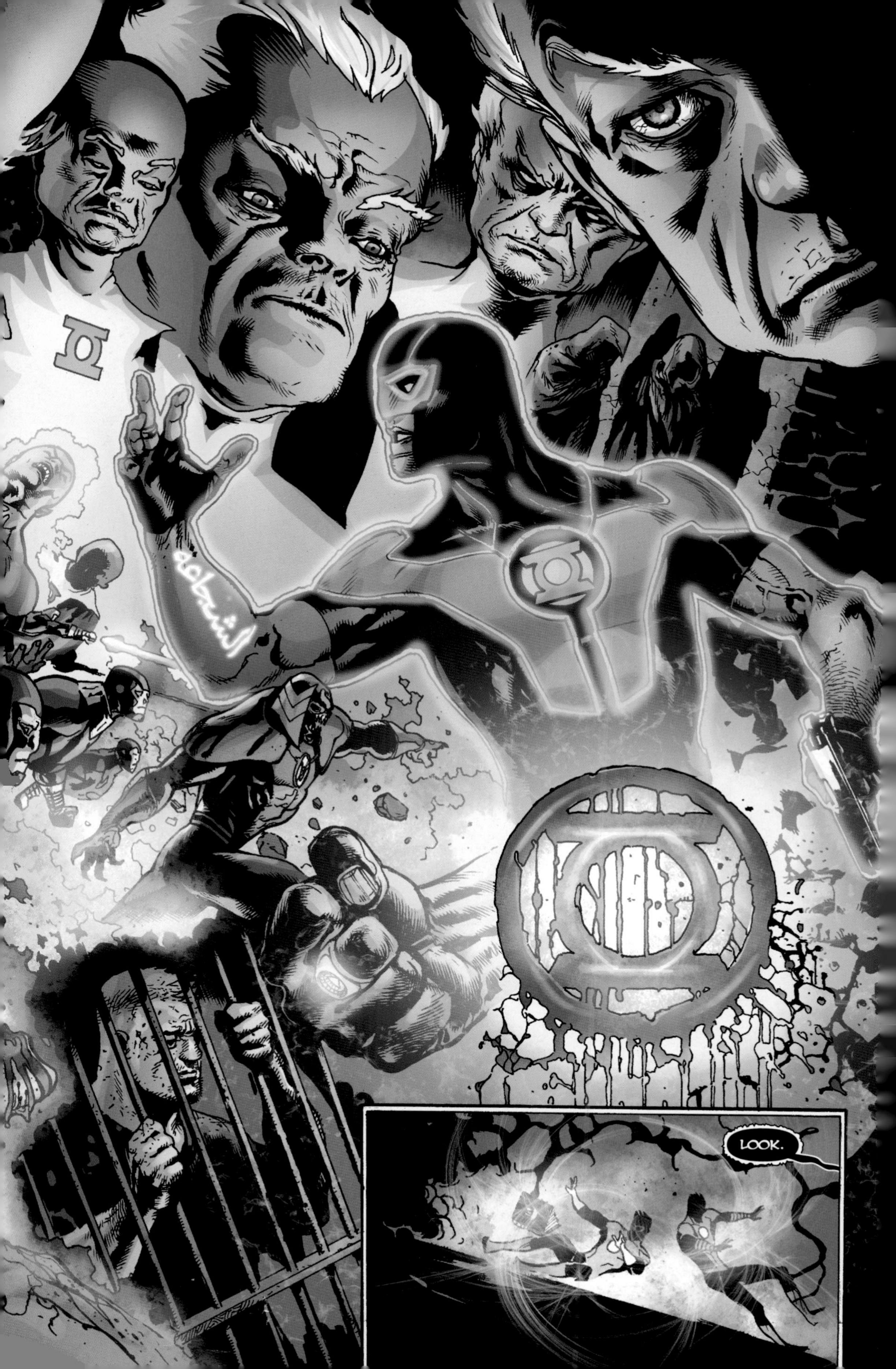
الشجاعه
LOOK.

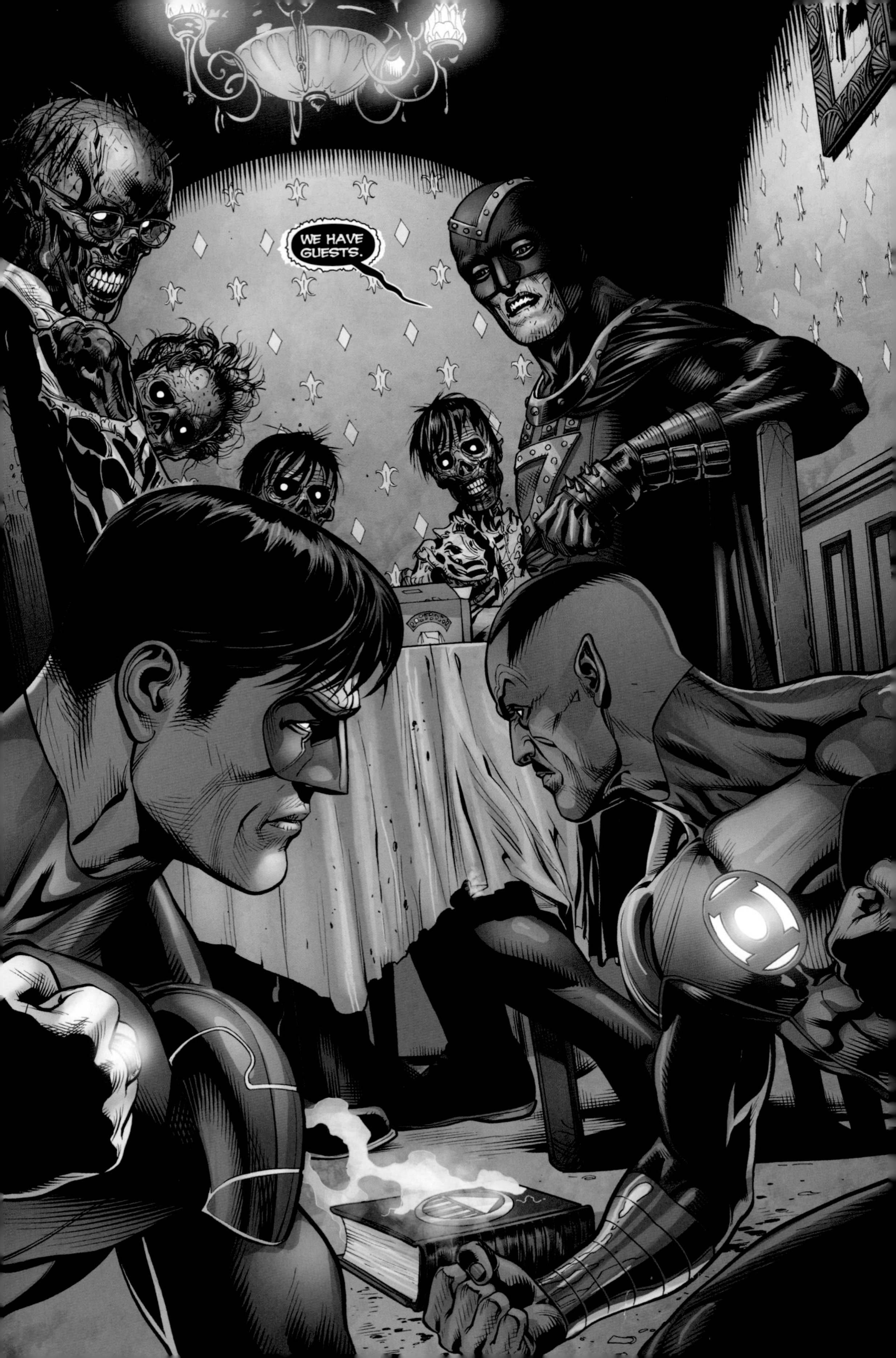
WE HAVE GUESTS.

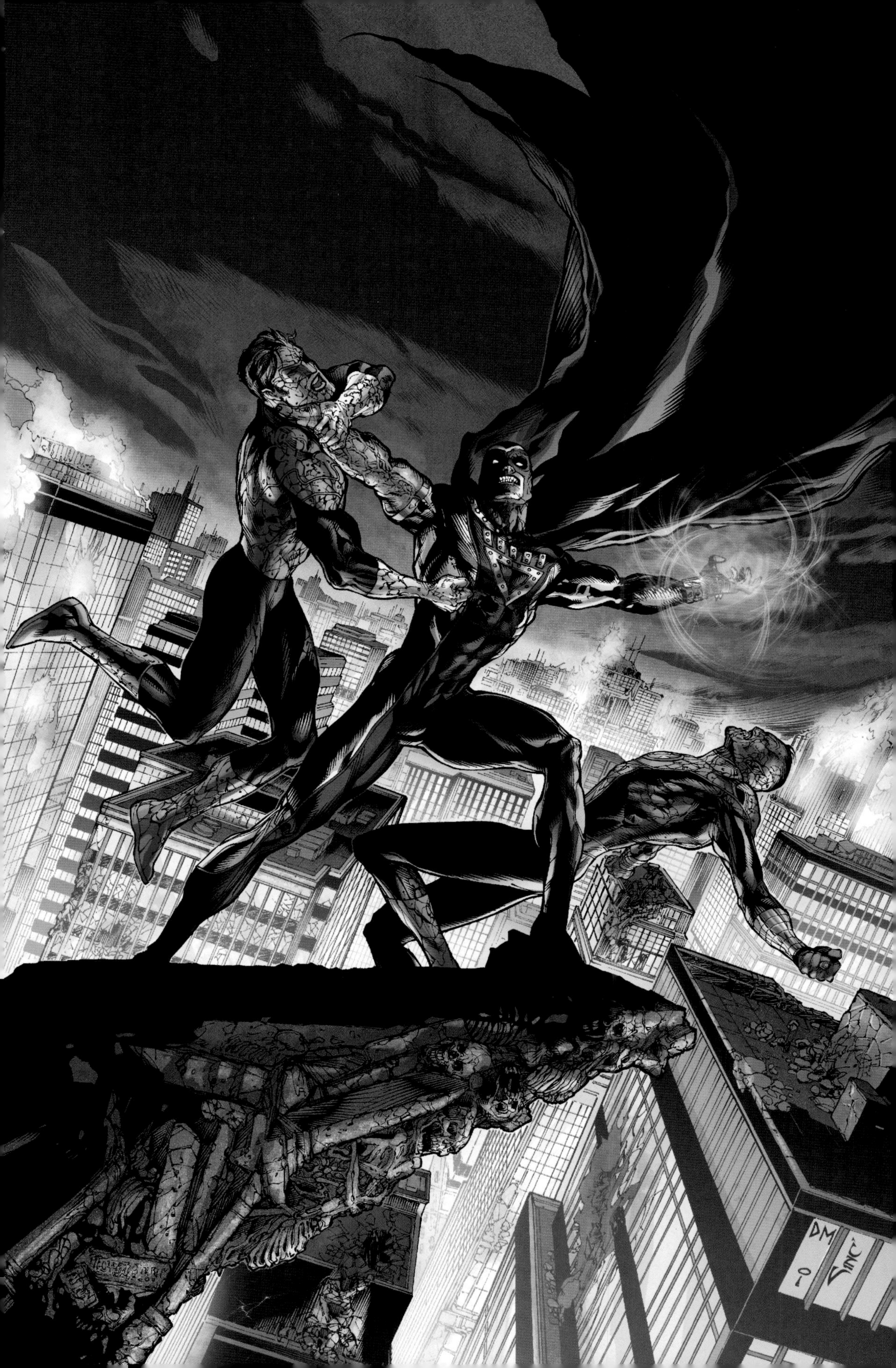

THE REVENGE OF BLACK HAND part two

GEOFF JOHNS writer **RENATO GUEDES & JIM CALAFIORE** artists **DOUG MAHNKE, MARK IRWIN & ALEX SINCLAIR** cover

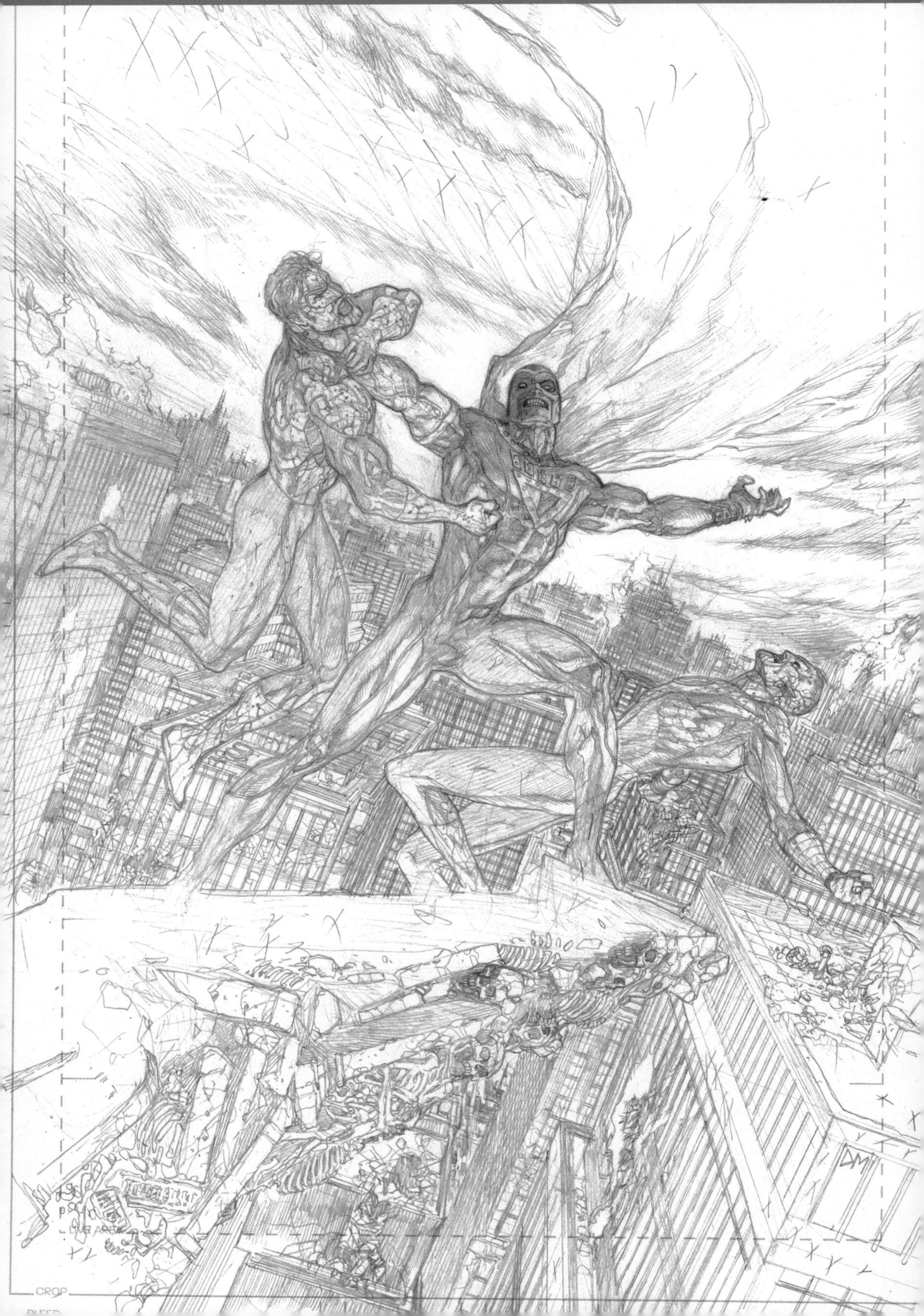

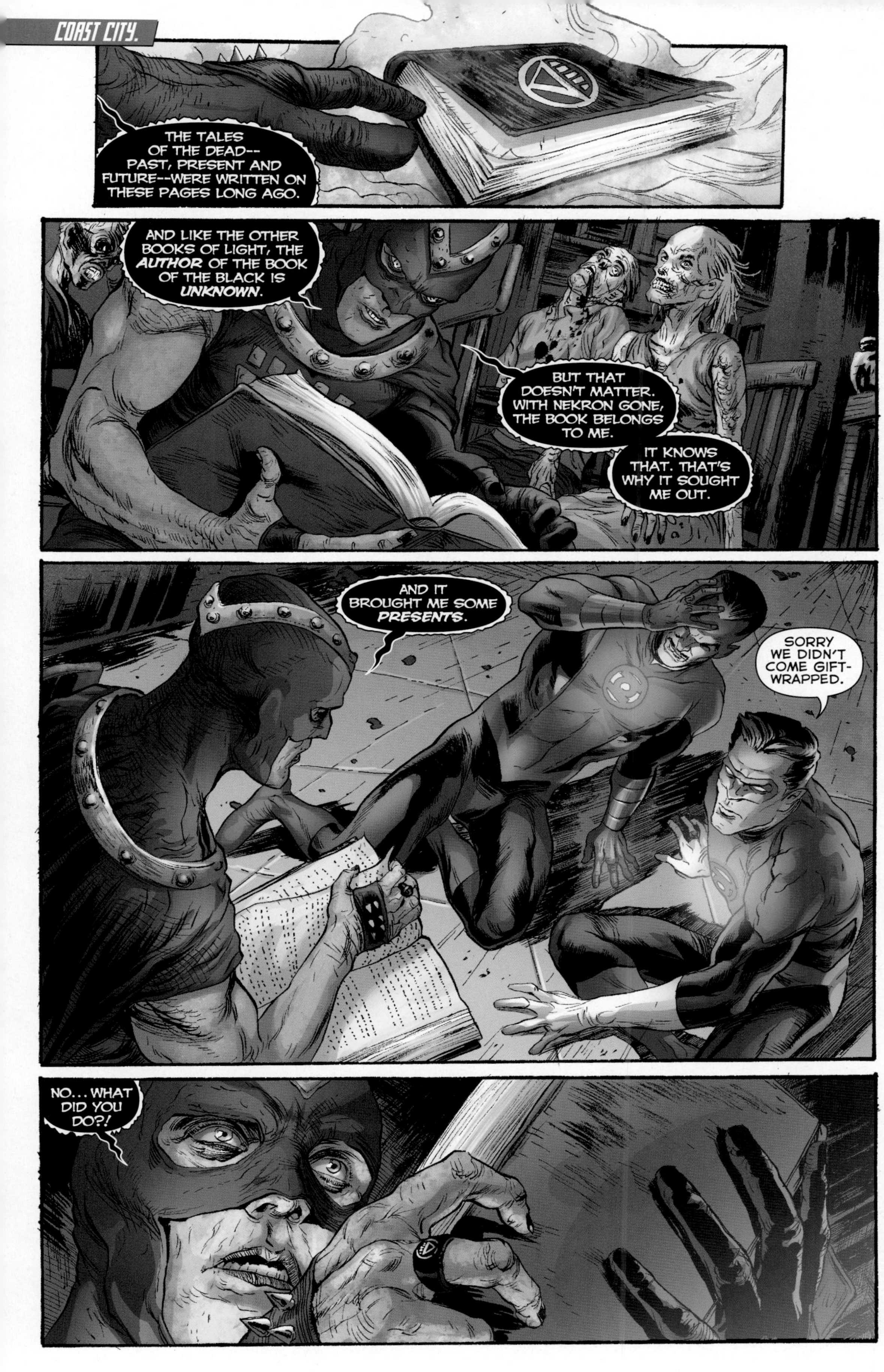
COAST CITY.
THE TALES OF THE DEAD--PAST, PRESENT AND FUTURE--WERE WRITTEN ON THESE PAGES LONG AGO.
AND LIKE THE OTHER BOOKS OF LIGHT, THE AUTHOR OF THE BOOK OF THE BLACK IS UNKNOWN.
BUT THAT DOESN'T MATTER. WITH NEKRON GONE, THE BOOK BELONGS TO ME.
IT KNOWS THAT. THAT'S WHY IT SOUGHT ME OUT.
AND IT BROUGHT ME SOME PRESENTS.
SORRY WE DIDN'T COME GIFT-WRAPPED.
NO... WHAT DID YOU DO?!

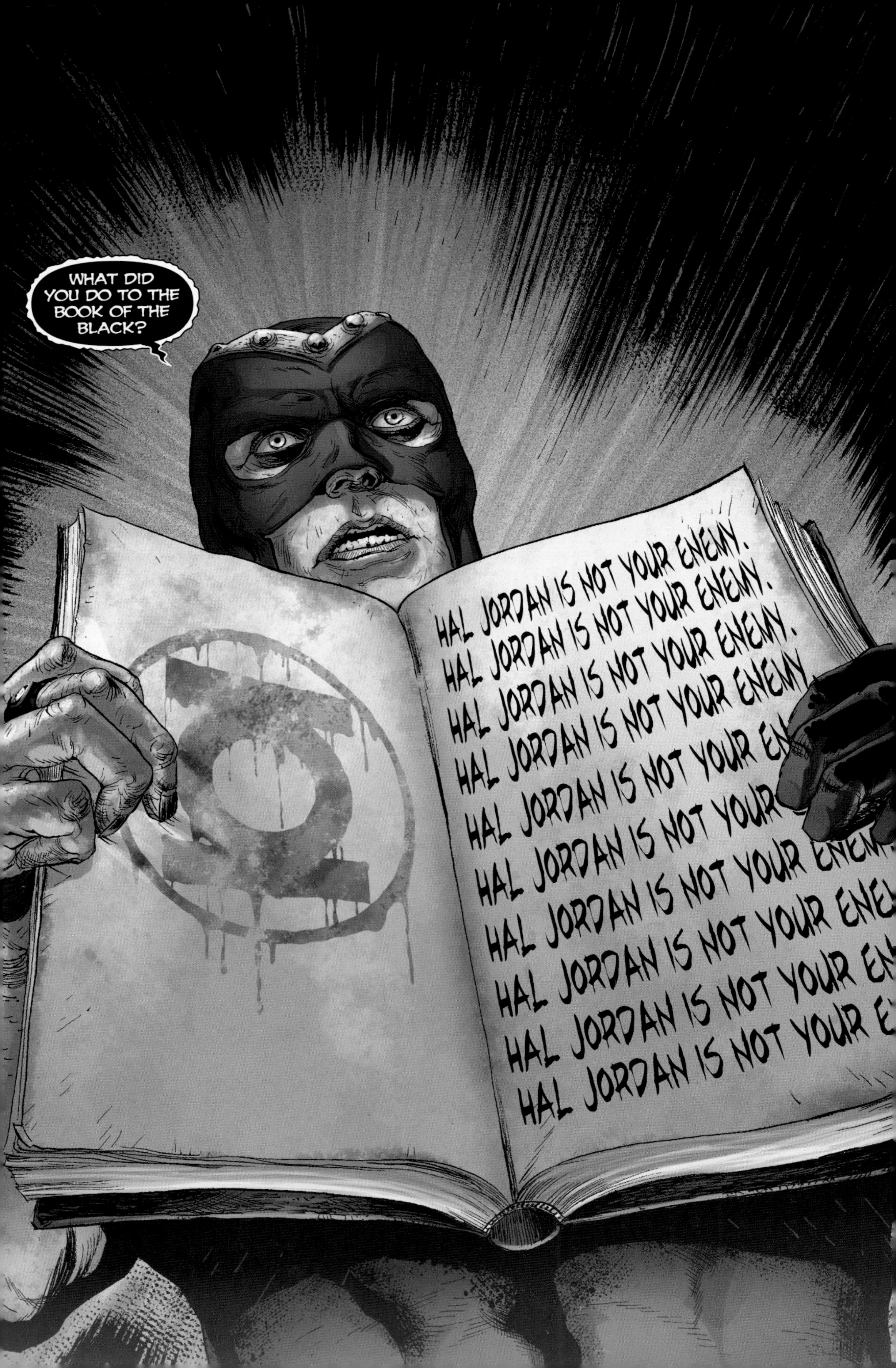
WHAT DID YOU DO TO THE BOOK OF THE BLACK?
HAL JORDAN IS NOT YOUR ENEMY.
HAL JORDAN IS NOT YOUR ENEMY.
HAL JORDAN IS NOT YOUR ENEMY.
HAL JORDAN IS NOT YOUR ENEMY
HAL JORDAN IS NOT YOUR
HAL JORDAN IS NOT YOUR
HAL JORDAN IS NOT YOUR
HAL JORDAN IS NOT YOUR
HAL JORDAN IS NOT YOUR
HAL JORDAN IS NOT YOUR
HAL JORDAN IS NOT YOUR
HAL JORDAN IS NOT YOUR

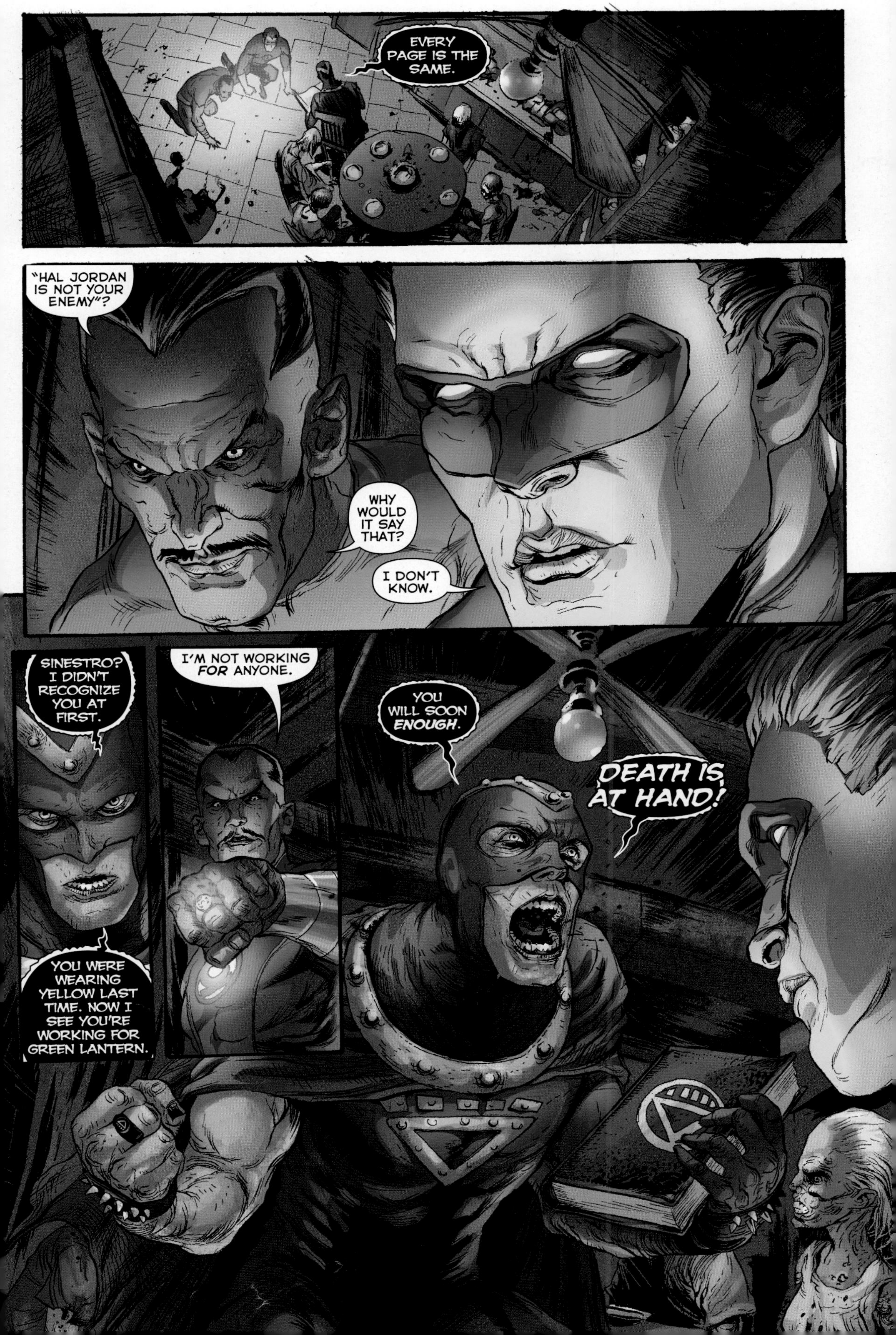
EVERY PAGE IS THE SAME.
"HAL JORDAN IS NOT YOUR ENEMY"?
WHY WOULD IT SAY THAT?
I DON'T KNOW.
SINESTRO? I DIDN'T RECOGNIZE YOU AT FIRST.
YOU WERE WEARING YELLOW LAST TIME. NOW I SEE YOU'RE WORKING FOR GREEN LANTERN.
I'M NOT WORKING FOR ANYONE.
YOU WILL SOON ENOUGH.
DEATH IS AT HAND!

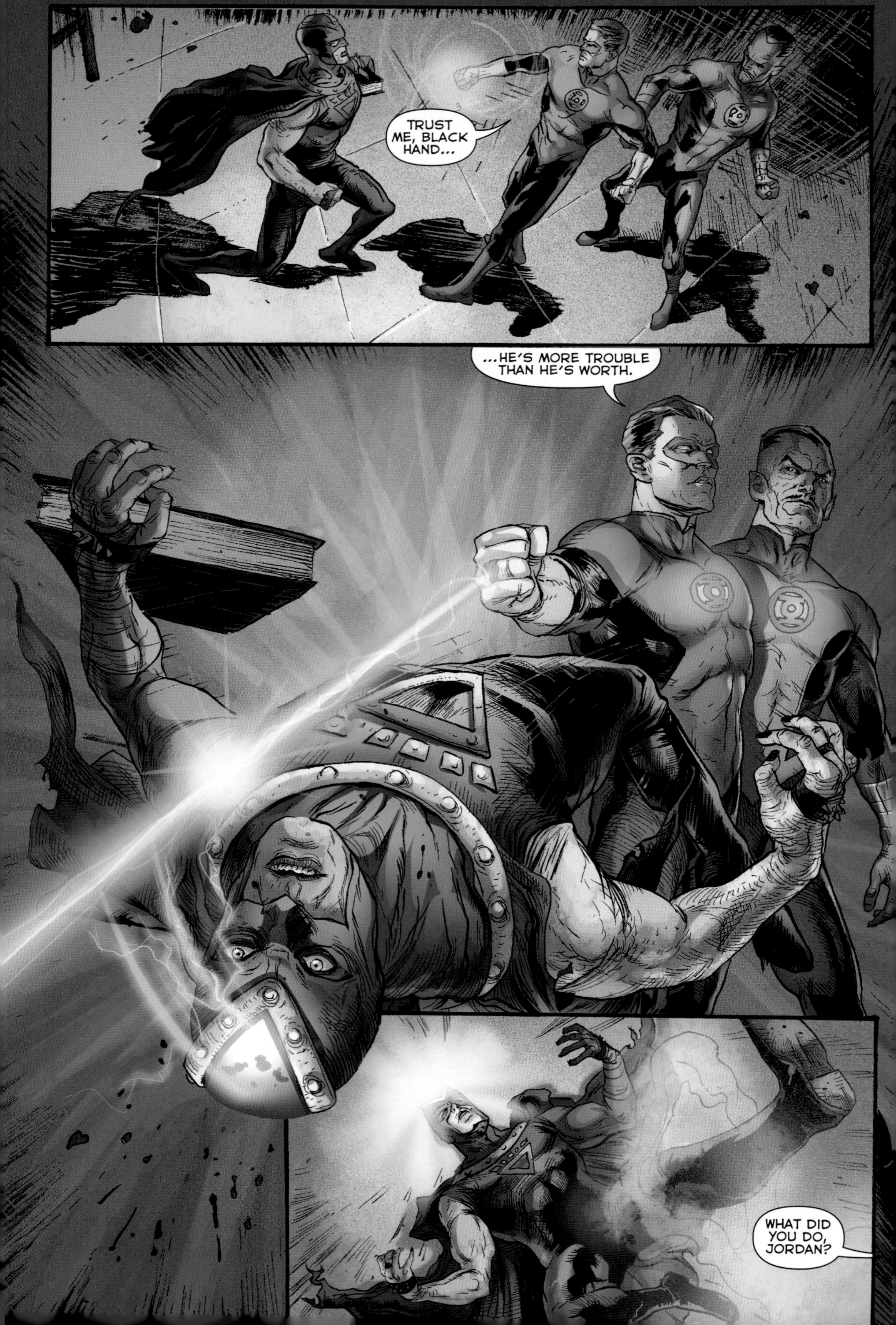
TRUST ME, BLACK HAND...
...HE'S MORE TROUBLE THAN HE'S WORTH.
WHAT DID YOU DO, JORDAN?

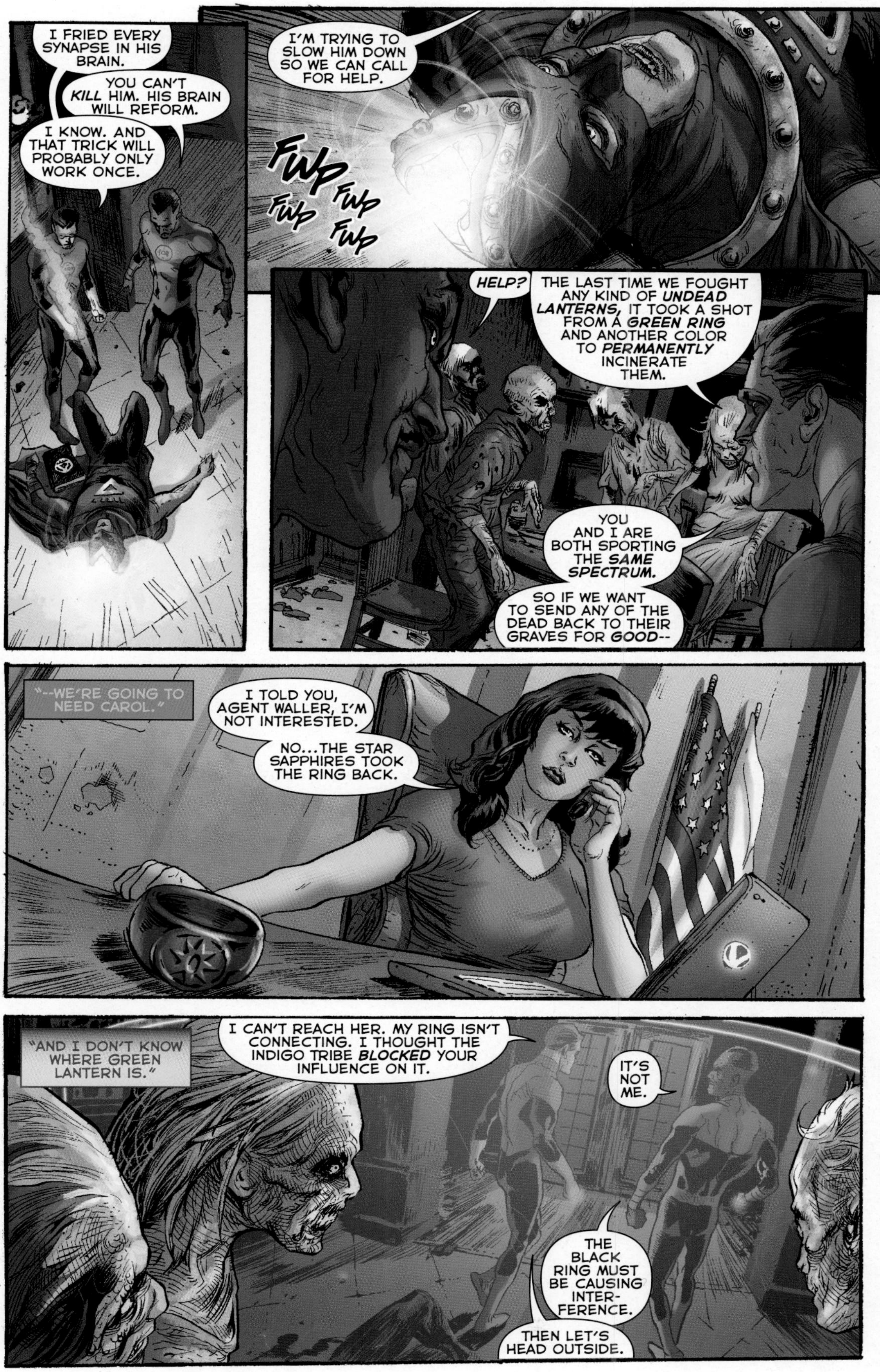
I FRIED EVERY SYNAPSE IN HIS BRAIN.
YOU CAN'T KILL HIM. HIS BRAIN WILL REFORM.
I KNOW. AND THAT TRICK WILL PROBABLY ONLY WORK ONCE.
I'M TRYING TO SLOW HIM DOWN SO WE CAN CALL FOR HELP.
FWP FWP FWP FWP FWP
HELP?
THE LAST TIME WE FOUGHT ANY KIND OF UNDEAD LANTERNS, IT TOOK A SHOT FROM A GREEN RING AND ANOTHER COLOR TO PERMANENTLY INCINERATE THEM.
YOU AND I ARE BOTH SPORTING THE SAME SPECTRUM.
SO IF WE WANT TO SEND ANY OF THE DEAD BACK TO THEIR GRAVES FOR GOOD--
"--WE'RE GOING TO NEED CAROL."
I TOLD YOU, AGENT WALLER, I'M NOT INTERESTED.
NO...THE STAR SAPPHIRES TOOK THE RING BACK.
"AND I DON'T KNOW WHERE GREEN LANTERN IS."
I CAN'T REACH HER. MY RING ISN'T CONNECTING. I THOUGHT THE INDIGO TRIBE BLOCKED YOUR INFLUENCE ON IT.
IT'S NOT ME.
THE BLACK RING MUST BE CAUSING INTER-FERENCE.
THEN LET'S HEAD OUTSIDE.

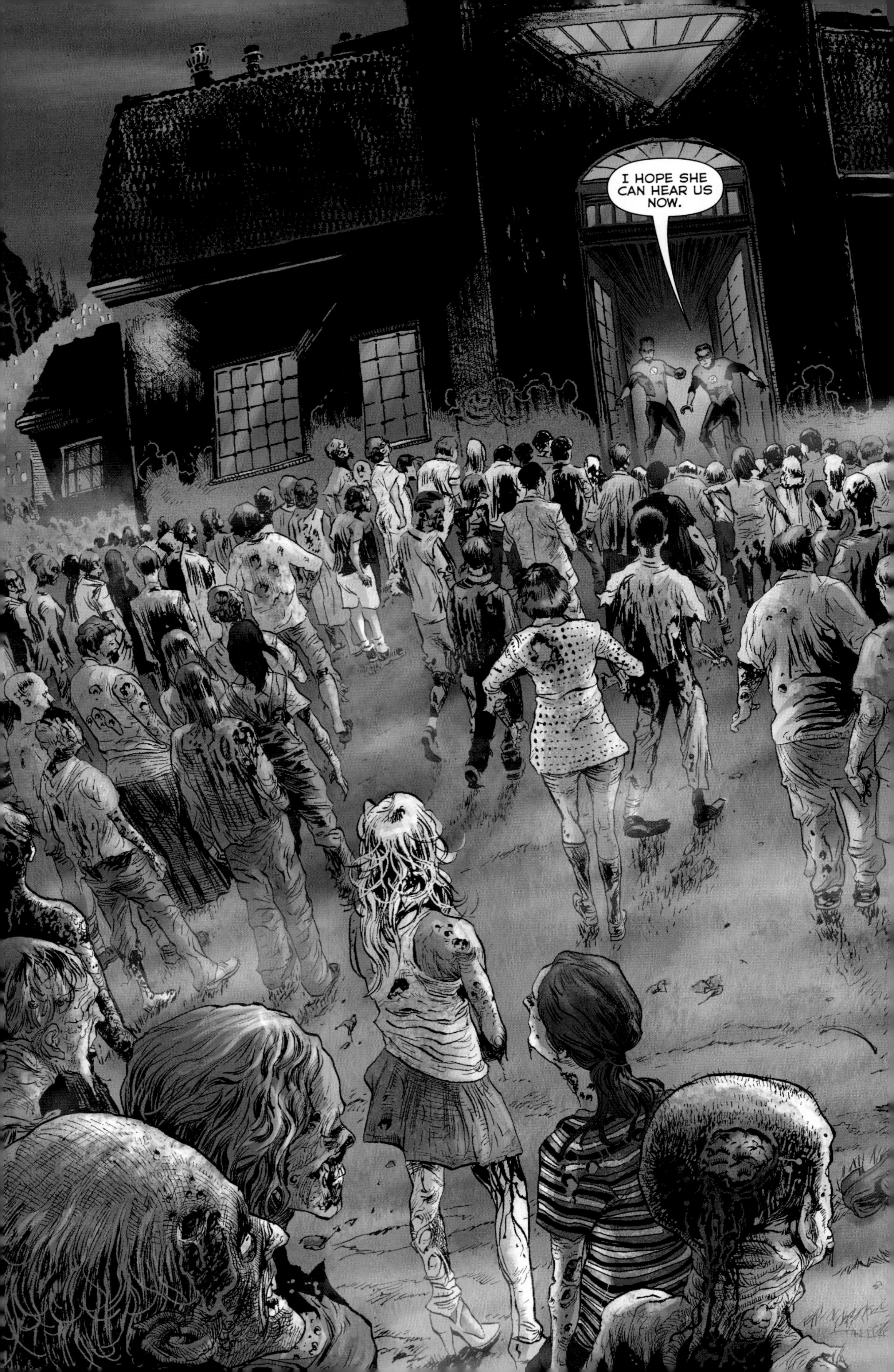
I HOPE SHE CAN HEAR US NOW.

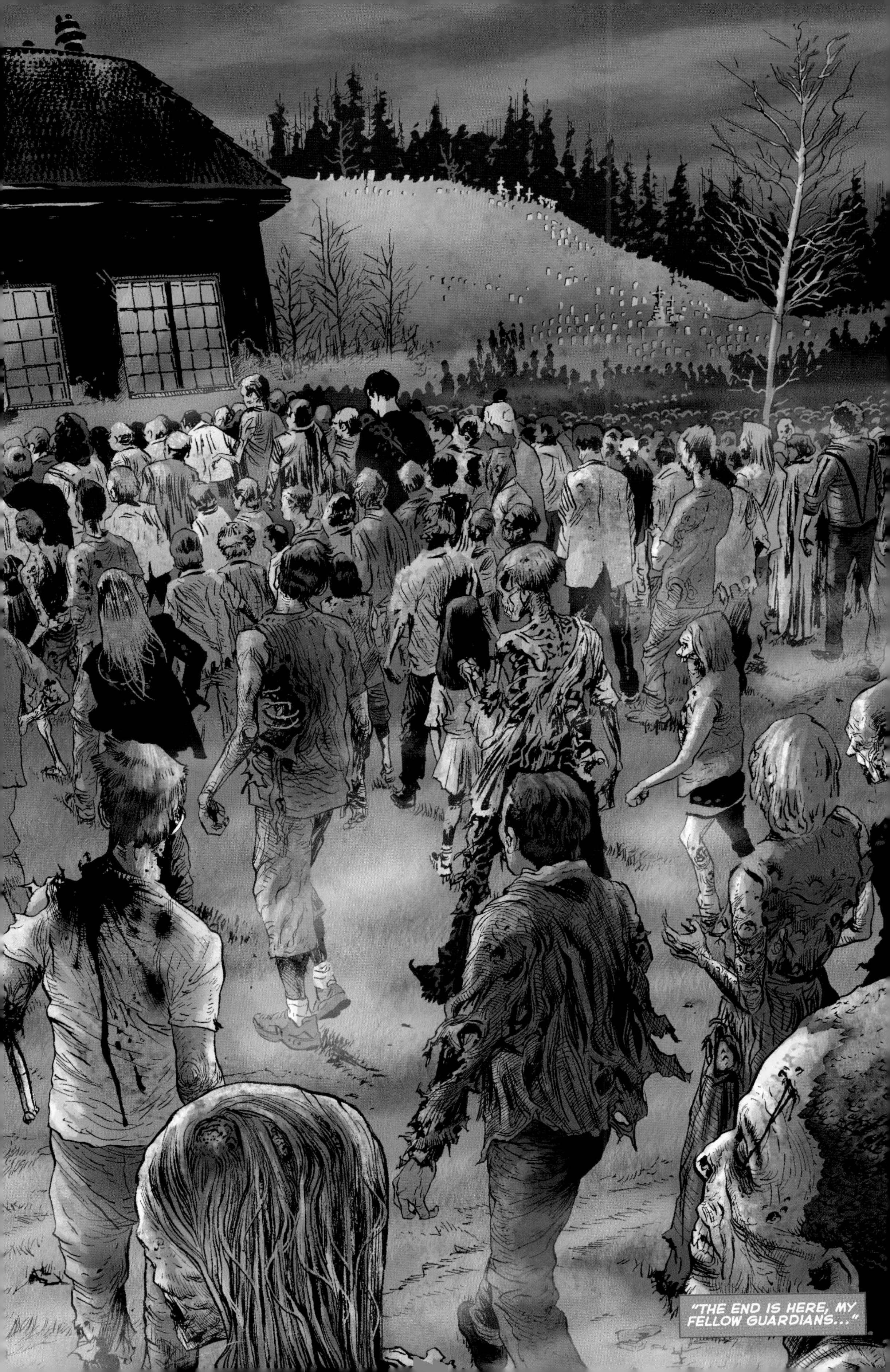
"THE END IS HERE, MY FELLOW GUARDIANS..."

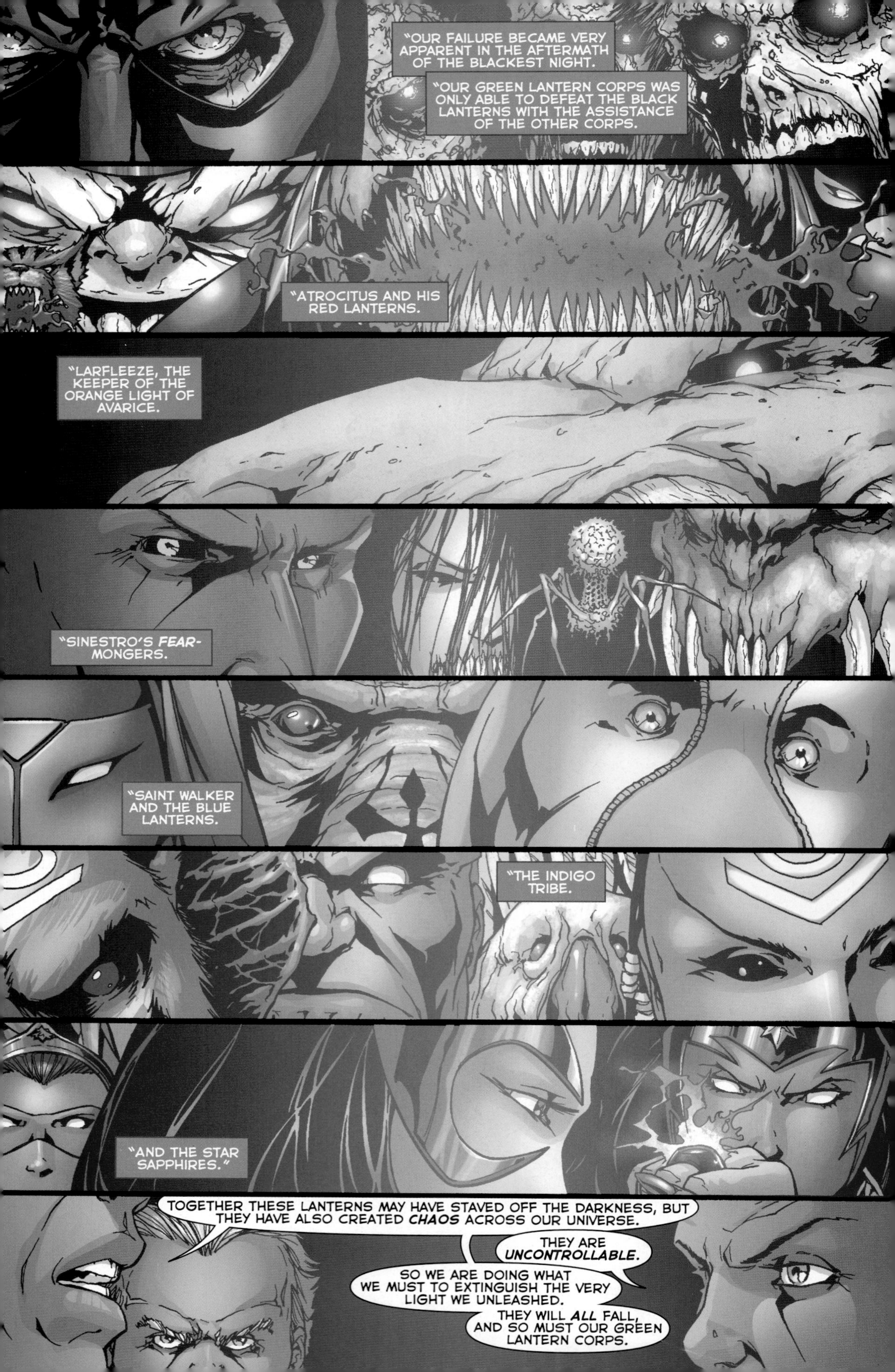
"OUR FAILURE BECAME VERY APPARENT IN THE AFTERMATH OF THE BLACKEST NIGHT.
"OUR GREEN LANTERN CORPS WAS ONLY ABLE TO DEFEAT THE BLACK LANTERNS WITH THE ASSISTANCE OF THE OTHER CORPS.
"ATROCITUS AND HIS RED LANTERNS.
"LARFLEEZE, THE KEEPER OF THE ORANGE LIGHT OF AVARICE.
"SINESTRO'S FEAR-MONGERS.
"SAINT WALKER AND THE BLUE LANTERNS.
"THE INDIGO TRIBE.
"AND THE STAR SAPPHIRES."
TOGETHER THESE LANTERNS MAY HAVE STAVED OFF THE DARKNESS, BUT THEY HAVE ALSO CREATED CHAOS ACROSS OUR UNIVERSE.
THEY ARE UNCONTROLLABLE.
SO WE ARE DOING WHAT WE MUST TO EXTINGUISH THE VERY LIGHT WE UNLEASHED.
THEY WILL ALL FALL, AND SO MUST OUR GREEN LANTERN CORPS.

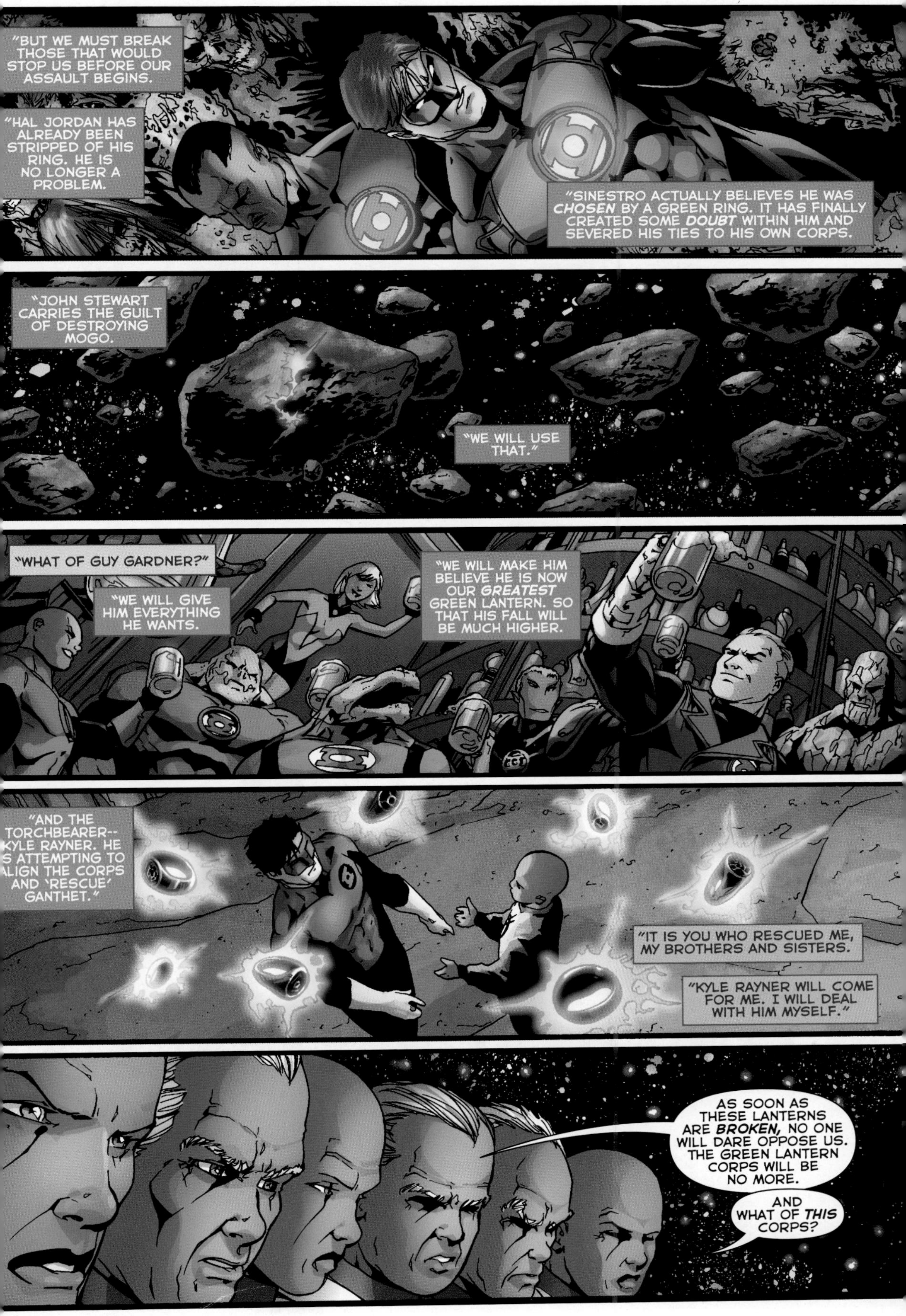
"BUT WE MUST BREAK THOSE THAT WOULD STOP US BEFORE OUR ASSAULT BEGINS.
"HAL JORDAN HAS ALREADY BEEN STRIPPED OF HIS RING. HE IS NO LONGER A PROBLEM.
"SINESTRO ACTUALLY BELIEVES HE WAS CHOSEN BY A GREEN RING. IT HAS FINALLY CREATED SOME DOUBT WITHIN HIM AND SEVERED HIS TIES TO HIS OWN CORPS.
"JOHN STEWART CARRIES THE GUILT OF DESTROYING MOGO.
"WE WILL USE THAT."
"WHAT OF GUY GARDNER?"
"WE WILL GIVE HIM EVERYTHING HE WANTS.
"WE WILL MAKE HIM BELIEVE HE IS NOW OUR GREATEST GREEN LANTERN. SO THAT HIS FALL WILL BE MUCH HIGHER.
"AND THE TORCHBEARER--KYLE RAYNER. HE IS ATTEMPTING TO ALIGN THE CORPS AND 'RESCUE' GANTHET."
"IT IS YOU WHO RESCUED ME, MY BROTHERS AND SISTERS.
"KYLE RAYNER WILL COME FOR ME. I WILL DEAL WITH HIM MYSELF."
AS SOON AS THESE LANTERNS ARE BROKEN, NO ONE WILL DARE OPPOSE US. THE GREEN LANTERN CORPS WILL BE NO MORE.
AND WHAT OF THIS CORPS?

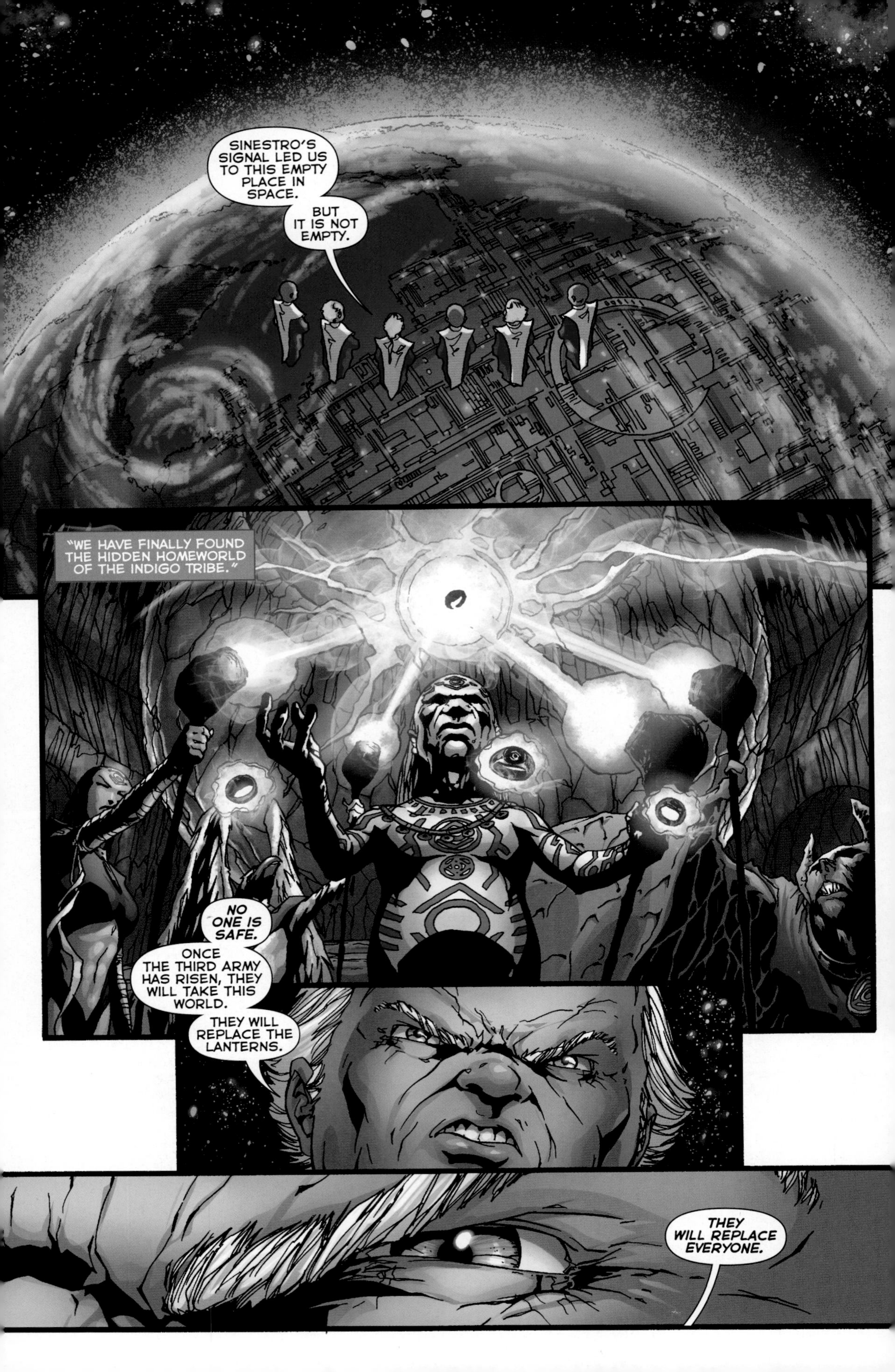
SINESTRO'S SIGNAL LED US TO THIS EMPTY PLACE IN SPACE.
BUT IT IS NOT EMPTY.
"WE HAVE FINALLY FOUND THE HIDDEN HOMEWORLD OF THE INDIGO TRIBE."
NO ONE IS SAFE.
ONCE THE THIRD ARMY HAS RISEN, THEY WILL TAKE THIS WORLD.
THEY WILL REPLACE THE LANTERNS.
THEY WILL REPLACE EVERYONE.

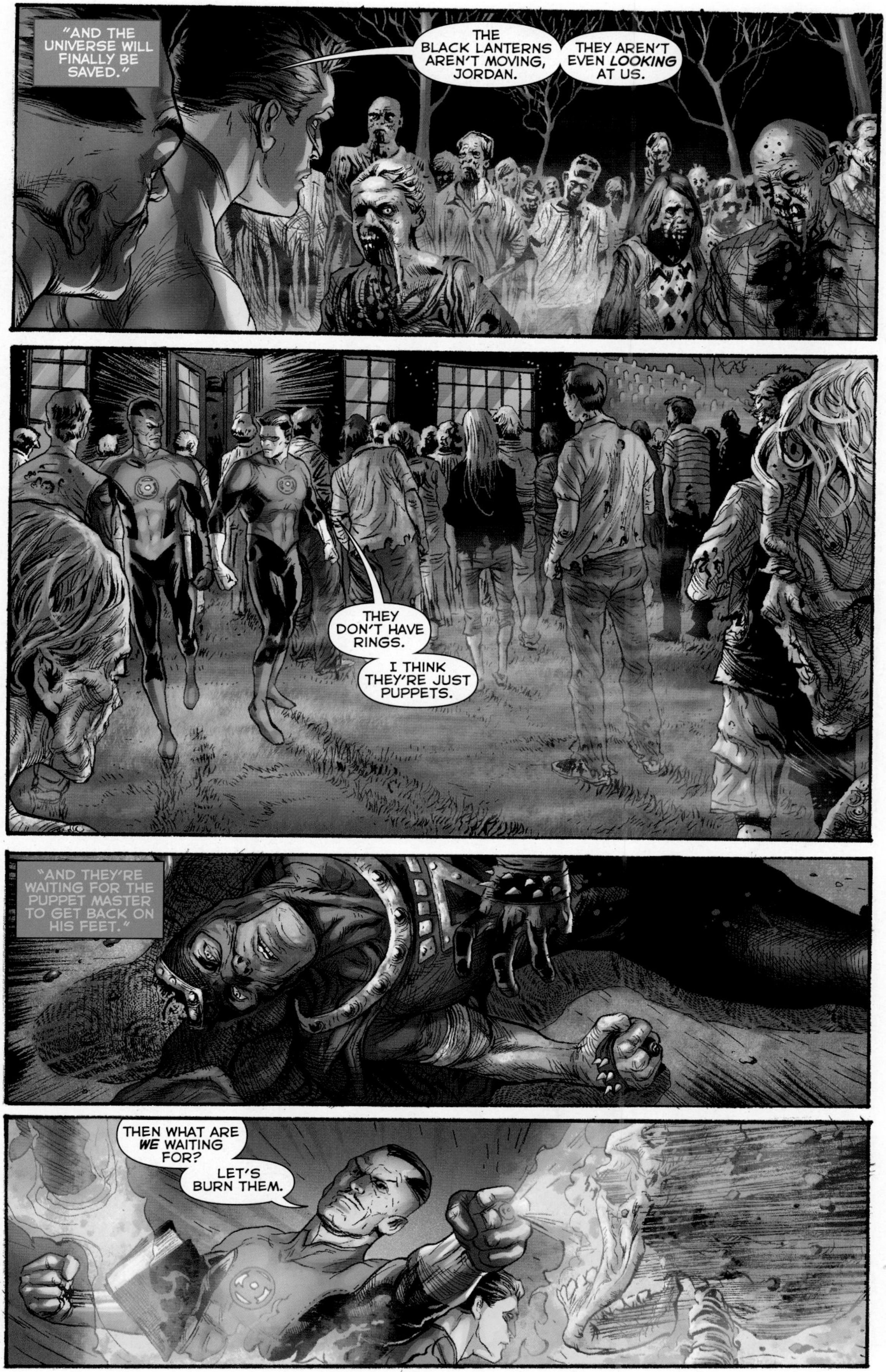
"AND THE UNIVERSE WILL FINALLY BE SAVED."
THE BLACK LANTERNS AREN'T MOVING, JORDAN.
THEY AREN'T EVEN LOOKING AT US.
THEY DON'T HAVE RINGS.
I THINK THEY'RE JUST PUPPETS.
"AND THEY'RE WAITING FOR THE PUPPET MASTER TO GET BACK ON HIS FEET."
THEN WHAT ARE WE WAITING FOR?
LET'S BURN THEM.

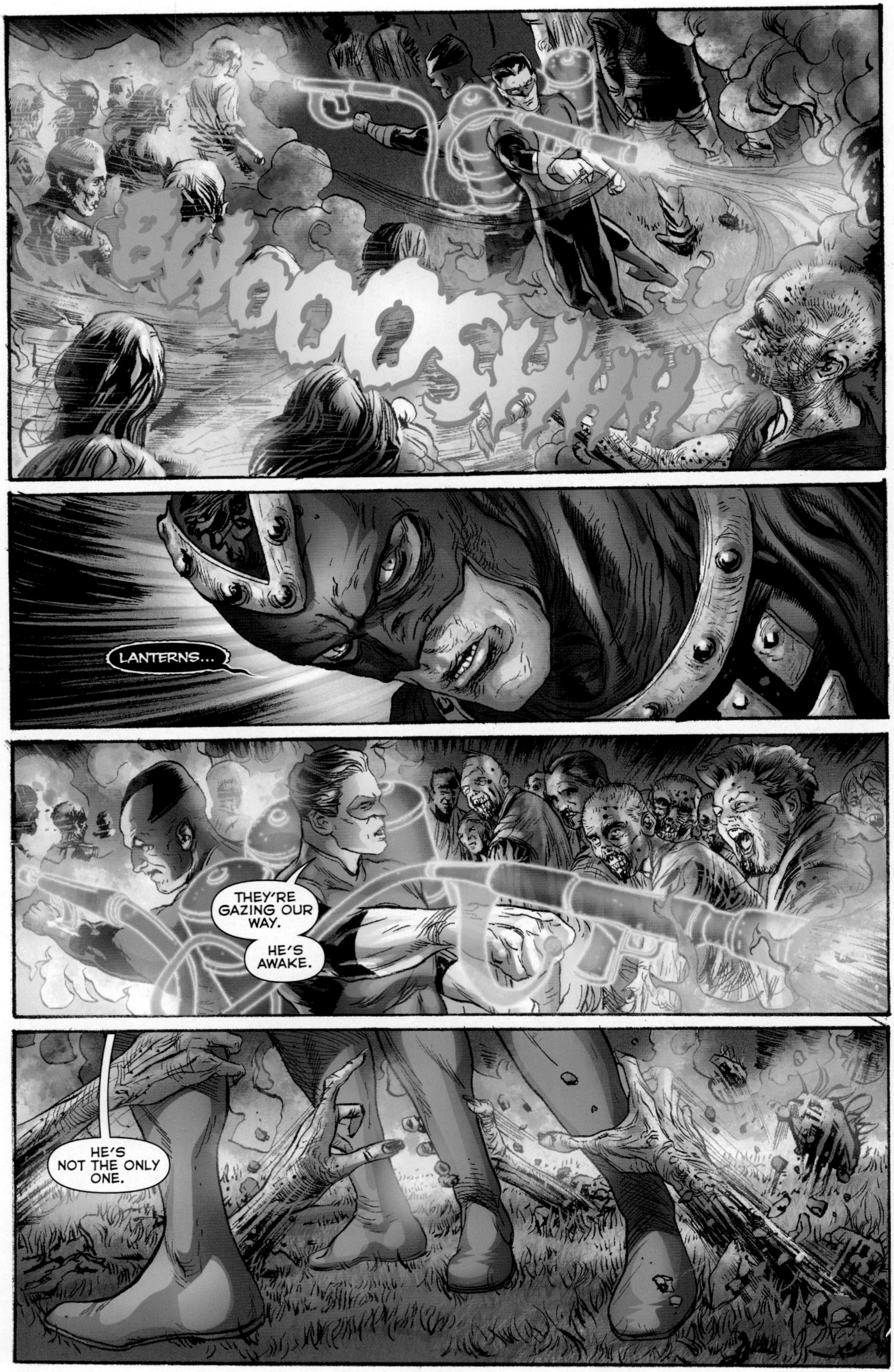
BWOOOSHHH
LANTERNS...
THEY'RE GAZING OUR WAY.
HE'S AWAKE.
HE'S NOT THE ONLY ONE.

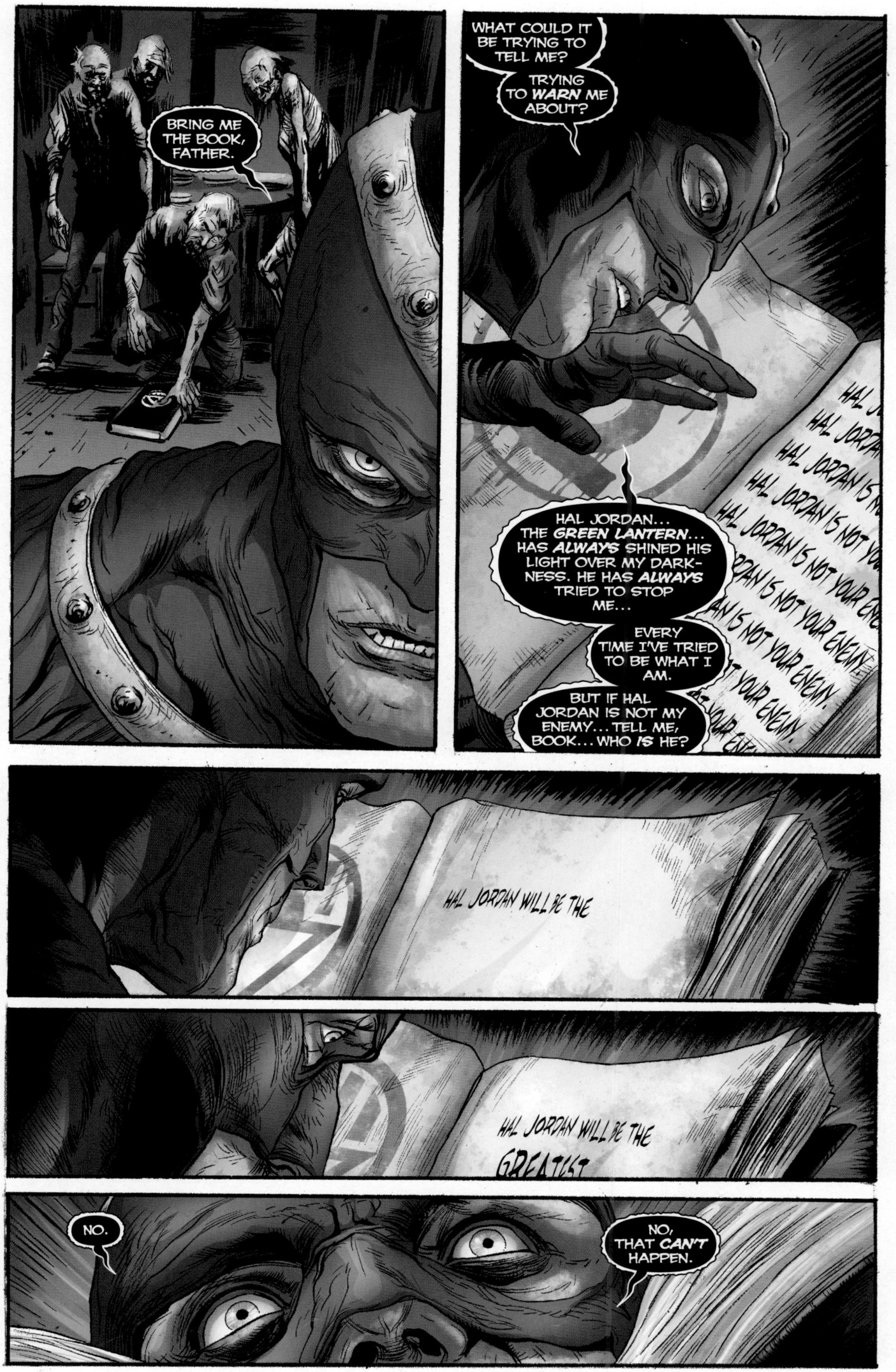
BRING ME THE BOOK, FATHER.
WHAT COULD IT BE TRYING TO TELL ME?
TRYING TO WARN ME ABOUT?
HAL JORDAN IS NOT YOUR ENEMY.
HAL JORDAN... THE GREEN LANTERN... HAS ALWAYS SHINED HIS LIGHT OVER MY DARKNESS. HE HAS ALWAYS TRIED TO STOP ME...
EVERY TIME I'VE TRIED TO BE WHAT I AM.
BUT IF HAL JORDAN IS NOT MY ENEMY... TELL ME, BOOK... WHO IS HE?
HAL JORDAN WILL BE THE
HAL JORDAN WILL BE THE GREATEST
NO.
NO, THAT CAN'T HAPPEN.

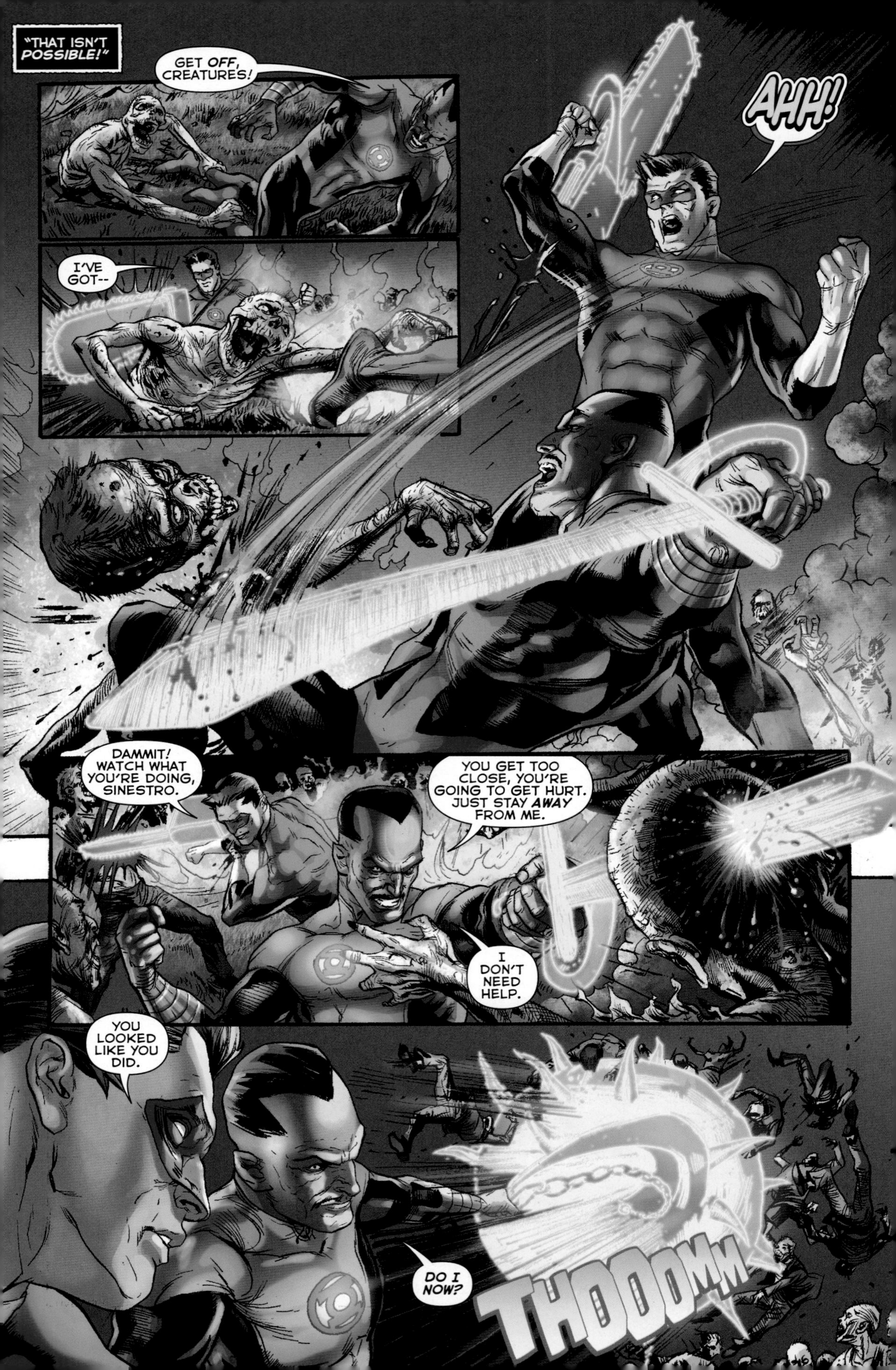
"THAT ISN'T POSSIBLE!"
GET OFF, CREATURES!
AHH!
I'VE GOT--
DAMMIT! WATCH WHAT YOU'RE DOING, SINESTRO.
YOU GET TOO CLOSE, YOU'RE GOING TO GET HURT. JUST STAY AWAY FROM ME.
I DON'T NEED HELP.
YOU LOOKED LIKE YOU DID.
DO I NOW?
THOOOMM

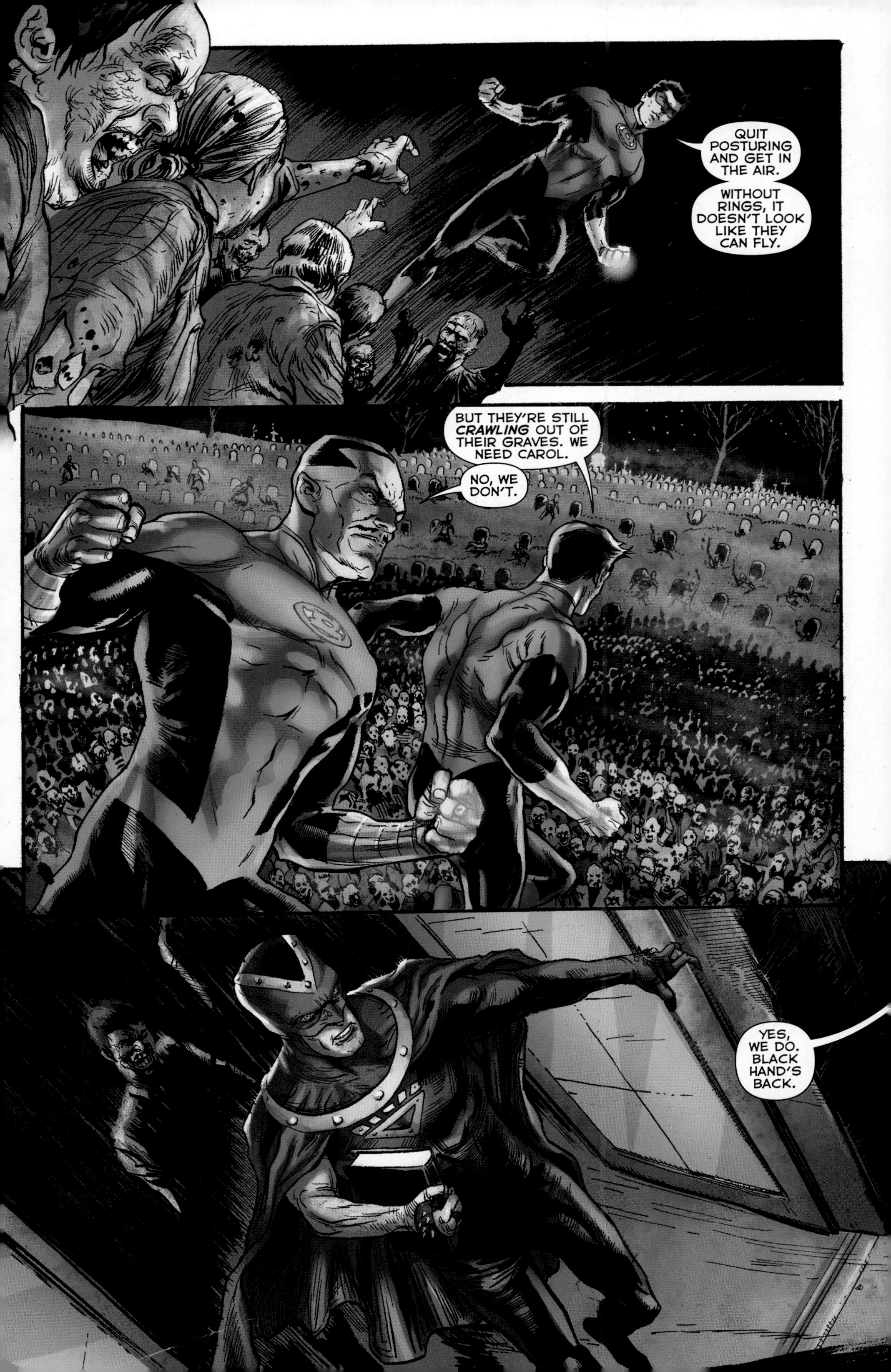
QUIT POSTURING AND GET IN THE AIR.
WITHOUT RINGS, IT DOESN'T LOOK LIKE THEY CAN FLY.
BUT THEY'RE STILL CRAWLING OUT OF THEIR GRAVES. WE NEED CAROL.
NO, WE DON'T.
YES, WE DO. BLACK HAND'S BACK.

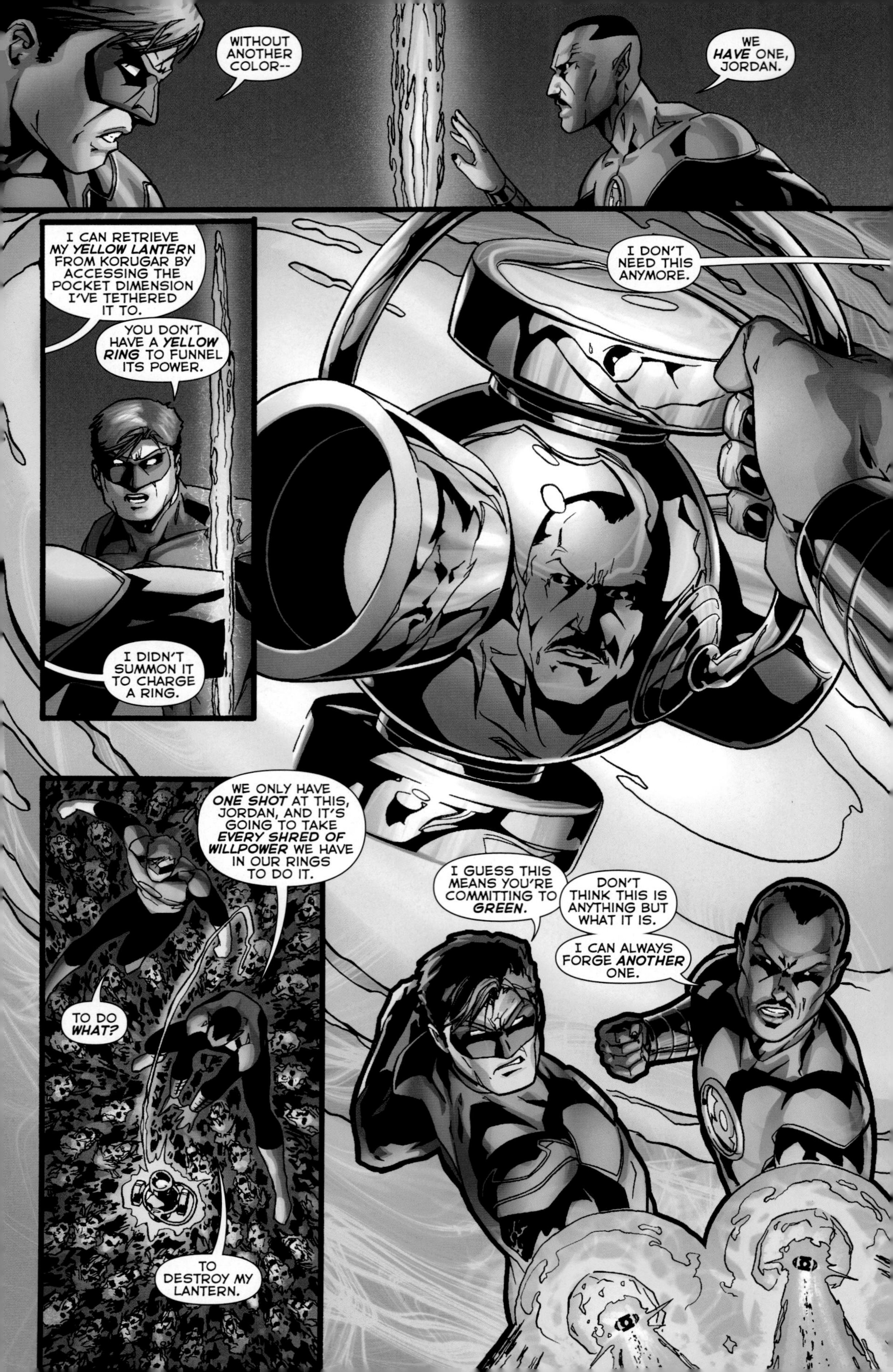
WITHOUT ANOTHER COLOR--
WE HAVE ONE, JORDAN.
I CAN RETRIEVE MY YELLOW LANTERN FROM KORUGAR BY ACCESSING THE POCKET DIMENSION I'VE TETHERED IT TO.
YOU DON'T HAVE A YELLOW RING TO FUNNEL ITS POWER.
I DIDN'T SUMMON IT TO CHARGE A RING.
I DON'T NEED THIS ANYMORE.
WE ONLY HAVE ONE SHOT AT THIS, JORDAN, AND IT'S GOING TO TAKE EVERY SHRED OF WILLPOWER WE HAVE IN OUR RINGS TO DO IT.
TO DO WHAT?
TO DESTROY MY LANTERN.
I GUESS THIS MEANS YOU'RE COMMITTING TO GREEN.
DON'T THINK THIS IS ANYTHING BUT WHAT IT IS.
I CAN ALWAYS FORGE ANOTHER ONE.

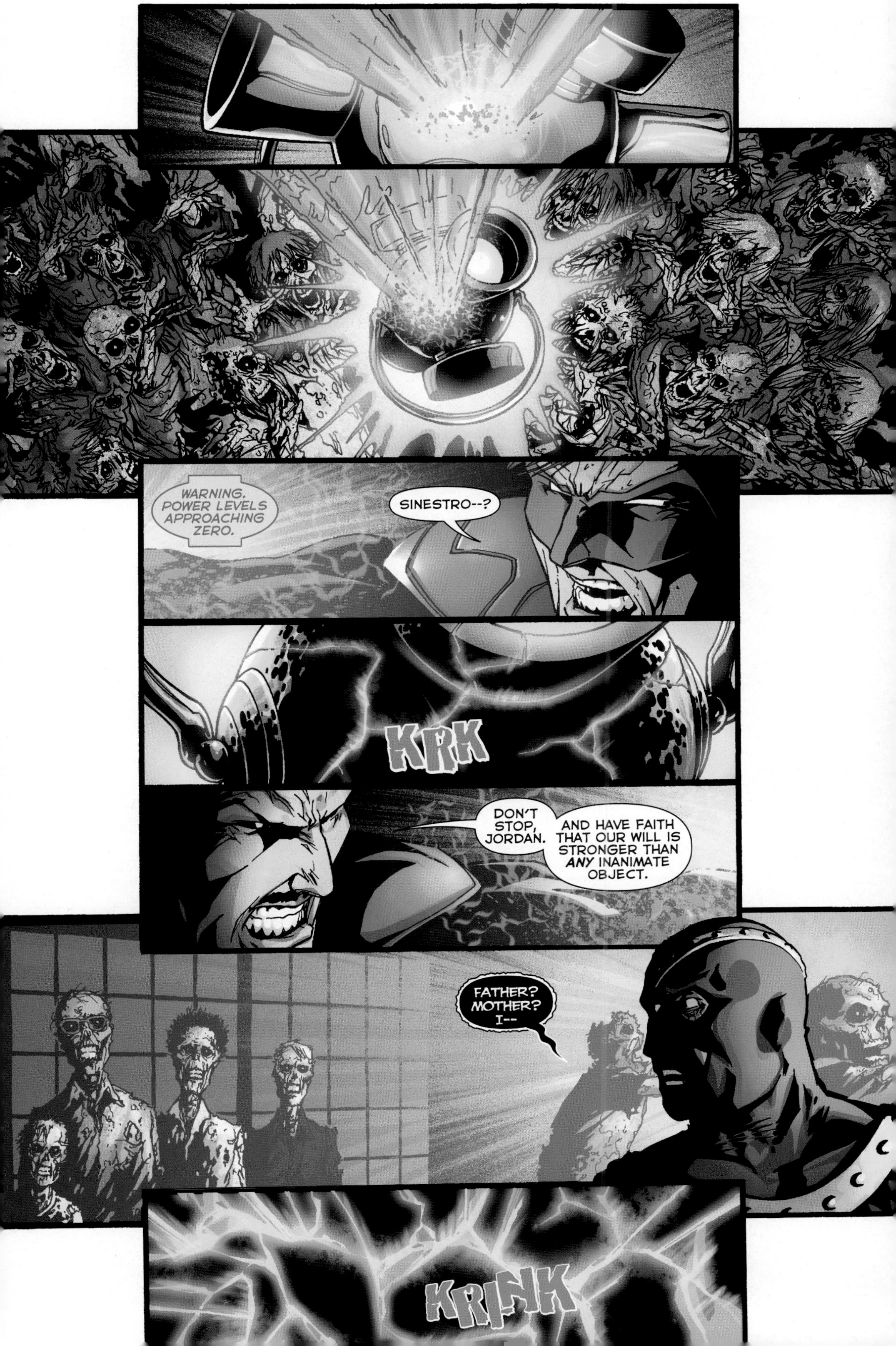
WARNING. POWER LEVELS APPROACHING ZERO.
SINESTRO--?
KRK
DON'T STOP, JORDAN.
AND HAVE FAITH THAT OUR WILL IS STRONGER THAN ANY INANIMATE OBJECT.
FATHER? MOTHER? I--
KRIRIK

CONNECTION SEVERED.

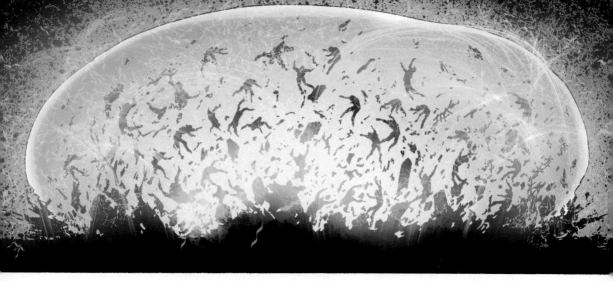

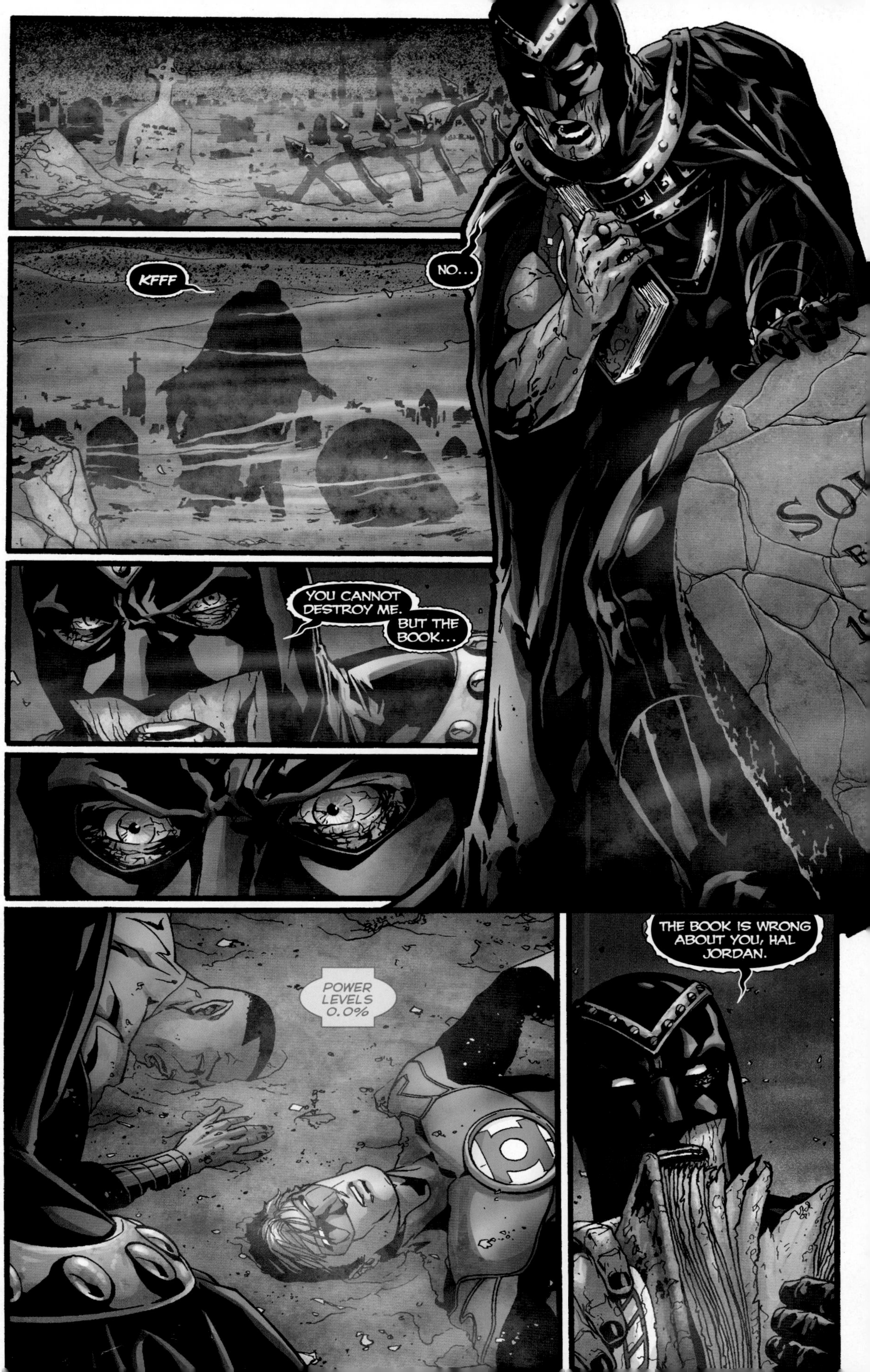
KFFF
NO...
YOU CANNOT DESTROY ME.
BUT THE BOOK...
POWER LEVELS 0.0%
THE BOOK IS WRONG ABOUT YOU, HAL JORDAN.

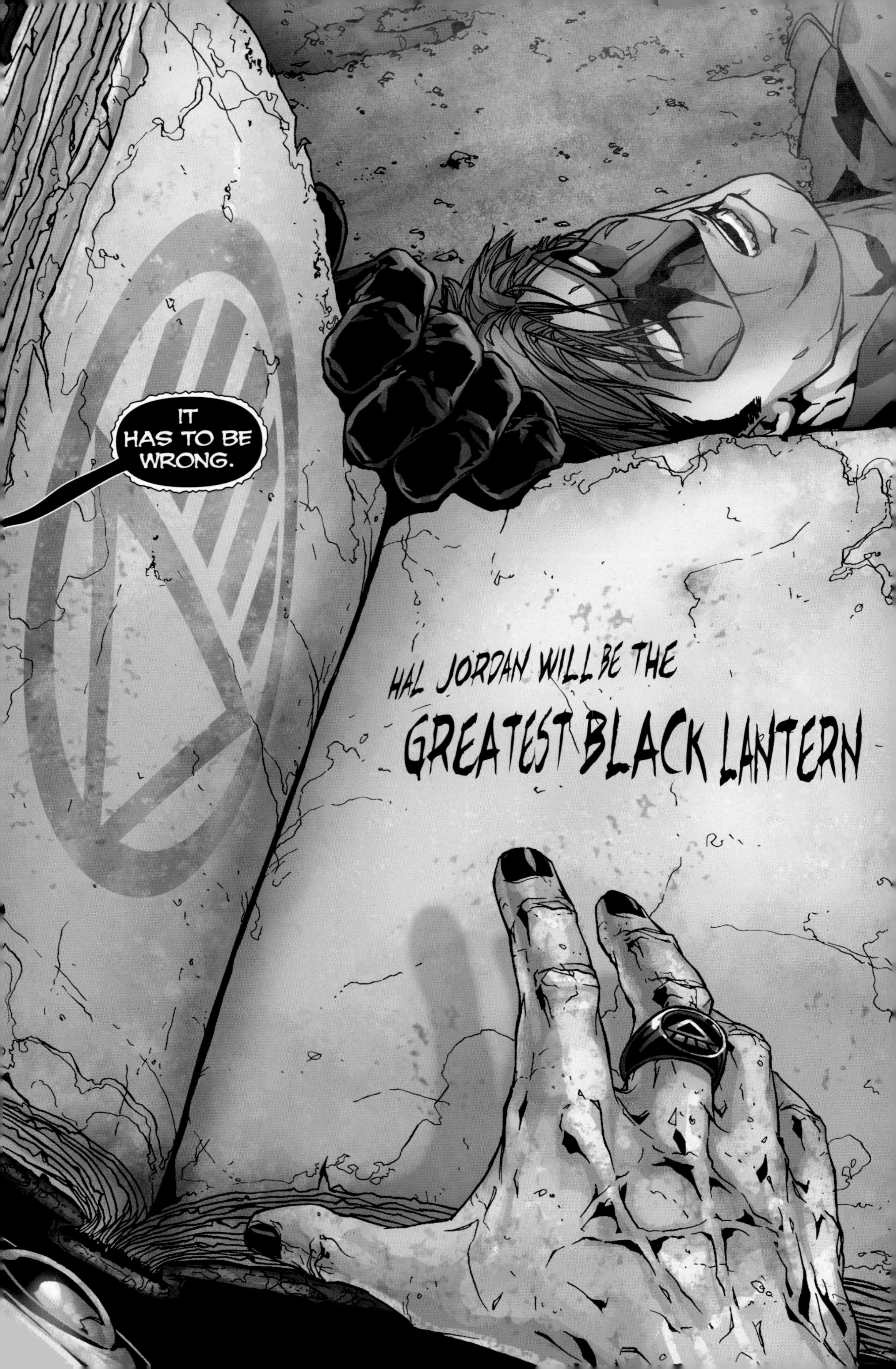
IT HAS TO BE WRONG.
HAL JORDAN WILL BE THE GREATEST BLACK LANTERN

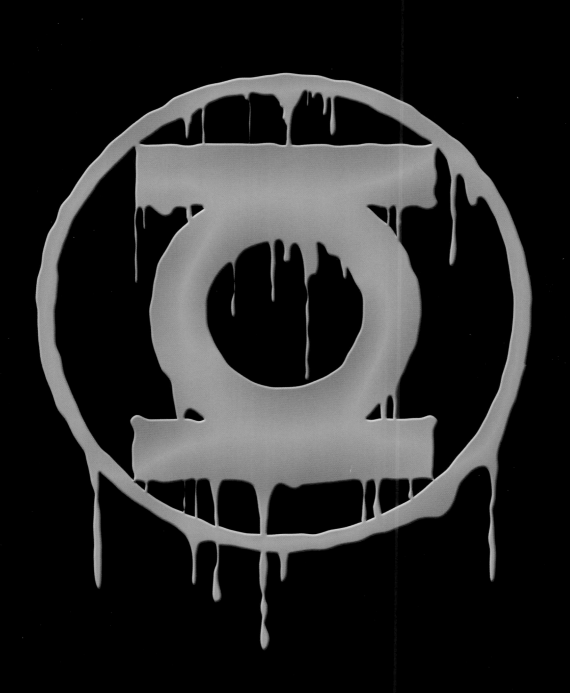

THE REVENGE OF BLACK HAND conclusion GEOFF JOHNS writer ETHAN VAN SCIVER artist

EPILOGUE PETE WOODS penciller CAM SMITH inker

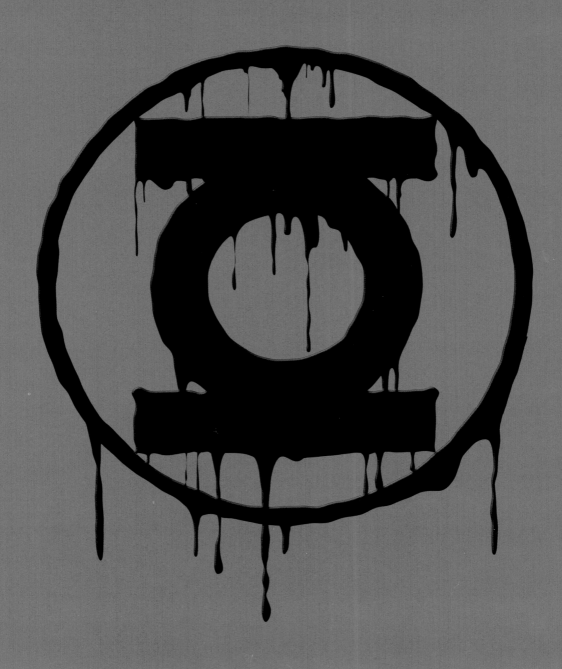

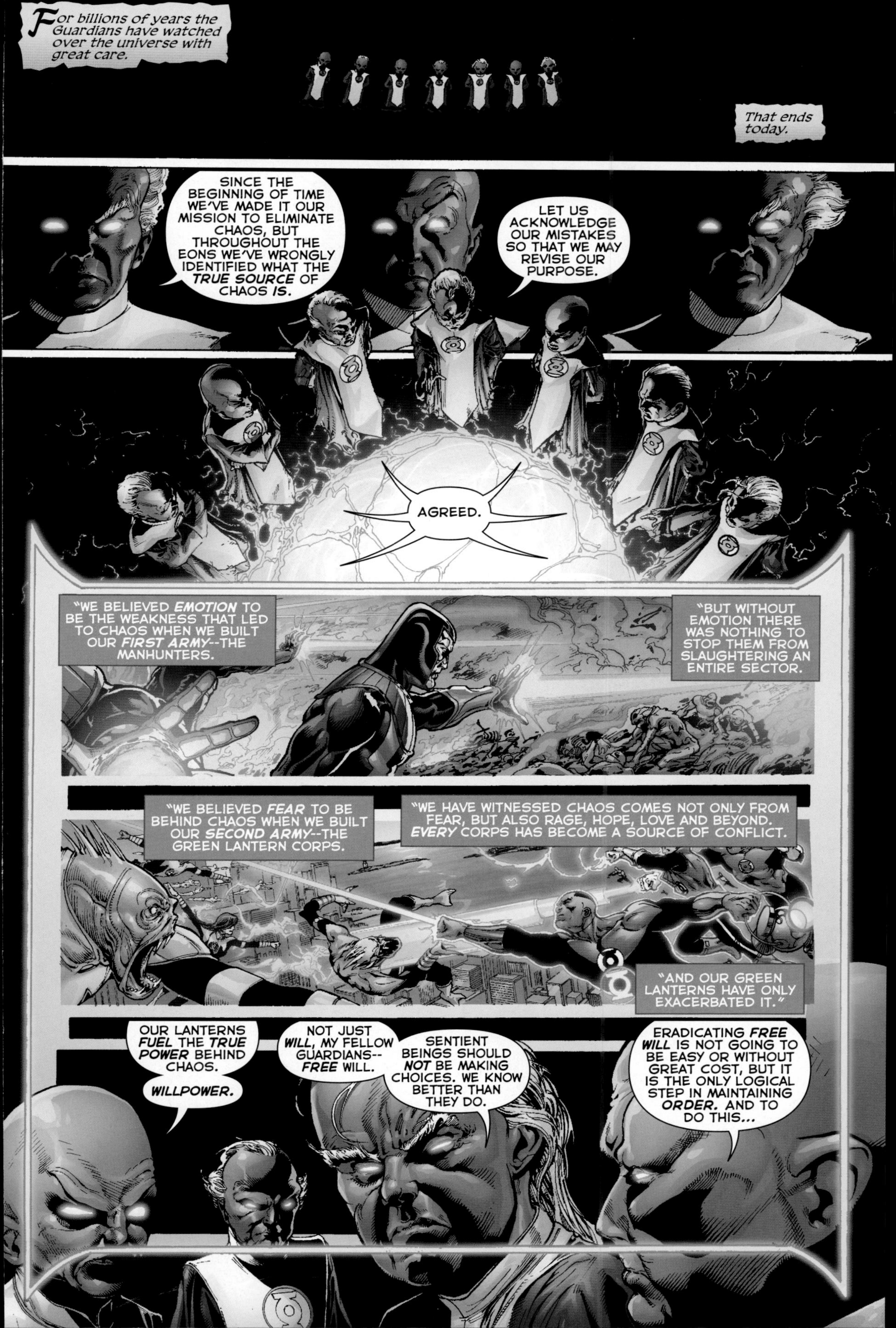

For billions of years the Guardians have watched over the universe with great care.
That ends today.
SINCE THE BEGINNING OF TIME WE'VE MADE IT OUR MISSION TO ELIMINATE CHAOS, BUT THROUGHOUT THE EONS WE'VE WRONGLY IDENTIFIED WHAT THE TRUE SOURCE OF CHAOS IS.
LET US ACKNOWLEDGE OUR MISTAKES SO THAT WE MAY REVISE OUR PURPOSE.
AGREED.
"WE BELIEVED EMOTION TO BE THE WEAKNESS THAT LED TO CHAOS WHEN WE BUILT OUR FIRST ARMY--THE MANHUNTERS.
"BUT WITHOUT EMOTION THERE WAS NOTHING TO STOP THEM FROM SLAUGHTERING AN ENTIRE SECTOR.
"WE BELIEVED FEAR TO BE BEHIND CHAOS WHEN WE BUILT OUR SECOND ARMY--THE GREEN LANTERN CORPS.
"WE HAVE WITNESSED CHAOS COMES NOT ONLY FROM FEAR, BUT ALSO RAGE, HOPE, LOVE AND BEYOND. EVERY CORPS HAS BECOME A SOURCE OF CONFLICT.
"AND OUR GREEN LANTERNS HAVE ONLY EXACERBATED IT."
OUR LANTERNS FUEL THE TRUE POWER BEHIND CHAOS.
WILLPOWER.
NOT JUST WILL, MY FELLOW GUARDIANS-- FREE WILL.
SENTIENT BEINGS SHOULD NOT BE MAKING CHOICES. WE KNOW BETTER THAN THEY DO.
ERADICATING FREE WILL IS NOT GOING TO BE EASY OR WITHOUT GREAT COST, BUT IT IS THE ONLY LOGICAL STEP IN MAINTAINING ORDER. AND TO DO THIS...

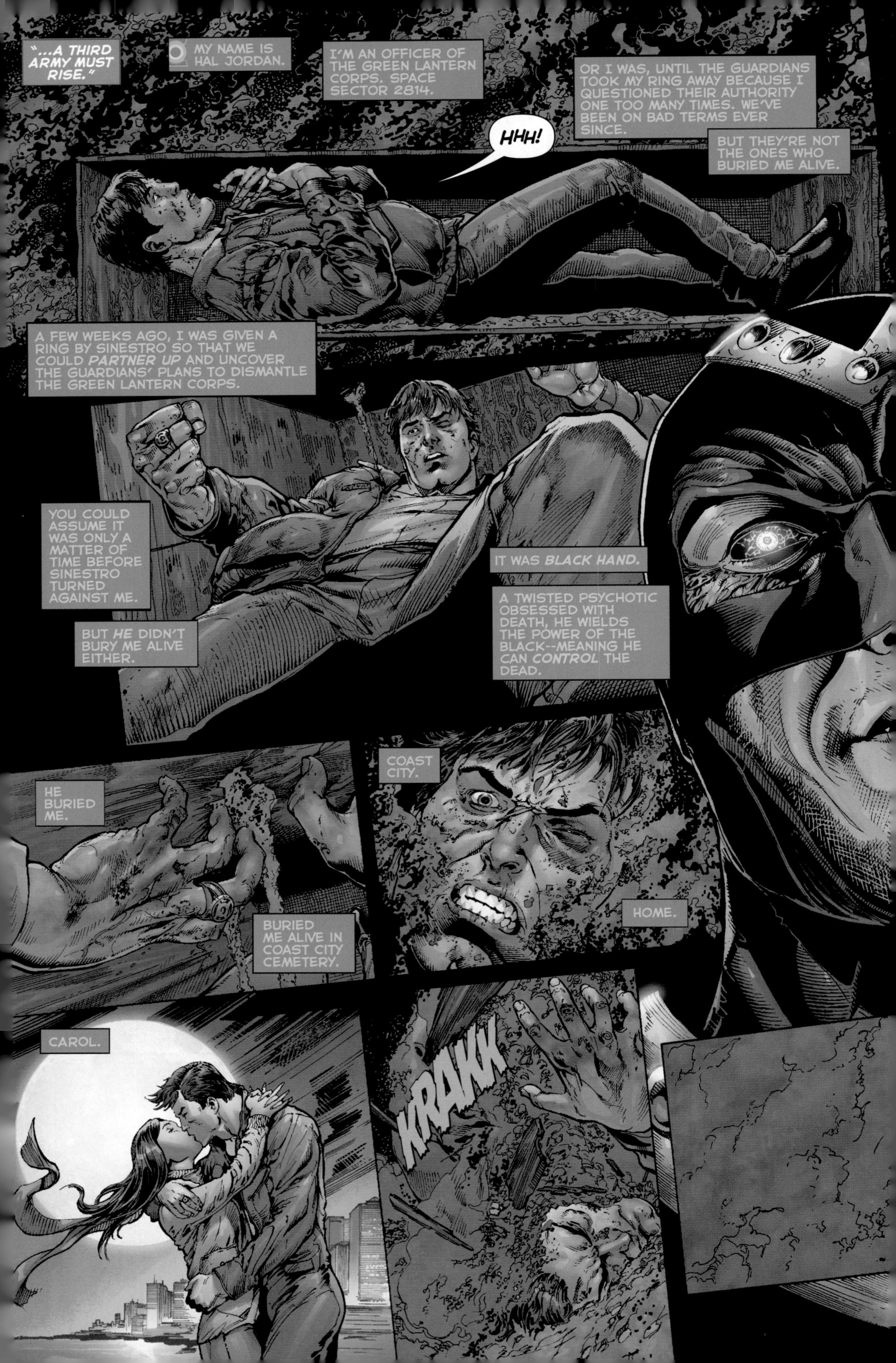
"...A THIRD ARMY MUST RISE."
MY NAME IS HAL JORDAN.
I'M AN OFFICER OF THE GREEN LANTERN CORPS. SPACE SECTOR 2814.
OR I WAS, UNTIL THE GUARDIANS TOOK MY RING AWAY BECAUSE I QUESTIONED THEIR AUTHORITY ONE TOO MANY TIMES. WE'VE BEEN ON BAD TERMS EVER SINCE.
HHH!
BUT THEY'RE NOT THE ONES WHO BURIED ME ALIVE.
A FEW WEEKS AGO, I WAS GIVEN A RING BY SINESTRO SO THAT WE COULD *PARTNER UP* AND UNCOVER THE GUARDIANS' PLANS TO DISMANTLE THE GREEN LANTERN CORPS.
YOU COULD ASSUME IT WAS ONLY A MATTER OF TIME BEFORE SINESTRO TURNED AGAINST ME.
BUT *HE* DIDN'T BURY ME ALIVE EITHER.
IT WAS *BLACK HAND.*
A TWISTED PSYCHOTIC OBSESSED WITH DEATH, HE WIELDS THE POWER OF THE BLACK--MEANING HE CAN *CONTROL* THE DEAD.
HE BURIED ME.
BURIED ME ALIVE IN COAST CITY CEMETERY.
COAST CITY.
HOME.
CAROL.
KRAKK

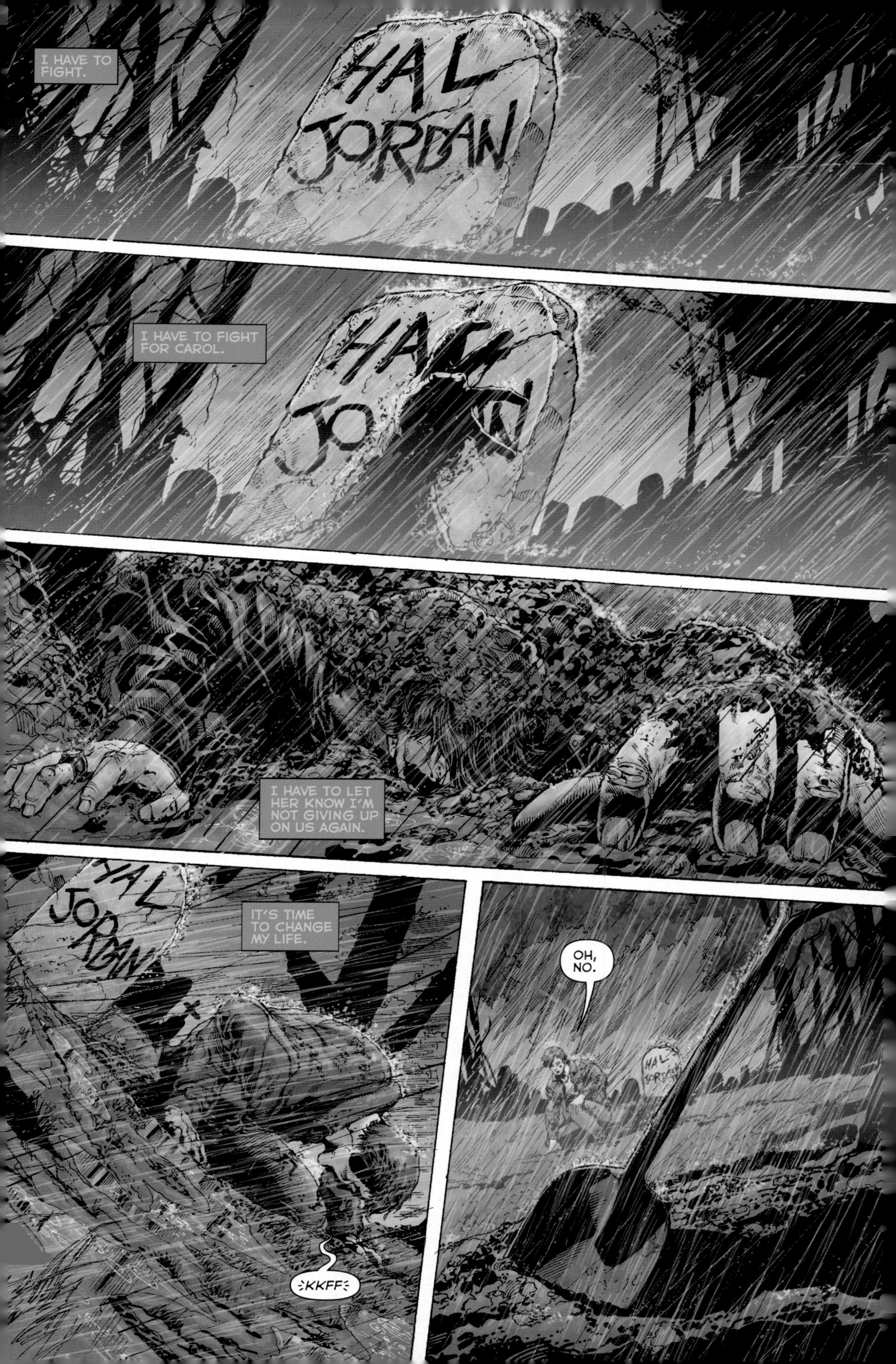
HAL JORDAN
I HAVE TO FIGHT.
I HAVE TO FIGHT FOR CAROL.
I HAVE TO LET HER KNOW I'M NOT GIVING UP ON US AGAIN.
IT'S TIME TO CHANGE MY LIFE.
KKFF
OH, NO.

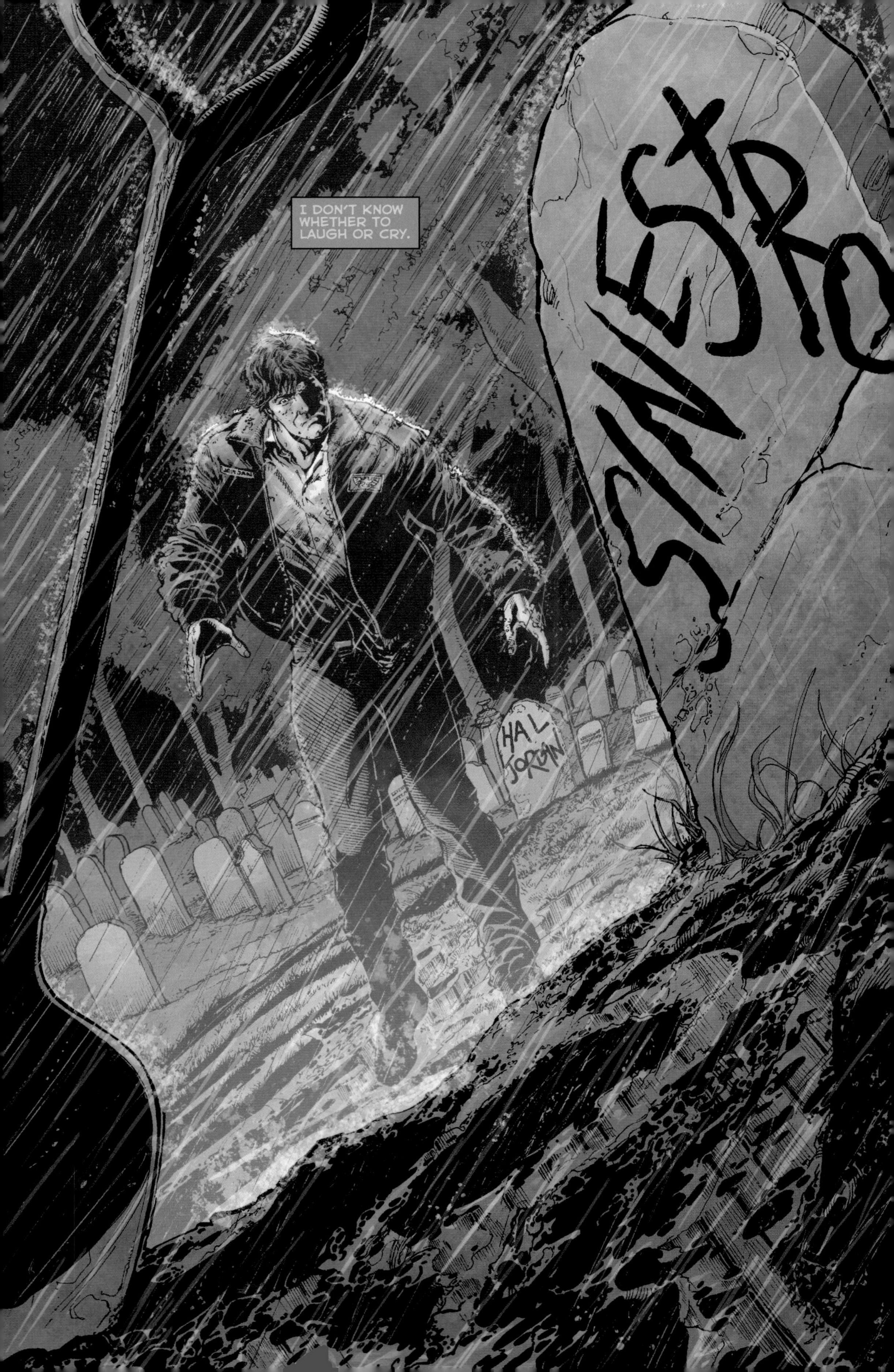
I DON'T KNOW WHETHER TO LAUGH OR CRY.
SINESTRO
HAL JORDAN

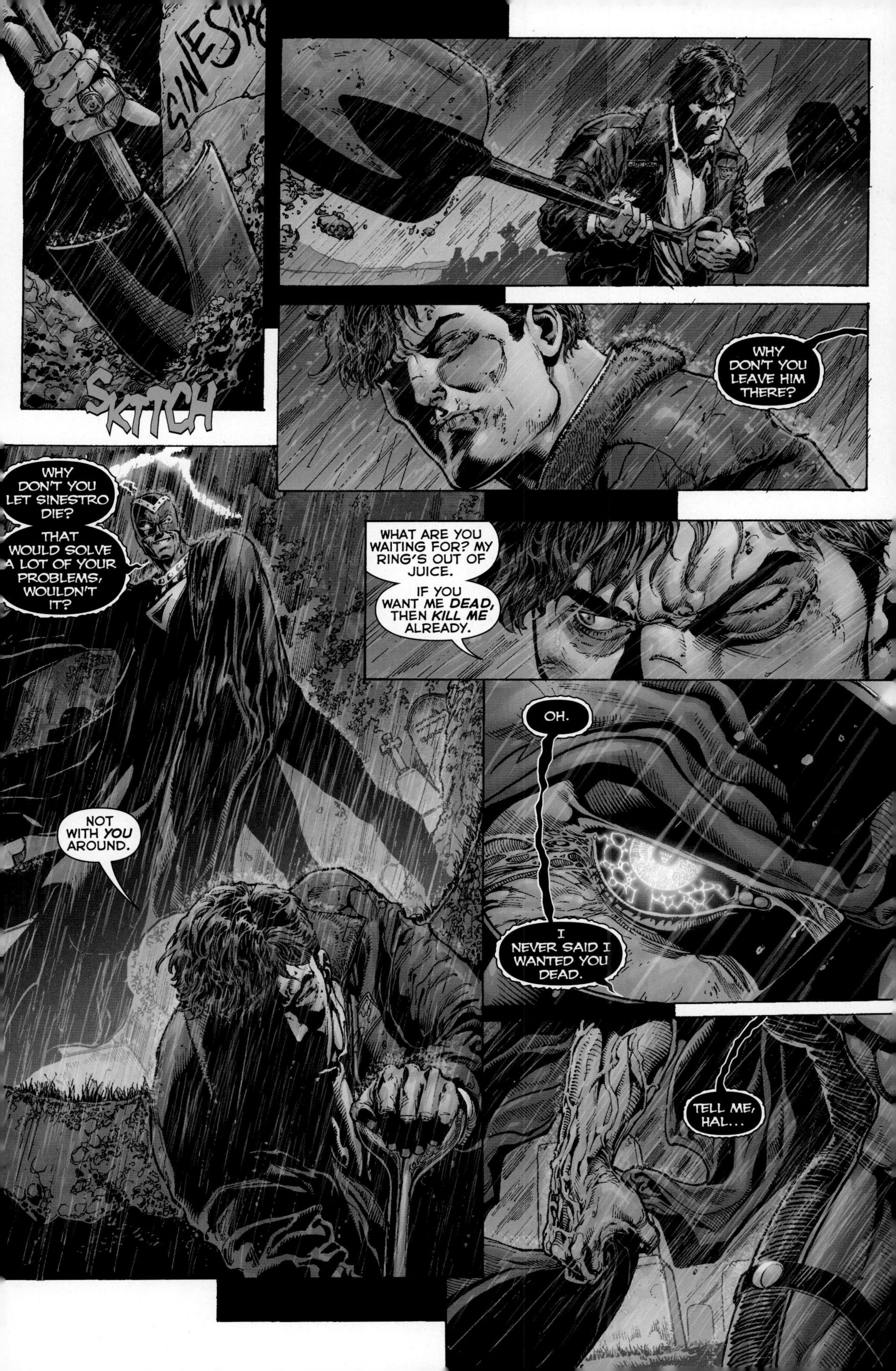
SINESTRO
SKTTCH
WHY DON'T YOU LEAVE HIM THERE?
WHY DON'T YOU LET SINESTRO DIE?
THAT WOULD SOLVE A LOT OF YOUR PROBLEMS, WOULDN'T IT?
WHAT ARE YOU WAITING FOR? MY RING'S OUT OF JUICE.
IF YOU WANT ME DEAD, THEN KILL ME ALREADY.
NOT WITH YOU AROUND.
OH.
I NEVER SAID I WANTED YOU DEAD.
TELL ME, HAL...

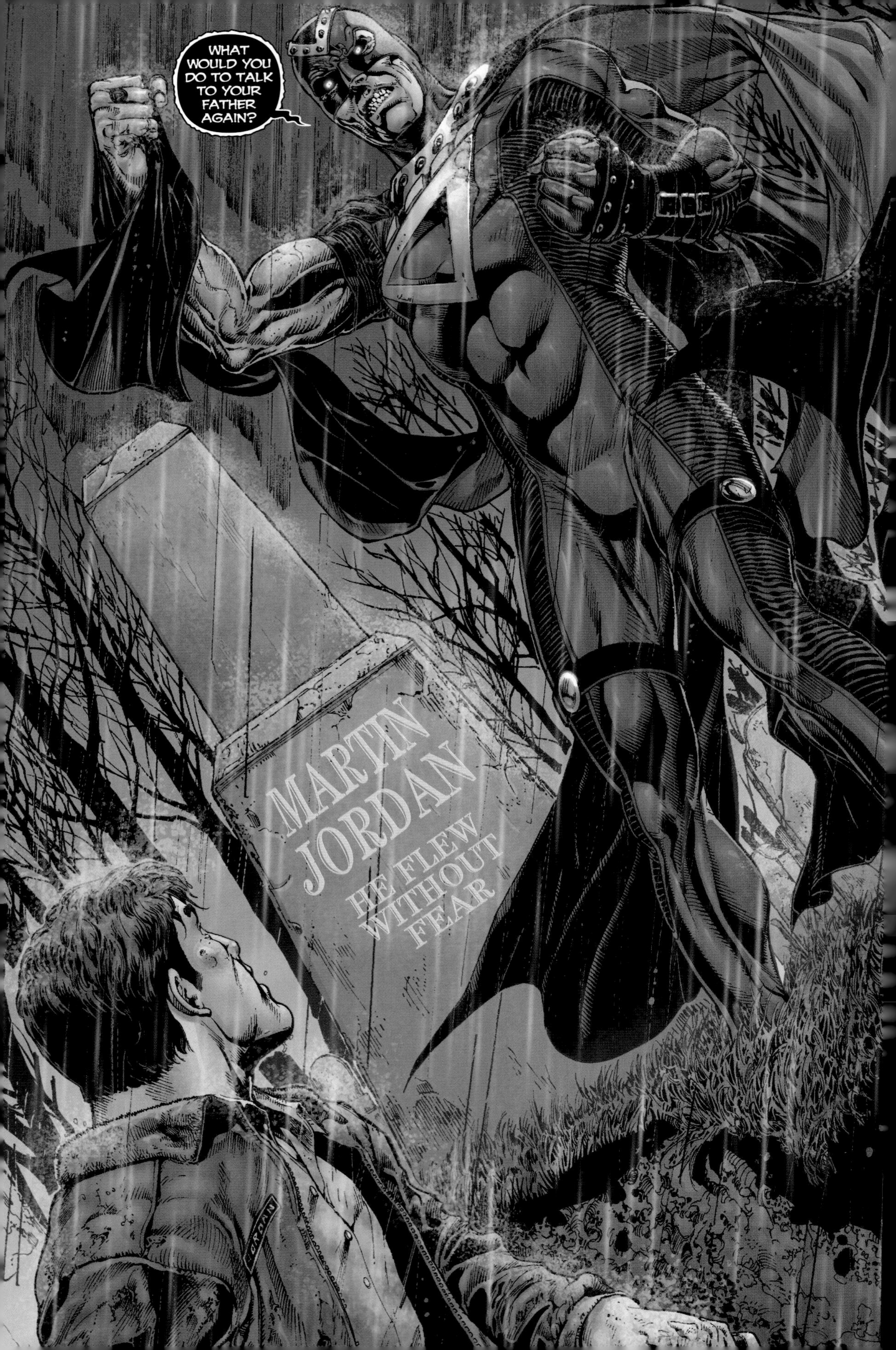
WHAT WOULD YOU DO TO TALK TO YOUR FATHER AGAIN?
MARTIN JORDAN
HE FLEW WITHOUT FEAR

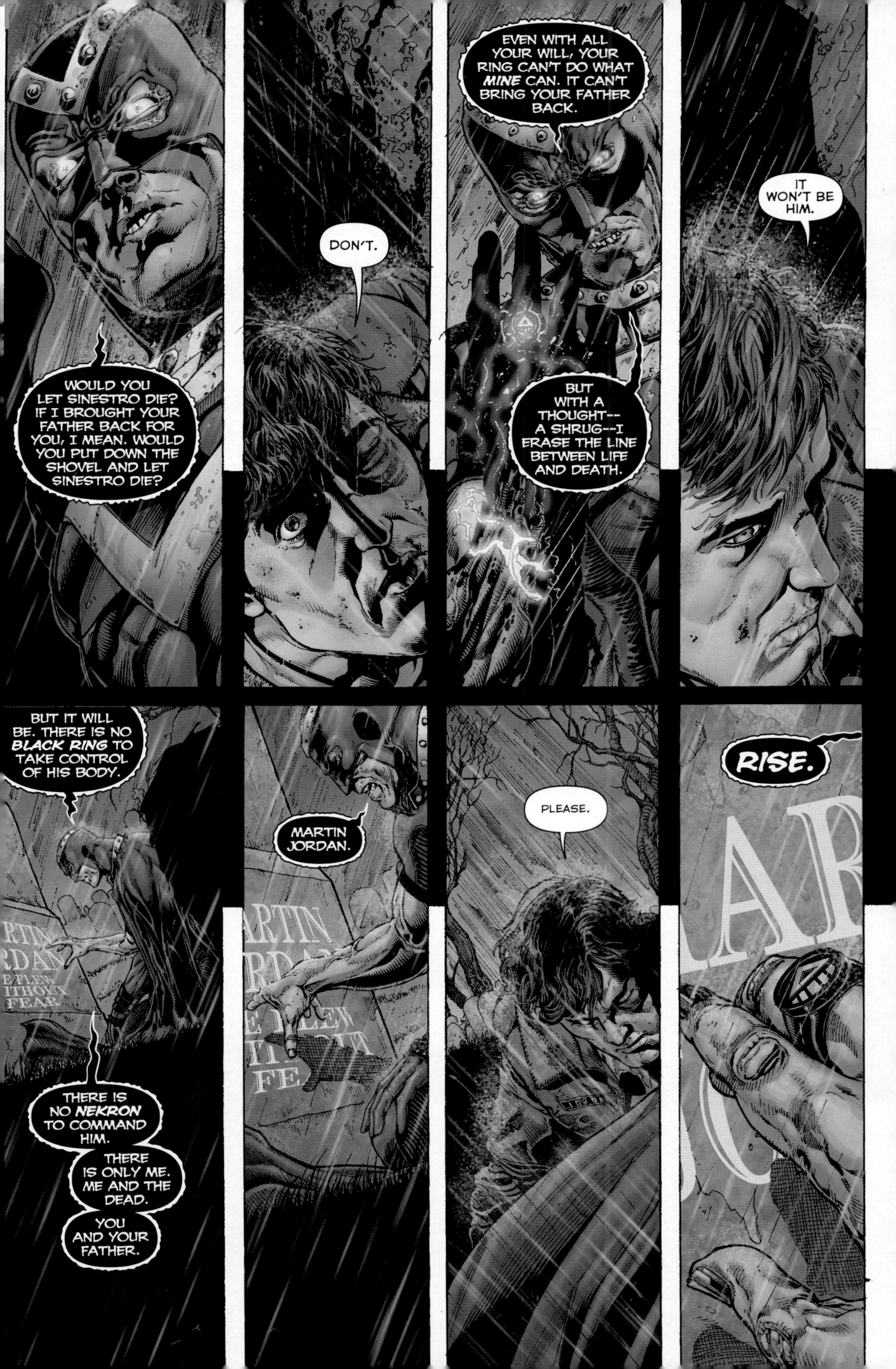
WOULD YOU LET SINESTRO DIE? IF I BROUGHT YOUR FATHER BACK FOR YOU, I MEAN. WOULD YOU PUT DOWN THE SHOVEL AND LET SINESTRO DIE?
DON'T.
EVEN WITH ALL YOUR WILL, YOUR RING CAN'T DO WHAT *MINE* CAN. IT CAN'T BRING YOUR FATHER BACK.
BUT WITH A THOUGHT-- A SHRUG--I ERASE THE LINE BETWEEN LIFE AND DEATH.
IT WON'T BE HIM.
BUT IT WILL BE. THERE IS NO *BLACK RING* TO TAKE CONTROL OF HIS BODY.
THERE IS NO *NEKRON* TO COMMAND HIM.
THERE IS ONLY ME. ME AND THE DEAD.
YOU AND YOUR FATHER.
MARTIN JORDAN.
PLEASE.
RISE.

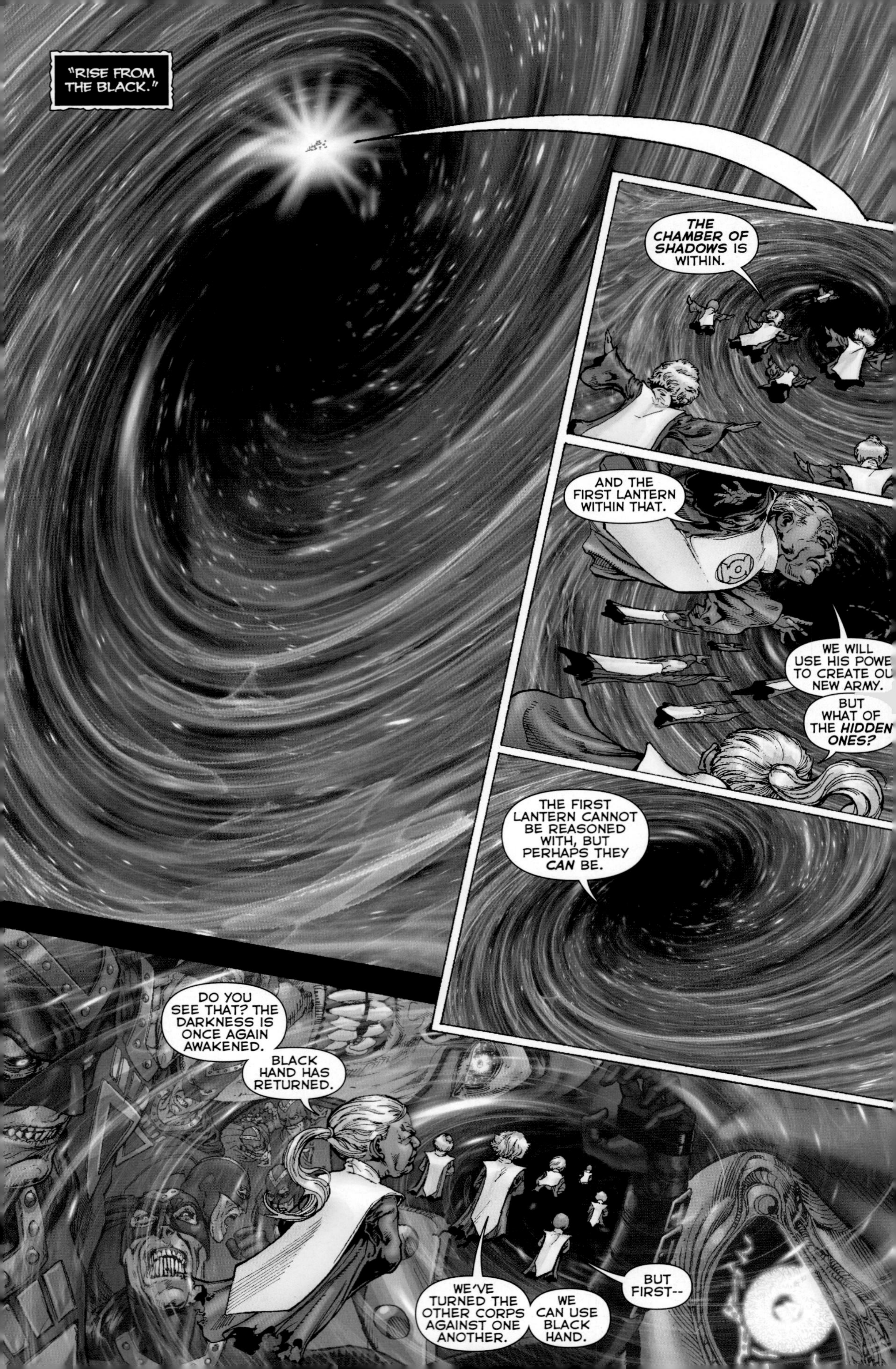
"RISE FROM THE BLACK."
THE CHAMBER OF SHADOWS IS WITHIN.
AND THE FIRST LANTERN WITHIN THAT.
WE WILL USE HIS POWE TO CREATE OU NEW ARMY.
BUT WHAT OF THE HIDDEN ONES?
THE FIRST LANTERN CANNOT BE REASONED WITH, BUT PERHAPS THEY CAN BE.
DO YOU SEE THAT? THE DARKNESS IS ONCE AGAIN AWAKENED.
BLACK HAND HAS RETURNED.
WE'VE TURNED THE OTHER CORPS AGAINST ONE ANOTHER.
WE CAN USE BLACK HAND.
BUT FIRST--

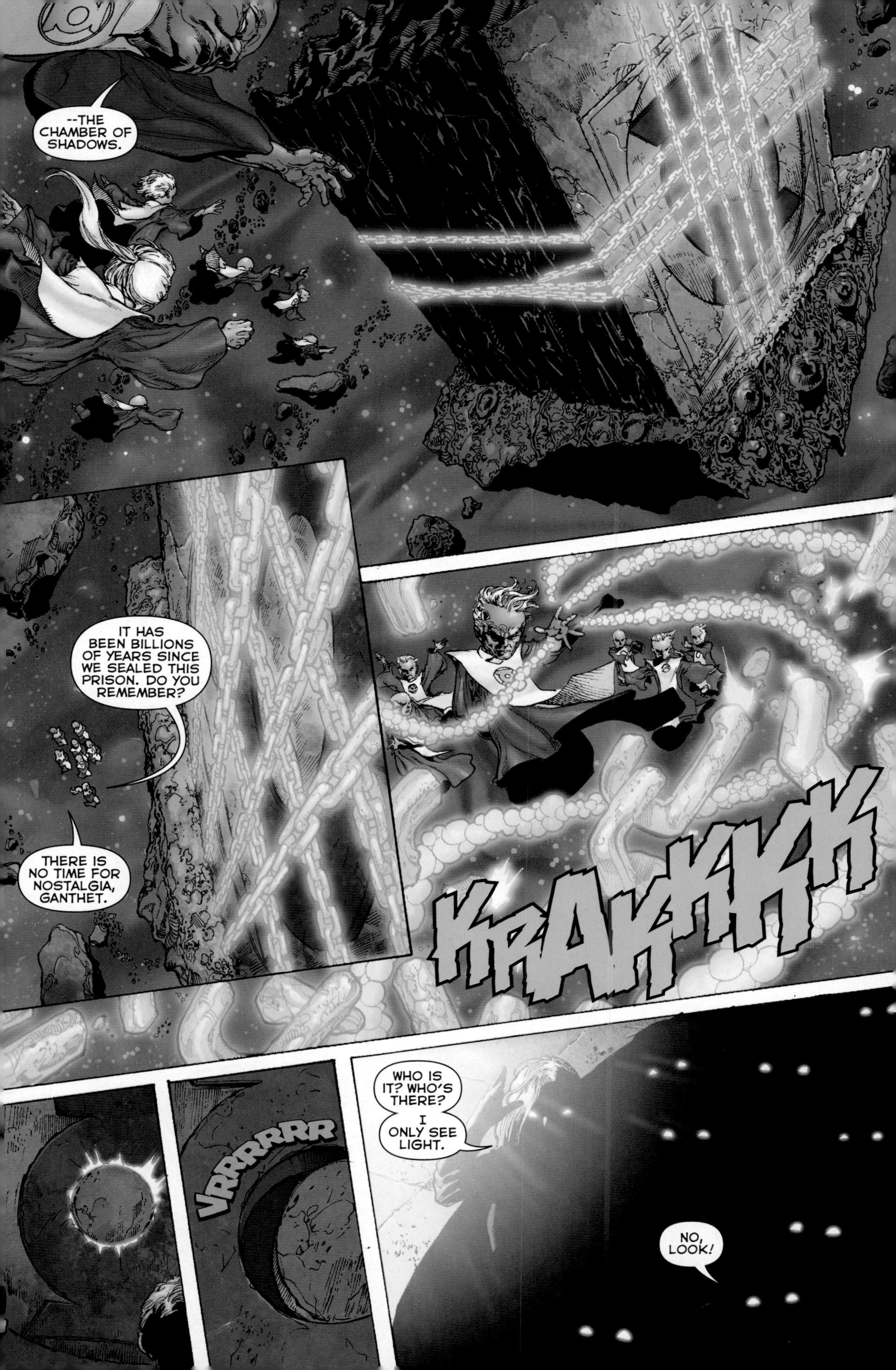
--THE CHAMBER OF SHADOWS.
IT HAS BEEN BILLIONS OF YEARS SINCE WE SEALED THIS PRISON. DO YOU REMEMBER?
THERE IS NO TIME FOR NOSTALGIA, GANTHET.
KRAKKKK
VRRRRRRR
WHO IS IT? WHO'S THERE?
I ONLY SEE LIGHT.
NO, LOOK!

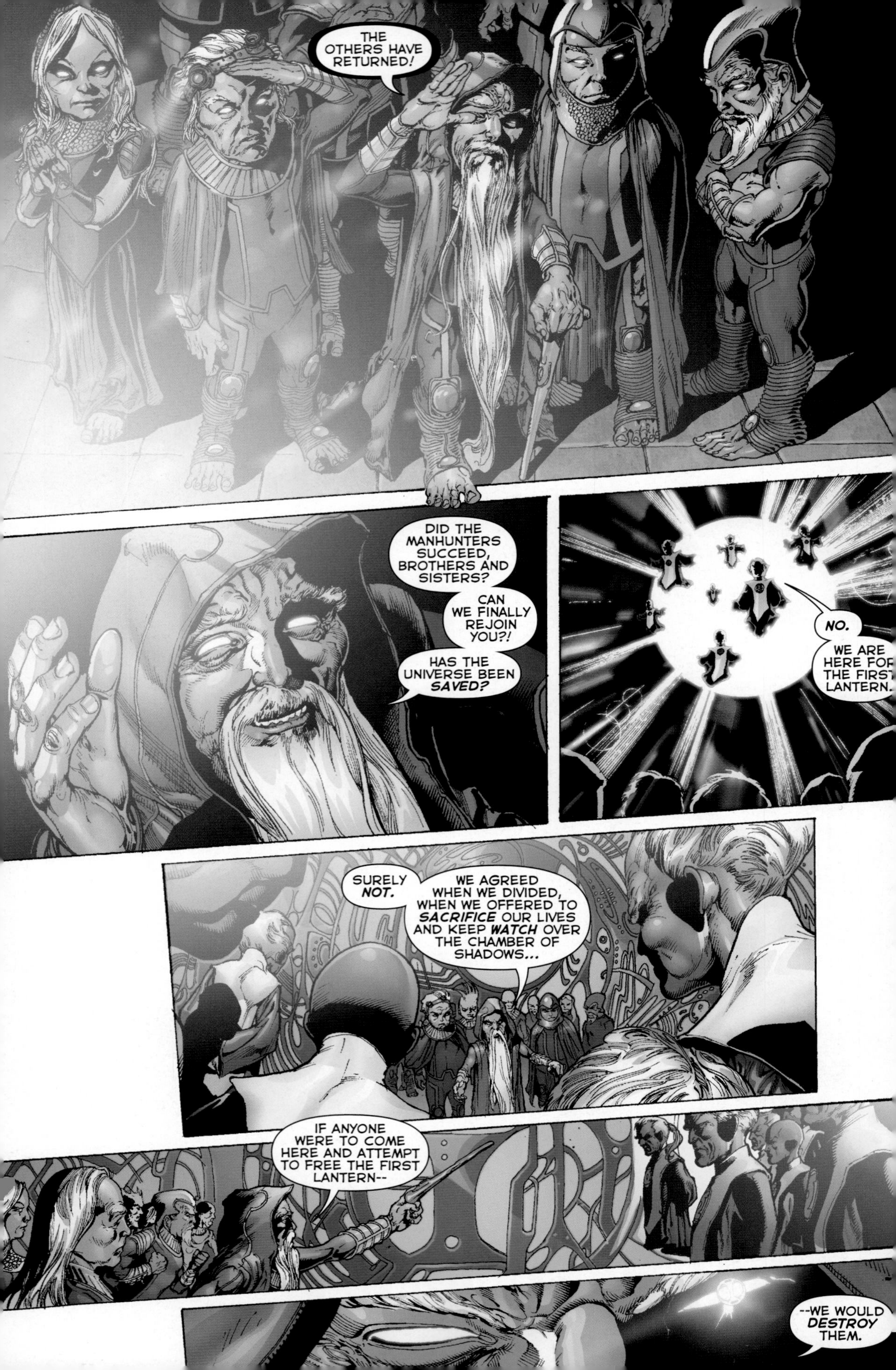
THE OTHERS HAVE RETURNED!
DID THE MANHUNTERS SUCCEED, BROTHERS AND SISTERS?
CAN WE FINALLY REJOIN YOU?!
HAS THE UNIVERSE BEEN SAVED?
NO.
WE ARE HERE FOR THE FIRST LANTERN.
SURELY NOT.
WE AGREED WHEN WE DIVIDED, WHEN WE OFFERED TO SACRIFICE OUR LIVES AND KEEP WATCH OVER THE CHAMBER OF SHADOWS...
IF ANYONE WERE TO COME HERE AND ATTEMPT TO FREE THE FIRST LANTERN--
--WE WOULD DESTROY THEM.

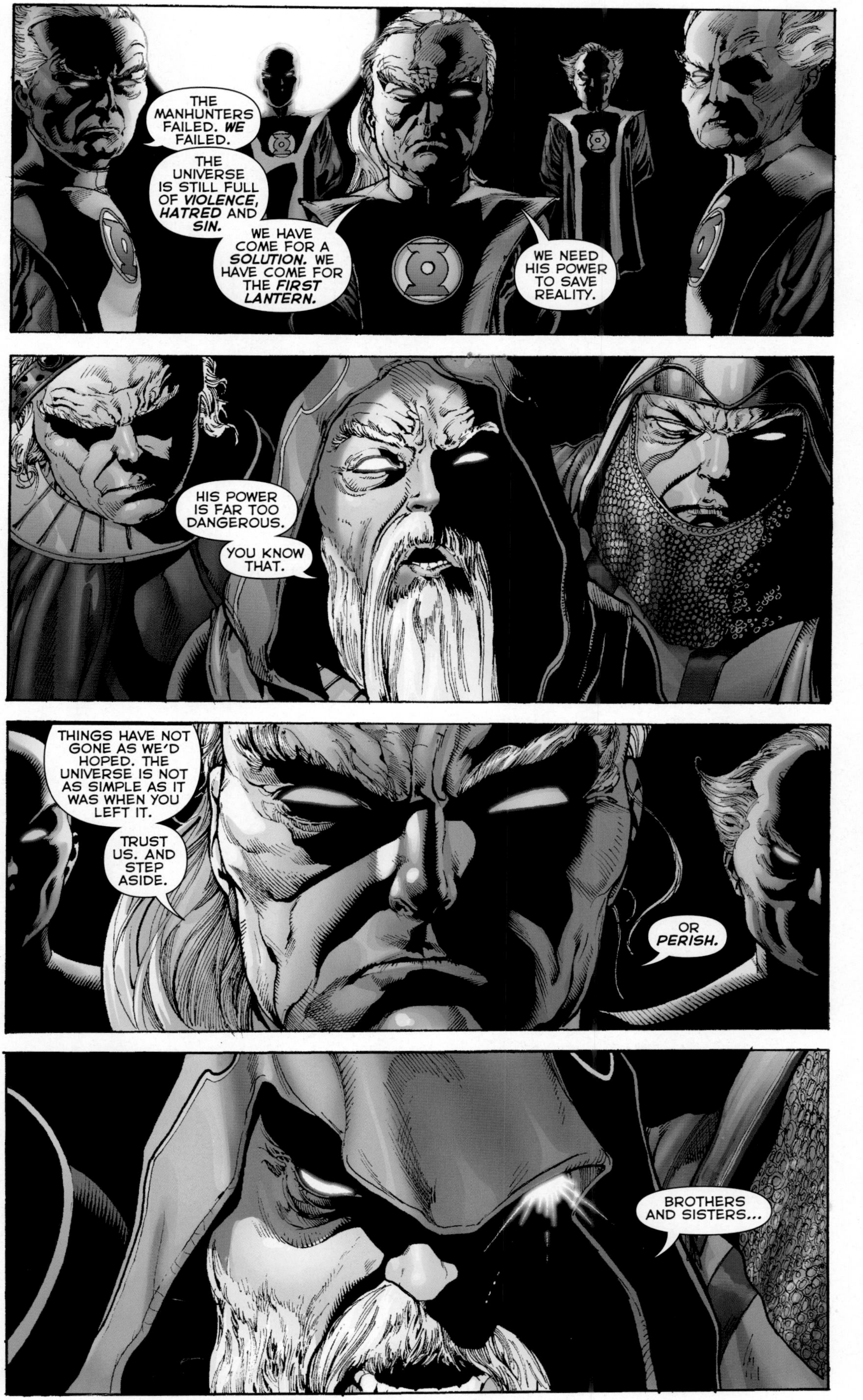
THE MANHUNTERS FAILED. WE FAILED.
THE UNIVERSE IS STILL FULL OF VIOLENCE, HATRED AND SIN.
WE HAVE COME FOR A SOLUTION. WE HAVE COME FOR THE FIRST LANTERN.
WE NEED HIS POWER TO SAVE REALITY.
HIS POWER IS FAR TOO DANGEROUS.
YOU KNOW THAT.
THINGS HAVE NOT GONE AS WE'D HOPED. THE UNIVERSE IS NOT AS SIMPLE AS IT WAS WHEN YOU LEFT IT.
TRUST US. AND STEP ASIDE.
OR PERISH.
BROTHERS AND SISTERS...

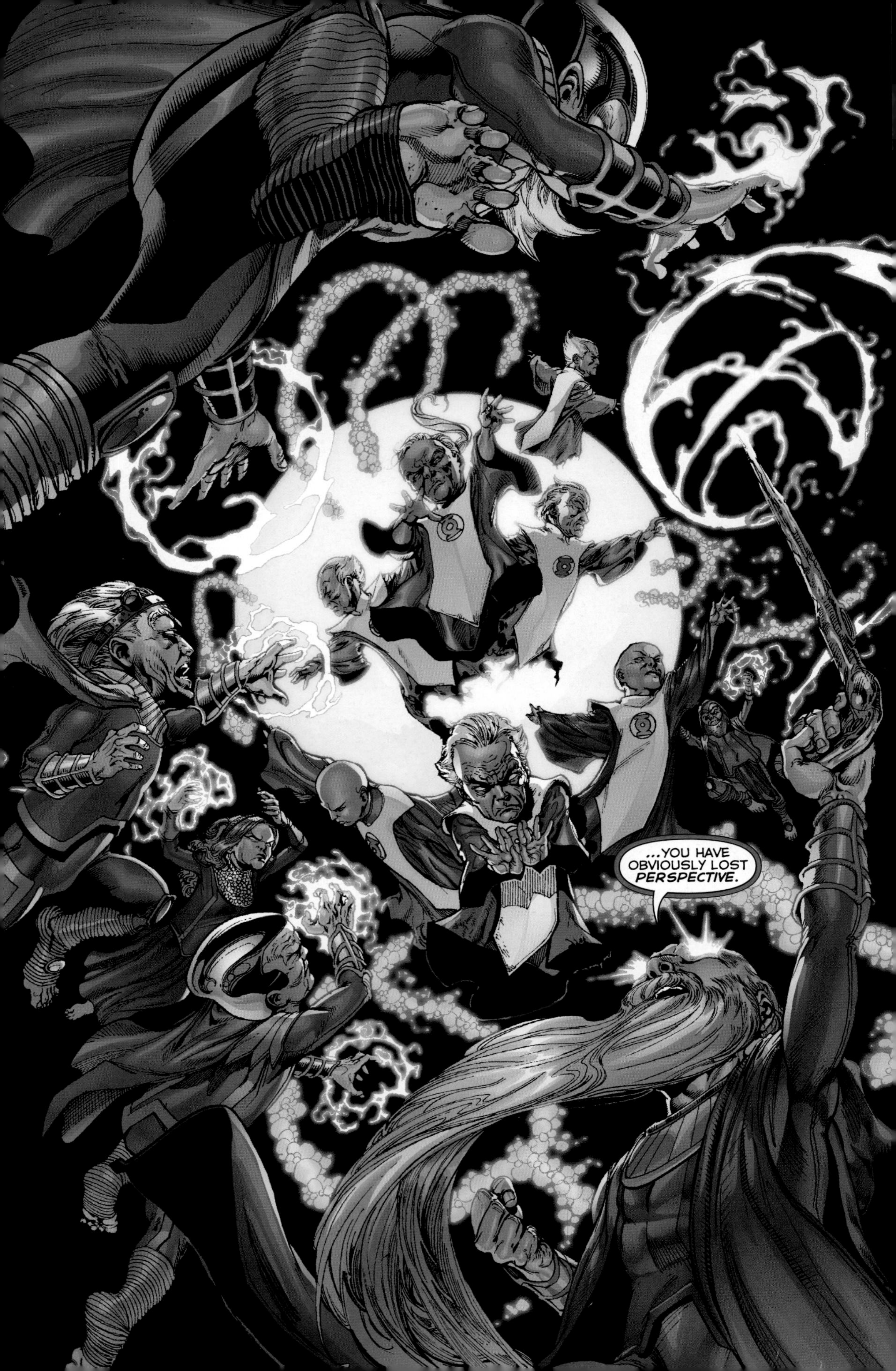
...YOU HAVE OBVIOUSLY LOST PERSPECTIVE.

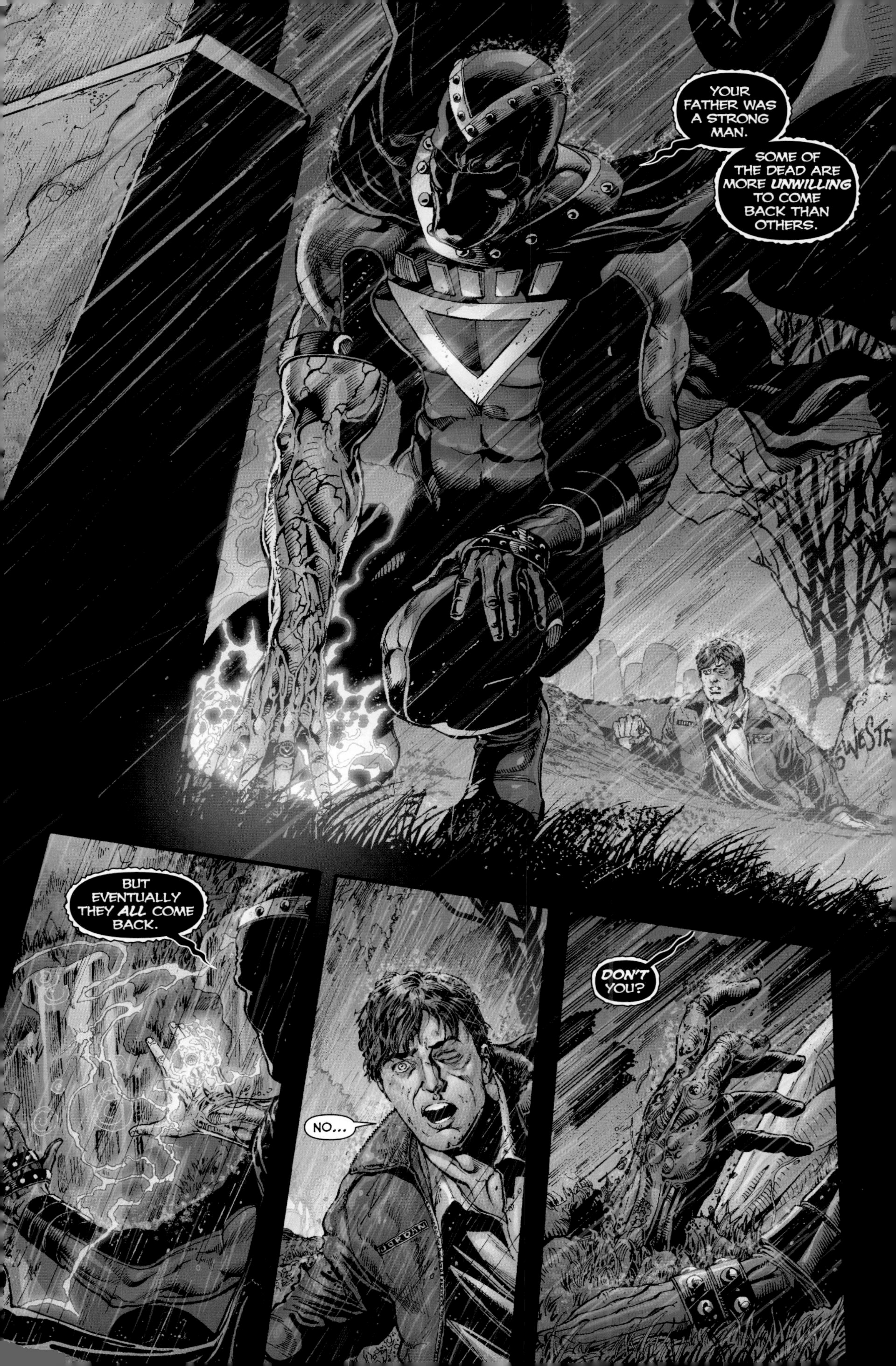
YOUR FATHER WAS A STRONG MAN.
SOME OF THE DEAD ARE MORE UNWILLING TO COME BACK THAN OTHERS.
BUT EVENTUALLY THEY ALL COME BACK.
NO...
DON'T YOU?
JORDAN

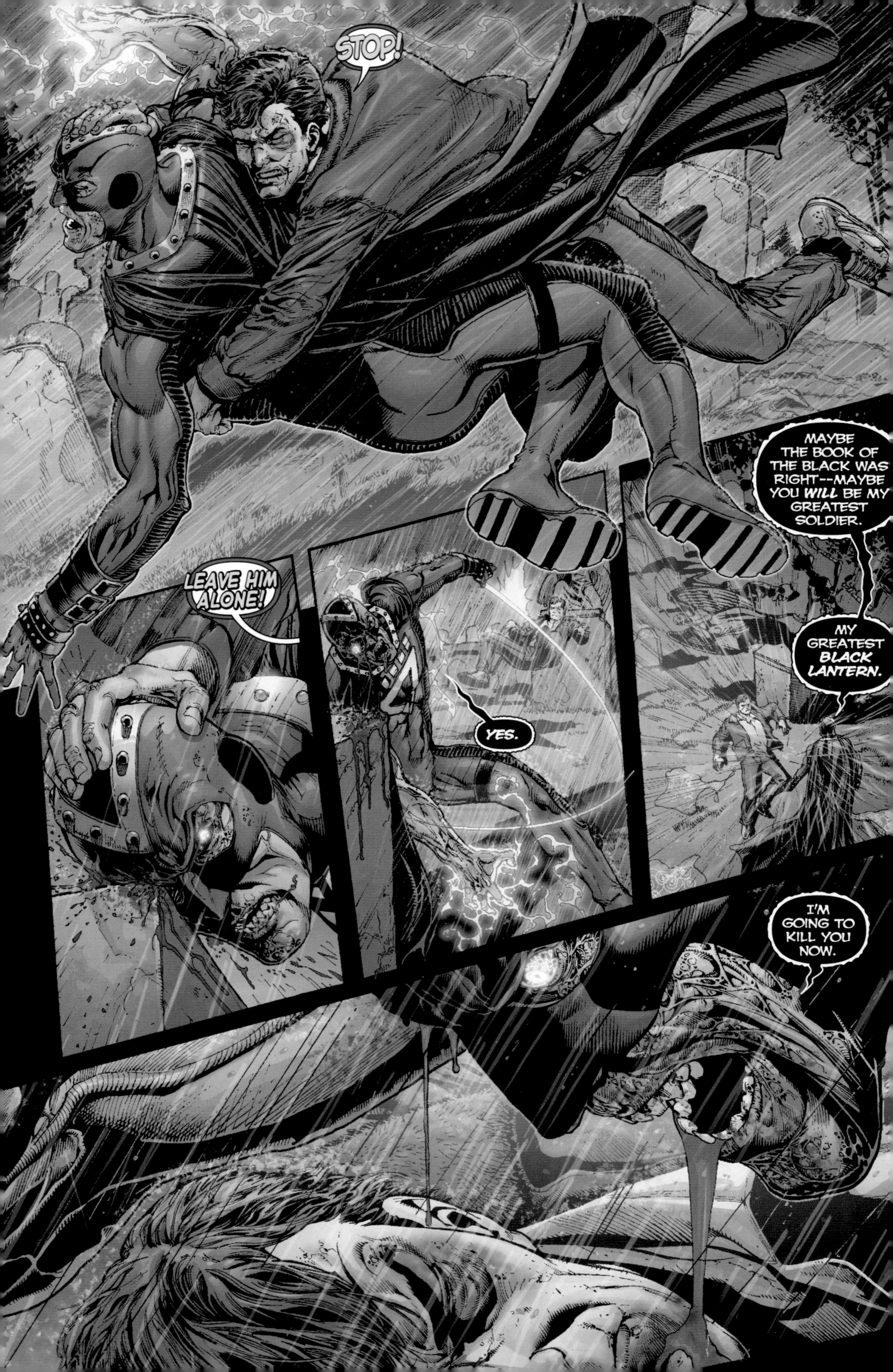
STOP!
LEAVE HIM ALONE!
YES.
MAYBE THE BOOK OF THE BLACK WAS RIGHT--MAYBE YOU WILL BE MY GREATEST SOLDIER.
MY GREATEST BLACK LANTERN.
I'M GOING TO KILL YOU NOW.

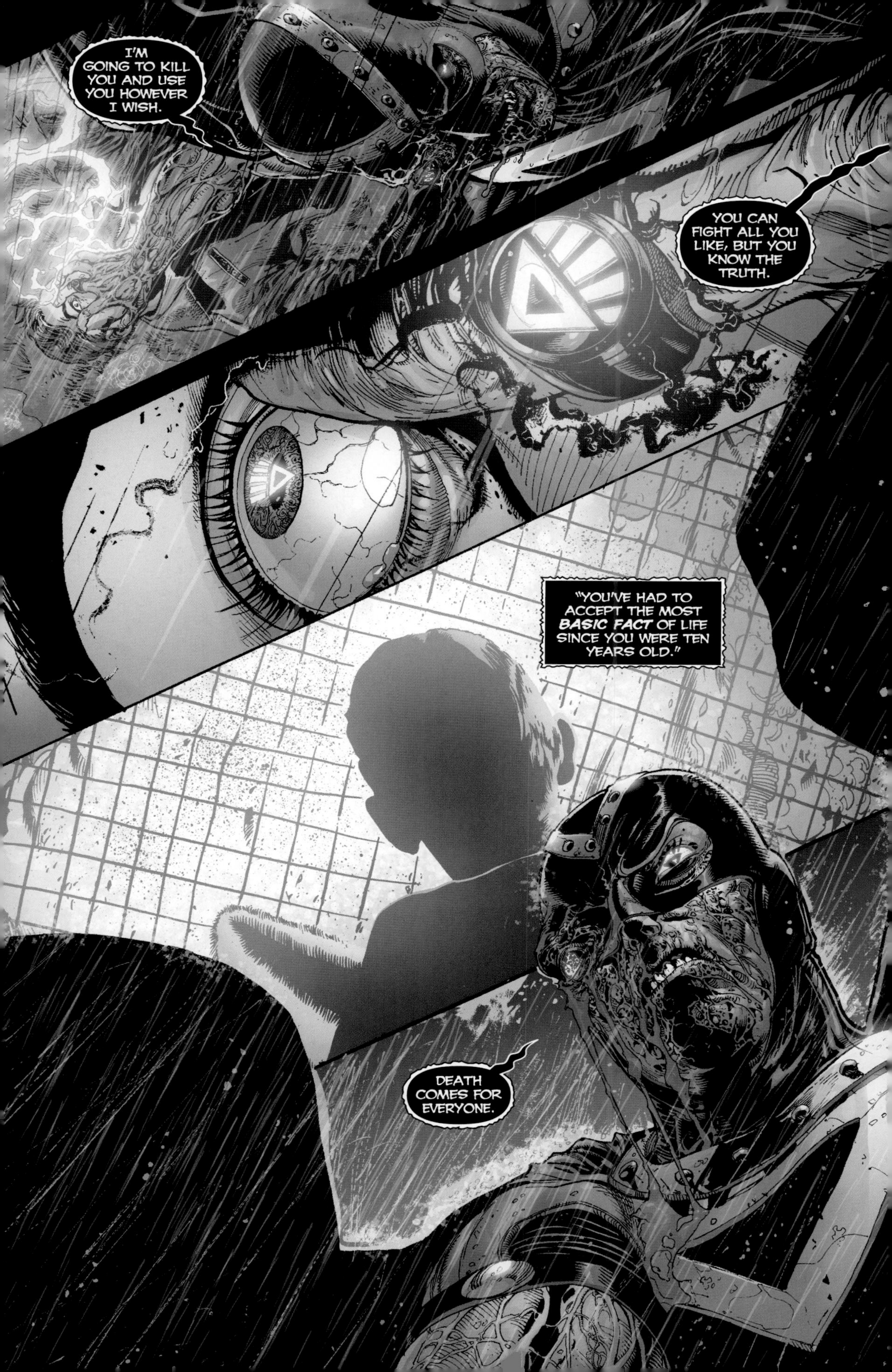
I'M GOING TO KILL YOU AND USE YOU HOWEVER I WISH.
YOU CAN FIGHT ALL YOU LIKE, BUT YOU KNOW THE TRUTH.
"YOU'VE HAD TO ACCEPT THE MOST *BASIC FACT* OF LIFE SINCE YOU WERE TEN YEARS OLD."
DEATH COMES FOR EVERYONE.

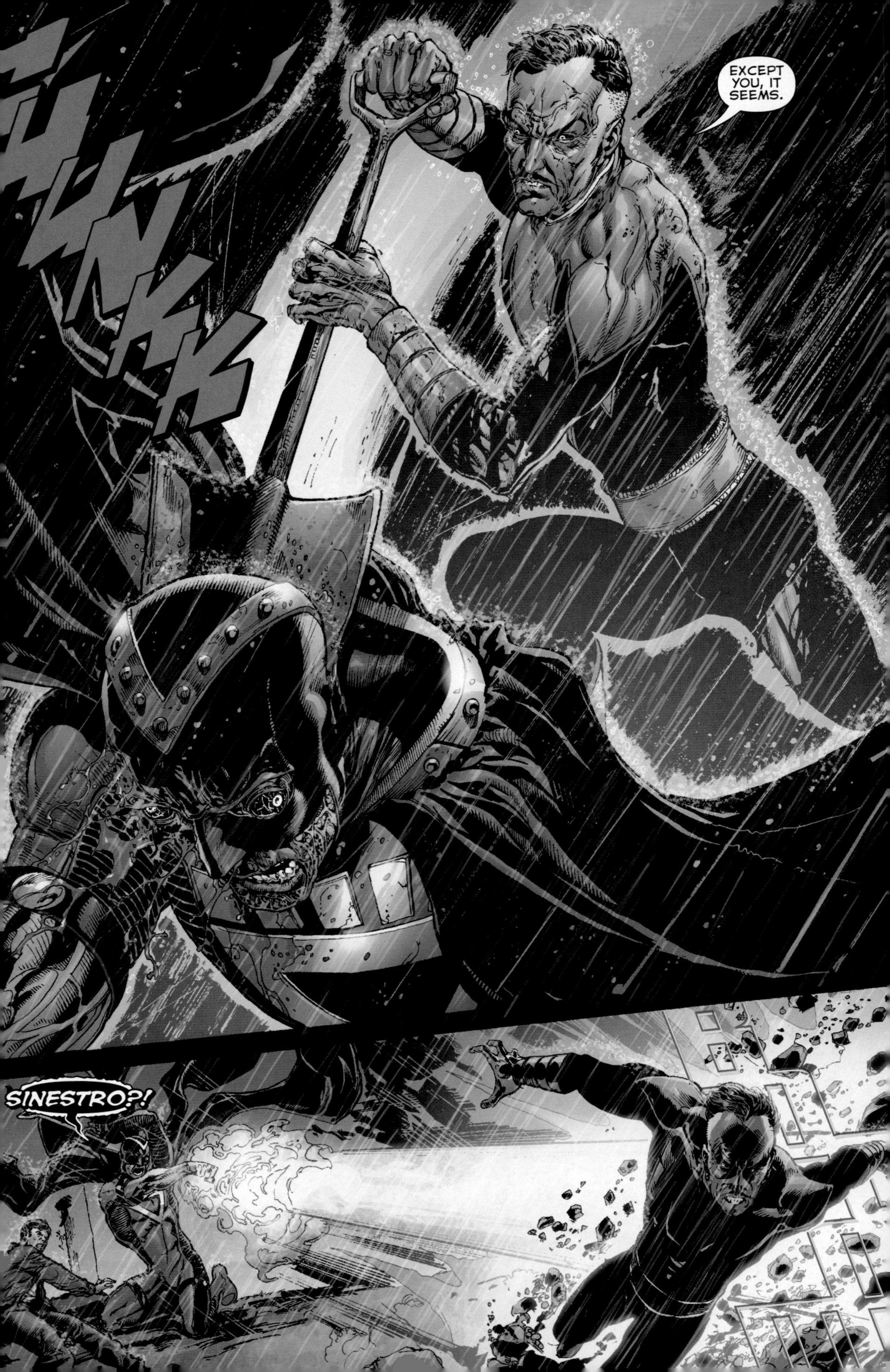
THUNK
EXCEPT YOU, IT SEEMS.
SINESTRO?!

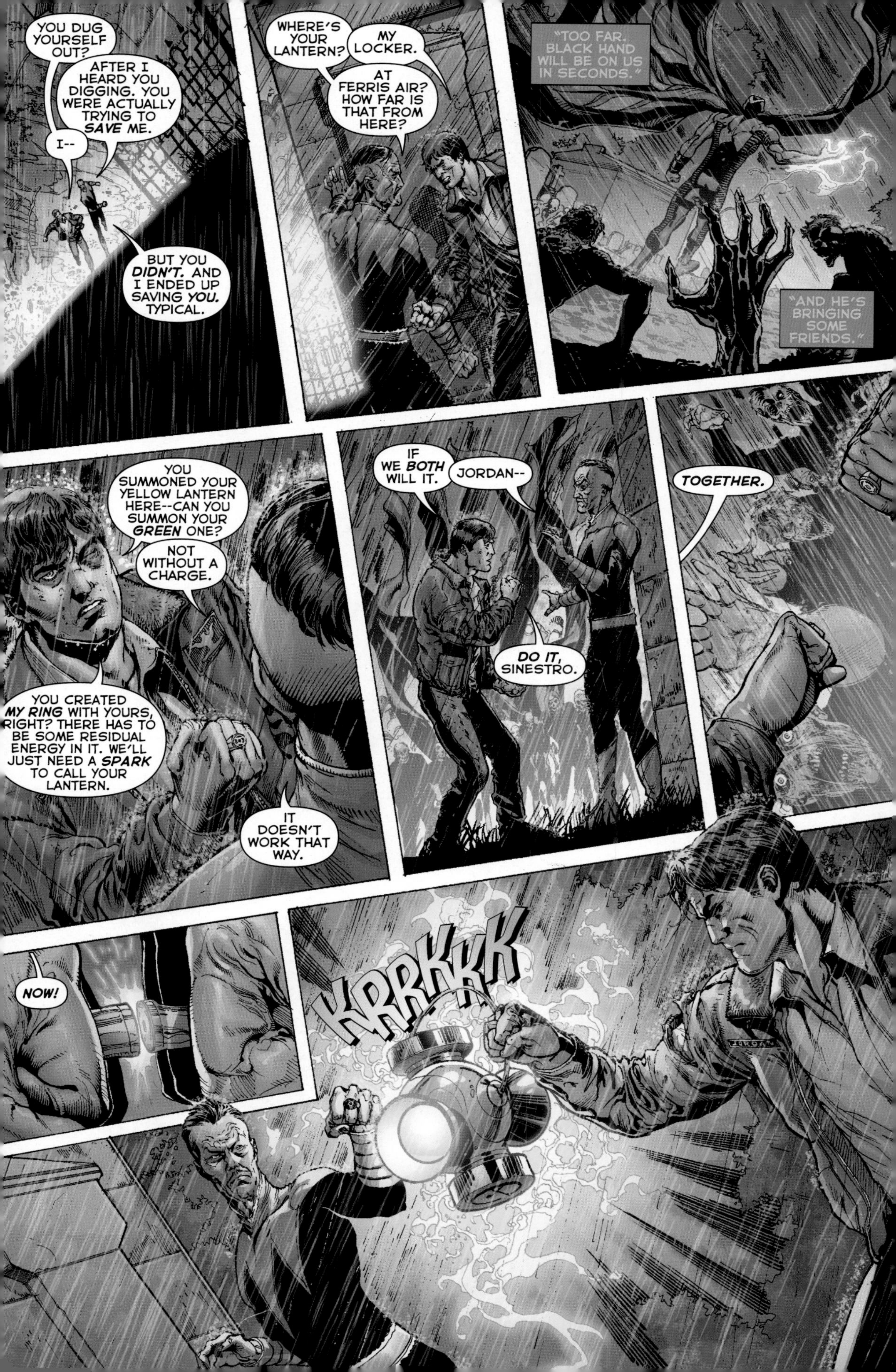

YOU DUG YOURSELF OUT?
AFTER I HEARD YOU DIGGING. YOU WERE ACTUALLY TRYING TO *SAVE* ME.
I--
BUT YOU *DIDN'T.* AND I ENDED UP SAVING *YOU.* TYPICAL.
WHERE'S YOUR LANTERN?
MY LOCKER.
AT FERRIS AIR? HOW FAR IS THAT FROM HERE?
"TOO FAR. BLACK HAND WILL BE ON US IN SECONDS."
"AND HE'S BRINGING SOME FRIENDS."
YOU SUMMONED YOUR YELLOW LANTERN HERE--CAN YOU SUMMON YOUR *GREEN* ONE?
NOT WITHOUT A CHARGE.
YOU CREATED *MY RING* WITH YOURS, RIGHT? THERE HAS TO BE SOME RESIDUAL ENERGY IN IT. WE'LL JUST NEED A *SPARK* TO CALL YOUR LANTERN.
IT DOESN'T WORK THAT WAY.
IF WE *BOTH* WILL IT.
JORDAN--
DO IT, SINESTRO.
TOGETHER.
NOW!
KRRKKK

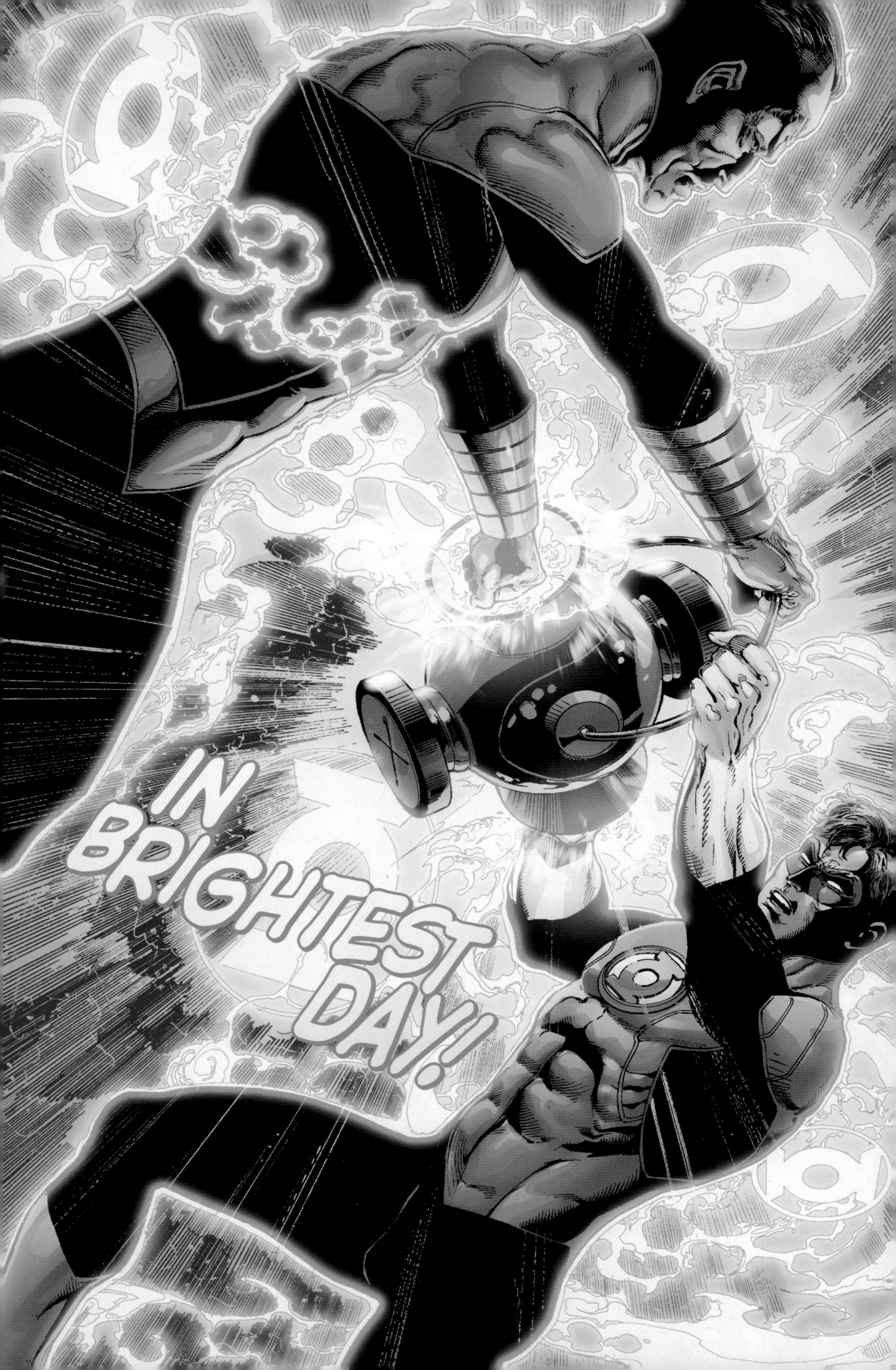
IN BRIGHTEST DAY!!

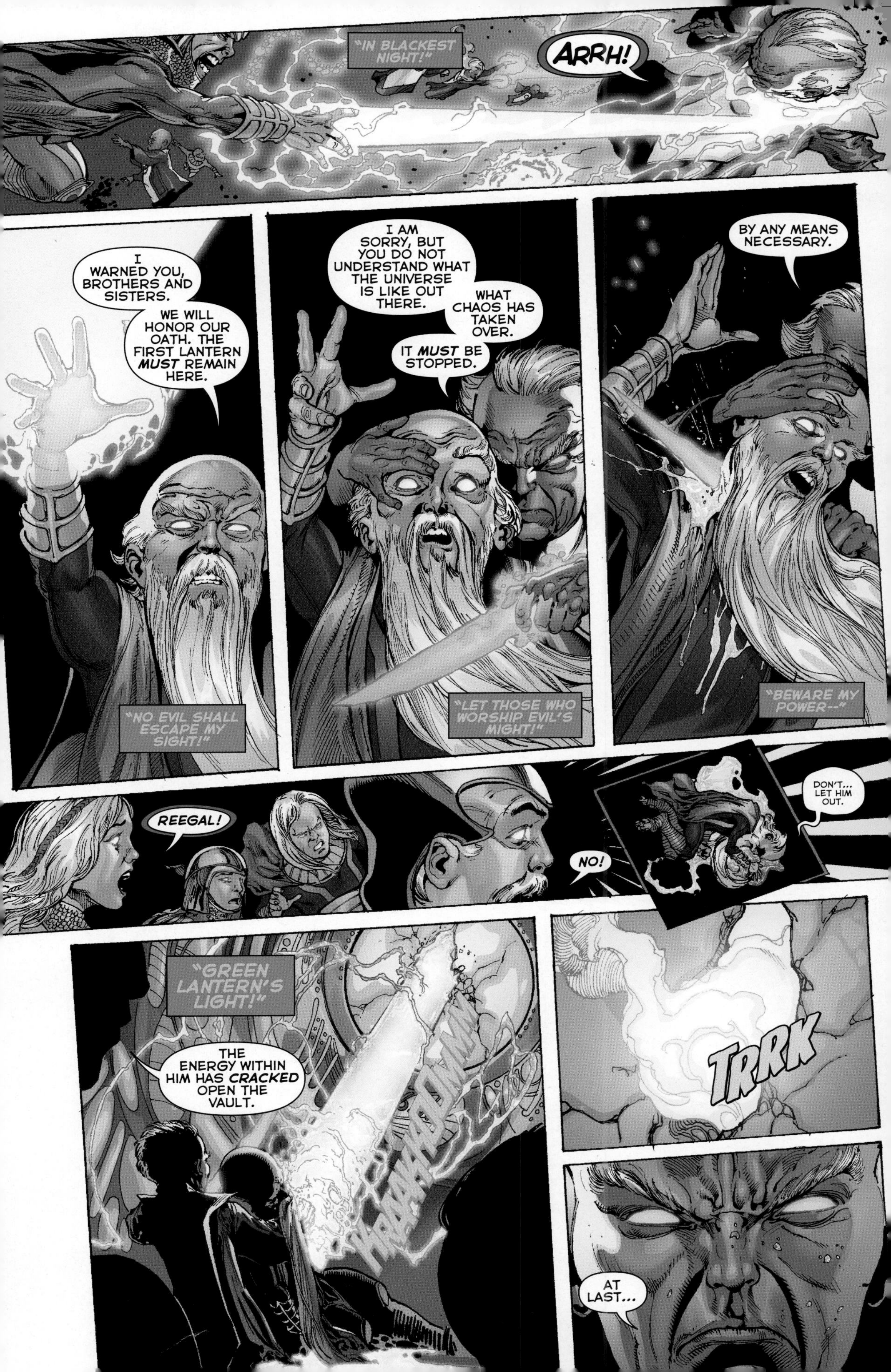
"IN BLACKEST NIGHT!"
ARRH!
I WARNED YOU, BROTHERS AND SISTERS.
WE WILL HONOR OUR OATH. THE FIRST LANTERN MUST REMAIN HERE.
"NO EVIL SHALL ESCAPE MY SIGHT!"
I AM SORRY, BUT YOU DO NOT UNDERSTAND WHAT THE UNIVERSE IS LIKE OUT THERE.
WHAT CHAOS HAS TAKEN OVER.
IT MUST BE STOPPED.
"LET THOSE WHO WORSHIP EVIL'S MIGHT!"
BY ANY MEANS NECESSARY.
"BEWARE MY POWER--"
REEGAL!
NO!
DON'T... LET HIM OUT.
"GREEN LANTERN'S LIGHT!"
THE ENERGY WITHIN HIM HAS CRACKED OPEN THE VAULT.
KRAAKOOMM
TRRK
AT LAST...

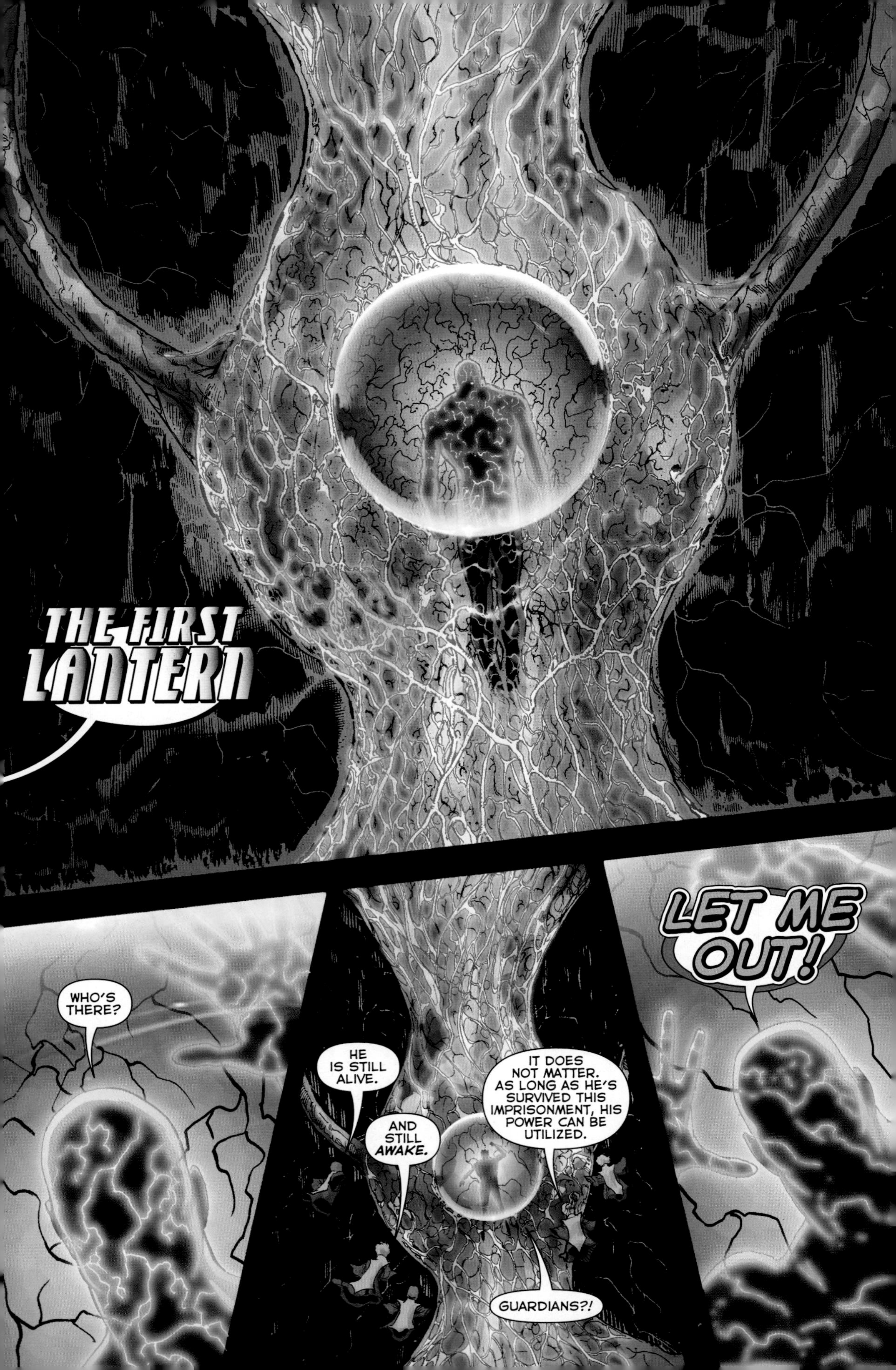
THE FIRST LANTERN
WHO'S THERE?
HE IS STILL ALIVE.
AND STILL AWAKE.
IT DOES NOT MATTER. AS LONG AS HE'S SURVIVED THIS IMPRISONMENT, HIS POWER CAN BE UTILIZED.
GUARDIANS?!
LET ME OUT!

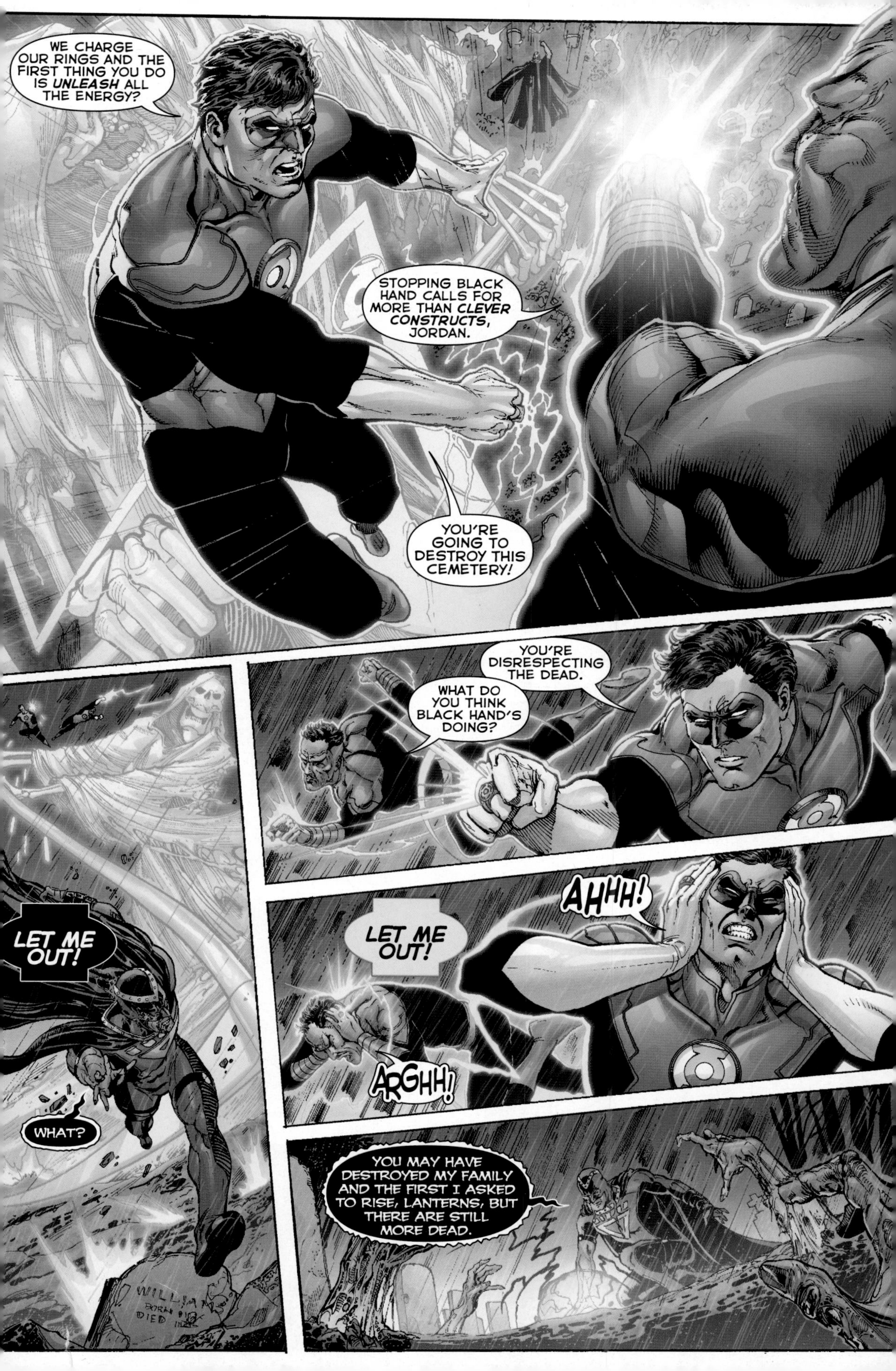
WE CHARGE OUR RINGS AND THE FIRST THING YOU DO IS *UNLEASH* ALL THE ENERGY?
STOPPING BLACK HAND CALLS FOR MORE THAN *CLEVER CONSTRUCTS*, JORDAN.
YOU'RE GOING TO DESTROY THIS CEMETERY!
YOU'RE DISRESPECTING THE DEAD.
WHAT DO YOU THINK BLACK HAND'S DOING?
LET ME OUT!
WHAT?
LET ME OUT!
AHHH!
ARGHH!
YOU MAY HAVE DESTROYED MY FAMILY AND THE FIRST I ASKED TO RISE, LANTERNS, BUT THERE ARE STILL MORE DEAD.

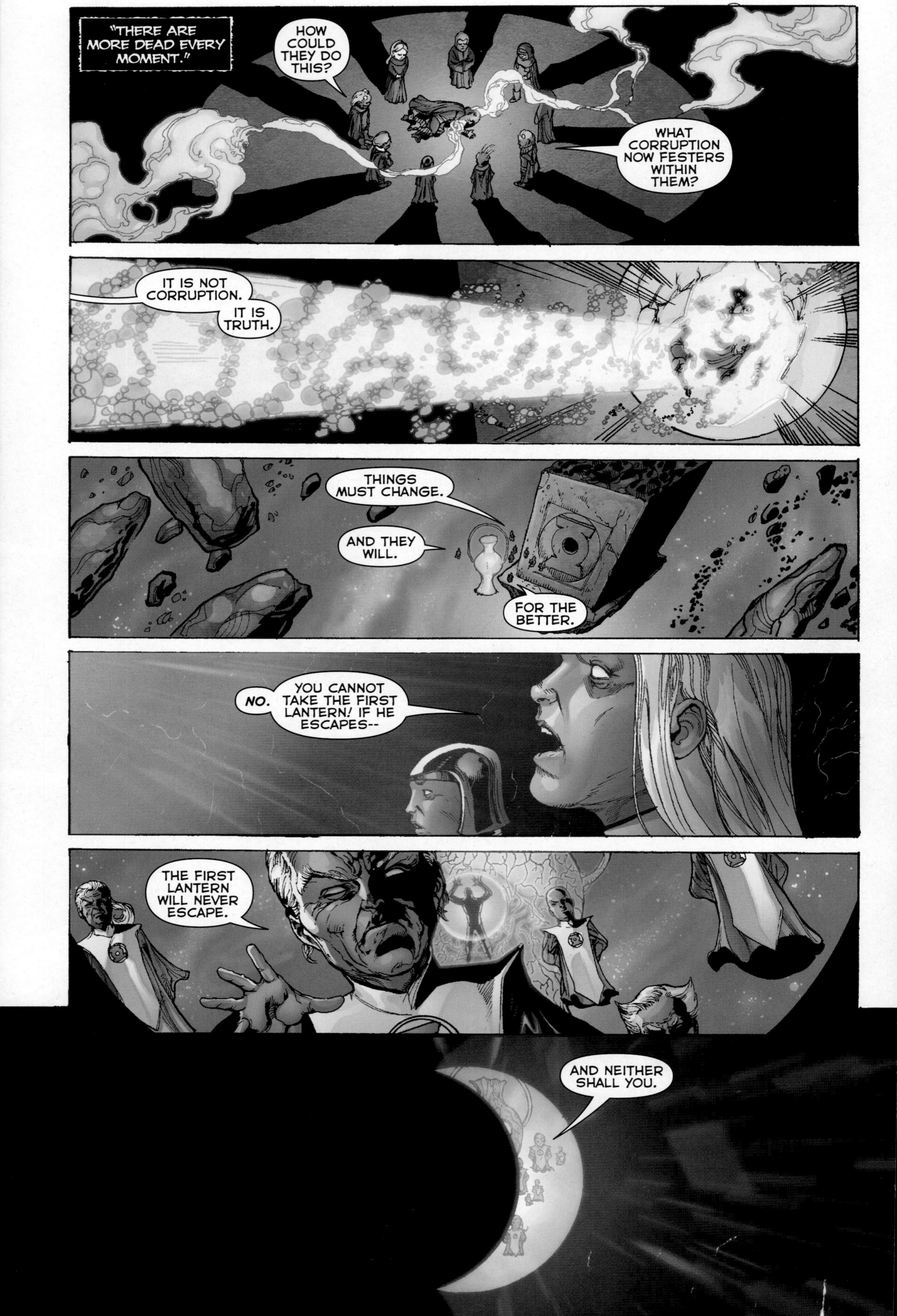
"THERE ARE MORE DEAD EVERY MOMENT."
HOW COULD THEY DO THIS?
WHAT CORRUPTION NOW FESTERS WITHIN THEM?
IT IS NOT CORRUPTION.
IT IS TRUTH.
THINGS MUST CHANGE.
AND THEY WILL.
FOR THE BETTER.
NO.
YOU CANNOT TAKE THE FIRST LANTERN! IF HE ESCAPES--
THE FIRST LANTERN WILL NEVER ESCAPE.
AND NEITHER SHALL YOU.

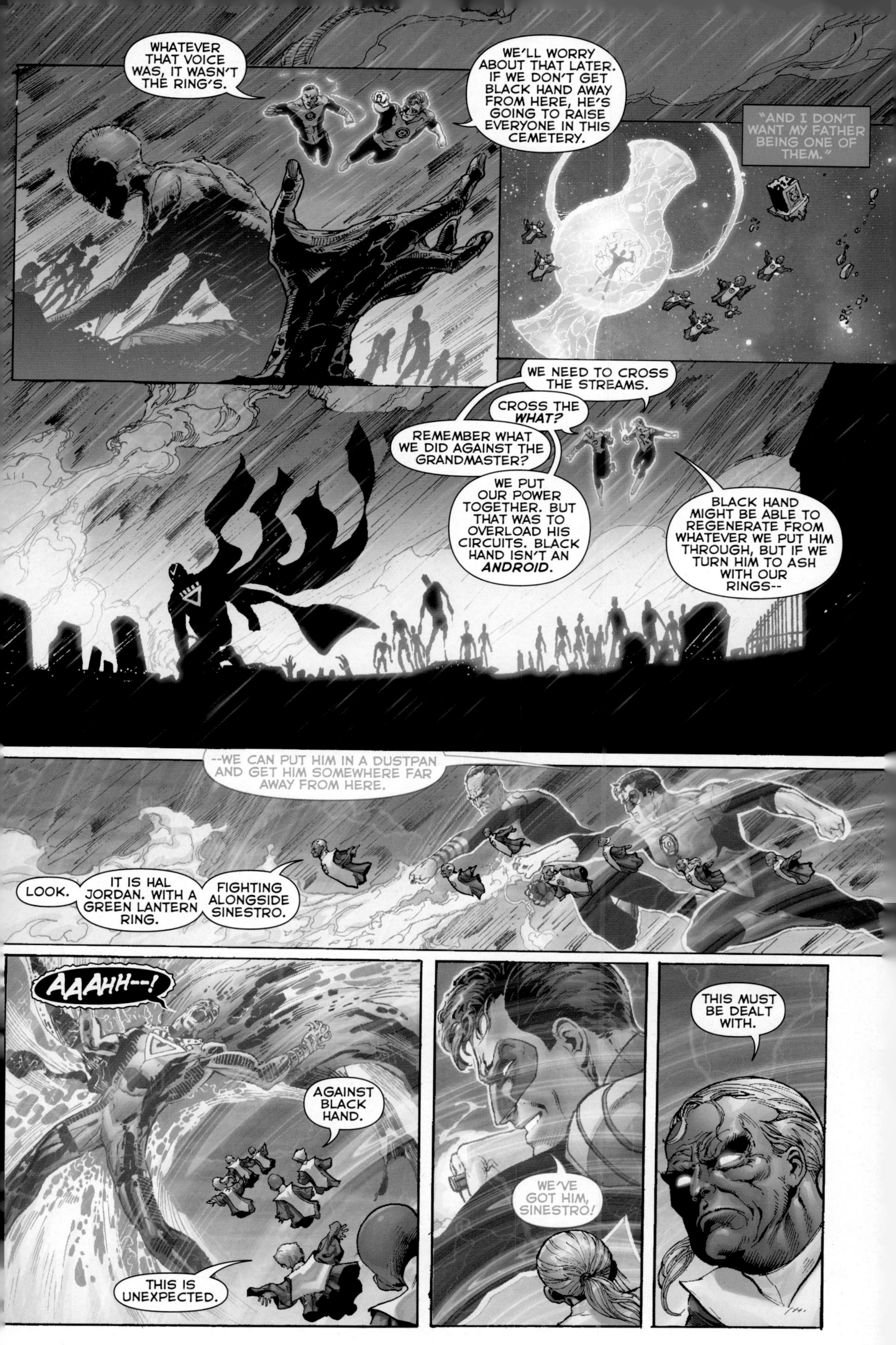
WHATEVER THAT VOICE WAS, IT WASN'T THE RING'S.
WE'LL WORRY ABOUT THAT LATER. IF WE DON'T GET BLACK HAND AWAY FROM HERE, HE'S GOING TO RAISE EVERYONE IN THIS CEMETERY.
"AND I DON'T WANT MY FATHER BEING ONE OF THEM."
WE NEED TO CROSS THE STREAMS.
CROSS THE *WHAT?*
REMEMBER WHAT WE DID AGAINST THE GRANDMASTER?
WE PUT OUR POWER TOGETHER. BUT THAT WAS TO OVERLOAD HIS CIRCUITS. BLACK HAND ISN'T AN *ANDROID*.
BLACK HAND MIGHT BE ABLE TO REGENERATE FROM WHATEVER WE PUT HIM THROUGH, BUT IF WE TURN HIM TO ASH WITH OUR RINGS--
--WE CAN PUT HIM IN A DUSTPAN AND GET HIM SOMEWHERE FAR AWAY FROM HERE.
LOOK.
IT IS HAL JORDAN. WITH A GREEN LANTERN RING.
FIGHTING ALONGSIDE SINESTRO.
AAAHH--!
AGAINST BLACK HAND.
THIS IS UNEXPECTED.
WE'VE GOT HIM, SINESTRO!
THIS MUST BE DEALT WITH.

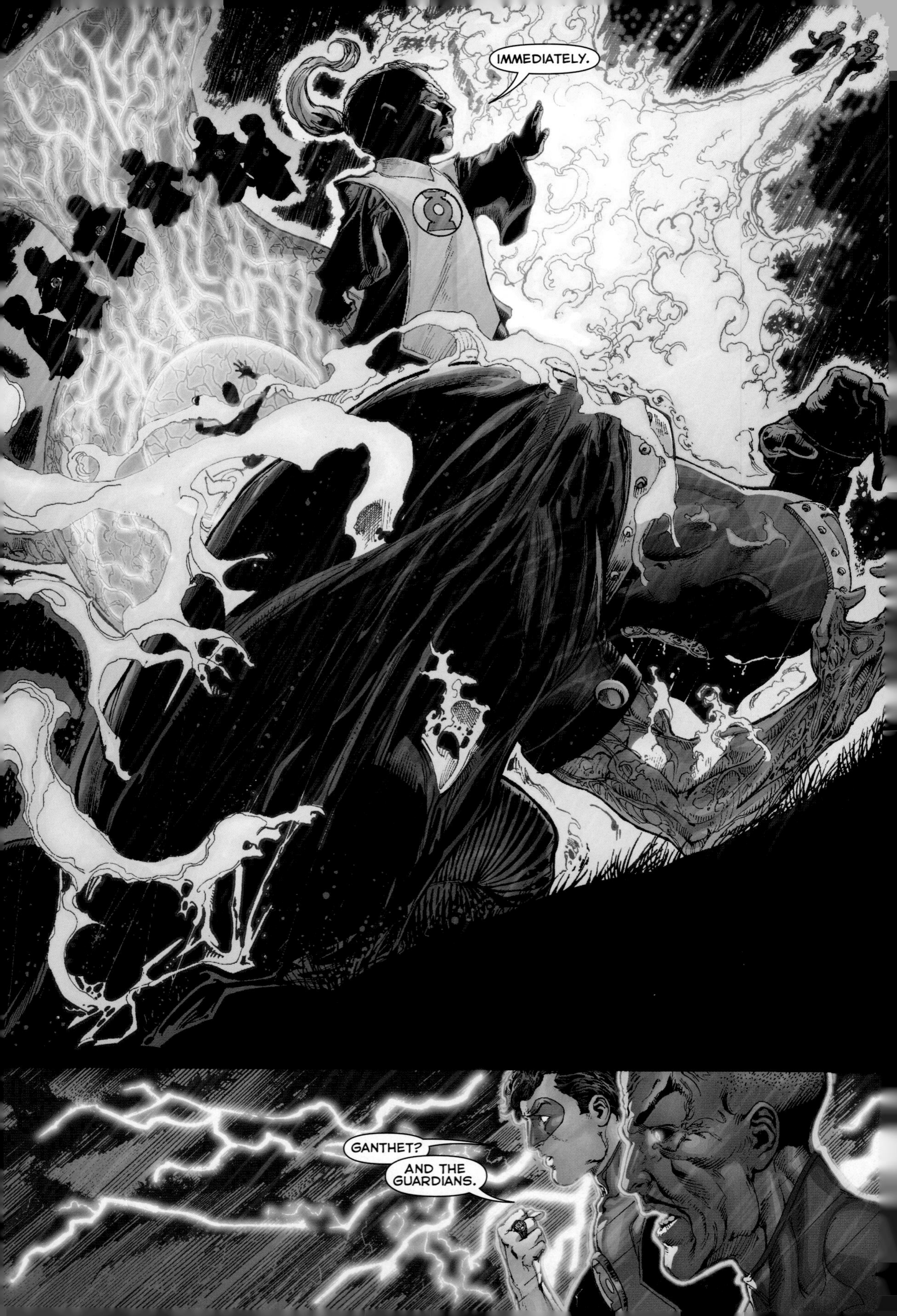
IMMEDIATELY.
GANTHET?
AND THE GUARDIANS.

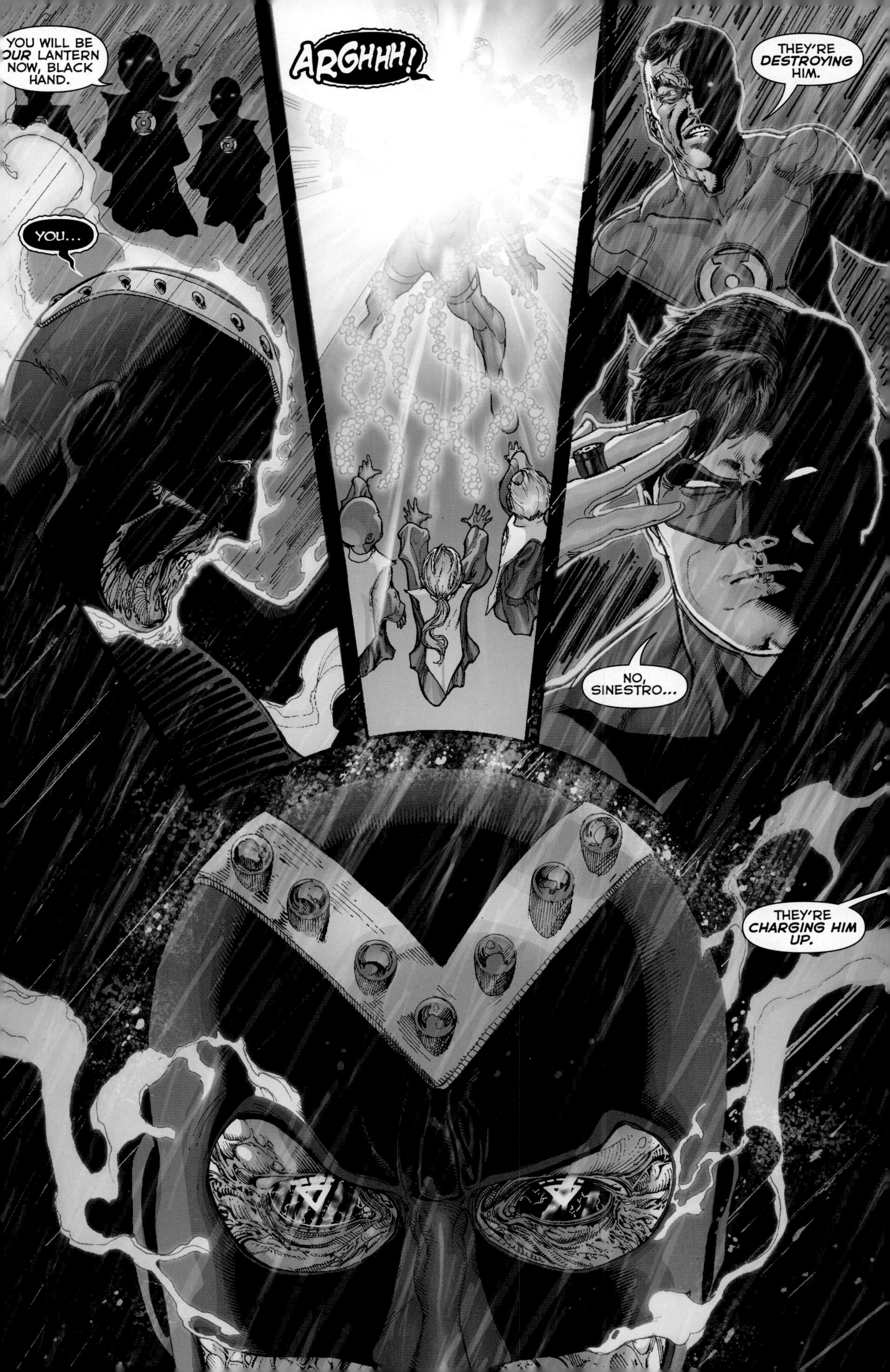
YOU WILL BE OUR LANTERN NOW, BLACK HAND.
YOU...
ARGHHH!
THEY'RE DESTROYING HIM.
NO, SINESTRO...
THEY'RE CHARGING HIM UP.

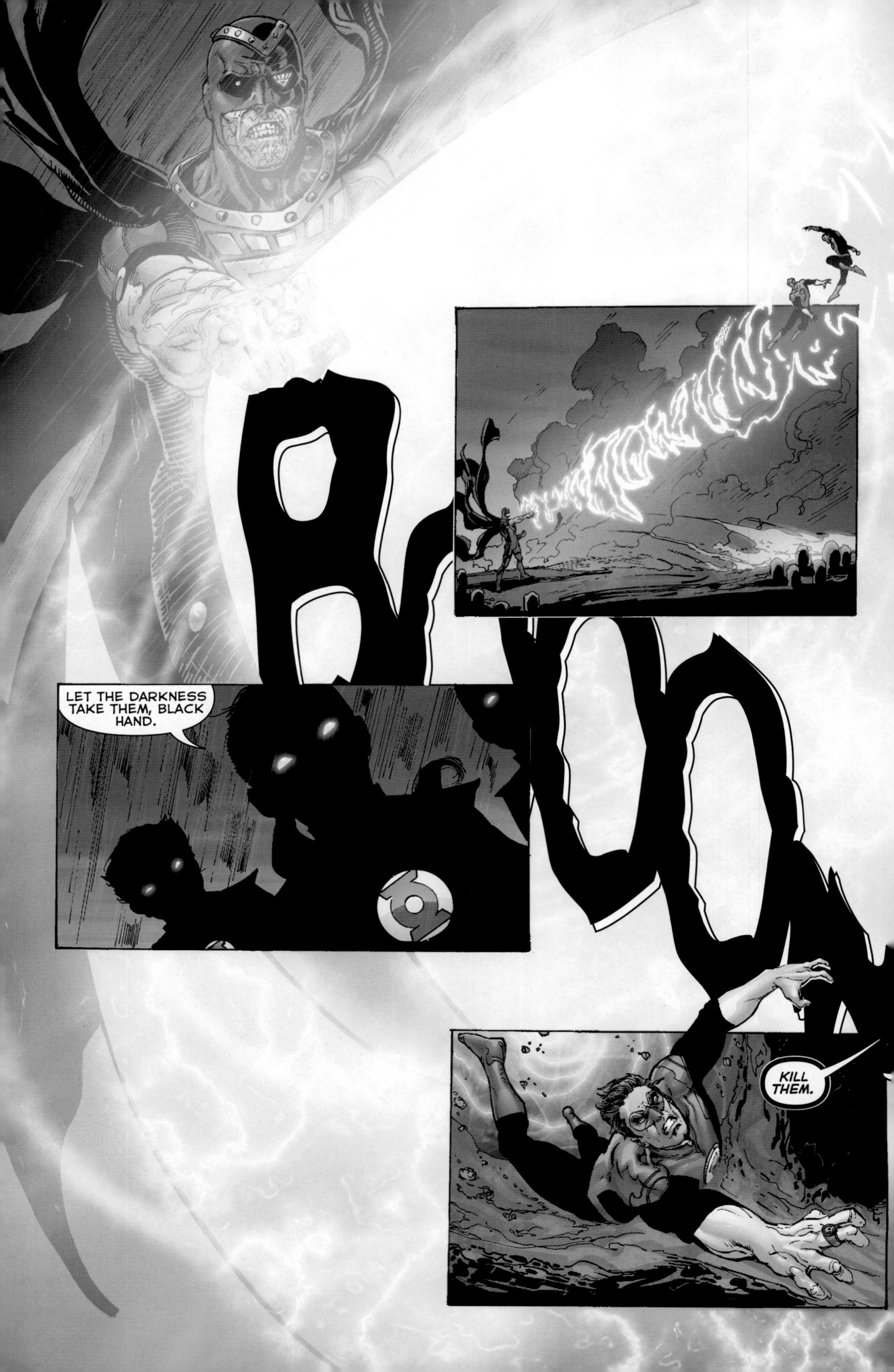
LET THE DARKNESS TAKE THEM, BLACK HAND.
KILL THEM.

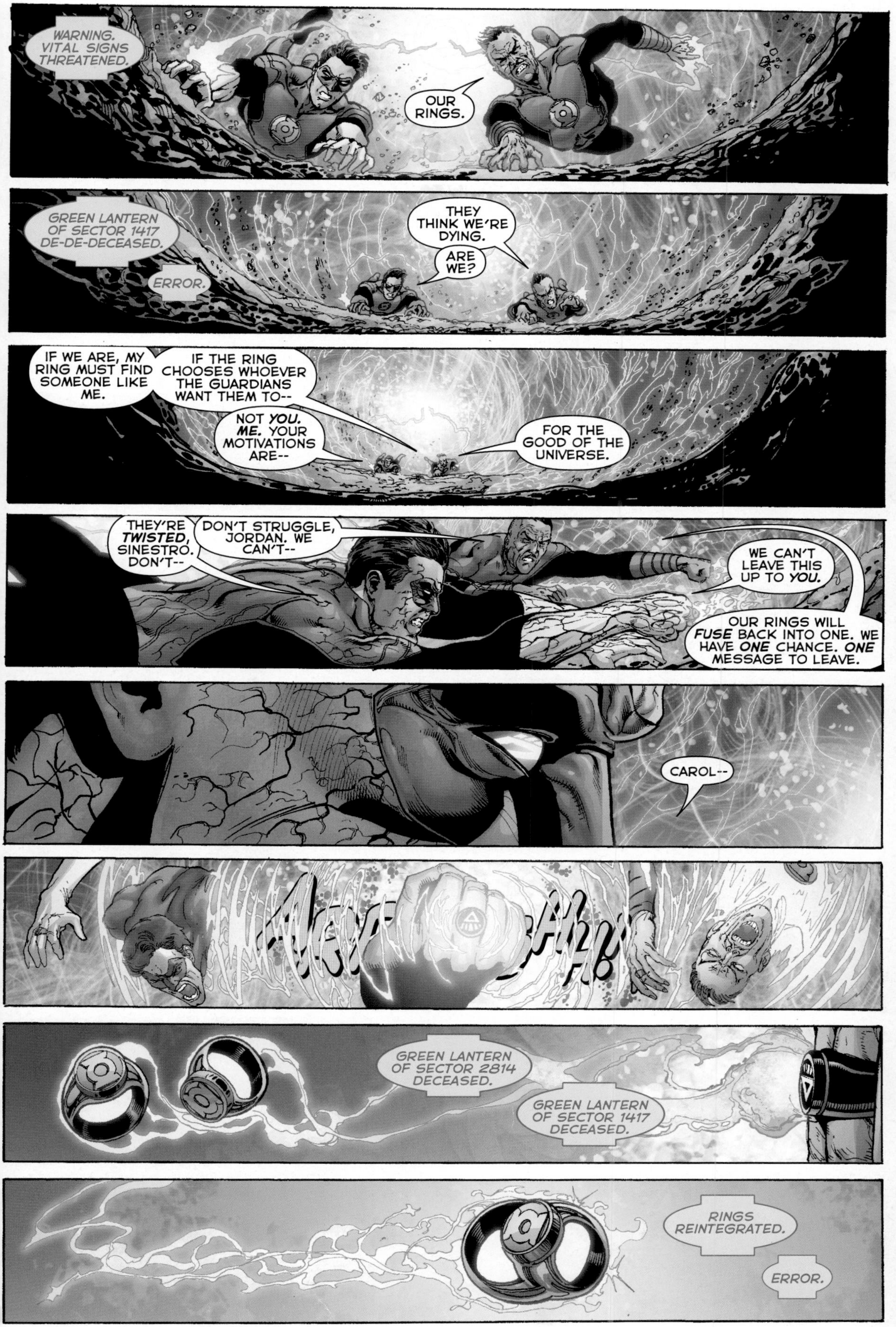
WARNING. VITAL SIGNS THREATENED.
OUR RINGS.
GREEN LANTERN OF SECTOR 1417 DE-DE-DECEASED.
ERROR.
THEY THINK WE'RE DYING.
ARE WE?
IF WE ARE, MY RING MUST FIND SOMEONE LIKE ME.
IF THE RING CHOOSES WHOEVER THE GUARDIANS WANT THEM TO--
NOT YOU. ME. YOUR MOTIVATIONS ARE--
FOR THE GOOD OF THE UNIVERSE.
THEY'RE TWISTED, SINESTRO. DON'T--
DON'T STRUGGLE, JORDAN. WE CAN'T--
WE CAN'T LEAVE THIS UP TO YOU.
OUR RINGS WILL FUSE BACK INTO ONE. WE HAVE ONE CHANCE. ONE MESSAGE TO LEAVE.
CAROL--
GREEN LANTERN OF SECTOR 2814 DECEASED.
GREEN LANTERN OF SECTOR 1417 DECEASED.
RINGS REINTEGRATED.
ERROR.

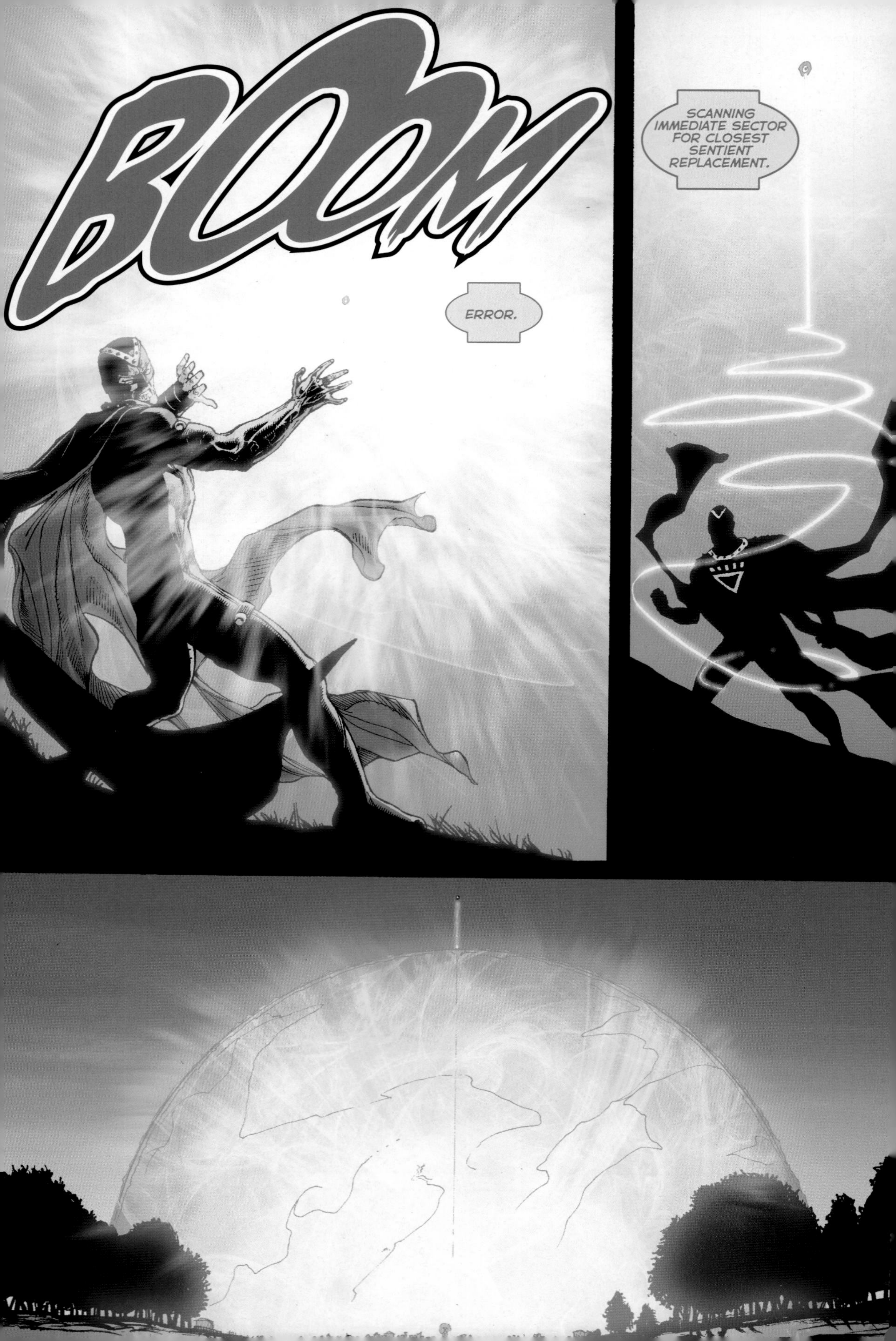
BOOM
ERROR.
SCANNING IMMEDIATE SECTOR FOR CLOSEST SENTIENT REPLACEMENT.

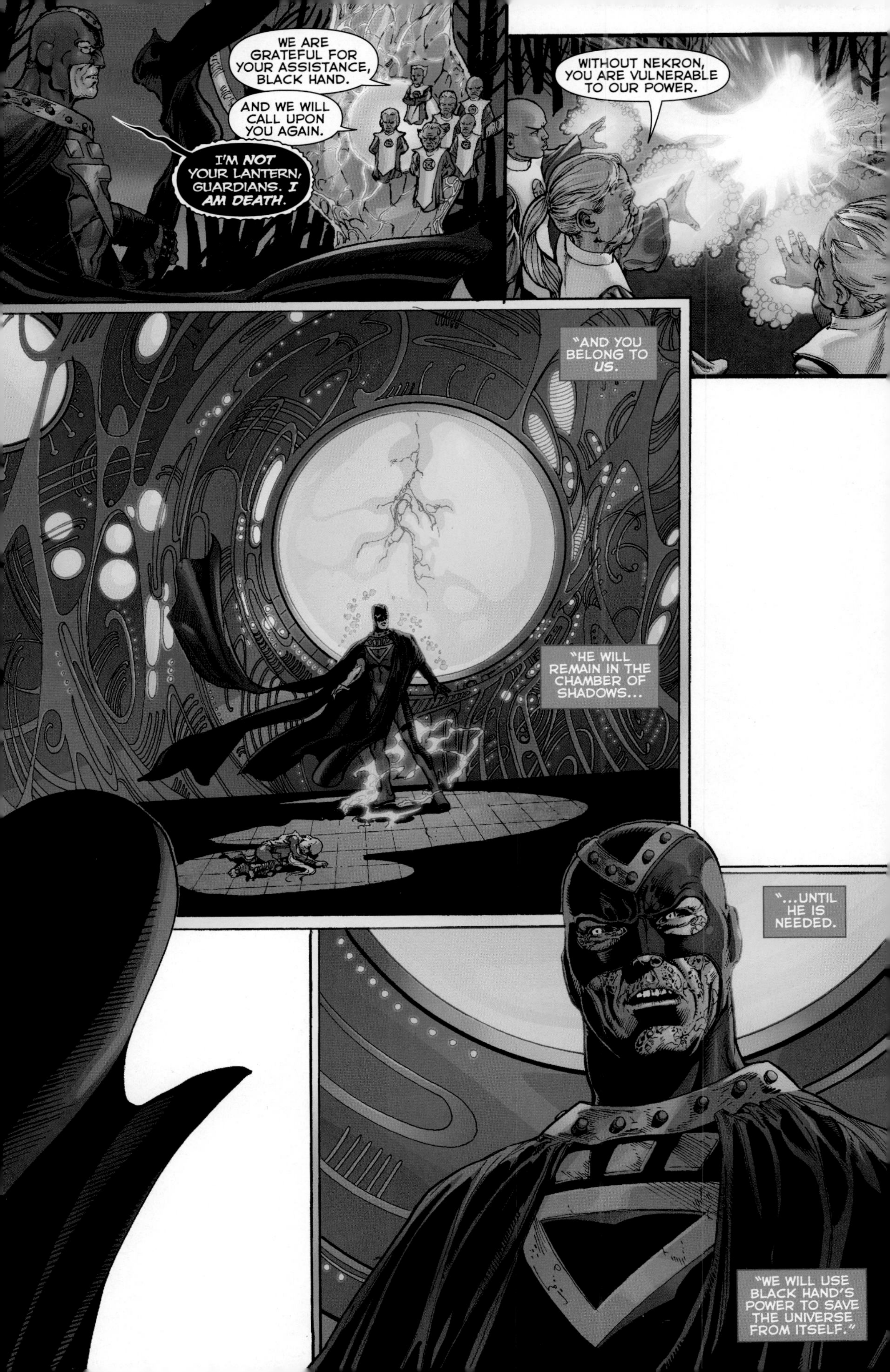
WE ARE GRATEFUL FOR YOUR ASSISTANCE, BLACK HAND.
AND WE WILL CALL UPON YOU AGAIN.
I'M NOT YOUR LANTERN, GUARDIANS. I AM DEATH.
WITHOUT NEKRON, YOU ARE VULNERABLE TO OUR POWER.
"AND YOU BELONG TO US.
"HE WILL REMAIN IN THE CHAMBER OF SHADOWS...
"...UNTIL HE IS NEEDED.
"WE WILL USE BLACK HAND'S POWER TO SAVE THE UNIVERSE FROM ITSELF."

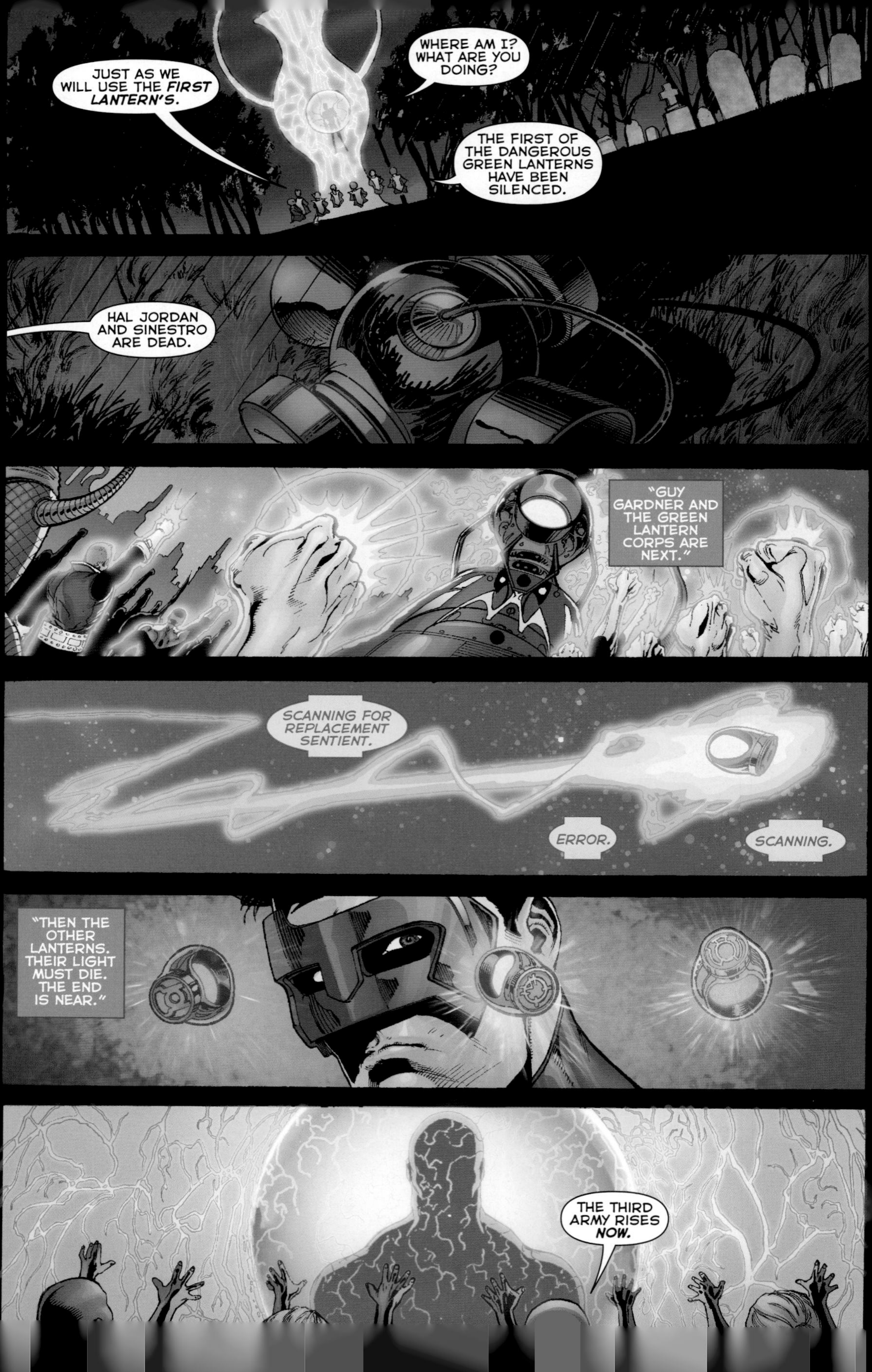

JUST AS WE WILL USE THE *FIRST LANTERN'S*.
WHERE AM I? WHAT ARE YOU DOING?
THE FIRST OF THE DANGEROUS GREEN LANTERNS HAVE BEEN SILENCED.
HAL JORDAN AND SINESTRO ARE DEAD.
"GUY GARDNER AND THE GREEN LANTERN CORPS ARE NEXT."
SCANNING FOR REPLACEMENT SENTIENT.
ERROR.
SCANNING.
"THEN THE OTHER LANTERNS. THEIR LIGHT MUST DIE. THE END IS NEAR."
THE THIRD ARMY RISES *NOW.*

EPILOGUE: THE FIRST SOLDIER

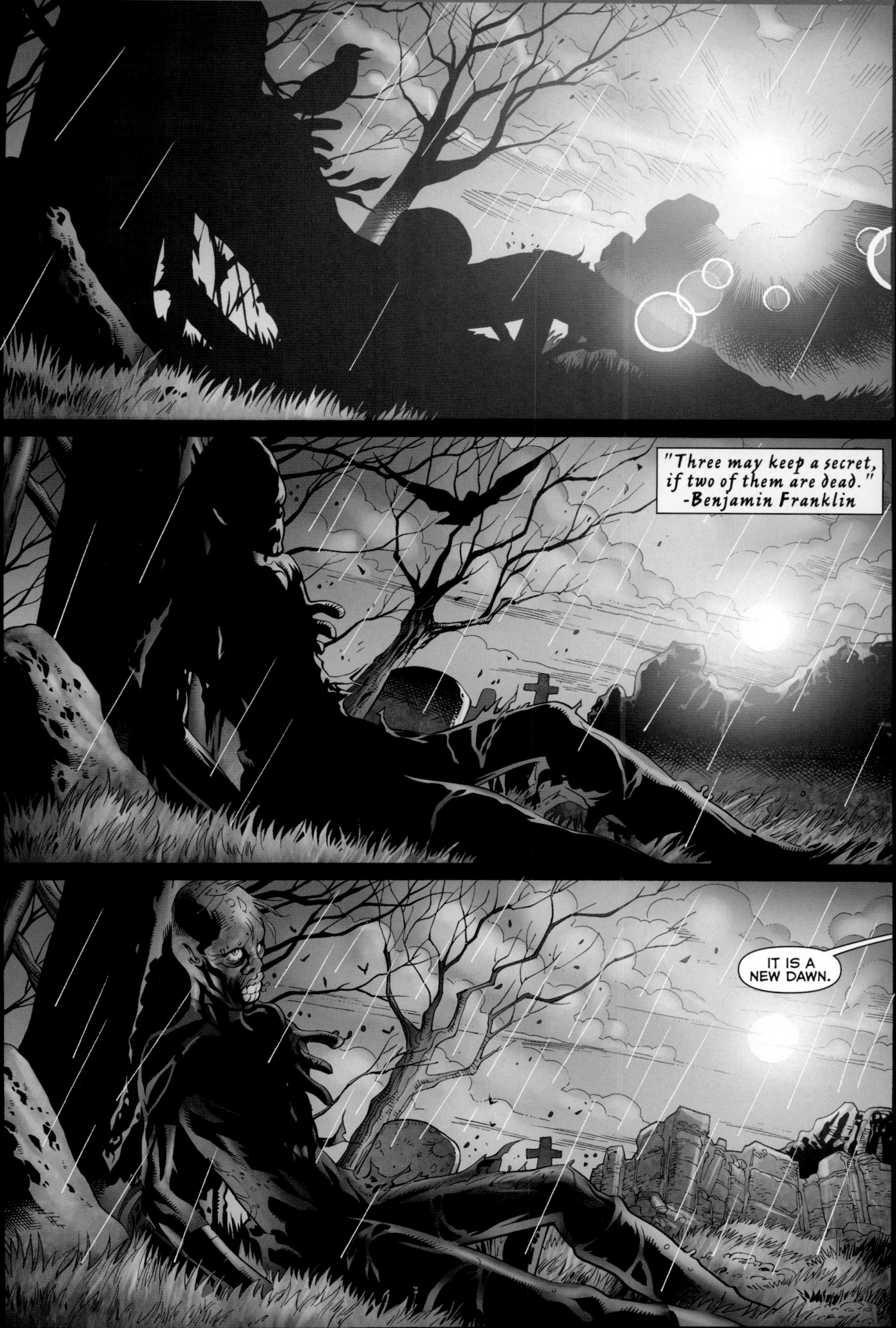

"Three may keep a secret, if two of them are dead."
-Benjamin Franklin
IT IS A NEW DAWN.

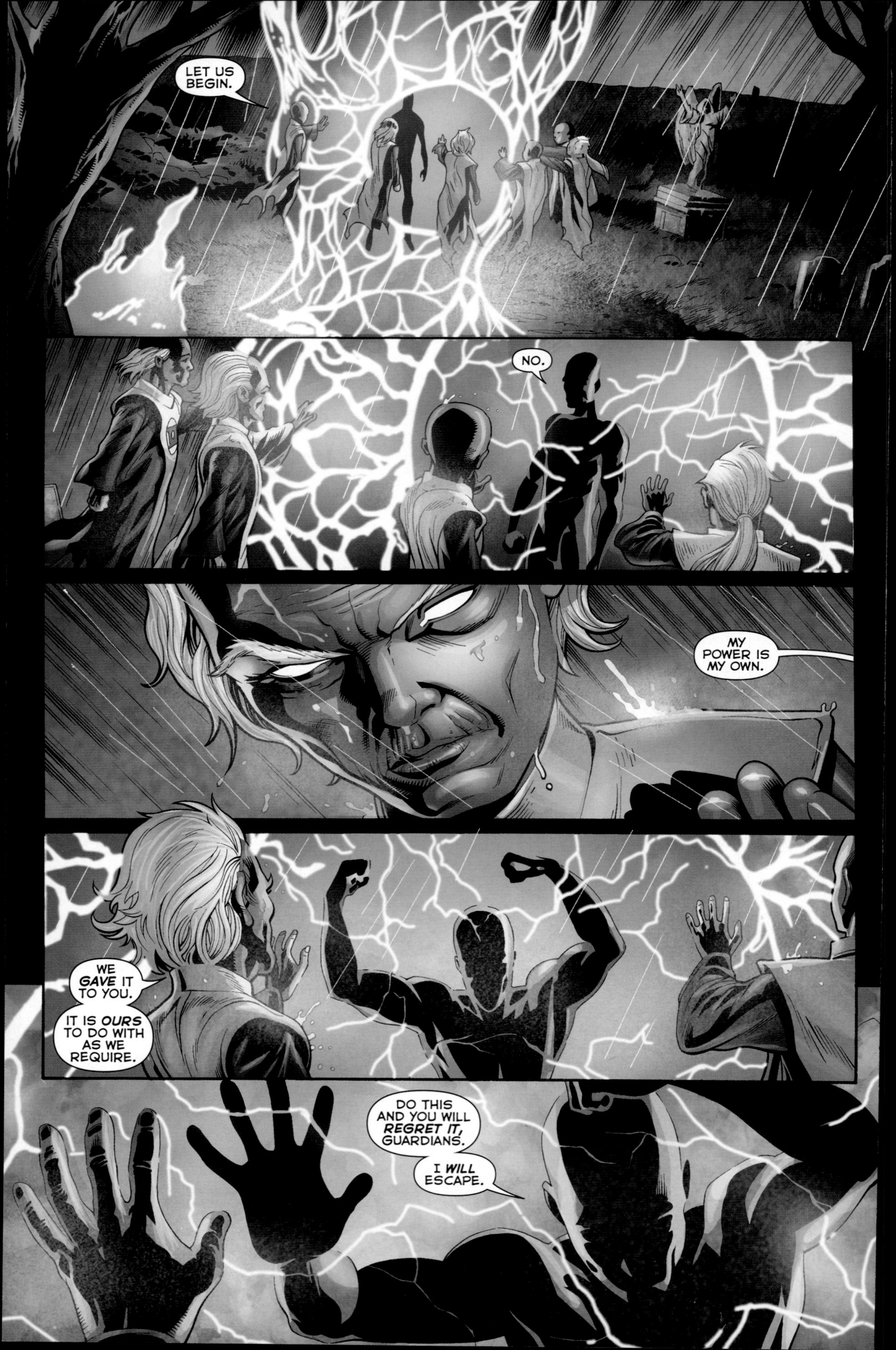
LET US BEGIN.
NO.
MY POWER IS MY OWN.
WE GAVE IT TO YOU.
IT IS OURS TO DO WITH AS WE REQUIRE.
DO THIS AND YOU WILL REGRET IT, GUARDIANS.
I WILL ESCAPE.

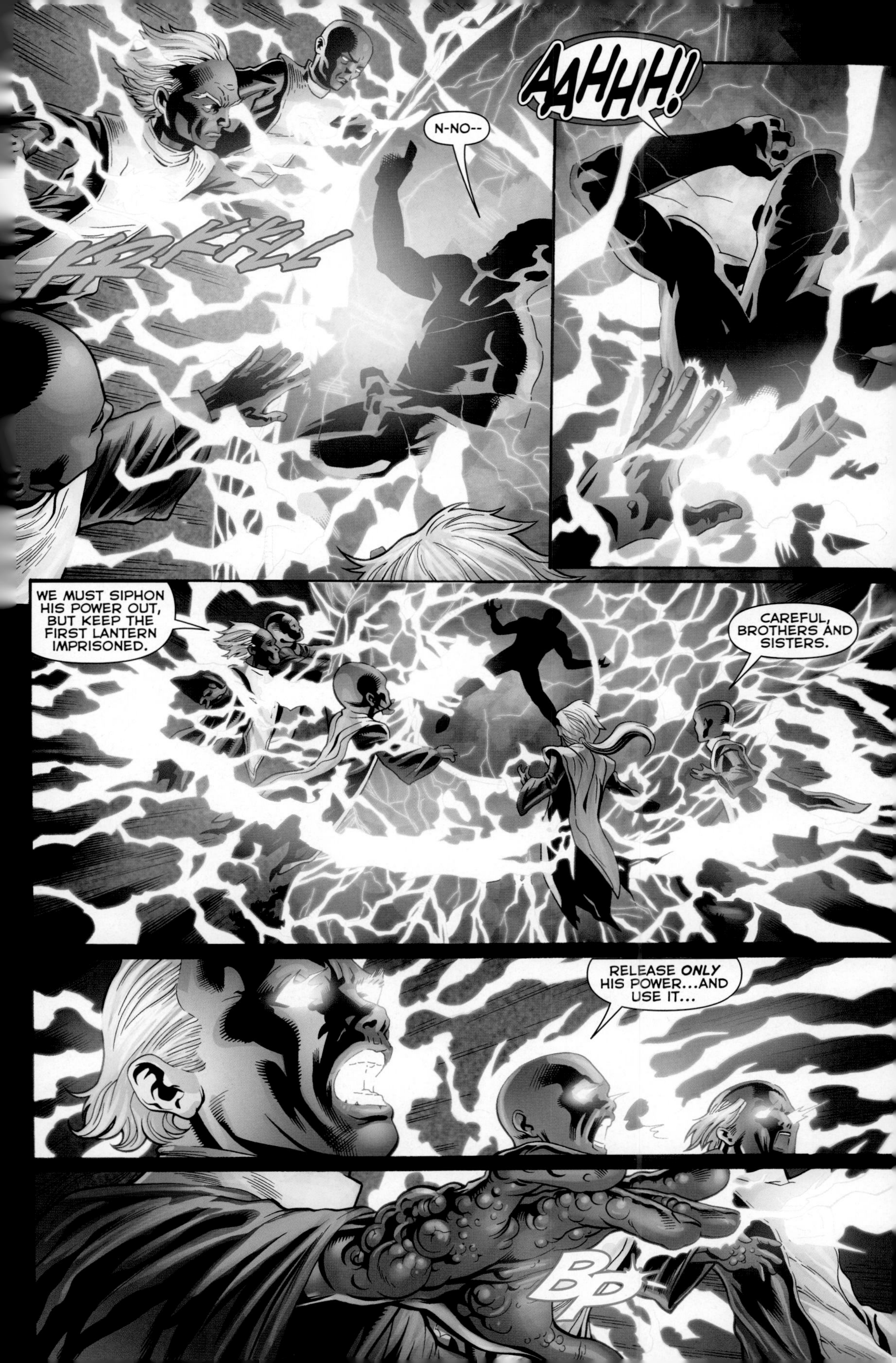
N-NO--
KRKKL
AAHHH!
WE MUST SIPHON HIS POWER OUT, BUT KEEP THE FIRST LANTERN IMPRISONED.
CAREFUL, BROTHERS AND SISTERS.
RELEASE ONLY HIS POWER...AND USE IT...
BBB

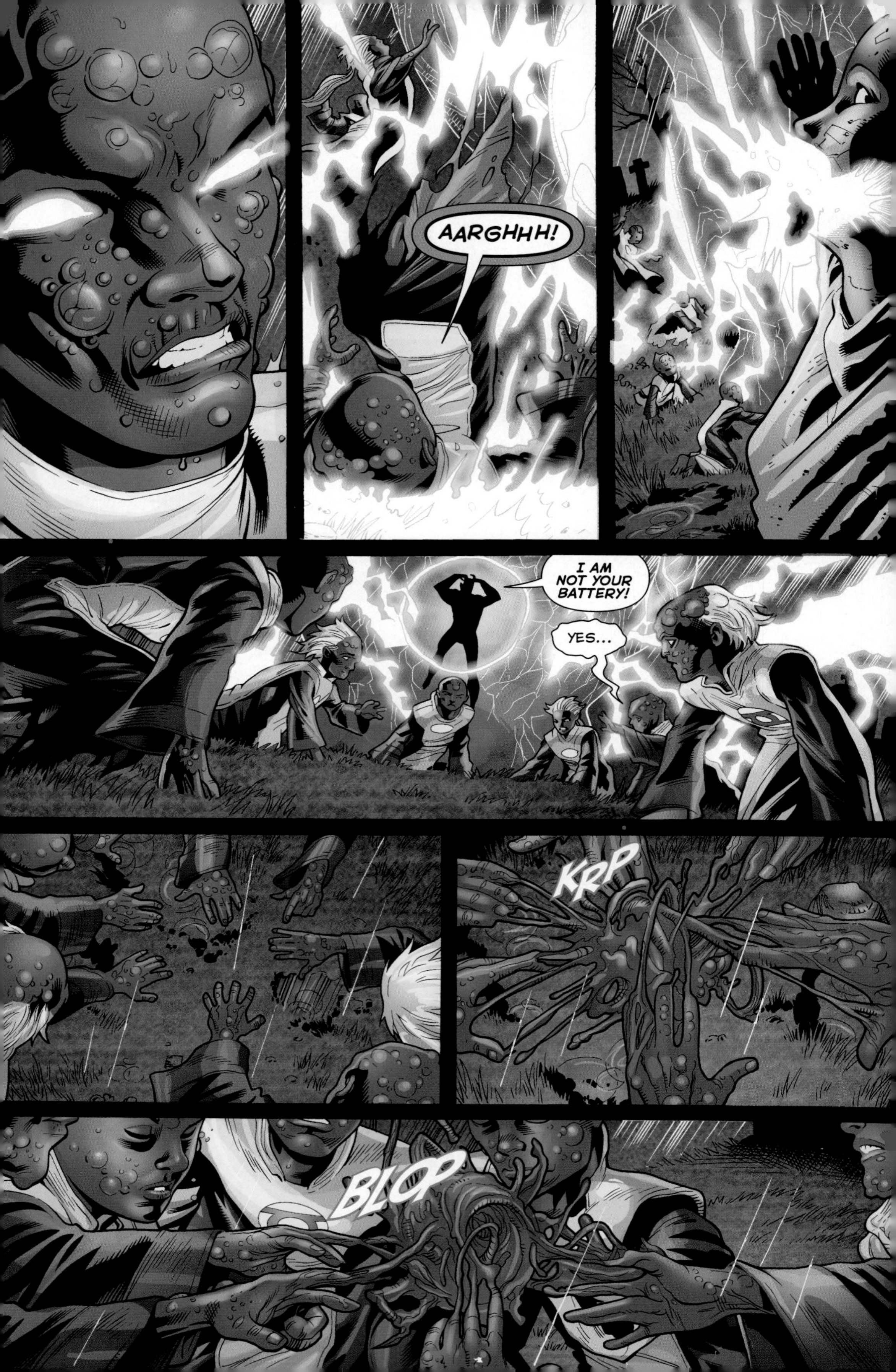
AARGHHH!
I AM NOT YOUR BATTERY!
YES...
KRP
BLOP

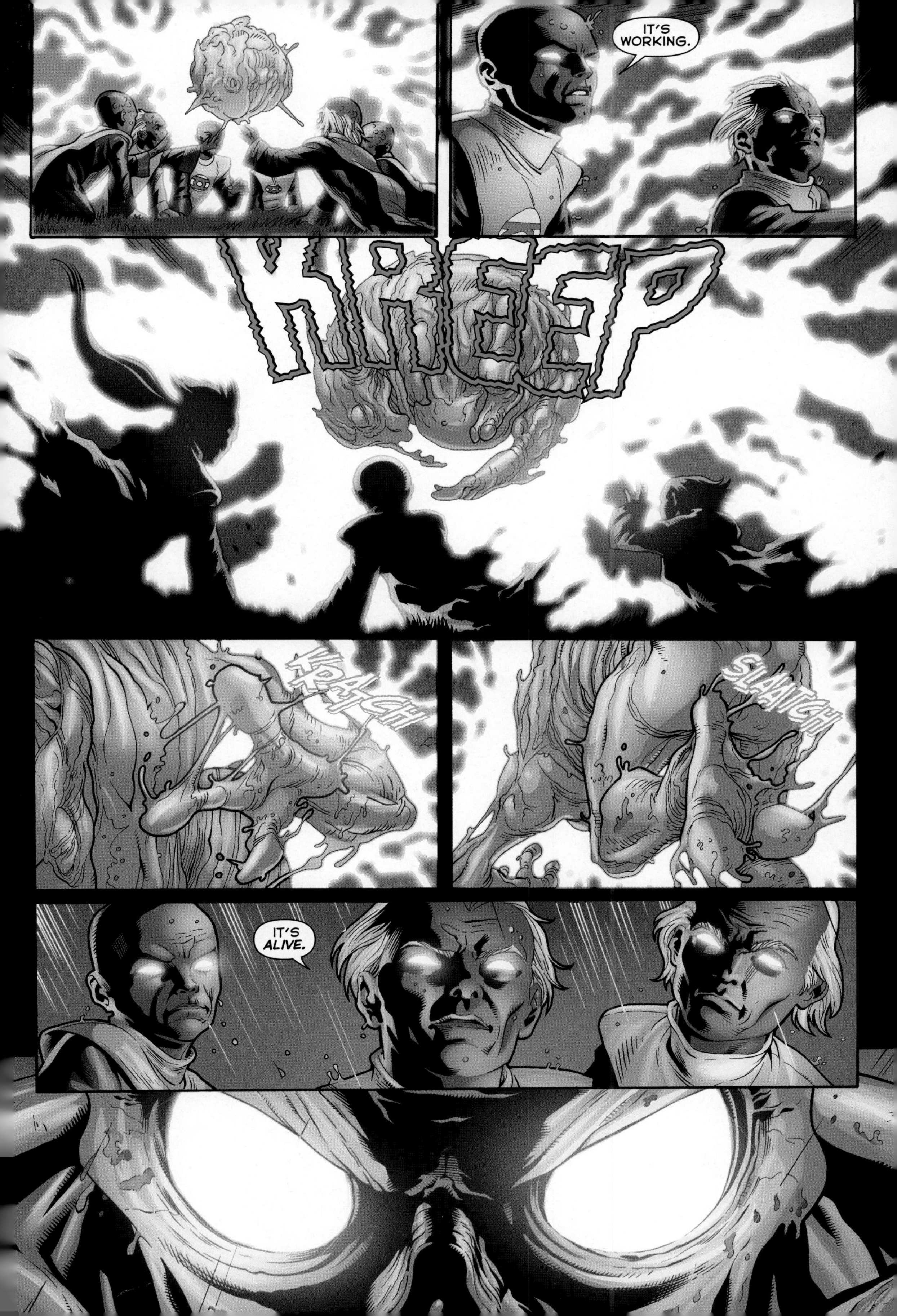
IT'S WORKING.
KRATCH
SLATCH
IT'S ALIVE.

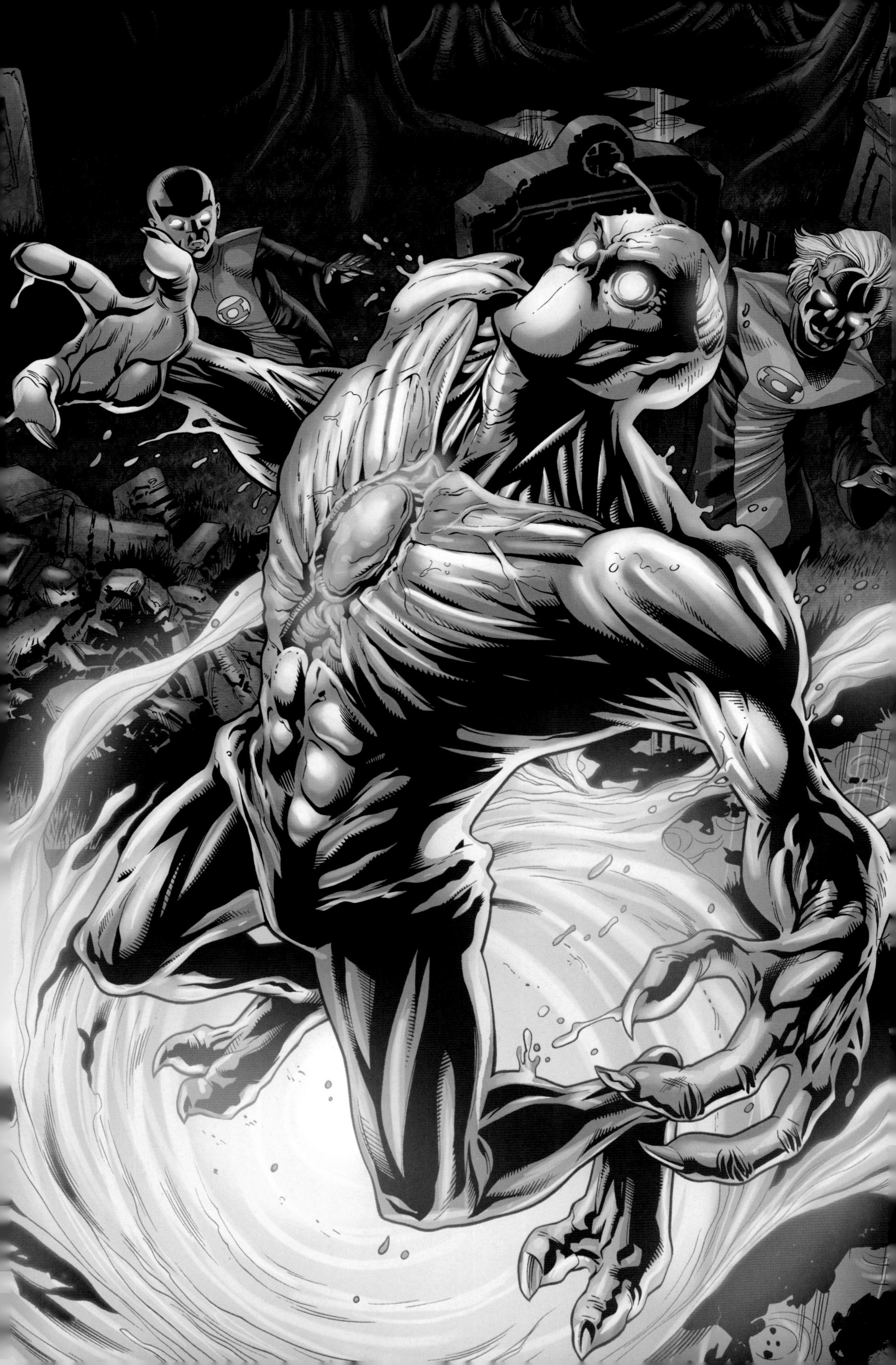

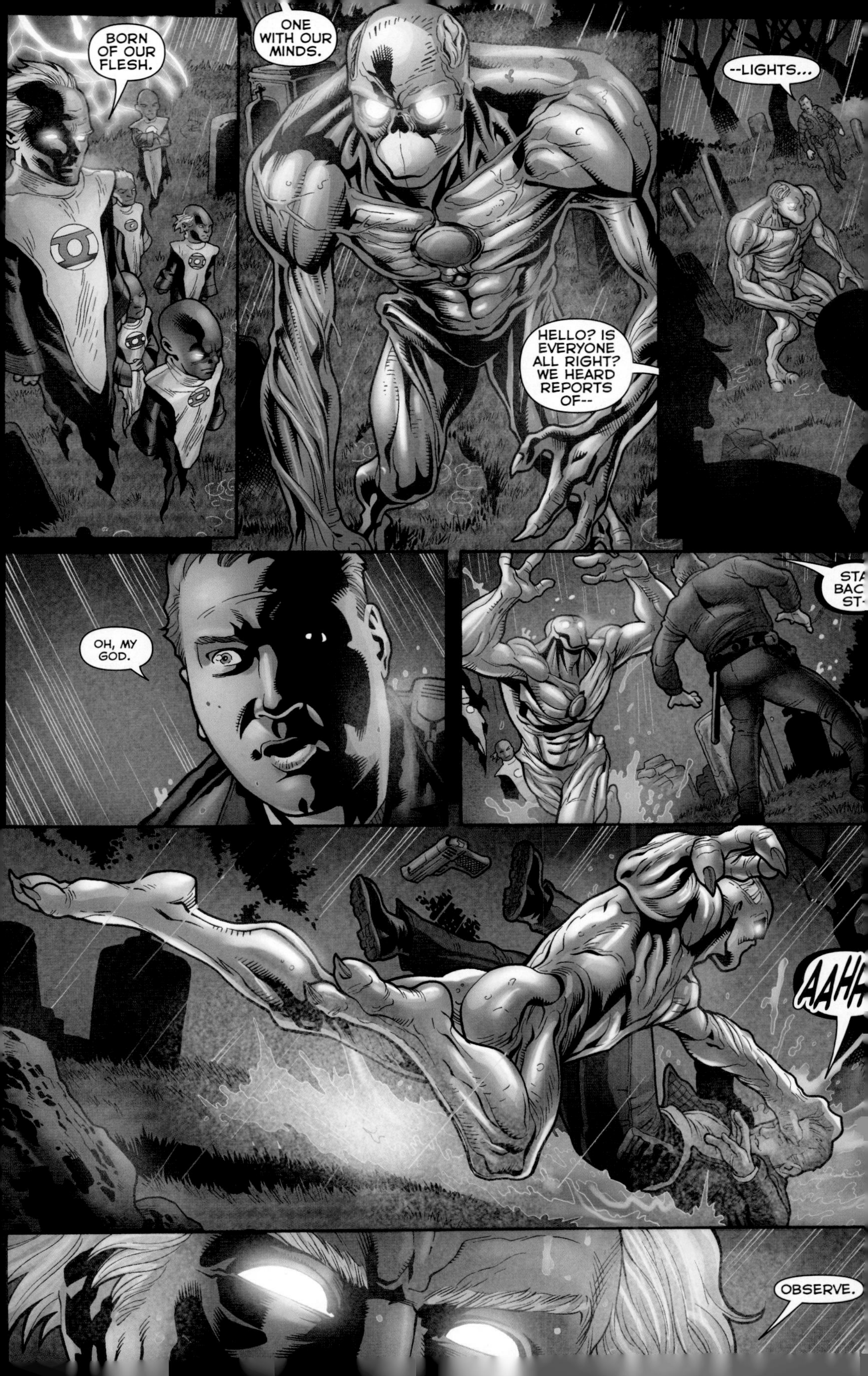
BORN OF OUR FLESH.
ONE WITH OUR MINDS.
--LIGHTS...
HELLO? IS EVERYONE ALL RIGHT? WE HEARD REPORTS OF--
OH, MY GOD.
STA BAC ST-
AAHH
OBSERVE.

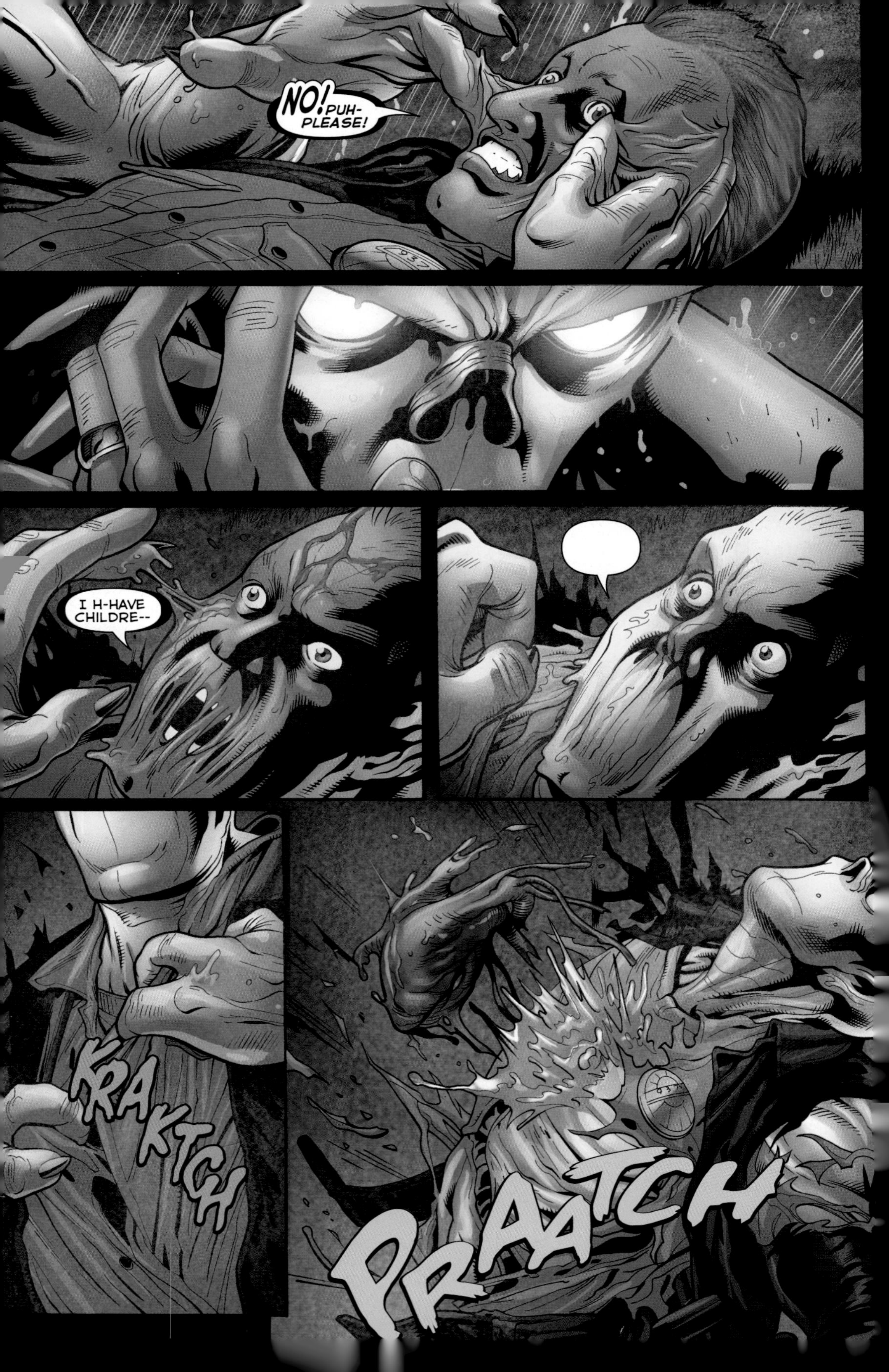
NO! PUH-PLEASE!
I H-HAVE CHILDRE--
KRAKTCH
PRAATCH

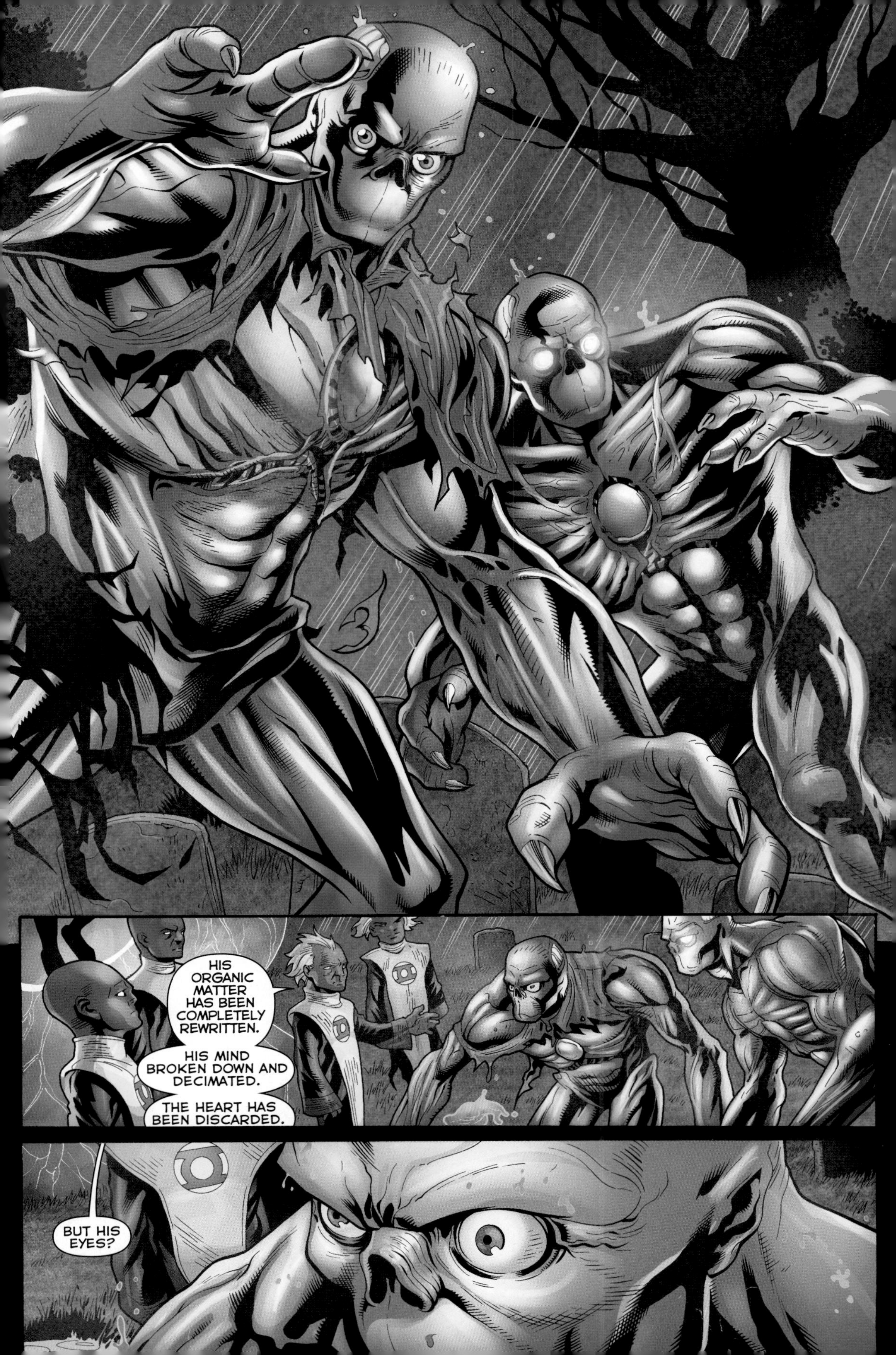
HIS ORGANIC MATTER HAS BEEN COMPLETELY REWRITTEN.
HIS MIND BROKEN DOWN AND DECIMATED.
THE HEART HAS BEEN DISCARDED.
BUT HIS EYES?

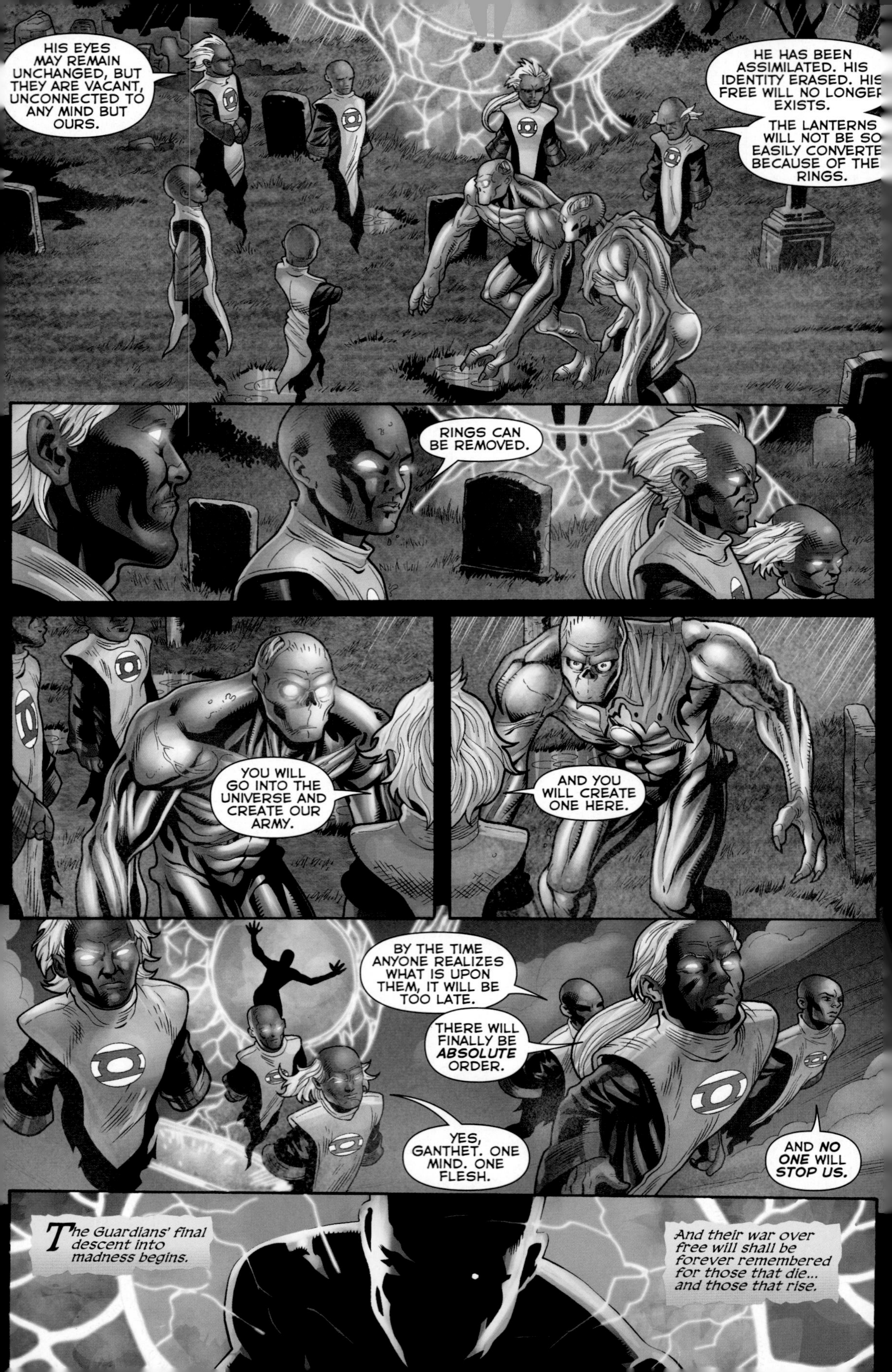
HIS EYES MAY REMAIN UNCHANGED, BUT THEY ARE VACANT, UNCONNECTED TO ANY MIND BUT OURS.
HE HAS BEEN ASSIMILATED. HIS IDENTITY ERASED. HIS FREE WILL NO LONGER EXISTS.
THE LANTERNS WILL NOT BE SO EASILY CONVERTE BECAUSE OF THE RINGS.
RINGS CAN BE REMOVED.
YOU WILL GO INTO THE UNIVERSE AND CREATE OUR ARMY.
AND YOU WILL CREATE ONE HERE.
BY THE TIME ANYONE REALIZES WHAT IS UPON THEM, IT WILL BE TOO LATE.
THERE WILL FINALLY BE ABSOLUTE ORDER.
YES, GANTHET. ONE MIND. ONE FLESH.
AND NO ONE WILL STOP US.
The Guardians' final descent into madness begins.
And their war over free will shall be forever remembered for those that die... and those that rise.

VARIANT COVER GALLERY

GREEN LANTERN 7
by Ian Churchill & Alex Sollozzo

GREEN LANTERN 8
by Dale Keown

GREEN LANTERN 9
by Gary Frank & Brad Anderson

GREEN LANTERN 8 Combo Pack
by Doug Mahnke, Mark Irwin & Alex Sinclair

GREEN LANTERN 9 Combo Pack
by Doug Mahnke, Mark Irwin & Alex Sinclair

GREEN LANTERN 10 Combo Pack
by Doug Mahnke, Christian Alamy & Alex Sinclair

GREEN LANTERN 11 Combo Pack
by Doug Mahnke, Christian Alamy & Alex Sinclair

GREEN LANTERN 12 Combo Pack
by Doug Mahnke, Mark Irwin & Alex Sinclair

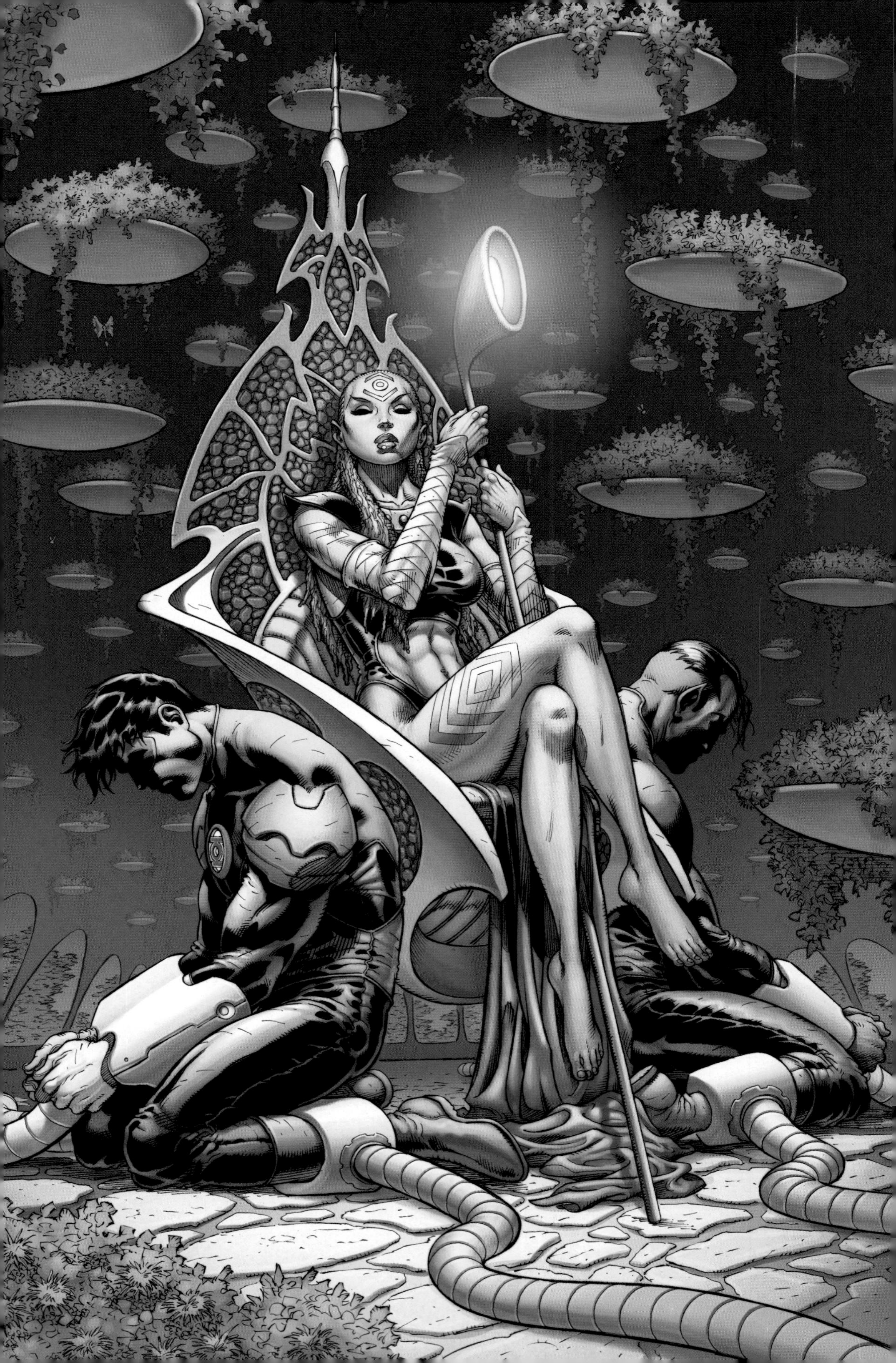

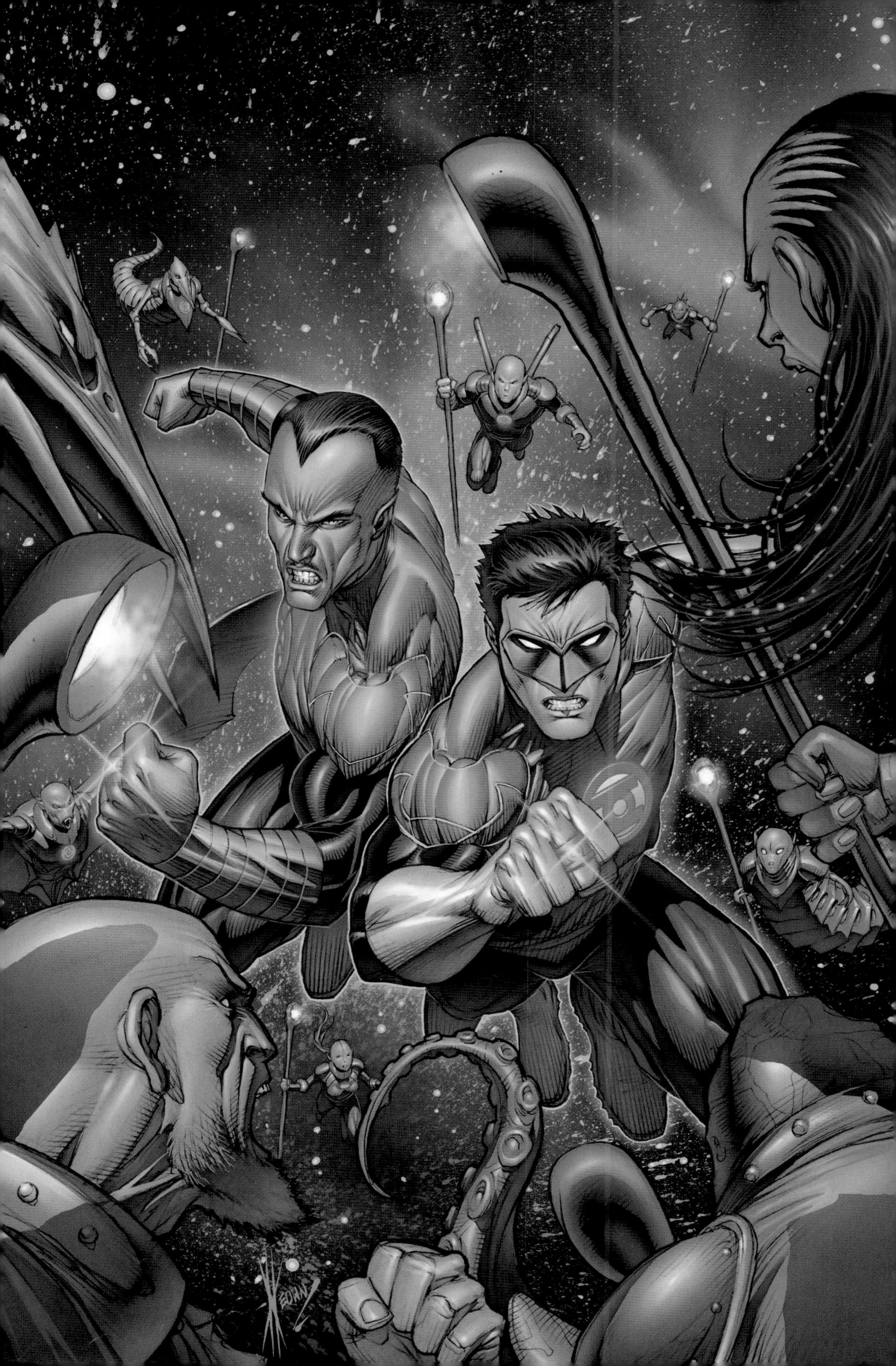

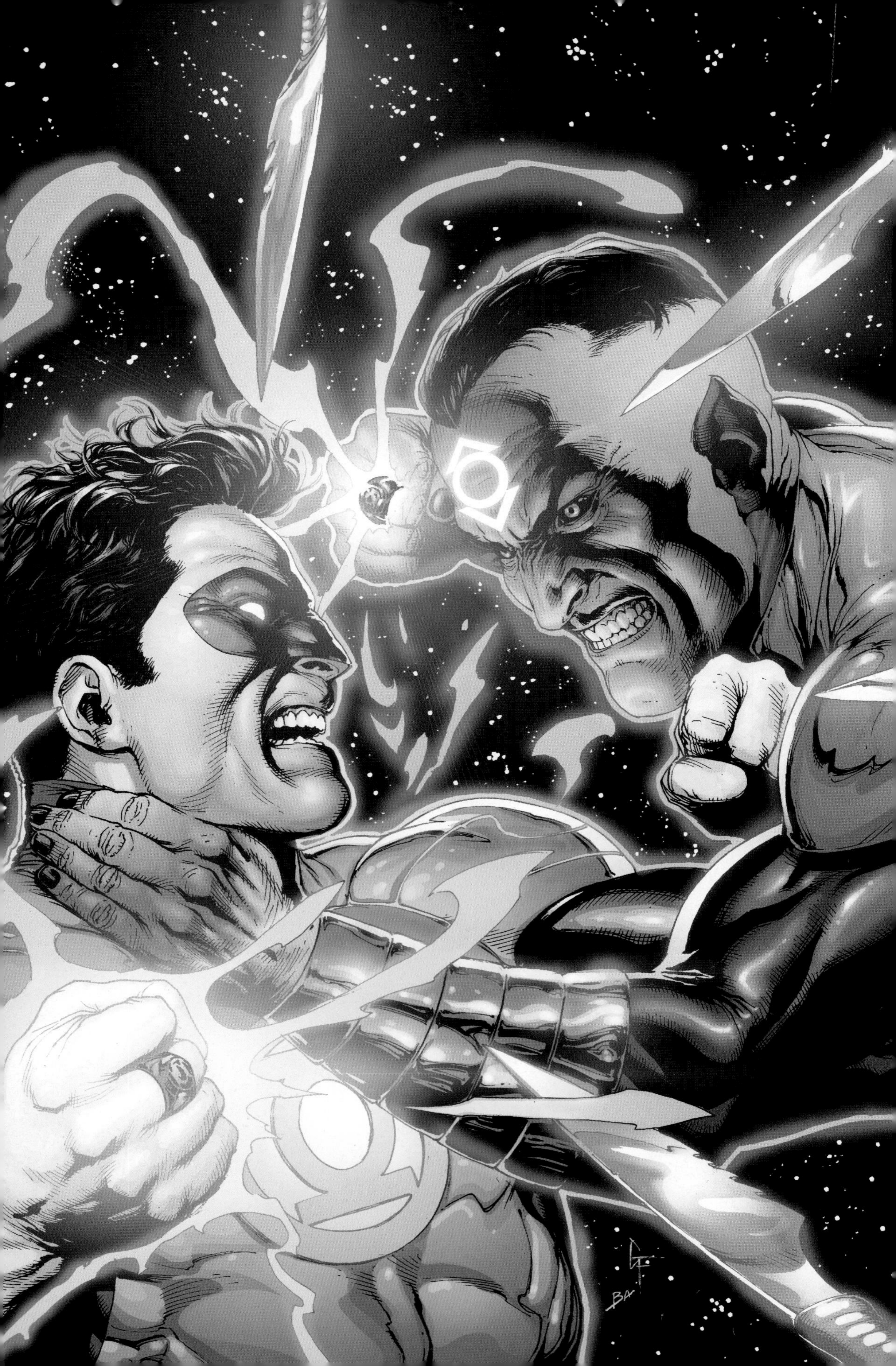

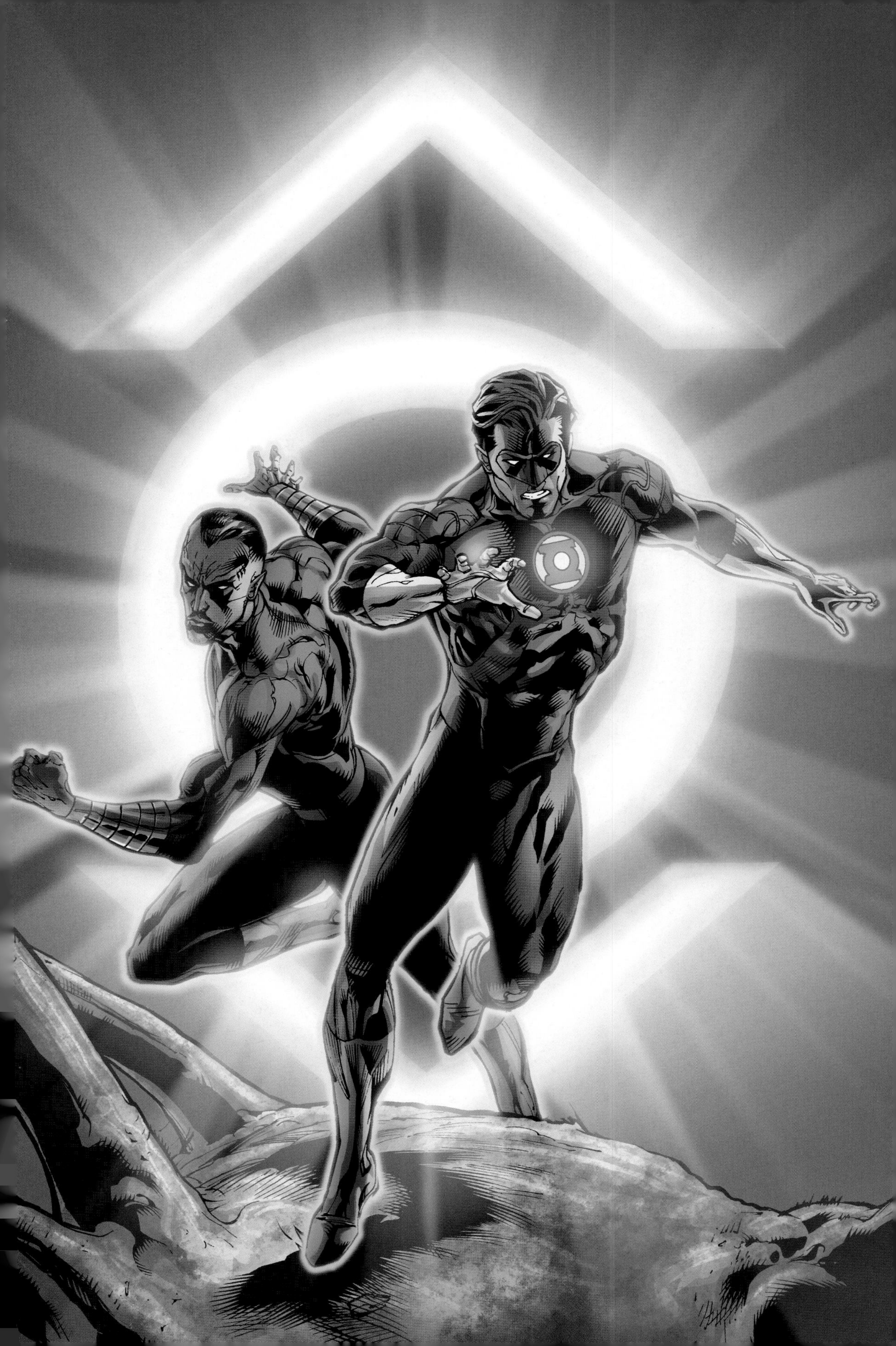

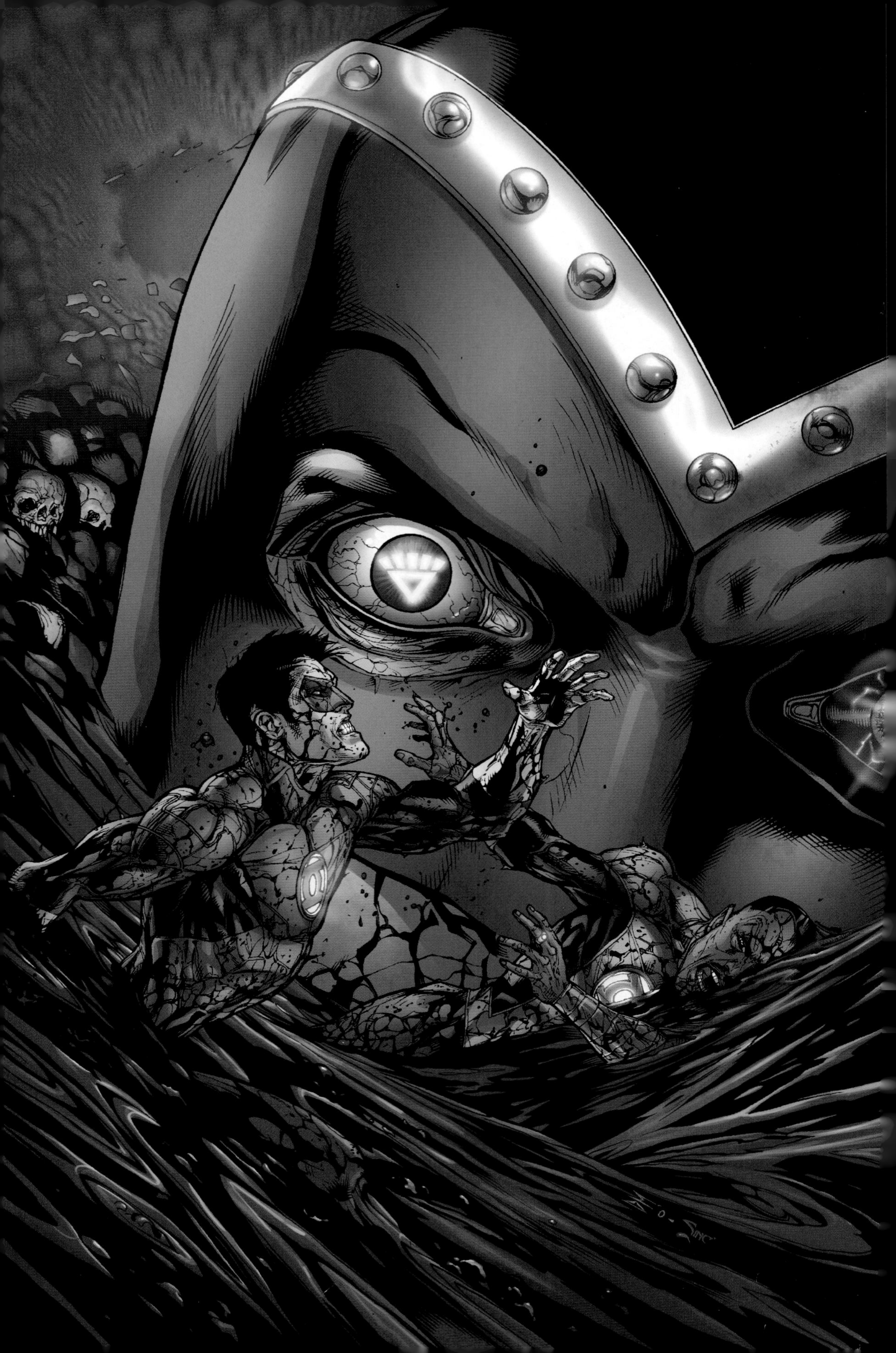

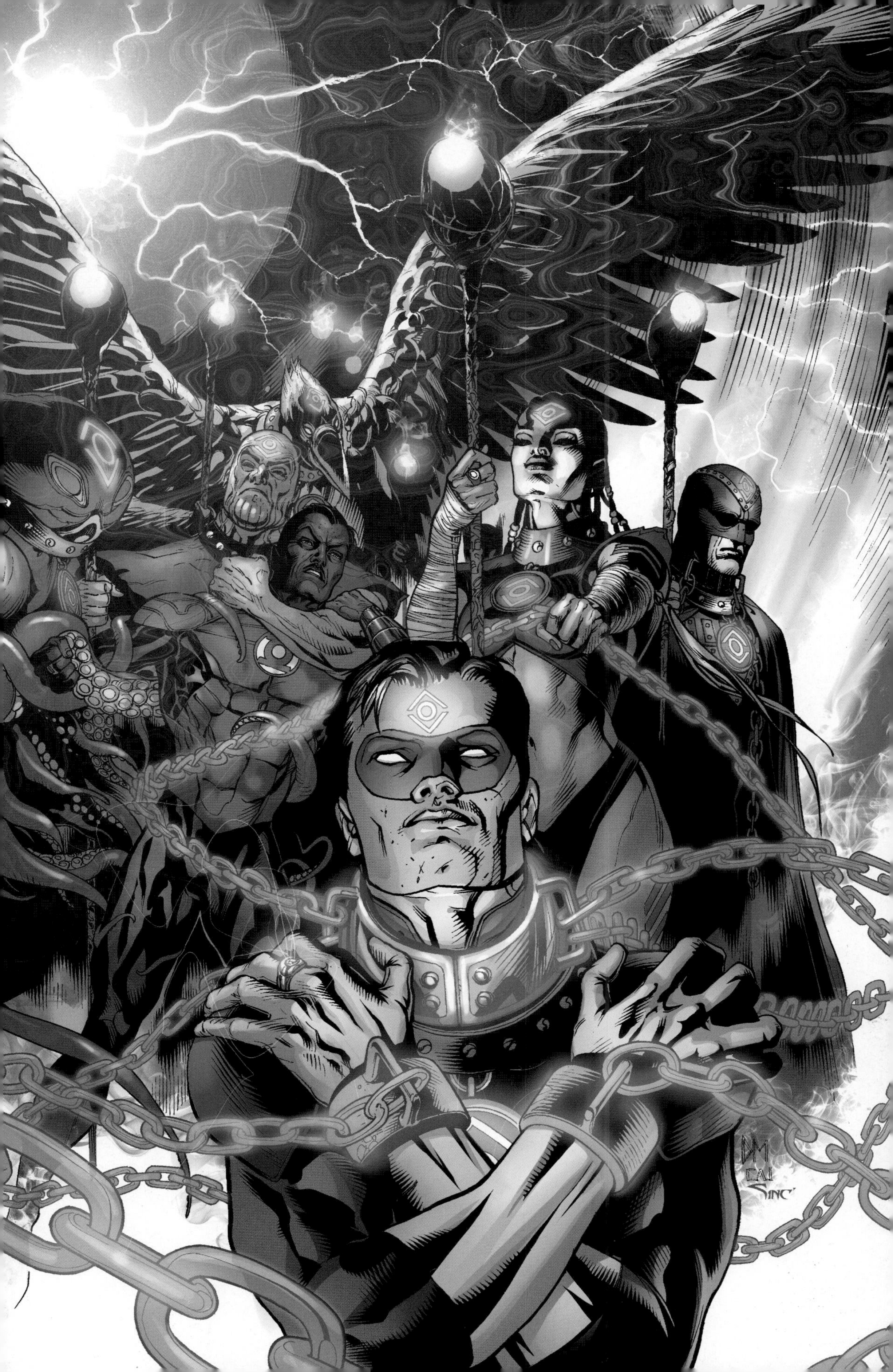

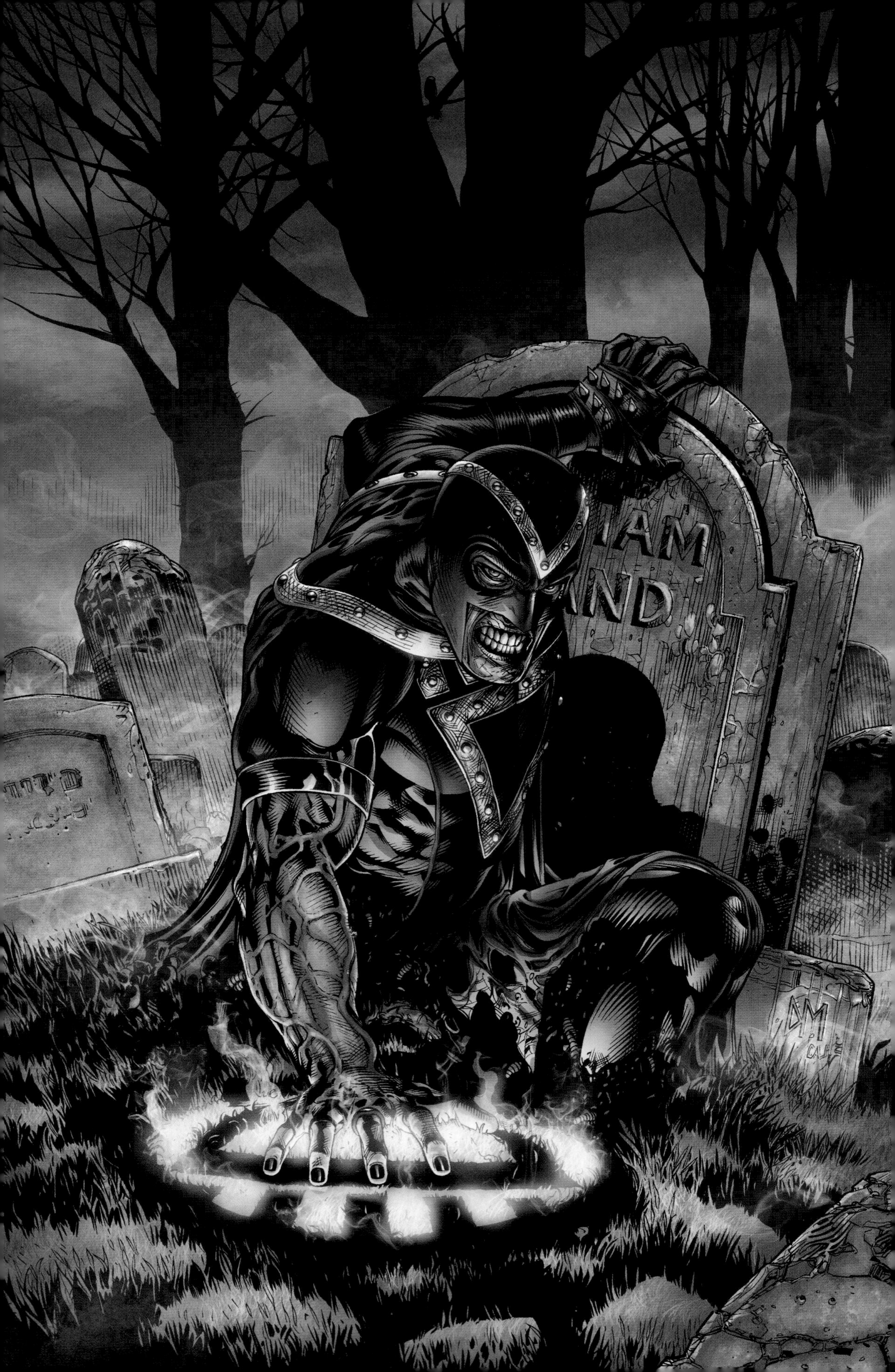
IAM
ND

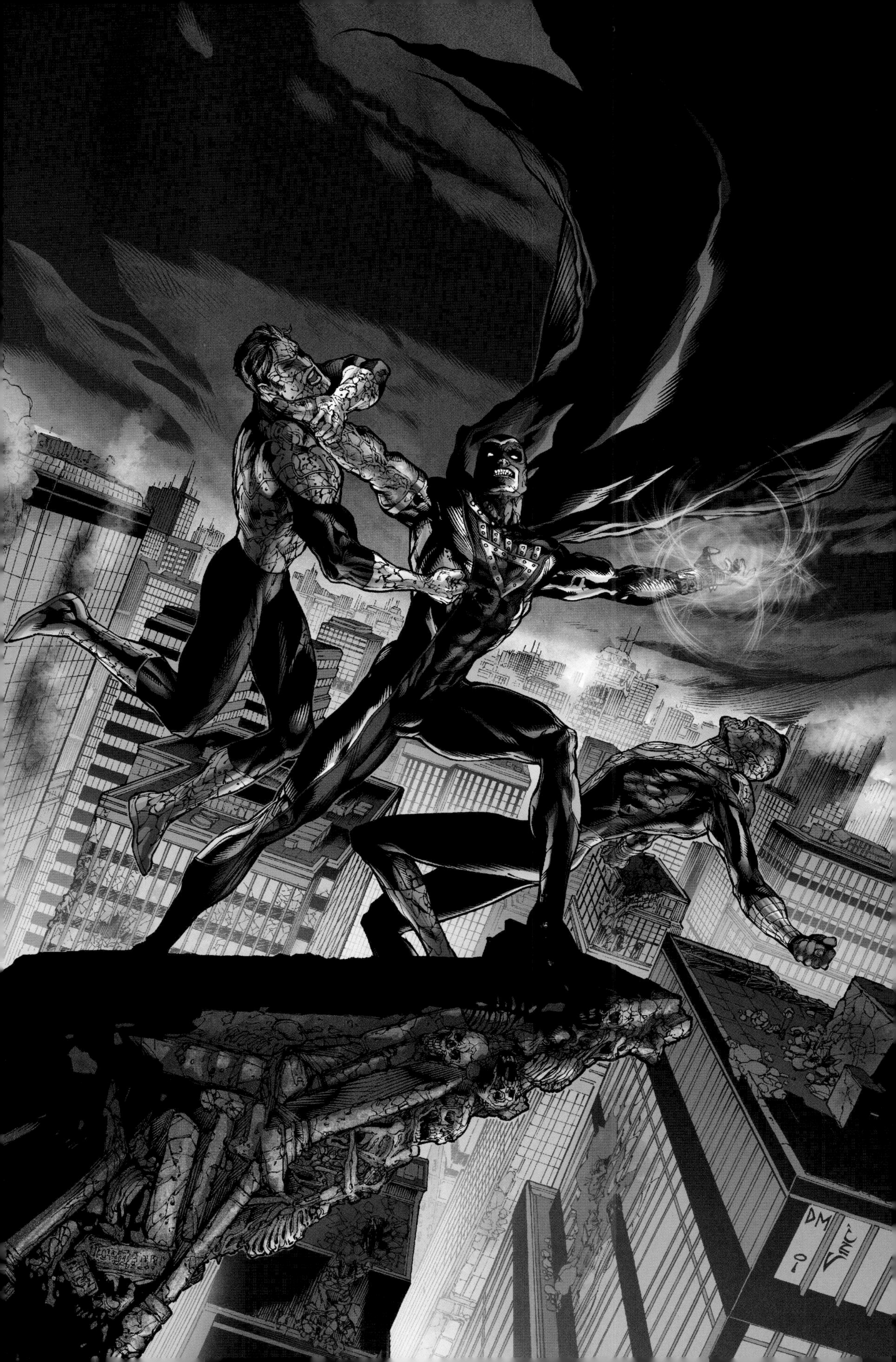

RISE OF THE

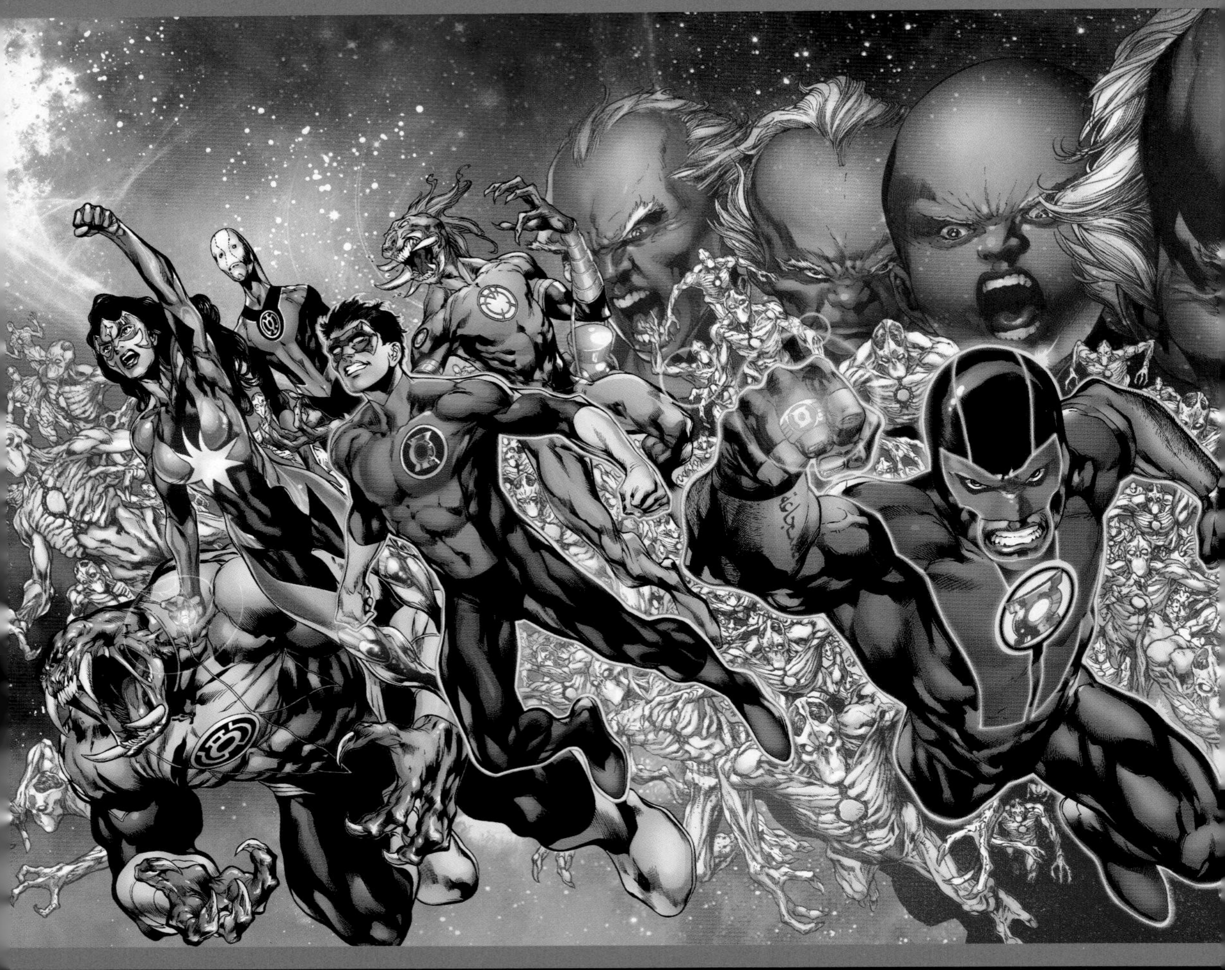

ABSOLUTE POWER CORRUPTS ABSOLUTELY — AND THE GUARDIANS

TIME IS FINALLY HERE. MISSION FOREVER

THIRD ARMY

THE GUARDIANS' THIRD ARMY RISES TO REPLACE
THE GREEN LANTERN CORPS — BUT HOW IS HORRIFYING
AND WHY WILL CHANGE THE GUARDIANS AND THEIR

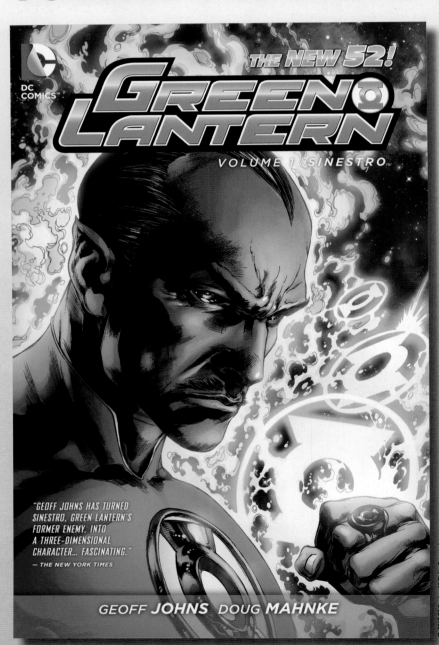

FROM THE WRITER OF *THE FLASH* & *ACTION COMICS*

GEOFF JOHNS
BLACKEST NIGHT with IVAN REIS

**BLACKEST NIGHT:
GREEN LANTERN**

**BLACKEST NIGHT:
GREEN LANTERN CORPS**

Read the Entire Epic!

BLACKEST NIGHT

BLACKEST NIGHT:
GREEN LANTERN

BLACKEST NIGHT:
GREEN LANTERN
CORPS

BLACKEST NIGHT:
BLACK LANTERN
CORPS VOL. 1

BLACKEST NIGHT:
BLACK LANTERN
CORPS VOL. 2

BLACKEST NIGHT:
RISE OF THE BLACK
LANTERNS

BLACKEST NIGHT:
TALES OF THE CORPS

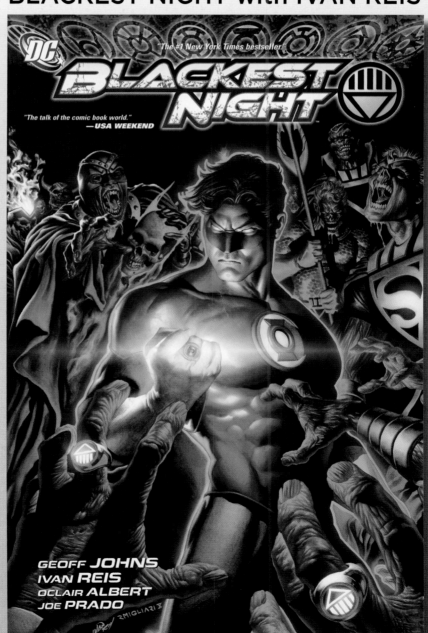

DC COMICS™

READ THE FOLLOW-UP TO THE *NEW YORK TIMES* #1 BEST-SELLING *BLACKEST NIGHT*

BRIGHTEST DAY
GEOFF JOHNS and PETER J. TOMASI

BRIGHTEST DAY VOL. 2

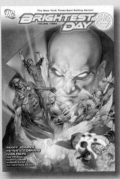

BRIGHTEST DAY VOL. 3

GREEN LANTERN: BRIGHTEST DAY

GEOFF JOHNS
PETER J. TOMASI
IVAN REIS
PATRICK GLEASON   FERNANDO PASARIN
ARDIAN SYAF   SCOTT CLARK   JOE PRADO